Doing Your Dissertation with Microsoft® Word

Doing Your Dissertation with Microsoft® Word

A comprehensive guide to using
Microsoft® Word
for academic writing

Updated for Word 2007 & 2010

By Jacques Raubenheimer
©2012

True Insight Publishing
Bloemfontein

Doing Your Dissertation with Microsoft® Word

A comprehensive guide to using Microsoft® Word for academic writing

Updated for Word 2007 & 2010

Published by True Insight Publishing

www.insight.trueinsight.za.com/word

Copyright © 2012 Jacques Raubenheimer

Requests can be made to trueinsight.consulting@gmail.com.

Limit of liability/disclaimer of warranty:

The publisher and the author make no representations of warranties with respect to the accuracy or completeness of the contents of this work, and specifically disclaim all warranties, including without limitation warranties of fitness for a particular purpose. No warranty may be created or extended by sales or promotional materials. The advice and strategies contained in this work may not be suitable for every situation. This work is sold with the understanding that the neither the publisher nor the author are engaged in rendering legal or other professional services related to this work. If professional assistance is required, the services of a competent professional person should be sought. Neither the publisher nor the author shall be liable for damages arising from the use or misuse of the content presented in this work. The fact that an organisation or website is referred to in this work as a citation and/or a potential source of further information does not mean that the author or the publisher endorses the information the organisation or website may provide or recommendations they may make. Further, readers should be aware that internet addresses listed in this work may have changed or ceased to exist between when this work was written and when it is read.

First published: 2012

ISBN: 978-0-86886-814-1

North American and Europe edition printed by Amazon CreateSpace

For more content from True Insight publishing, please visit http://insight.trueinsight.za.com.

DEDICATED TO

GERT HUYSAMEN

WITHOUT WHOM THERE WOULD HAVE BEEN NO

PHD DISSERTATION, AND THUS,

WITHOUT WHOM THIS BOOK WOULD NOT HAVE BEEN BORN.

Acknowledgements

As with any book, there is a whole list of people without whom this book would not have seen the light of day.

First simply must be all the students, through the years, who have brought their dissertation-in-Word problems to me, the solving of which has formed an important part of my own learning.

Inus Janse van Rensburg, for writing the forward to this book.

Leo Kirsten, who was a sounding board for my ideas when I needed someone who works with a lot more equations than I do (see Chapter 17).

Dap Louw, who encouraged me and advised me along the long path that lies between an idea and an actual publication.

Louis Venter and all the support staff at the University of the Free State's Unit for the Development of Rhetorical and Academic Writing (UDRAW) for providing the base from which I could do the first presentations of my course (from which this book grew) in 2005, and for continued moral support in the years since.

Jo Hall of the UFS Library and Information services, for help with the ISBN no.

Anneke Denobli and **Sonja Loots**, for their advice.

Stefan Dippenaar of MyBook for advice and for getting all the things in place to actually get this printed.

JP Nell for patiently putting up with me when I need Shumani Printers to print the book copies in a hurry because I have spent too long writing.

Daleen, my long-suffering wife, who probably believes I am actually married to the PC. I would rather look into your two eyes than my PC's two monitors. Really. Together with her, **Matthew** and **Michael**, two sons without comparison, who have had to sacrifice so many story-reading sessions so that their father could tell another story—this one. I love you all.

The **Lord Jesus Christ**, without whom even a book like this would have no meaning.

Credits

Table of Contents

ix

Figures

Instruction Sets

Tables

Application Entries

Macro Listings

In the final stage of every post-graduate study one abides to a daily struggle between keeping laboratory instrumentation in working order, trying to reproduce previous results and conducting the final reactions and literature investigations between 2 and 3am. As if this is not enough, you are constantly reminded of the difficult task of compiling all the random data stating that "A + B turns yellow" into a well written, perfectly presented, easy to read manuscript—a tall order indeed!

This manuscript you write is so important that you will have placed your working experience on hold to investigate a couple of thoughts and expose these on a few pages; pages that will carry your findings to the oh-so-important Professors who will decide the fate—or maybe I should say the worthiness—of your work. How can the significance of this document (whether a thesis or dissertation) be overemphasised? And so also the significance of the way it is presented, formatted and laid out?

Also, how is it that proper training in document formatting is so often regarded as general knowledge among students? It is true that there is so much to learn ("so many reactions, so little time") but proper training in document formatting can save hours during the preparation of one's manuscripts.

I met Dr Jacques Raubenheimer due to a shared interest in the sole thing keeping an academic from insanity: Rock climbing. Among our friends and fellow students with the smell of climbing gear and fingers being chalked too frequently, I came to learn about his course in which he taught post graduate students to properly format their theses and dissertations. It might have been my constant complaining ("the little numbers jump around," or "I have to re-label all the figures. Again!") that made him invite me to his next course. A couple of weeks later I attended a well presented and very informative, detailed course on thesis layout. Still today this investment is number one on my list of money well spent. If only I had invested in it sooner!

It is with great honour that I can say to every reader "devour the words on these pages" it will truly make a difference, because detail does matter.

June 2012

Dr J. Marthinus Janse van Rensburg
PhD (Inorganic Chemistry)

Chapter 1
Introduction

Let me start by describing to you the way I have seen so many typical students type their theses. You type a heading: "Chapter One<Enter>Introduction." Then you grab the mouse. Select the text. Format it as a heading should be formatted. Then select the next paragraph and resume typing—of course, if you don't have a "next" paragraph, when you press **Enter**, Word helpfully formats the new paragraph in the same manner as you just formatted your heading, when means you end up having to strip that formatting away! Pretty soon, you get very frustrated. You have to apply all those changes. You have to remember what headings get formatted in which way. You have to figure out what the next number is for the heading that you are about to type. You end up thinking to yourself: "There must be a better way!" There is. And you're going to learn it.

To illustrate this, I examined my own PhD dissertation. It has a total of 15 419 paragraphs (granted, a lot of them are in table cells—12 619 cells, in 74 tables, leaving 2 800 other paragraphs). It has 149 standard headings, and a fair amount of other headings (such as for tables and figures). Counting only the main set of these, the total comes to 288—Table 1 shows the formatting settings for these headings used in the dissertation. As you can see, a total of 3 234 formatting settings were made for these headings (actually a lot more, but the point is amply illustrated). Now what if that number could be reduced to just 377 (89 + 288)? That would lead to a more than 88% increase in efficiency!

Table 1   *Formatting Settings in Dissertation*

Heading	Occurrences	Formatting settings	Total number of formatting operations
Heading 1	7	13	91
Heading 2	24	12	288
Heading 3	44	10	440
Heading 4	51	10	510
Heading 5	23	7	161
Chapter Title	3	14	42
Chapter Subtitle	22	10	220
Table/Figure Captions	114	13	1482
Totals	**288**	**89**	**3234**

There are other examples I will refer to. I have twice had students tell me that it took them about a week[1] to make all the changes required when their promoters ask them to switch two chapters around. If you think about it, a lot must be done: The text must be selected, cut and pasted. All the headings (text headings, table and figure headings, etc.) have to be renumbered in both chapters. All references throughout the entire document to the tables and figures and other headings in the document have to be fixed. All the page numbers have to be changed. The table of contents must be redone (and the list of tables and list of figures). It's a huge amount of work. I have also had to do this in my

---

[1] "A week" is a very vague term when it comes to quantifying work. I estimate, conservatively, that a PhD student working on a full dissertation would take about 10 hours of work to complete this task.

own theses. It takes me less than a minute. I am not joking—I just get Word to do all the work for me.

1.1 Where this book came from

I was blessed with terrible handwriting[2]—the only subject I ever got an F for in school was for writing in Sub A (Grade 1). Just in case you were wondering, I came close with a few other subjects, though. Why would that be a blessing? In 1993, as a third year University student, I had to submit my first typewritten assignment. I couldn't type, so I found a typist, and the ordeal began. The typist struggled to read my handwriting, and thus there were many corrections, and corrections upon corrections, and soon I realised that if this was going to be the norm (typewritten submissions)—and it was—then I was going to have to learn to type myself. And so, in my honours year (1994), I got access to the university's computer lab for post graduate students—a small anteroom with two PCs (I kid you not!). We still worked on 5in floppy disks, and the PCs were x386 DOS PCs with Word for DOS version 6. And so I began to teach myself Word. As time moved on, I started working for the university, and was given better hardware and software to work on. I submitted my Master's thesis in 1997, using Word 97. There, already, I was using many of the features you will see in this book. And I have never looked back since. I did a PhD, submitted with Word 2002 (aka Word XP), and just last year submitted a second Master's thesis, using Word 2007. Each time, I endeavoured to apply more of the principles you will be learning in this book (e.g., even though I own a copy of a RMS programme—ProCite—I purposefully used the MSWord 2007 Bibliography tool for my referencing).

However, knowing what I had learned, I set about teaching other students the same skills. This led to a course on using MSWord for your thesis, and that led to this book. I make a grand boast in this book—I estimate that if you use the principles in this book, you could submit your PhD thesis about a month earlier. I have had students who have attended my course, who have told me that they think my estimate is about right. Of course, that is very subjective, and it is in no way empirically determined—it is really just a thumb-suck. It will vary depending on the scope of the document you are producing, so a Master's student doing a mini-thesis won't be able to expect to save that much time. It also depends on what you know before you work through this book, although my own experience has been that students vastly overestimate their knowledge of Word, and their mouths hang open when I show them tools that have been available in Word for more than a decade and which they had no idea existed.

But this course is not just aimed at saving you time. I also have worked through a fair number of theses in my work at the university. And, with some exceptions, I can almost immediately tell whether the person typing the thesis knows Word or not. It is so easy for mistakes to creep in (after all, you'll be working on your thesis late at night at least some of the time). Page numbers and tables of content don't correlate. Heading numbers and table and figure numbers falter (either a number gets repeated or it gets skipped). Formatting always suffers (e.g., some headings are bold and italics, some are just bold).

---

[2] And so we see how even the failures of our lives may very well be used to prepare us for the successes of our future.

And the litany just goes on and on. The principles of this book are aimed at helping you create a better quality—dare I say "professional"—product. And to do that faster. So you win on both fronts: You save time and you get a better end result. Life doesn't normally work like that. Your thesis content won't work like that. Generally, to get the best results, you have to put in the most effort. But thanks (most of the time) to the enterprising folks at Microsoft, when it comes to the typing of your thesis, the opposite is true. And the sole purpose of this book is to show you how.

1.2   Who this book is for

Microsoft Word is a strange beast. It can do amazing things, and it can just as easily be amazingly frustrating. Many students these days are finding that it is easier to type their dissertations and theses[3] than to write them and have them typed by someone else. Equally, many professional typists find themselves inundated with work (not only dissertations), and creating large documents with Word is becoming the norm. This course is aimed at you, the student or typist who is faced with this daunting task. But it will also help other users of Word, even academics writing short articles will benefit. Word has a vast array of very powerful tools to help you complete the task. If only you know about them, and how to use them. This course is intended to introduce you to the tools at your disposal, and also how to use them effectively and efficiently, not as in Figure 1.

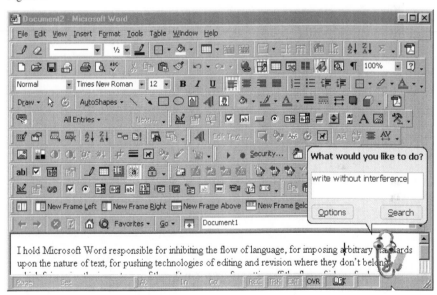

Figure 1   *Ineffective use of Word[4]*

---

[3] A first explanation: I will, henceforth, mostly use only the word "dissertation" to refer to dissertations, theses, and other forms of large documents.

[4] I have no idea who created this image. It was one of those jokes sent via e-mail from the previous millennium. I can only assume that this person would still gripe about the new ribbons in Word 2007/2010 too.

This, of course, was one of the reasons why Microsoft decided to go with the new Fluent® ribbon interface introduced in Microsoft Office 2007. Of course, judging from the reaction many users had to *that*, one wonders whether they succeeded. But, for better or worse, ribbons are here to stay. The irony is that, despite the fact that the ribbons were meant to bring the so-called "hidden" features of the programs[5] out to where people could see them, people still don't know and use the features of Word which you will be discovering in this book.

Also, Word sometimes displays strange behaviour, which is often caused by settings the user is unaware of. While the hidden settings in Figure 2 (please excuse the strong language—I did not create this joke) are bogus, the fact is that most users don't understand the settings that Word really does have. I want to show you those settings, and explain to you how to use them. Here again, the new interface doesn't seem to have helped much in this regard.

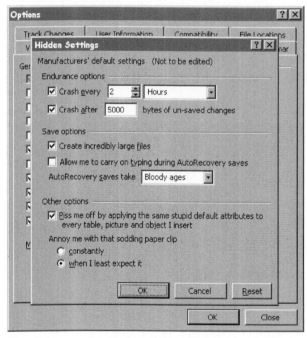

Figure 2   *Does Word have hidden settings?*[6]

From all of this, I hope you will gather that this is an advanced book in using Microsoft Word[7]. This is not for beginners. But, by the same token, don't be discouraged. Even if

---

[5] Another word on spelling. In the US, "program" refers to a timetable, and "programme" to a computer program. In the rest of the English-speaking world, it's just the opposite. I will be using, of course, South African English spelling in this book.

[6] Found at http://word.mvps.org/Tutorials/LightRelief/WordOptions.htm.

[7] I have made some notes, and one day would think about writing a more introductory level book on Word.

you know nothing about Word, after having mastered the skills in this book, you will be the envy of all your friends and colleagues—you *can* master Word.

1.3   What this book teaches you

The focus in this book is not just about how to master Word, however. While this is definitely not a book on writing skills, it does focus on many of the theoretical things you need to know about writing, publishing, and typesetting, to get a professional end product—the dissertation you want to submit. You will be learning about things that are not specific to Microsoft Word, although if Word cannot do them, you won't be learning about them. This book, then, is not about using Word per se, but about how to type a good dissertation or thesis, and about how to use Word to accomplish this.

I also have to tell you what this book does *not* teach you. Because I consider this to be an advanced book, I do not discuss *everything* there is to know about Word (I seriously doubt that such a book exists—not even Microsoft's own help files describe all the features of Word, as I will point out in this book—see, for example, section 3.2.3.2, p. 40). I have made some choices about what I consider to be prerequisite knowledge, and those things are not discussed here. Of course, I am not providing that list, but you will see that many aspects of things like setting fonts, changing paragraph settings, selecting and moving text, and many other topics are *not* covered in this book. If you think something should be included, you could always make a suggestion for a future edition. But consider first whether it shouldn't be something you should already know before starting with this book.

1.4   Application boxes

I have not only been using these principles now for well over a decade, but I have also been helping countless Masters and PhD students apply them in their own work, helping them when they get stuck. As such, I may not have "seen it all," but I definitely have seen a lot. What I want to try and do here is also present you with little boxes containing examples of how this work can be applied in practise (or at least, how it has been applied by someone else). Look out for the Application boxes which give detail about how the principles you learn in this book can be applied to practical problems students experience when typing their thesis or dissertations.

1.5   Instruction sets

An idea I have been using in my course guides for some time now is what I call Instruction Sets. Basically, in the world of computers, there is often more than one way of doing something. Most guides show one way, and this can confuse people when others do it in a different way. Also, when people sit down and what they see on the screen in front of them doesn't look like the book, then they get confused. My aim with the instruction sets is to show you all the ways of doing something. You can then choose what works best for you, although I will not be leaving you rudderless—you will soon see that I will be advocating a very particular way of working in Word. The way in which the Instruction sets work is explain in section 2.2, p. 25.

1.6   Layout of this book

Finally, you will see that this course does not follow the layout of most computer training courses. We don't work through the ribbons, from left to right, top to bottom. We also don't give you a random array of disparate tasks, and show you how to do them using the computer, leaving you with an unsorted plate of spaghetti that makes no sense. The layout of the course follows the coherent process of typing a large document such as a dissertation. What is the first thing you need to know, and what after that? And so you will proceed right through to the end. Because of this, you may find us visiting and then later revisiting some of the same tools, as the context determines—for example, the "Outlining" toolbar is discussed in the sections on document navigation (Chapter 11) as well as creating master documents (Chapter 12). This approach is perhaps best evident in Chapter 14 on using Word's reviewing tools. Instead of discussing, for example, how to add, edit, navigate between, and delete comments, we discuss how to review a document (which covers adding and editing comments), and how to work through document revisions (which covers navigating between, and deleting comments). Or, as one final example, AutoCorrect and AutoFormat settings are discussed in section 4.3, but Math AutoCorrect (which is in the same dialog) is discussed in section 17.3.

In short, this means that I have tried to demonstrate the use of the tools in their proper context. I hope that you will find this approach meaningful, not confusing.

1.7   Use of fonts

Most of the book is written in Times New Roman, 12pt, with varying sizes of Garamond for the headings. However, to help distinguish the instructions you are called to follow, parts of the interface (e.g., ribbon names, dialog names, option buttons, check boxes, list boxes, combo boxes, text boxes, buttons, etc.) are displayed in Segoe UI, which is the default font for window title bars, menus, etc. in Windows 7.

1.8   Some terminology

It will help to clarify some terminology to be used in this book.

Firstly, I have discovered that often, people don't know the names of all the things they find on their keyboards. I will use the names for the various keyboard symbols listed in Table 2. This is, technically, a combination of British and US English, although I think it is the closest thing I could find to officially recognised South African terms, and these are the terms I feel familiar with.

Table 2   *Symbol names*

Symbol	Name used in this book	Symbol	Name used in this book
{}	Braces	?	Question mark
()	Parentheses	!	Exclamation mark
[]	Brackets	@	At sign
~	Tilde	#	Hash
<>	Angle brackets	$	Dollar
`	Grave accent	%	Per cent
´	Acute accent[a]	^	Caret (circumflex)
.	Period	&	Ampersand
...	Ellipsis	*	Asterisk
,	Comma	|	Bar
'	Apostrophe	/	Forward slash
"	Quotation mark	\	Backslash
;	Semicolon	-	Hyphen
:	Colon	_	Underscore

a: Not on a standard keyboard: **Ctrl** + ` then **Space**

1.9   Thesis tools

Yes, yes. I am fully aware that some of the readers of this book will already be in a tight spot. You might not have time to master all these techniques. Can't I just give you some tools that will help you get your thesis fixed without having to slog through a whole book like this?

Well, the truth is, I can. And I will. Please visit www.insight.trueinsight.za.com/word. There you will find the following:

- **Further tips and techniques** that I will add to the site as I become aware of them.
- **Links** to useful sites mentioned in this book (e.g., to BibWord, discussed in section 13.4, p. 296).
- My own rendition of the **SA Harvard** style for BibWord.
- **Templates** that you can use to get the heading styles and the heading numbering and page numbering right without even having to master the content of this book. But beware. If you don't know how these things work, you could still easily mess up those templates, and your thesis as a result. Having those templates will help, but it's not a perfect, bullet-proof fix. The only thing that will really help you, as with most areas of life, is your own knowledge and expertise, which I hope you will get form working through and applying the content of this book.
- A set of **Word uTIlities** (macros I have written for Word) that will help you apply some of the principles discussed in this book. The tools are packaged in what is known as a Global Template for Word, but you needn't worry about those details. From the website, you simply download the WorduTIlities.exe file, and then double click on it to install it (after having made certain that MSWord is not running). It should do the rest all on its own. If it installed

successfully, you will have a uTIlities ribbon added to your Word interface (Figure 3).

Figure 3   *Word uTIlities ribbon*

These uTIlities do the following:

- **Register keyboard shortcuts:** Use only once, attempts to register the keyboard shortcuts suggested in section 2.3.2 (p. 30). *No longer on the ribbon.*
- **Fit Hyperlink:** Resolve the problem with adding long hyperlinks discussed in Application 13.2 (p. 295) by automatically adding no-width breaks at the appropriate places.
- **Captioned figure:** I discuss this in Application 8.2, p. 164. I provide a macro there (Macro Listing 1), but I might as well include it in the tool set, so here it is. This resolves the problem of having captions separate from the figures to which they refer. It pastes a figure already copied to the clipboard, and adds a caption.
- **Insert a numbered equation:** A solution to the problem of numbered equations, as discussed in section 17.1.7 (p. 412, and macro shown on p. 415). You won't find another one like this out there.
- **Reauthor Comments:** Very popular with journal editors and the like. Allows you to do something you cannot do manually—change the listed author of comments in a section of a document, or a whole document. Note that for some odd reason which only the people at Microsoft know (or do not even know), this can only reconfigure comment authors, not change (insertions/deletions) authors. Change authors can be changed, but it requires manual XML editing. This is tangentially related to the topic discussed in Chapter 14 (from p. 301). I am working on something to try and do the impossible, but only when I'm not busy writing this book. If you really need it done, see the back pages for information about the consultation service.
- **Style Summary:** Examines a document and generates a complete list of the styles found, and used, in the document. Can also count the number of occurrences of each used style (some styles are listed as used, but do not occur any more, and are thus, technically, unused), although this does take some time to complete. Styles are discussed in Chapter 6, from p. 91.
- **Share template:** Ensure that all of a set of documents use the same template. Very relevant if you are doing your thesis with each chapter in a separate document, as discussed (and not recommended, by the way) in section 12.2, from p. 270.
- **Combine documents:** Also relevant to the strategy of doing your thesis across multiple documents. Takes several documents, and merges them into one document. This does not use the Master document structure to do this (discussed in section 12.2.1, p. 271), but rather actually copies and pastes each successive document into the main document. This means that it is a once-off operation.

8

- ❧ **Copy to new:** This tool is relevant if you follow my advice (p. 265) and do your thesis in one document only. What if you need to send just one chapter of your thesis to your promoter? The techniques discussed in section 12.1 (p. 266) and section 5.2.3 (p. 85) makes this an easy enough operation, but since I am sure there will be someone who considers this too much work, I have automated the process: Select your chapter (again, see section 12.1, p. 266), and click the button. If I hurry, I can do the whole operation in less than 15 seconds.

- ❧ **Backup:** Creates a backup of the current document. This employs the strategy I discuss in Application 12.2 (p. 267) for backing up your document. Basically, a one-click backup of the document that works on a system which allows an easy to follow timeline of your thesis. By far the most popular and most-used tool in the set!

- ❧ **Bookmark manager:** In all honesty, Word's built-in Bookmark dialog is severely lacking. Here is my replacement for it, that does what I believe a bookmark manager should do. Us it to rename bookmarks (which Word's tool cannot do), reposition bookmarks, add and delete bookmarks, and see a complete, sortable list of all the bookmarks, either in the whole document, or just in a selection. Bookmarks are discussed in section 11.2 (p. 240).

- ❧ **List Bookmark:** Compiles a list of all the bookmarks in the current document, and writes it to a table in a new document (similar to the style summary above) so that you can print it out, etc.

- ❧ **And more tools are being added!**

1.10   *Microsoft and I*

The further I progressed with writing this book, the more I realised that I would have to put in a little paragraph like this, so if you're reading this chapter, here it is! Microsoft did not pay me to write this book, nor do I get any benefit from Microsoft from writing this book. I am not a so-called Microsoft Word MVP (Most Valued Professional) , although I am a so-called Microsoft MCT (Microsoft Certified Trainer). While only Microsoft itself appoints MVPs based on their contribution to the worldwide community of users (e.g., Microsoft Word users for Word MVPs), anyone can become an MCT—you just need to do some exams and pay a membership fee (you also need to maintain a certain approval level in your training, meaning it's probably easier to lose your certification than it is to actually get it!). This means that being a MVP is a big deal, and being a MCT is not (that's to put me in my place keep me humble).

I do confess to enjoying Microsoft products (you should see me with Excel), but like most other "power users" (I am arrogant enough to call myself that) it always ends up being something of a love-hate affair (I have the same position with some Apple products I use, I just think some Apple aficionados are too blinded by single-minded devotion to see any flaws in anything from the world of Jobs). So you will see me, throughout this book, extolling all the virtues of Word, but at the same time, also taking Microsoft to task (not that I have any hope of them ever listening) for oversights, bugs, and just plain silly things they do. I sometimes get the impression that some of the newer recruits at Microsoft have no idea what their predecessors actually did, nor the inclination to study it up and figure it out—so we often find things that have worked perfectly, being changed, in the name of progress, to versions that no longer work as well. Go figure!

I will, thus, also offer some solutions to problems in Word, sometimes, again, I am even arrogant enough to think that my solutions are better than those provided by Microsoft (my Bookmark Manager—one of the Word uTIlities I have created—and my solution to creating captioned equations—p. 412—are examples). But please remember that Word is a Microsoft product, for which they should get their full credit (and, where due, blame!), and please remember that I also make mistakes (more than you know).

1.11   A final word before we begin

Beware. The techniques you are about to learn are extremely powerful. Please *do* use these techniques at home—the only way to master them is through practise (just reading this book is not enough). But please also note that powerful techniques also come with the capability of making a great big mess. Please do make backups before trying something you don't know. And when you do make a mess, please do persevere, and try again, not just until you get it right, but until you actually understand what it is you are doing—that is the only way you will learn.

I have put a lot of effort into this book. As I mentioned earlier, I started presenting this material in 2005 (for Word 2003). I started working on this version of the book that you have in your hand (which contains some of that early material) on 8 June 2009. To date, I have spent somewhat less than 319 hours working on this document alone. And that does not include the time spent developing the uTIities, or the time spent reading up and learning better about how Word works. This book contains 146 437 words. The document is 27Mb on disk. All to teach you the intricacies of using Word for typing your thesis or dissertation—I really, really, want you to work better with Word.

It is my hope, then, that you will find the book useful, and also, importantly, enjoyable, and that you will also become a Word master.

Chapter 2
Different strokes for different folks: Accessing tools

I must explain one concept to you as well before we start. It concerns how the instructions in this manual are presented. I have a concept (no, unlike the big guns out there, I haven't trademarked it!) which I call "instruction sets." Imagine a room in a house with more than one door (kitchens and dining rooms often fit this description). This means that there is more than one way to get into that particular room. For example, I could walk from the passage into the kitchen, or I could walk down the passage, into the dining room, through the dining room, and then into the kitchen (that, in computer terms, would normally be using the mouse). Now on the computer, there often exists more than one way to get a job done. This is also especially significant when it comes to the interface for a specific command—you can often perform a certain command with a keyboard combination, through the menu (with the keyboard or the mouse), through a toolbar (with the mouse), or with a context menu (with the mouse *or* the keyboard). Knowing these various paths has made the transition from Office 2003 to Office 2007 surprisingly painless for me. Now that may be salt in your wounds, as it is a bit late to learn about that now, but then again, it's never too late to learn something new.

2.1 *Getting things done*

Before I introduce what I call "Instruction Sets," I want to examine the various "paths" to performing tasks briefly.

2.1.1 Keyboard shortcuts

Firstly, keyboard combinations (from now on, I will use the proper term: "**keyboard shortcuts**") commonly combine an indicator key[8] (which may, or may not, make sense) with one or more access keys[8] (Ctrl, Alt and Shift) to initiate certain commands. For example, we have all heard the rhyme "Cut, Copy, Paste." Now that rhyme will help you learn three easy keyboard shortcuts that work in any computer program I know (i.e., they are universal). The (understandable) indicator is C for Copy. Now look at your keyboard. You will see the keys X, C, V near the bottom left. Those keys are Cut, Copy, Paste (X for Cut and V for Paste don't make sense without their proximity to the C key). Pressing **Ctrl + C**[9] while you are typing is a lot quicker than stopping your typing, grabbing the mouse, and then selecting copy (through one of the methods still to be described), and then returning to your keyboard. Wherever possible, I try to teach myself keyboard shortcuts to speed up my work. I will describe the process I use for this briefly in 2.2. Also note that your keyboard has a right-click key—the right click brings up the context menu—(typically, between the Ctrl and Alt keys on the right of the keyboard, or **Shift + F10**). This is useful for when you wanted to right click on a word,

---

[8] This is my own terminology, so don't try to look it up in a computing encyclopaedia.

[9] Note that while it is strictly speaking more correct to use a lower case to indicate a key used without the Shift key, and an upper case to indicate a key used with the Shift key, I will follow convention and always use uppercase letters, as the keys on keyboards use uppercase letters.

for example when a word is misspelled and you would like to use the context menu to correct it. Context menus are discussed in section 2.1.5 below.

2.1.2   Accelerator keys

Normally, every command a program can perform can also be accessed through the **menu**, or, in Office 2007, the ribbons. In fact, I hate it when the menus are incomplete—that is to say, when certain functions are only hidden in obscure context menus or keyboard shortcuts (fortunately, there are very few of those). It thus pays to familiarise yourself with the menu of the program you are working with, so that you know where to find the command you are looking for. Note that the main menu items represent themes or sets of commands (also note that third-party vendors—or you!—can create extra menus and toolbars for most programs). The location of certain commands under certain menus is sometimes debatable. This is very interesting, as in the re-organisation of the Microsoft Office user interface, some things have indeed shifted around a bit. For example, in Word 2003, you would insert a table by selecting the menu Table, Insert, Table. In Office 2007, it is now on the ribbon Insert, Table.

Let me teach you some more about menus and ribbons. Firstly, note that a menu actually (sort-of) consists of three "columns." The instructions are on the left (actually the middle, with icons to their left), and the right of the menu will show some additional information. Look at the File menu below (Figure 4): Some of the items actually show the keyboard shortcuts to the right (have you ever seen that?!), and some have a small rightward-pointing triangle, indicating a sub-menu. Note that some instructions end with a "..." indicating that a dialog (or sometimes a pane) will be called up, and you will have to complete the dialog for the instruction to be completed. I will step you through a dialog in a minute.

Also note that each menu item has one letter underlined, and that, in the context of the menu, that letter is unique (i.e., no other menu item has the same letter underlined). This is known as an **accelerator key**, and allows you to drive the menu with the keyboard (i.e., without the mouse). You will see that each submenu again has (as far as possible) a unique letter underlined. The way to drive the menus with the keyboard is to press and release the Alt key, and then to type the accelerator keys for the functions you want. In this way, I could, for example, copy (in Word 2003 and earlier) with Alt, E, C. Of course, there is no reason why I would want to do that, because **Ctrl + C** is quicker, but for some often-used functions with no keyboard shortcut, this is incredibly useful. And if you have the bad fortune of having to work on a laptop with only a fiddly touch pad or joystick and no proper mouse, knowing how to operate the menus with the keyboard becomes very handy.

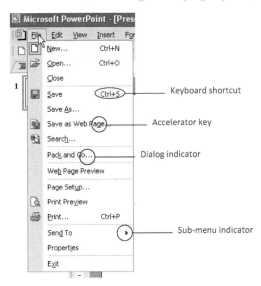

Figure 4   *PowerPoint 2002 File menu*

So what does all this talk of menus help when we are working with Word 2007 or 2010, where menus have (almost) ceased to exist? Microsoft Office also allows you to operate the ribbons with accelerator keys. Just press Alt, and you will see the keys for each ribbon appearing as tooltips next to the ribbon tab. Press a ribbon's key or keys[10], and that ribbon will be displayed, together with accelerator keys for every item on the ribbon. For example, in Figure 6, when Alt is pressed, the top part of the figure appears. Then when H is pressed, the Home ribbon is displayed, and the accelerator keys for all items on the Home ribbon are displayed, as in the bottom part of the figure. Note that keyboard shortcuts are not displayed any more (as was the case in the old menus), but can still be seen in the form of a tooltip that appears when the mouse is held over the tool. Throughout this book, whenever a command is mentioned, its accelerator key or keys will be indicated by underlining, or, if the letters involved do not appear in the word, then as a footnote.

---

[10] The ribbon now includes two-character accelerators, such as JT for the Table Design ribbon in Microsoft Word.

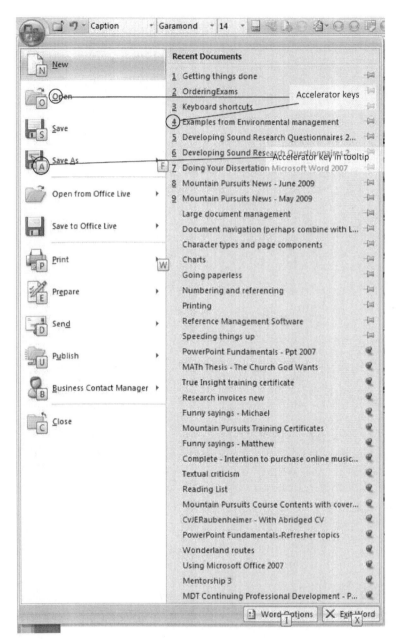

Figure 5　　　　*Word 2007 Office menu (Similar to the old "File menu")*

Figure 6   *Operating Ribbons with the keyboard*

2.1.3   Ribbons

The important thing to note is that ribbons replace both toolbars and menus, although chiefly toolbars. Many of the tools previously found on toolbars are now located on the ribbons. Suffice it to say that normally, the tools on the ribbons are invoked with the mouse (but can, as already indicated, be invoked with the keyboard). If you click on any ribbon tab, that ribbon with all its tools will appear. Click on the tool, and the job is done. If you have a mouse with a scroll wheel, you can also hold your mouse over the ribbons, and use the scroll wheel to move back and forth between ribbons.

Each ribbon is divided into a number of groups (also known as chunks). These groups always appear in the same order, and the tools in each also appear in the same order. Thus the Home ribbon in Word contains the Clipboard, Font, Paragraph, Styles, and Editing groups, in that order.

Dialog indicators have also changed in the new interface, being the small square with an arrow pointing diagonally down to the right in the bottom right corner of certain groups on the various ribbons (these can be clearly seen at the bottom right of the Clipboard, Font, Paragraph, and Styles groups of the Home ribbon in the top part of Figure 6). Having said that, the ribbons replace toolbars and menus together, and some of the ribbon tools are actually miniature menus, with the more traditional dialog launchers on them (Figure 7 shows the Borders tool in the Paragraph group on the Home ribbon as an example).

Figure 7   *Home ribbon | Paragraph group | Borders menu*

The ribbons also make extensive use of split buttons (split either horizontally or vertically). For example, the Paste button on the Home ribbon has a paste icon on top, and an arrow on the bottom. If you just want to paste, click on the top part. If you want to do an out-of-ordinary paste (i.e., view other paste options), then click on the arrow. The default option (the one shared by the other half of the split button) is normally the first in the extra list (i.e., it is redundant). You will even find split buttons on the Office menu (Save As and Print), and, of course, they work in the same way there.

A new feature on the ribbons is galleries. These basically consist of a variety of options to choose from, and have two scroll buttons at the right which allow you to move through the gallery one row at a time (see the up ⏶ and down ⏷ arrows in Figure 8), or, at the bottom right, a More ⏬ button which will expand the entire gallery (sometimes obscuring what you want to see, hence the row-by-row scroll buttons). Galleries are often live previewed, meaning that whatever you have selected will be displayed as if the gallery option had been applied.

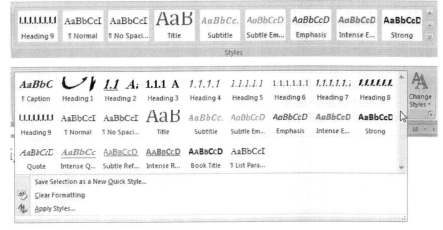

Figure 8   Styles gallery—Home ribbon, and Styles gallery expanded

Note that the ribbons are very context-specific. Firstly, Word will decide how to display the ribbon tools based on the available space on the screen. What this means is that if you work on two different computers with two different size screens and/or different screen resolutions, the tools on the ribbons may appear to be different—relax, the tools are always the same, and are always in the same place, they sometimes just look a bit different (I know, it's confusing). Secondly, you may find Word jumping between ribbons from time to time, depending on what you just did, and you will also find that certain ribbons only appear in certain contexts. For example, just because you can see a table on the page in front of you, doesn't mean Word is going to give you the two table ribbons (Table Tools | Design and Table Tools | Layout. Oh no, you first have to move into the table (click or move with the keyboard) before it will yield and supply the ribbons you want. And when you move away from the table, the ribbons obediently disappear out of the way.

Finally, you can minimise the ribbons in entirety as well. The simplest way to do this is to toggle them off and on with the **Ctrl + F1** keyboard shortcut. Alternatively, right click on any ribbon or click on the arrow on the right of the Quick Access Toolbar (Instruction set 1).

Instruction set 1   *Minimising and maximising ribbons*

Shortcut	Ctrl + F1
Left click	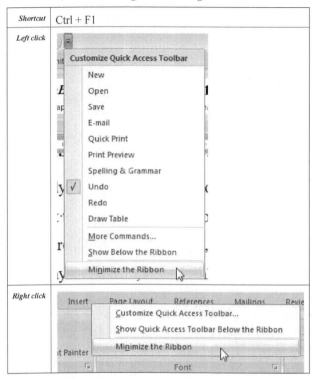
Right click	

2.1.4   Quick Access Toolbar

A new productivity tool introduced in Office 2007 is the Quick Access Toolbar[11] (see the very top row of Figure 6), which allows you to add your own buttons for tools you commonly use. What makes the Quick Access Toolbar useful is the ability to add tools not already on the ribbons—this is your own little piece of real estate, which you can use to customise the way you work in Word.

The Quick Access Toolbar contains three buttons by default: Undo, Redo, and Save. Strictly speaking, space on the Quick Access Toolbar is at a premium, and all three of those can be run from the keyboard (**Ctrl + Z**, **Ctrl + Y** or **F4**, **Ctrl + S** respectively), but I like the ability to undo and redo multiple actions (the Undo and Redo buttons are also split buttons), so I tend to keep at least the Undo button (my main motivation is that I also use it, ironically, to teach myself keyboard shortcuts, but more about that in section 2.2). But I normally ditch the Redo and Save buttons. Then the task at hand for you is to keep thinking while you work. When you find yourself struggling to access a tool, or find that a tool you use a lot is not on the ribbon (e.g., it is in a dialog box), then you need to stop and add the tool to the Quick Access Toolbar.

---

[11] Already being referred to on the Net as the "QAT."

Adding tools to the Quick Access Toolbar is relatively simple: Click on the arrow on its far right, and select one of the most popular commands from the list, or select <u>M</u>ore commands... to open the Word Options dialog on the Quick Access Toolbar tab (Figure 9).

Instruction set 2   Customising the Quick Access Toolbar

Keyboard	Alt | F | I | C (Select the <u>F</u>ile Tab, Word Opt<u>i</u>ons, and then go to the <u>C</u>ustomize Ribbon tab)
Left click	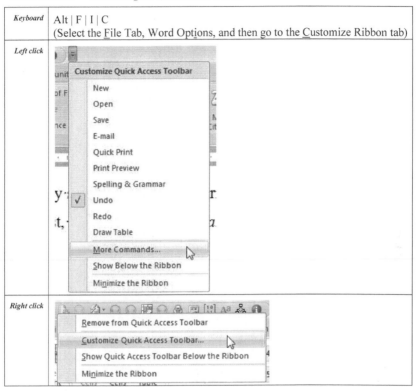
Right click	

The Word Options \| Quick Access Toolbar dialog basically consists of two parts. On the left you will find all the tools that Word has. On the right is the Quick Access Toolbar. The left part organises the Word tools for you in various ways to help you find them. First there is a list of what Microsoft, on the basis of its research, believes to be the most popular tools. Pulling down the list will show you some other options. Working from below, you can find commands on any of the ribbons, or you can add macros that you are using or you can browse through the quite extensive list of all of Word's commands, or, very usefully, you can find a listing of all the tools that are not on the ribbons (these are typically the tools that you either access from dialogs, or even more obscure locations). The two parts are separated by <u>A</u>dd and <u>R</u>emove buttons. Once you have found the tool you are looking for, you can thus add it to the Quick Access Toolbar, and if you have tools on the Quick Access Toolbar that you feel you no longer want to use, you can remove them to make space for other tools. Quite obviously, you first need to select the tool you are adding or removing, and less obviously, the add and remove buttons can quite simply be replaced by a double click on the tool.

The right part simply represents the Quick Access Toolbar. What is on the top of the list, will appear on the left of the Quick Access Toolbar, and so on. Use the spin buttons on the right of the list to reorder the items on the Quick Access Toolbar. To nix the whole thing and go back to the original ("factory") setting, click on Re̲set. To change the icon associated with any tool, click on M̲odify....

Finally, note that you actually can have as many Quick Access Toolbars as you like. Right at the top, you will find the setting "For all documents (default)." This is where you build the Quick Access Toolbar that is always displayed in Word. However, from the same list, you can select any of the currently open documents, and build a new Quick Access Toolbar for that document. Those tools will then only be displayed when that document is active (i.e., not just open, but actually the document you are working on—minimise the document, and its Quick Access Toolbar will disappear). Note that this Quick Access Toolbar will appear to the right of the default Quick Access Toolbar, ensconced in a faint vertical rectangle.

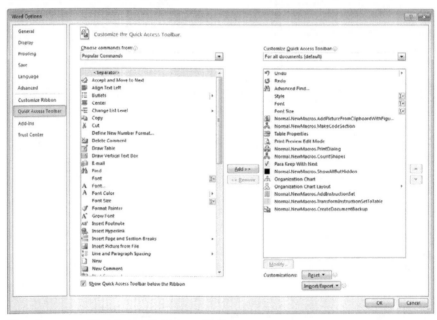

Figure 9   *Word Options: Quick Access Toolbar*

Once you have your Quick Access Toolbar loaded with all sorts of goodies, you need to decide where to keep it. You have two choices—above or below the ribbons. Simply right click on it, or click on the arrow on its far right, and select S̲how Below the Ribbon to move it down. Do the same, this time selecting the same menu item, which now reads $\underline{S}$how Above the Ribbon to move it up[12]. Both positions have their advantages and their disadvantages: Above saves a miniscule amount of vertical screen space. Below gives you more horizontal screen space for tools added to the Quick Access Toolbar, and also brings those tools a bit closer to where your mouse normally is. However, if you drive with the keyboard, note that each tool you add to the Quick Access Toolbar is given its own accelerator, and that makes this last point moot.

Figure 10   *Quick Access Toolbar above and below the ribbons*

Application 2.1   *Quick Access Toolbar*

If you write and use macros a lot, you may find yourself adding them to the Quick Access Toolbar very quickly—especially macros that you use repeatedly. What else can you add to the Quick Access Toolbar? Firstly, I try to keep it clear for tools I really can't access any other way. This means that I generally steer clear of things like Save (Ctrl + S), New (Ctrl + N), Print (Ctrl + P), Print Preview (Ctrl + F2), etc. However, if you look at some of the examples already used (Figure 6, Figure 10), you will notice that I have added three tools from my Home ribbon to the Quick Access Toolbar on my computer—three tools that take up a lot of space: Style, Font, and Font Size. My reasoning was simple: Because I work with styles a lot (see Chapter 6), I always want to be able to see, as I move around and do things in my document, what the current settings are for the paragraph I am in. Now by and large, the reasoning behind the new Fluent User Interface® has been to reduce the effort needed to perform a task. While Microsoft have succeeded in this, overall, there have always been some trade-offs (Print Preview, via the mouse, has become a drag—either Ctrl + F2 it, or add it to the Quick Access Toolbar). Another drag is that in the old UI, the toolbars were always displayed (unless you "accidentally" lost them), and I could thus always see this information. In the new UI, I need to switch to the Home ribbon to see this, and that is a drag when all I actually wanted to do was a quick check with a glance of my eye. So now I put them up there where I can see them, and it has helped a lot. This is also encouraged by the fact

---

[12] If you really like doing things the longest way possible, you can do this from Word Options | Customize as well.

*that the keyboard shortcuts which used to take you to the Font and Font Size tools on the toolbars in previous versions of Word (**Ctrl + Shift + F** and **Ctrl + Shift + P**, respectively), now both open the Font dialog, and this is often unnecessary for what I want to do. So again, having these tools on the Quick Access Toolbar means I can access them with the assigned accelerators, and I have the functionality of my old tools back.*

Finally, please, bear in mind that when you add tools to the Quick Access Toolbar, it really should be the tools that you use a lot, and that you cannot access via other means—you really don't want Word to end up like Figure 1.

2.1.5   Context menus

The last place from which you can access tasks is the **context menus**. These are an attempt to bring the tasks you would most commonly need in a certain situation right to you, through the use of the right mouse button. This means that what the context menu consists of will depend on what you are busy doing at that point in time. Sometimes the tasks you might want to use would not be on the context menu, meaning that you will have to learn, through use, when the context menu is a good option and when not. Note also that I said (on p. 11) that the context menus can be driven with the keyboard or the mouse. I think the mouse does not need explanation, but note that on the bottom right of the main part of a standard keyboard (or in any number of places on laptop keyboards), you will find the following special keys, normally in this order: Alt, Windows (⊞), Right Click/Context menu (▤), and Ctrl. Using the **Right Click key** (or pressing **Shift + F10**) is the same as right-clicking with the mouse on whatever is selected, or on the item at the cursor or the I-beam (depending on where you are working), and the context menu also has accelerator keys which can be driven with the keyboard (no need to press Alt now). Microsoft Office 2007 introduces a mini-toolbar together with the context menu (see Figure 11), although this only appears when the mouse is right-clicked, not when the context menu is invoked from the keyboard.

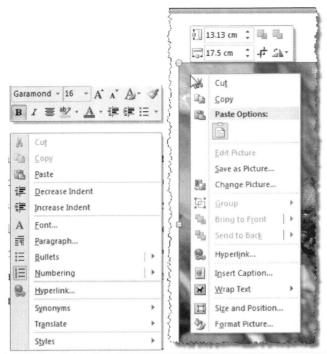

Figure 11   Context menu and Mini-Toolbar (text and picture)

2.1.6   Dialogs and Panes

Dialogs are like go-betweens, facilitating a dialogue between you and the program, so that it can get the necessary information it needs from you in order for it to be able to complete its task. A newer feature (okay, it's not so new any more) in Microsoft Office is the use of panes. Panes can be located to the left (e.g., the Office Clipboard pane), to the right (e.g., the Mail Merge Wizard pane in Word) or even below the screen (e.g., the Reviewing Pane in Word, which can now appear to the left as well). Panes basically contain the same parts as dialogs, and some panes have actually just replaced dialogs from previous versions. Interestingly, after a history of moving a number of dialogs to panes over various previous versions of Office[13], Microsoft has reduced the number of panes significantly in Office 2007 (could panes have been a pain?). Also note that in Office 2007, dialogs and panes are now launched from the dialog launcher buttons (⬜) at the bottom right (level with the group name) of the relevant groups on the various ribbons.

To understand how to operate a dialog box (and to understand the instructions for the tasks you will be performing in this course), it helps to know what the names of all the bits and pieces are (the same as you appreciate your surgeon knowing his anatomy…).

---

[13] Yes, just like there once was a time when ribbons did not exist, so also there was a time when panes did not exist. Maybe you're too young to have experienced that. Once upon a time TV also did not exist…

Just a note in general before I get stuck into the detail: Note that many of the settings in dialogs are also controlled by accelerator keys. In this instance, you hold the Alt key down *while* pressing that key, and the relevant part of the dialog is automatically selected or invoked. This is quicker than grabbing the mouse to click on that part, and then typing in whatever you want. If you don't want to jump around in a dialog like that, you can also navigate through dialogs one item at a time with the **Tab** key, moving from one setting to the next (and you can reverse the order with **Shift + Tab**). So you can "type, Tab, type, Tab," your way through a dialog rather than "type, grab mouse, move mouse, click mouse, type…" (you get the picture).

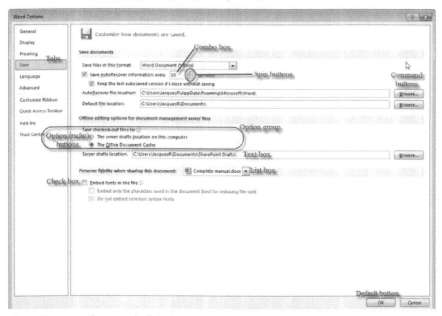

Figure 12	Anatomy of a dialog box

2.1.6.1   Option groups

Dialogs often contain numerous settings which are grouped according to their function. Option groups normally contain settings from which you may choose only one option (see below).

2.1.6.2   Check boxes and option buttons

When you have to select from various options, check boxes and/or option buttons (a.k.a. radio buttons) are used. Check boxes normally allow you to select multiple options at the same time, while option buttons allow you to select only one option from that particular option group.

Toggle buttons (not shown, and seldom used) are similar to check boxes, in that they turn certain functions on or off (similar to light switches), or a set of two option buttons, in that they switch between the two available options.

2.1.6.3   Text boxes, list boxes, and combo boxes

When you need to enter in something, a text box is used. An example of this is when you have to give a name for a file that you are saving. When you have to choose from a list of predefined options, list boxes are used. A combo box is like a list box, except that it has the option of typing in your own value—in other words, it combines the functionality of a text box and a list box. Note that spin buttons are often used to set the value of a combo box, especially when it is a numerical combo box. However, the increment chosen for the spin button can determine whether it is actually useful or not. For example, if I want to set the left indentation of a paragraph in Word's Paragraph dialog to 9cm (where the increment is in tenths of a centimetre), I will have to click the spin button 90 times! But because it is a combo box, I can just type "9" (one keystroke instead of 90 mouse clicks is quite a big difference). You can also type in list boxes, although then, what you type is not physically entered into the box, it merely serves as a guide for navigating through the list (e.g., if I type a R in the Alignment list box of the Paragraph dialog, it automatically takes me to the first—and in this case only—R in the list: Right alignment) which is still faster than opening and selecting from the list with the mouse.

A further point to note about the combo box and list box tools is that they often allow you to select more than one item at a time (known as multi select). This is done in one of two ways: To select a whole group, click on the first item, hold the Shift key in, and then click on the last item (or hold the shift key down and move with the arrows). To select a number of disparate items, click on them while holding the Ctrl key in (this cannot, to my knowledge, be done with the keyboard).

2.1.6.4   Command buttons

Command buttons perform certain tasks (the most common being the OK and Cancel buttons, or open more dialogs (in which case, this is often indicated by the "…"). Note that dialogs often have a default button, which can be identified by its being highlighted, even when it is not selected. When a default button exists, you can activate it from anywhere in the dialog (almost anywhere—the exception is when you are in certain list or combo boxes) simply by pressing Enter.

2.1.6.5   Tabs

Often dialogs contain so many settings that they cannot fit into the available space. So the dialog gets broken into tabs. Each tab contains a group of settings (supposedly) governed by the thematic title of the tab. The tabs shown in Figure 12 are newer ones, running vertically down the left side, whereas the older style tabs run horizontally across the top.

2.2   Instruction sets

Because I dislike over-using the mouse (it is a slow, cumbersome tool, especially when working with text), I tend to like alternatives to getting jobs done. So I use a lot of accelerator keys and keyboard shortcuts. However, I realise that some people find it difficult to kick their mouse addiction (note: It's not that I hate the mouse, I do use it—

really!—it's just that I know how the mouse can slow me down, so I try to avoid using it *unless* it helps me speed things up). So for those people whose mice seem to stick to their palms, and for the sake of completeness, I list as many ways of getting a command initiated as possible—hence the instruction sets. Here's how they work—below is what the instruction set for Copy would look like—you can see that the keyboard shortcut, the ribbon accelerator (keyboard), the ribbon image (or wherever you would click with your left mouse button), and the context menu item (accessed with the right mouse button, typically) are all shown:

Instruction set 3   Example of Copy

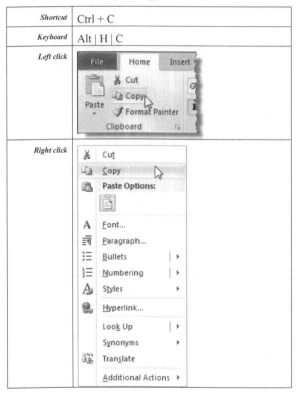

Shortcut	Ctrl + C
Keyboard	Alt | H | C

Note that, depending on the task at hand, some of the methods in the set might not be shown. That merely indicates that that avenue (e.g., a keyboard shortcut) does not *yet* exist for that task. In certain circumstances, most often when there is only one (default) way of performing a certain task, I will not use an instruction set, but will explain the process in the text. Also, note that I will often be using the instruction sets as an abbreviated form of demonstrating in these notes how certain tasks should be activated. In other words, the standard way of doing it would be to show you a screen capture of me actually doing the task, as in Figure 13 (below) from PowerPoint 2002. However, this does not necessarily show you all the ways of doing what you want to do, and it also does not make provision for changes in what the user sees (e.g., if the users sees the abbreviated menu which does not look like my screen capture, or users open a dialog on a different tab than my screen capture, they get confused). Relax, though, this doesn't mean that you won't be seeing screen captures, just that I will be using them only when necessary, and giving you more complete information in an instruction set whenever I can.

Figure 13   *Screen capture of Copy command on the Edit menu*

To further explain the instruction sets, take a look at Instruction set 3 again. In the *Left click* image, you can see the Ribbon tab (the Home ribbon in this case), the Ribbon group (the Clipboard group in this case), and the button to click on is highlighted. Note that when you hold your mouse over this button, a screen tip naming and explaining that particular button will appear—this might not be shown in my instruction set.

Some people seem to struggle to know where to find the tools when they look at these instructions. Yes, strictly speaking, I could have labelled a nice little 1 in a nice little circle above the Home ribbon in the image, and then had a nice little 2 in a nice little circle on the Copy button (or even a 2 on the Clipboard group, and a 3 on the copy button). I did not do that, though, but I always went to great pains to include the ribbon tab (which will always be highlighted in the same way that Word naturally highlights them) and the entire ribbon group to which the tool belongs. Thus, when looking at these instructions, get into the habit of looking for the highlighted tab first, and then the highlighted tool on the ribbon. If you do that, you should have no problem finding the tool. Here and there, when tasks requiring complex sequences are involved, I did illustrate the process step by step (see Figure 190 on p. 254 for an example).

Also bear in mind that the Ribbons are dynamic. Figure 14 shows the same group as is found in Instruction set 3, but on a different screen. What is happening is that the program figures out how much space it has on the screen depending on the screen resolution, and then either expands or scrunches up the ribbons to fit into the available space. So don't allow that to throw you off. It's still the same command in the same place, it just looks a little different.

Figure 14   *Expanded vs Condensed Clipboard group*

The next thing to bear in mind with the instruction sets is the sets of symbols that I have chosen to use. Compare the *Keyboard* and the *Keyboard shortcut* boxes. Note that in the *Keyboard* listing (which shows the ribbon accelerator), the command is Alt | H | C. The bar | indicates that the keys are pressed *in succession* (i.e., in this instance, press and then release the Alt key, then press and release the H key, and then press and release the C key). In the *Shortcut* box, the command is **Ctrl + C**. The + indications that keys must be pressed *simultaneously* (i.e., press and hold the Ctrl key, then also press the C key, and then release both). Also note that, strictly speaking, c=c and C=Shift + c (i.e., when you just press the C key on the keyboard, you get a lowercase c, but when you hold down Shift and press the same key, you get an uppercase C). However, I will always be using the uppercase symbol to denote any letter key, as is the custom on the keyboard itself, and will explicitly indicate when the Shift key is needed (e.g., **Ctrl + Shift + C**). This applies to the instruction sets, as well as to the list of keyboard shortcuts in Appendix A (starting on p. 497). In the *Right click* box (which shows the context menu), you will note that the C is underlined, indicating the accelerator key for that, should you wish to operate the context menus via the keyboard (as explained in 2.1.5).

A final thought about instruction sets and the new Quick Access Toolbar (mentioned in section 2.1.4 on p. 18) is that, even though it starts out with a default collection of only three buttons (Save, Undo, and Redo), *all* Word commands can be added to it. Of course, you wouldn't want to do that, because you would have no space left to work on your screen. But because every command can be added, I won't mention that in each and every instruction set. Thus, whenever you see an instruction set, note that you can also create your own "shortcut" by adding the command to the Quick Access Toolbar, or you can assign your own keyboard shortcut to it, as will be described in section 2.3.2, p. 30).

2.3   Using keyboard shortcuts

One day, we will speak to our computers, or just wave our hands. One day. But for this generation, we will still do most of our work with a keyboard. And a mouse. But if you really want to work at your fastest, you will want to learn to use the mouse only when necessary, and to maximise your use of the keyboard—it just makes sense to be able to do a lot of your Word formatting, etc. on the keyboard, even as you type your text. To do this, you will want to master the use of keyboard shortcuts. Below, I will outline a strategy for learning Word's existing keyboard shortcuts, and I will also show how easy it is to create your own customised keyboard shortcuts in Word.

2.3.1   Learning to use keyboard shortcuts

If you really want to boost your productivity, you will want to learn how to use the keyboard for more than just typing text—the keyboard is a powerful tool for performing commands on the computer, in many ways more powerful than the mouse, especially because many commands need to be activated while typing text. To type, stop, grab the mouse, do the command, then come back to the keyboard and resume typing is a very slow process, while to type, do the command on the keyboard, and then continue typing is much faster. I must add here that I am not a mouse-hater. It's nothing personal. In fact, I do use my mouse quite a bit, although only when I know it is the fastest way to

28

do the job. I just hate working slowly, and I have realised how much the mouse can slow you down.

How, then, do you learn keyboard shortcuts? Please not by trying to memorise lists of keyboard shortcuts—you will have forgotten 90% of them within the month, or, if you do remember them, might find yourself in the auditions for Rain Man II.

The most important skill to acquire is to awaken your curiosity concerning keyboard shortcuts. Become as curious as a little child again. When you are typing, you sometimes press the wrong keys on the keyboard, and some interesting things can happen on the screen. Most people grab the mouse (their first mistake!), click undo (their second mistake—**Ctrl + Z** is quicker), and simply continue working, never wondering what has just happened, instead just thankful that they were able to recover. Rather, stop to analyse what has happened, and look at the undo stack (If you must use the mouse, click, not on undo, but on the arrow on the right of undo, or use the keyboard accelerator to bring up the list immediately—quicker again) to see what the program calls the action you just accomplished (even if unwittingly). Next, decide whether this is useful to you. For example, do you change line spacing a lot? If you just accidentally changed the line spacing of your paragraph with the keyboard, then this is your opportunity to learn how to do that purposefully[14]. If what happened is not something you would use, move on and forget about it. If it is useful to you, then you should try to figure out what it was that you typed to activate that action. If you can't figure it out, *then* you can try to find the action in a list of keyboard shortcuts (I have provided the most complete list I could in Appendix A, starting on p. 497), or in the help files (just open help, type "keyboard shortcuts", and viola! a nice long list). All you need to do now is to practise it a few times, and start using it-you will have learned it without ever having had to memorise it.

A large number of keyboard shortcuts can just be learned by being observant—I have already pointed out that keyboard shortcuts are permanently listed across certain menu items in many programs. When you notice one, decide whether it is useful, and if it is, start using it. You can also get the Microsoft Office applications to teach you to use keyboard shortcuts by including them in the screen tips on the ribbons: Go to the Advanced tab of the *Application*[15] Options (all of this, of course, is Alt | F | T | A on the keyboard), then in the Display group, activate Show shortcut keys in ScreenTips (Figure 15). Then, when you hold your mouse over any tool on the ribbon, the screen tip will include the shortcut key (if it exists, and not quite always—e.g., the clear formatting keyboard shortcut[16] is not shown in its screen tip). Many functions for which keyboard shortcuts do not exit can still be accessed very quickly from the keyboard by using the accelerator keys.

---

[14] Ctrl + 1 = Single line spacing, Ctrl + 2 = Double line spacing, and Ctrl + 5 = One and a half (1.5) line spacing, if you were wondering.

[15] i.e., Word, Excel, PowerPoint, Access, etc.

[16] It's Ctrl + Spacebar, by the way.

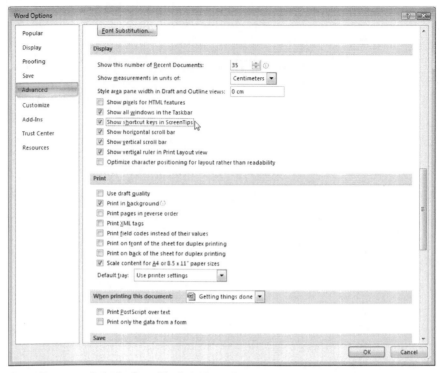

Figure 15   *Activating ScreenTips for keyboard shortcuts*

We have discussed now how to *discover* keyboard shortcuts. But they are only any good if you can *remember* them. The last point to using keyboard shortcuts is that the best way to remember them is to relate them to use. There is no sense in memorising a list of keyboard shortcuts that you will never use. For example, unless you are Danish or Norwegian, does it really help you to know that "**Ctrl + /**" adds a slash through the letters o and O in MSWord? Rather, when you find yourself doing a certain task repetitively with the mouse, know that Marx's comment was wrong: It is not religion that is the opium of the masses, but the mouse which is the true opiate of the masses (of course, Marx knew nothing about what was to come). This is the time that you must refuse to accept the status quo, and go to the trouble of finding out (as described above) what the keyboard shortcut is for that function. Because it relates to a function you use often, it will take no time at all to practise the shortcut so much that you will never forget it. Learn your keyboards shortcuts like that—one at a time, discovering what they are and then applying them in practise, until they stick.

2.3.2   Creating keyboard shortcuts

One of Word's most brilliant features is the ability to easily create your own keyboard shortcuts[17]. The Customize Ribbon tab of the Word Options dialog (Figure 9, p. 20),

---

[17] While you can theoretically create your own keyboard shortcuts in all of the Microsoft Office programs, Word is by far the best in this regard.

has a Keyboard shortcuts: Customize... button at the bottom. Selecting this opens the Customize Keyboard dialog (Figure 16). This dialog is again organised in such a way as to help you find the tool to which you want to assign a keyboard shortcut—first the Categories group lists all the ribbons, finishing with the All Commands section if you really cannot find the tool. Over and above that, a separate section at the bottom of this list allows you to assign keyboard shortcuts to macros, fonts, AutoText entries, styles, and even common symbols. To find the command, simply select (in the Categories list) the ribbon on or other group to which to tool belongs, and then find the tool in the Commands list on the right (which is sorted alphabetically, although since this list uses Word's own internal nomenclature for the tools, it is a bit cryptic). When you have selected the tool, the dialog will show you whether any keyboard shortcuts already exist for it, and what they are. If a shortcut exists, it will be shown in the Current keys list— use it and learn it (note the order). If none exists, your next task is to choose a keyboard shortcut for yourself, and to enter it in the Press new shortcut key text box. If it is already assigned to another tool, this will be indicated just below the Current keys list. If this keyboard shortcut is already assigned to a tool, first consider finding an unassigned keyboard shortcut for the tool you want, or decide whether you can do without the tool to which it is currently assigned. Once you have your shortcut, select the Assign button to assign it to your tool (if it is already assigned to another tool, this will be replaced). If you see that a tool has multiple keyboard shortcuts, you can always select the ones you don't use and then select Remove, although, because keyboard shortcuts can be reassigned as and when you please, this form of housekeeping is hardly necessary. If you also find that you have really made a mess of the keyboard shortcuts, you can click on the Reset All... button to go right back to the keyboard shortcuts Word had out of the box.

Apart from the ability to use this dialog to assign keyboard shortcuts (which we will discuss shortly), I sometimes use this dialog to discover keyboard shortcuts as well (in addition to the Word Help files, already discussed).

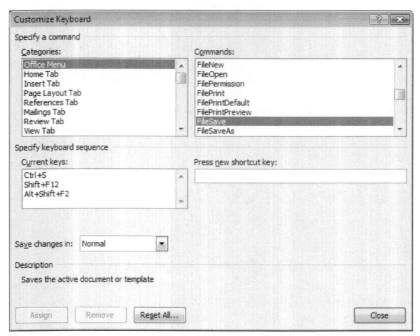

Figure 16   Customize Keyboard dialog

Application 2.2   Keyboard shortcuts

*Figure 16 shows that three different keyboard shortcuts exist for Save. **Ctrl + S** is an almost universal keyboard shortcut (there is not a program I have worked on that does not use **Ctrl + S** for Save). That means that the **Shift + F12** and **Alt + Shift + F12** are really redundant. These can be useful for other tools you would want to assign keyboard shortcuts to.*

*In Chapter 6 you will learn about using styles. Remember that keyboard shortcuts in Word can be used for more than just standard tools. Some of the good keyboard shortcuts to learn are those for the heading styles[18]. However, you will also learn, I hope, to avoid the Normal style like the plague, and to rather use the Body Text style. However, there is no keyboard shortcut for the Body Text style, so I created my own. Using exactly the process described above, I assigned the keyboard shortcut **Ctrl + Alt + B** to it (this is an unassigned combination, as shown in Figure 17), which, by virtue of the association of the B with Body Text, and the Ctrl + Alt already used for some of the heading styles (as shown in footnote 18) is also easy to remember.*

*Another keyboard shortcut I can recommend creating is one for inserting a section break (discussed in section 7.1.1.1 on p. 120). To help me remember it, I have made it similar to the keyboard shortcuts for adding other breaks (**Ctrl + Enter** adds a page break, and **Ctrl + Shift + Enter** adds a column break). Thus I chose **Alt + Shift + Enter** (look for InsertSectionBreak in the list of commands).*

---

[18] Ctrl + Alt + 1 for Heading 1, Ctrl + Alt + 2 for Heading 2, Ctrl + Alt + 3 for Heading 3.

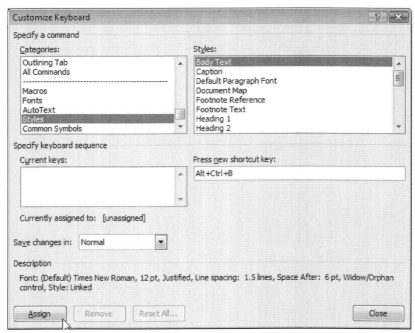

Figure 17   *Assigning a keyboard shortcut to the Body Text style*

2.4   Toggle Keys

Another useful function that you can activate on your PC that is not actually related to Word is the Toggle Keys feature of Windows (available since Windows 95). Click on Start, Settings, Control Panel, and then double-click on the accessibility Options icon. Under the Keyboard tab, select the Use Toggle Keys[19] option, and under the General tab, make sure that the Turn off accessibility features after idle for: option is not selected. Once this has been done, the computer will beep every time you press one of the Lock keys (**Caps Lock**, **Num Lock**, **Scroll Lock**) on the keyboard. This is especially useful in Word for people like me who tend to hit the **Caps Lock** key when they wanted to press the **A** key, and end up typing a whole sentence all capitalised before realising the mistake.

---

[19] Note that the Windows default shortcut for activating this setting is to hold the Num Lock key down for five seconds.

Chapter 3
Building blocks: Character types and page components

It helps to get a good grip on fonts and font types right from the start. As such, we will be taking a cursory look at the science of typography as well. Since this is not an academic work per se, I am going to take the liberty I would not normally take of referring you to WikiPedia. Here are some links you can follow that will give you a general introduction:

http://en.wikipedia.org/wiki/Typography

http://en.wikipedia.org/wiki/Typesetting

http://en.wikipedia.org/wiki/Glyph

http://en.wikipedia.org/wiki/Type_design

http://en.wikipedia.org/wiki/Serif

http://en.wikipedia.org/wiki/Sans-serif

3.1   Fonts

Fonts are wonderful things. They allow us to give different expressions to the same words. As you will see from the links provided, there is still a lot of debate about which fonts are best for what purpose. Remember that a font plays a dual role: It creates a certain feeling of aesthetics, and it influences legibility. And if you think fonts and font choices aren't important, read this article from Time magazine: "The Font War: Ikea Fans Fume over Verdana" (http://www.time.com/time/business/article/0,8599,1919127, 00.html).

I am not, however, going to give you a treatise on font selection. Rather, all I want you to do is take note of some things:

First, you may have no choice on what font to use. Some universities (unfortunately, in my opinion) are very prescriptive in what fonts should be used for what portions of a thesis. The aim of this, of course, is to increase uniformity. That in itself might not have been so bad except for the fact that these universities so often choose such drab fonts! But if the people in the university's administration bureaucracy prescribe the font, you are fighting a losing battle—just do what they say and get it over with.

Second, if you do have a choice, I would like you to think consciously about which font you choose. Your choice will tell your readers something about your personality. And it will make your thesis look more visually appealing if you choose an attractive, readable font. Studies seem to indicate that on printed paper, serif fonts read better (while the converse is true on screen, with its lower resolution). I once heard of a PhD student who purchased a font to use in his dissertation so that it would look unique. While I probably think that is a bit desperate, I will provide you with information on finding fonts and font tools below.

Here are some links to font information on the Internet:

Crabby's Font Facts. This is a short tutorial on the Microsoft website. Note that it consists of four parts:

http://office.microsoft.com/en-za/redir/HA001116430.aspx

http://office.microsoft.com/en-za/redir/HA001119384.aspx

http://office.microsoft.com/en-za/redir/HA001119655.aspx

http://office.microsoft.com/en-za/redir/HA001137126.aspx

A further great resource is the Microsoft Typography page:

http://www.microsoft.com/typography/default.mspx

You could, of course, even design your own fonts—the tools can be found on the Microsoft Typography page.

3.1.1 Collecting fonts

So what if you need fonts? Well, a good place to start is to take stock of what you've got. This article from Microsoft will tell you which fonts you got when you installed Microsoft Office:

http://office.microsoft.com/en-gb/powerpoint-help/fonts-that-ship-with-different-versions-of-office-HA010282644.aspx?CTT=1

And this page will show you all the fonts installed with all Microsoft products (one at a time, though):

http://www.microsoft.com/typography/fonts/default.aspx

Then you can get information on downloading and installing fonts here:

http://office.microsoft.com/en-gb/powerpoint-help/download-and-install-custom-fonts-to-use-with-office-HA010288084.aspx?CTT=1

Many links to places where you can find free and commercial fonts are here:

http://www.microsoft.com/typography/links/default.aspx

Here you can find a macro that will tell you which fonts you can access in Word:

http://support.microsoft.com/kb/q209205/

Some more fonts can be found at these sites:

(you guessed it): http://www.fonts.com

http://www.myfonts.com

http://www.dailyfreefonts.com

http://www.clipart.com/en/se/fonts

http://www.dingbatpages.com

http://www.fontlab.com

http://www.fontsquirrel.com

http://www.stixfonts.org

http://opensiddur.org/2010/07/unicode-compliant-and-open-source-licensed-hebrew-fonts/

Once you have those fonts, you can compare them using a pangram (a sentence containing all the letters of the alphabet). The most commonly used pangram is, of course, "the quick brown fox jumps over the lazy dog." Type this sentence out, copy and paste it multiple times, and format each one in the font you want to look at.

A brief tutorial showing how to install a font can be found here: http://www.microsoft.com/typography/TrueTypeInstall.mspx.

3.1.2   Character width

As is evident from the links provided above, one major distinction between fonts is that of serif vs. sans-serif fonts. However, another distinction that you need to keep in mind is that between monospace and proportional space fonts. With the old typewriters and early printers, the various keys were fixed to rods which were hit from behind against a ribbon to imprint the letter on the page. Because of the mechanics of these devices, the letters were all evenly spaced. The early computers also used these printers, and fonts were thus created which looked the same as they would on the printed page—in monospace. With the advent of better printing technology (from the now-obsolete dot-matrix printers to modern laser and inkjet printers), proportional space fonts were developed.

In proportional space fonts, each character occupies only the minimum horizontal width needed for its proper display. In monospace fonts, all the characters have the same width. Thus in *Courier*, probably one of the most famous monospace fonts around, an *i* and a *w* occupy the same amount of horizontal space on the printed page. In *Times Roman*, a proportional space font, an *i* occupies much less horizontal space on the printed page than a *w*, as is shown below:

Courier: iw
Times Roman: iw

Most modern fonts are proportional space, as they display much better, although this does mean that aligning your text will not be as easy as it may seem if you are using a proportional space font. For example, in the accompanying picture, it can be seen that the user has had to type in two spaces to align the number in the second row of a table with the number in the first row, even though the second row is only one digit shorter than the first (a better means of aligning numbers like this in a table will be discussed in 15.6.3).

Remember also that fonts can be attached to styles. This means that you can use a number of fonts in your document, giving it variety and a better look. It does, however, also mean that you will want to create a style for each font that you use. The reason for this is simple: Consistency. If you use only one style (e.g., "Normal") and then apply a range of different fonts to it, you can hardly expect the look of your document to be consistent without great effort. And the larger the document, the greater the effort. On the other hand, if you define various styles, with the same or different fonts, that you use in specific instances, you get a consistent look for your document. The most basic example of this is choosing the font that you want the majority of your text, your written work, to appear in, and setting the "Body Text" style with that font. Then, all the paragraphs that are made "Body Text" will look exactly the same. Some places where you may want to use other fonts are in your heading, table and figure titles, for example, or in the acknowledgements section of your dissertation.

3.2   Character types and classifications

If you want to really use Word for all it's worth, you need to know some technical details about the way the characters in your document are strung together. These will be dealt with in two broad classifications, after which you will be introduced to some characters that will help you put a shine to your dissertation.

3.2.1 Printing and non-printing characters

Mostly, what you see in Word is what you will get. If you type a letter 'g,' then you should expect to have a letter 'g' printed on your page. Most, characters, then, are "printing characters." However, some characters (called *non-printing characters*) can be made to appear on the screen, but do not print on the printed page. These include the carriage returns, hidden text, optional hyphens, etc., which will be discussed below. Also, the way in which non-printing characters are displayed is obviously different to the way in which they will be printed out (e.g., a tab is displayed on the screen with an arrow but prints as an extended white space).

By default, Word does not show most typographical characters. This may seem nice, but it is not very useful for high-quality work. One of the first things you should do is learn to work with these typographical characters visible. The simplest way to do this is to go to the Word Options dialog, and then in the Display tab, select the Show all formatting marks check box, as shown in Figure 18, or by clicking the Show/Hide (¶) button in the paragraph group of the Home ribbon, or, my preferred method, by using the keyboard shortcut **Ctrl + Shift + ***:

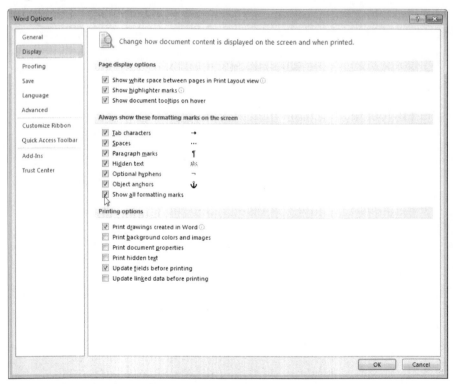

Figure 18   *Word Options: Showing all formatting marks*

As you can deduce from the other options in this section, this will allow you to see all the tab characters, spaces, paragraph marks (hard carriage returns), optional hyphens and hidden text in your document. These different characters will be dealt with in greater detail below, but here is a visual representation of what they look like on-screen:

- Tab characters   →
- Spaces   ·
- Optional hyphens   option¬al
- Hidden text   hidden
- Paragraph marks   ¶

Seeing these characters gives you far more control over what is happening in your document. For instance, it helps you pick up many typographical errors which might otherwise slip by, such as too many spaces between words. Also, your brain quickly adapts to these little intruders on the screen, so that they become less disturbing as you go along. In fact, if you have worked this way for any length of time, you may find it very hard to work without them again.

Now, having discussed characters in general, there are some attributes of characters (both normal and special) that deserve mentioning:

3.2.2   Breaking and non-breaking characters

Non-breaking characters differ from normal characters in that they exercise control over how Word is allowed to break lines (or not). Generally, these characters only come into play when their placement approaches the end of the line, although they do sometimes alter text spacing within a line as well. Again, most characters are breaking—when Word finds them at the end of a line, it is allowed to break the line there (of course, Word breaks lines at the word level, and not the character level, and thus, unless hyphens are used, Word will break lines in between words).

3.2.3   Characters of interest

3.2.3.1   Carriage returns

Every time you press the Enter (Return) key, a hard carriage return (¶) is inserted. A hard carriage return ends the paragraph, and thus, of necessity, the line. By contrast, when you press Shift + Enter a soft carriage return[20] (↵) is inserted. Soft carriage returns end the line, but not the paragraph. This is important, because in certain instances (e.g., a new "paragraph" in a bulleted list[21], but which is still part of the current point; or a heading which contains two lines[22]) you may want to end the line, but not the paragraph. Soft carriage returns are also useful for styles that are normally applied to single-line paragraphs and have large preceding or trailing spaces but now have to be applied to two successive lines, where the intervening spaces are not desired (actually, both examples mentioned in footnote 22 fall into that category, although

---

[20] Also called a "Manual line break" or a "Text wrapping break."

[21] An instance of this is used on p. 77.

[22] All the headings in this document use soft carriage returns to separate the heading number ("Chapter x") from the heading title, and double-barrelled headings (first line ending with a colon) also use soft carriage returns to separate the two elements.

additional elements come into play in each example). On the other hand, inserting soft carriage returns at the wrong place can have interesting effects on your text spacing within the line, especially with justified paragraphs (these problems may, however, be overcome through the use of non-breaking spaces—cf. 3.2.3.4.2).

3.2.3.2 *Style separator*

The style separator is not a character you will use a lot, but when you do, it becomes incredibly useful. The style separator is totally undocumented—there are no references to it in the Word help files, but I believe that it was introduced somewhere around Word 2003. The style separator is added by pressing **Ctrl + Alt + Enter**. What it does is to allow you to essentially combine two different paragraphs, with possibly different paragraph formatting, into one (old hands at Word used to do this by making a paragraph mark hidden, but the style separator remains a more elegant solution). One place the style separator is discussed in this book is in section 17.1.7 (p. 412).

3.2.3.3 *Hyphens and dashes*

If you thought a hyphen was a hyphen was a minus, then guess again. There's a whole array of those stripy-thingies for you to learn about and use in Word:

3.2.3.3.1 Regular hyphens

When you press the hyphen key (next to the zero key on the number line of a standard keyboard), a regular hyphen is inserted. You can use this to create purposeful hyphenation or to create compound words (such as "set-up," "Add-Ins" or "re-apply"). If the word is at the end of the line, the regular hyphen stays on the line, and the part of the word succeeding the regular hyphen drops to the next line (provided it cannot fit onto the current line). Regular hyphens are thus printing characters, as well as breaking characters.

3.2.3.3.2 Optional hyphens

When you press **Ctrl + -** (i.e., adding the Ctrl key to the hyphen key), you get an optional hyphen. You can use optional hyphens to show Word where you would want it to break a word, should it break over a line. Obviously, you need to follow proper grammar rules (e.g., put the hyphen between syllables), but Word doesn't check that for you—you can insert optional hyphens anywhere in a word, including where it doesn't belong. However, optional hyphens only come into play when they are needed—i.e., when the word has to break over the end of a line. Otherwise they do not print out. Optional hyphens are thus sometimes printing and sometimes non-printing characters, and sometimes breaking and sometimes non-breaking characters. It all depends on the positioning of the word on the line.

3.2.3.3.3 Non-breaking hyphens

These characters are easy to identify. They are always non-breaking characters, and always printing characters. You can insert them by pressing **Ctrl + Shift + -** (i.e., adding the Ctrl and Shift keys to the hyphen key). These are used in compound words, and force Word to treat the entire compound word as a whole unit (i.e., the whole word is transposed to the next line if it cannot fit into the current line, and is not broken[23]).

3.2.3.3.4 En dashes

An en dash is a typographical dash that is the same width as a lowercase "n." You can insert it in one of three ways: **Ctrl + -** (not hyphen, but *minus*—i.e., adding the Ctrl key to the minus key on the top right of a standard keyboard's number pad); or with **Alt + 0150**; or by inserting it from the Special Characters tab of the Insert Symbol dialog. En dashes are meant to be used to denote number ranges (e.g., "1–10"). Although there is a bit of a space on either side of the en dash, it functions the same way as a regular hyphen does—Word breaks the "word" containing the en dash immediately after the dash, should that "word" be at the end of a line.

3.2.3.3.5 Em dashes

Typographically, an em dash is as wide as a lowercase "m." However, Word's em dash is twice as wide as the en dash, regardless of the horizontal size of the letters in that font (see the discussion of mono- and proportional space fonts in 3.1). Having said that, the actual size of the em dash may vary from font to font, and so it might not always be twice the size of an en dash—it's very confusing, I know.

An em dash is inserted it in one of three ways: **Ctrl + Alt + -** (not hyphen, but *minus*— i.e., adding the Ctrl and Alt keys to the minus key on the top right of a standard keyboard's number pad); inserting it from the Special Characters tab of the Insert Symbol dialog, or (using the AutoCorrect feature of Word) by typing two hyphens in a row followed by a word. Em dashes are meant to be used to create breaks in sentences, similar to the way that parentheses are. An example of this is in the last sentence of the preceding paragraph. Em dashes break in the same way that en dashes do.

3.2.3.3.6 Hyphenation tool

Instruction set 4   Hyphenation

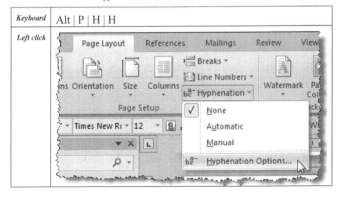

---

[23] Of course, you could force the word to break elsewhere with an optional hyphen, but this would not be grammatically correct in any case.

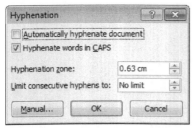

Figure 19   *Hyphenation tool*

Word has a hyphenation tool (Instruction set 4) that can manually or automatically hyphenate your document. The instructions are reasonably self-explanatory. However, you should bear the following in mind:

- I recommend that you take the time to apply this tool manually, as I am not certain that I would trust Word to do this right all the time in a large document containing much technical jargon, as dissertations are wont to be. However, the advantage of selecting the "Automatically hyphenate document" option is that every time you make changes to the document, Word will automatically re-hyphenate the document.

- Because Word inserts optional hyphens with this tool, you *shouldn't* end up with hyphens mid-line (no promises on that, though). However, my advice is to use the tool (if you choose to use it at all) at the very end of your process, just before you print out your dissertation (cf. Chapter 19, especially 19.4.8 and 19.7 (pp. 484–495). If you hyphenate your document, and then make changes, the *manual* hyphenation will become redundant.

- You can exempt paragraphs from being hyphenated by this tool by selecting the 'Don't hyphenate' option from the Line and Page Breaks tab of the Paragraph dialog, or by setting the proofing of the paragraph (or text) to '(no proofing)' under the 'Tools, Language, Set Language...' dialog. This can be done at the style level as well, so that all paragraphs of a certain style are automatically exempted from hyphenation.

- The hyphenation tool is language dependent. You may thus not be able to use it on other languages than English without the necessary additional components being installed (dictionary and hyphenation tool).

3.2.3.4   Spaces

Again, there are a myriad of spaces, when you probably thought there was only one.

3.2.3.4.1   Regular spaces

This is the normal space inserted every time you press the space bar on your keyboard. What is especially important is that Word adjusts these spaces evenly when a paragraph is justified. Thus normally these spaces have a fixed width (determined by the font type and size), but in justified paragraphs, these spaces have variable widths. Word also breaks a line at the space nearest the end of that line.

3.2.3.4.2 Non-breaking spaces

If you want to prevent a line from breaking between two words, you would have to use a non-breaking space. This is inserted by pressing **Ctrl + Shift + Space bar**. As a matter of fact, Word is so serious about not breaking a line in a non-breaking space, that if a word is too long to fit on a line (i.e., the whole word is longer than a single line[24]), but is preceded by a non-breaking space, Word will break the word instead! Note also that in justified paragraphs, Word does not adjust the width of non-breaking spaces. If a sentence has very long words, for example, it could happen that there are overly large spaces between all the words, barring those containing the non-breaking spaces.

One place where these spaces are very useful is in the last line before a soft carriage return in a justified paragraph. Ordinarily, Word will space the words out across the whole line, but with non-breaking spaces, they all appear on the left, as they should. Another example is one where you may be including Scripture references in your document, and not want the reference to be broken should it occur at the end of a line. Then you could insert something like this: John°3:16[25]. Incidentally, this is also a typical place where you might want to use non-breaking hyphens: John°3:16-21. A further typical example is when you mention sums of money. I might not want the currency indicator to be separated from the amount, or portions of the amount to be broken up: R°10°000.00[25].

3.2.3.4.3 No-width breaks

There are two of these: The no-width optional break and the no-width non-break. I can't quite think of contexts where I would want to use the latter, but the former can be quite useful in breaking long entries where you do not want a hyphen to appear. Figure 20 shows how it is added from the Special Characters tab of the (Insert) Symbol dialog—note the sentence displayed just underneath the dialog, where the I-beam has been positioned (even though you can't see it) just after the backslash after the folder name AppData. Figure 21 shows what this break looks like when it has been inserted, and when it is printed (or print previewed). Because it has no width, it is essentially invisible. This piece of text, by the way, is found in section 5.1 (p. 81).

---

[24] Of course, this probably won't happen in a standard document, but can happen in some languages, such as Afrikaans, where composite words (e.g., "tandheelkundigestudentevereenigingsvoorsitster") are made. It may easily happen in text that is broken into columns, though.

[25] The symbol I used here is actually not the non-breaking space, but the degree symbol, which looks like a non-breaking space on the screen. The non-breaking space, of course, does not print out, which is a bit of a problem for a manual such as this!

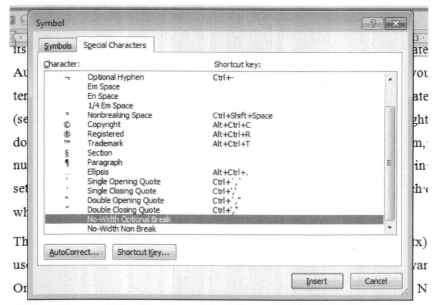

c:\Users\JacquesR\AppData\Roaming\Microsoft\Templates\Normal.dotm¶

Figure 20   *Adding a No-Width Optional Break*

On·my·Windows°7·pc,·the·current·location·for·the·Normal·template·is:·c:\Users\JacquesR\AppData\⧉
Roaming\Microsoft\Templates\Normal.dotm¶

On my Windows 7 pc, the current location for the Normal template is: c:\Users\JacquesR\AppData\
Roaming\Microsoft\Templates\Normal.dotm

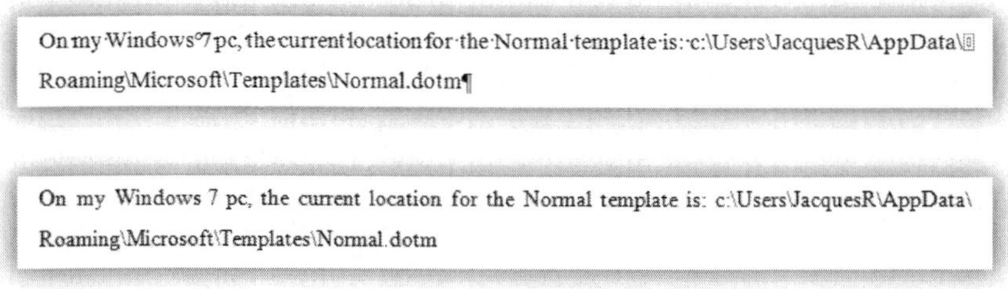

Figure 21   *No-Width Optional Break in text and previewed*

3.2.3.4.4   En spaces

An en space, as you may have guessed by now, is a space that is as wide as a lowercase n. The symbol Word uses for an en space looks similar to the symbol for a non-breaking space, but it has a certain amount of white space preceding it. Word does not adjust the spacing of en spaces in justified paragraphs (similar to non-breaking spaces), although it does break lines after en spaces where needed (in contrast to non-breaking spaces). You can insert an en space from the Special Characters tab of the (Insert) Symbol dialog.

3.2.3.4.5   Em spaces

As before, an em space, is a space that is as wide as a lowercase m. The symbol Word uses for an em space looks similar to the symbol for a non-breaking space, but it has a certain amount of white space preceding it and succeeding it. Word does not adjust the spacing of em spaces in justified paragraphs (similar to non-breaking spaces), although it does break lines after em spaces where needed (in contrast to non-breaking spaces).

44

You can insert an em space from the Special Characters tab of the (Insert)Symbol dialog.

Chapter 4
The right Word in the right place:
Automated text input and correction

Word contains a whole number of tools which can help you work better and faster. The small amount of time taken to learn these tools is quickly made up by your increased speed.

4.1   Copying and pasting

Before I get to "automated replacing," I have a brief topic that does not warrant a chapter of its own, and so I am sticking it here are the start of this chapter.

By the time you get to a manual like this, it is pretty much assumed that you know how to cut, copy, and paste. However, Word does contain some interesting features that make even this a more powerful set of tools that you might realise.

4.1.1   The office clipboard

For some odd reason, many people are not aware of the Office Clipboard. This tool is much like a car's spare tyre—it's always there, although you hardly ever need it. But when you do need it, it turns out to be immensely useful.

The Clipboard is opened from the dialog launcher of the Clipboard group on the Home ribbon (Instruction set 5). It is opened as a pane docked to the left of the Word window—Figure 22—but since it is a pane, the title bar can be grabbed and it can be dragged to float anywhere you position it).

Instruction set 5   Opening the Office Clipboard

Shortcut	Ctrl + C + C *(must be activated from the Clipboard options first)* *(something must be selected for the keyboard shortcut to work).*
Keyboard	Alt | H | FO
Left click	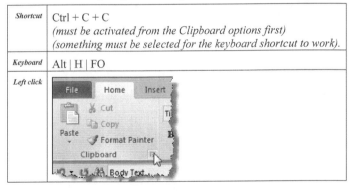

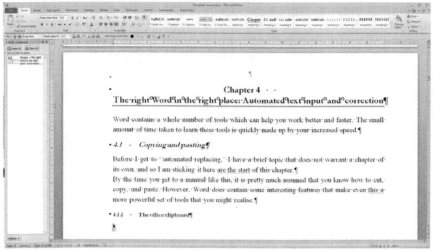

Figure 22   *Office clipboard in Word window*

Once the Clipboard has been opened, it "harvests" everything you copy in any of the Office applications—up to 24 items can be harvested. These items can then be pasted simply by positioning the I-beam in the desired place, and clicking on the item to be pasted in the Clipboard. Each item also has a drop-down menu (Figure 23) which allows you to either paste that item, or to delete it from the clipboard, thus freeing up space for other items.

Figure 23   *Office Clipboard item drop-down*

Note that, as can be seen from the top of Figure 23, the Clipboard also has two buttons which allow you to either Clear All items from the Clipboard or to Paste All items from the Clipboard, in the order in which they occur, at the present insertion point.

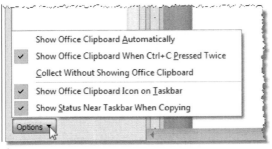

Figure 24   *Office Clipboard options*

You would want to take a few seconds to set the Clipboard Options (at the bottom left of the Clipboard—Figure 24) so that it will work the way that suits you best. Remember that if the first and third of these options (which are discussed below) are turned off (and they are, by default), then copying or cutting anything without first having opened the Clipboard will not result in that item being added to the Clipboard. These are the available options, what they mean, and how I prefer to use them:

📖 Show Office Clipboard Automatically: The minute you copy or cut anything, the Clipboard is opened and the item is added to the clipboard. I keep this off, because most of the time I just want to do a once-off copy/cut and paste, and hassling with the Clipboard in those instances is unnecessary.

📖 Show Office Clipboard When Ctrl+C Pressed Twice: Activates the Office 2003 keyboard shortcut (**Ctrl + C + C**) for the Clipboard. I find this useful, although note that something must be selected for this keyboard shortcut to work (i.e., you must actually be copying something).

📖 Collect Without Showing Office Clipboard: The safest alternative to always having the Clipboard's functionality at hand, but not having to hassle with the Clipboard unless you actually want to paste something from it. Everything you cut and copy is added all the time, although the Clipboard is not opened.

📖 Show Office Clipboard Icon on Taskbar: Adds an icon to the Windows Taskbar Notification Area. This icon will be there when the Clipboard is open, but will only be displayed there even though the Clipboard is not open when the third option (collect without showing) is on and at least one item has been added to the Clipboard. You can also right click on this icon to Stop Collecting, to Clear the Clipboard, or to open the Clipboard in the active Office application.

Figure 25   *Office Clipboard icon on Windows Taskbar*

📖 Show Status Near Taskbar When Copying: An optional extra which can be used in conjunction with, or independently of, the above option. Shows a small tooltip informing you of how many items have been added to the Clipboard (Figure 26).

Figure 26   *Office Clipboard status displayed on Windows Taskbar*

A last thing to remember about the Clipboard is that it is not the Word Clipboard, but the Office clipboard. As I mentioned before, it harvests up to 24 items from all the different Office applications. Figure 27 shows content in the Clipboard from PowerPoint, Access, Excel and Word. This makes it incredibly useful for multiple-item cross-application copying and pasting.

Figure 27   *Office Clipboard showing content from various Office applications*

4.1.2   The Word Spike

The Spike is an old tool in Word (you won't even find a reference to it in the Word 2010 help files). However, it still does have its uses. As you read through this description, you might realise that the Spike has, to some extent, been superseded by the Office Clipboard, but if you know how to use the Spike, you may find that, for applications within Word, it is still quicker to use than the Clipboard. It's pretty much a case of using the best tool for the specific task at hand.

The first step to using the Spike is to understand how it works behind the scenes. When you "spike" your first entry, Word actually creates an AutoText entry (see 4.4 below), called the "Spike." If you were then to "spike" something else, Word would then append that to what is already in the Spike. Note that you cannot select non-contiguous items—Word will only add the last selection to the Spike. So if you want to copy or cut two sentences that are, for example, at the start and end of a paragraph, you might as well just use the clipboard. However, if those two sentences are separated by many pages, it's quite easy to spike the first, then go to the second and spike it (you could, of course, use the Office clipboard discussed above). Note, though, that when something is "spiked," it is cut from the document. Also note that the Spike can contain anything you can put into a Word document—text, tables, pictures, etc. The Spike, then, serves as a sort of secondary clipboard.

Now, how to use the Spike. Simply select whatever it is that you want to spike, and press **Ctrl + F3**. This will cut the selection to the Spike. If you only wanted to copy to the Spike, simply undo (**Ctrl + Z**)—the selection will be restored, but will also remain in the Spike. Each time you thus spike something, it gets appended to what is already there (you could even append multiple copies of the same thing with a **Ctrl + F3**, **Ctrl + Z** repetition). To then insert the contents of the Spike into your document (or even another document), simply press **Ctrl + Shift + F3**. This will insert the contents of the Spike, and then also empty the Spike (Word actually deletes the AutoText entry it created). If you want to insert the Spike's contents without clearing the Spike, simply type the word "**spike**" and press **F3**.

If you really want to use the Spike without the keyboard shortcuts (although, to Word purists, that would be akin to heresy), the two tools "Spike" and "Insert from Spike" can be added to the QAT, as was discussed in section 2.1.4 (p. 18).

4.1.3   Paste Special

Copying or cutting and pasting is, most of the time, a straight and simple affair. But if you think that all there is to pasting is pasting, then you are creating a lot of unnecessary work for yourself.

First, Word allows you to set how pasted information is treated. treated. When you paste, the Paste Options button will appear at the pasted site, and clicking on this tooltip (or pressing Ctrl), will bring up a list of options that will allow you to change what was pasted (Figure 28). As you hold the mouse over each option, Word will preview the resultant change for you.

Figure 28   *Changing the format of what was pasted*

Furthermore, you can click on the Set Default Paste… option or just open the Word Options dialog and go to the Advanced tab to find the Cut, copy and paste settings (Figure 29). Figure 30 shows the Smart cut and paste Settings dialog, with the settings for Word 97–2000 style pasting, and Word 2002–2010 style pasting, or you can modify these settings to suit your own preferences (under the Custom heading). These options are reasonably self-explanatory, but if you would like to read more about what each of these options entails (especially the settings for smart cut and paste), you can consult this page from Microsoft (2012): http://office.microsoft.com/en-us/word-help/control-the-formatting-when-you-paste-text-HA010215708.aspx.

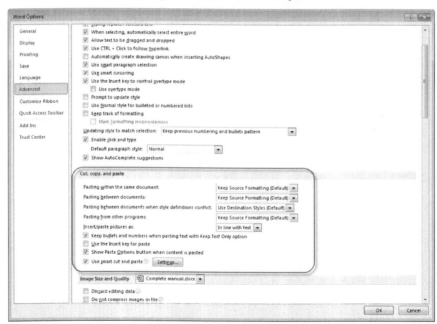

Figure 29   *Word Options: Advanced: Cut, copy and paste*

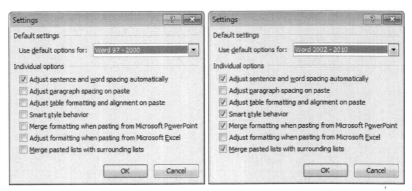

Figure 30   *Smart cut and paste settings*

That, though, has only brought us through the ways in which we can change the result *after* we have pasted. Paste Special, though, allows us to paste in a different way from the outset. As can be seen in Instruction set 6, the paste options as also available when right-clicking to paste, or when clicking on the bottom part of the Paste split button on the Home ribbon. These options are essentially the options that are available when using Paste Special. As is also the case with the paste options, holding the mouse over each option, will let Word preview the resultant change for you.

Instruction set 6   Paste Special

Shortcut	Ctrl + Alt + V
Keyboard	Alt | H | V | S
Left click	
Right click	

If you were to use the keyboard shortcut, or select the Pastel Special... option from the Home ribbon, the Paste Special dialog will open (this is no longer available from the right click menu). However, this dialog often gives additional options not available from the paste options. For example, Figure 31 (which is for the same copied selection of text used for Figure 28 and Instruction set 15), allows the text to be pasted with formatting (in this instance, Formatted Text and HTML Format will give the same result), without formatting (Unformatted Text or Unformatted Unicode Text), or converted to a picture, or added as an embedded Word document. It pays to become familiar with the Paste Special options especially when copying and pasting from other programs, as the options that will be made available will vary for each different program.

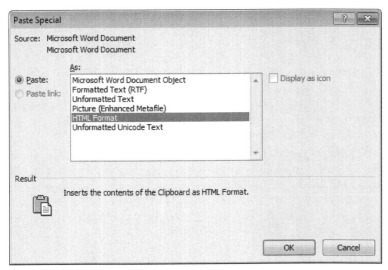

Figure 31   *Paste Special dialog*

4.1.4   Format painter

The Format painter is an incredibly useful tool in Word (actually, in all of the Office applications). Firstly, it does exactly what the name suggests: It copies formatting, but not the actual item copied. And it copies *all* the formatting, including the style of the selected item—you can even select just a paragraph end mark to copy the style of that paragraph (this is useful if character styles are applied over and above the paragraph style). You can even copy formatting without having selected anything (in contrast to the operation of the normal clipboard). Secondly, it operates with its own "clipboard," meaning that if you have copied something with the Format Painter, you can copy and cut other things without losing what is stored in the Format Painter clipboard (this is only lost when you copy other formatting, as it can only hold one item at a time, just like the standard clipboard).

Instruction set 7   *Format Painter*

Shortcut	Ctrl + Shift + C Ctrl + Shift + V
Keyboard	Alt | H | FP
Left click	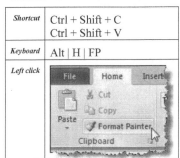

The Format Painter is one of those tools that just works better with the keyboard. Nonetheless, if you are using the mouse, there are two modes in which the Format

Painter can be used. Firstly, select, or even just position the I-beam within, the item whose formatting you want to copy. Then click on the Format Painter button, and the mouse pointer will change to an I-beam with a paintbrush on its left. Then click on the word or paragraph, or click and drag over the selection to which the formatting must be pasted, and the formatting will be pasted, while the mouse pointer will revert to normal. If you want to copy and then paste the copied formatting multiple times, simply double click on the Format Painter button. Now, each time the formatting is pasted, the mouse pointer will remain as the I-beam with the paint brush. To stop pasting formatting (and get your normal mouse point back), simply click once on the Format Painter button, press Esc, or just start typing.

To use the Format Painter with the keyboard, simply select, or even just position the I-beam within, the item whose formatting you want to copy. Then use the keyboard shortcut **Ctrl + Shift + C**[26]. You won't see anything happen, but know that the formatting has been pasted. The advantage to this method is that you can continue working, and can paste the formatting at any time (if formatting was copied with the Format Painter button and the mouse, the formatting also remains in the Format Painter clipboard, but cannot be pasted with the mouse once you have started working—it can only be pasted with the keyboard). To paste the formatting, click on the word or paragraph, or click and drag over the selection to which the formatting must be pasted, and press **Ctrl +Shift + V**[27].

I use this most often to copy and paste styles, such as the style I use in this book to indicate the user interface (see section 1.7 on p. 6). This is also useful for ensuring that all numbered paragraphs are using the same multilevel list (see my critique of how Microsoft has changed this feature in section 8.1 from p. 145).

4.2   Understanding fields

Without fields, this would have been a very short book. Fields do most of the work in Word, and various fields are referred to throughout this book. However, since various fields are discussed in more detail throughout this book, I will here limit myself to a brief discussion of what fields are, and how they work.

Fields act as placeholders where Word can decide, based on rules that you specify, what information to display at the time (e.g., when the document is printed). This means, that in a sense, you cede control of that piece of your document over to Word, but if you do it right, what you are actually doing is letting Word do the work of finding and filling in the required information for you at a certain point. As an example, this book, contains over 4500 fields. Every single heading number, table, figure application, macro listing and instruction set number, every cross-reference, every page number—all of these are done with fields. If you look at the statistics that I provide about this book in section 1.11 (p. 10), then note that all of those were done with fields too.

---

[26] Remember that Ctrl + C is the keyboard shortcut for normal copying.

[27] Remember that Ctrl + V is the keyboard shortcut for normal pasting.

Of course, there is a lot to know and learn about fields. Someone could (and someone should) write a book just on Word's fields[28]. Each field is a whole topic of its own, but here I just want to touch on some general points that should be kept in mind for all fields.

4.2.1   Field settings

Firstly, you can decide when and where Word should update its fields. Fields are generally updated each time you open your document, but you can additionally instruct Word to update the fields in the document before you print it out—this setting is in the Word Options dialog, Display tab, Printing Options group (Figure 32). The advantage to this is that the fields will never contain "outdated" information (e.g., if you copy and paste a figure or table caption, both the original and the copy will, until updated, contain the same number, as will any cross-references to either). However, note that in a large document, this can take some time to complete. You can manually update a selected field by pressing F9, or, of course, the whole document's fields with **Ctrl + A, F9**.

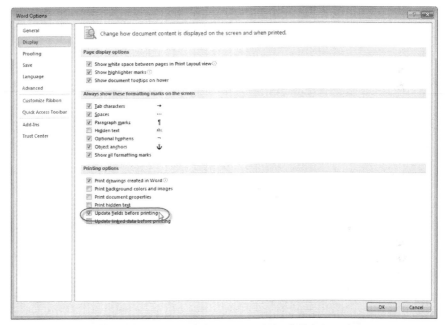

Figure 32   *Word Options dialog: Display settings—updating fields before printing*

The Word Options dialog (Advanced tab, Show document content group) also allows you to toggle between showing the field codes and the values those fields return,

---

[28] Having said that, somehow I doubt that there would be many of people who would buy it—it would probably be too technical for most. The only such "book" I am aware of is Allen Wyatt's e-book *Enhancing Word Documents with Dynamic Fields* (which I have not read). You can find more information on this at http://store.tips.net/ T010094_Enhancing_Word_Documents_with_Dynamic_Fields.html.

as well as how fields are shaded (Figure 33). The keyboard shortcut for this is **Alt + F9**. You can also toggle between the field codes and the field value for an individual field with **Shift + F9**. The former setting does this: The field code for the cross-reference to Figure 33 in the first sentence of this paragraph is { REF _Ref336020354 \h } , and the field value is, of course, Figure 33. The latter setting determines how fields are indicated in the document. I prefer the default setting, which is When selected. This means that when you click on a field, it is indicated with grey shading (see the previous two examples in this paragraph), and when you have not clicked on the field, it appears just like normal text. It may be useful, at times, to set this to Always, in which case you will be able to see all the fields without actually having to select them, but I do not recommend that you select Never from this list.

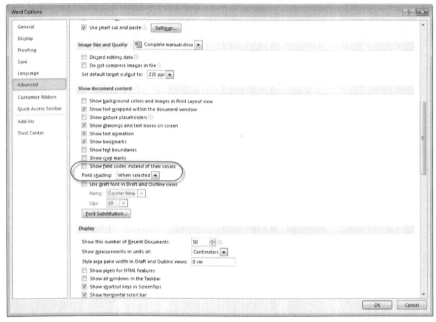

Figure 33   *Word Options: Display of fields*

4.2.2   Inserting fields

The next thing is learning how to insert fields into your document. The good news is that, most times, this process is automated. For example, if you insert a table or figure caption, or a cross-reference, or a heading number, Word adds the required field, with all the required information, automatically. However, there will be times when you will want to add fields manually. Depending on what you want to do, you could either manually type the field, or use the Field dialog. As Instruction set 8 shows, you type the field by first pressing **Ctrl + F9**. This adds a field, which will look like this: { }. Note that you cannot type the braces yourself—you must use Ctrl +F9 to add them. Then click inside the braces, and type the required field information.

Generally, fields all follow this syntax: { Field_name Parameters Switches }. Although parameters are required in most fields, they are optional with some fields, and absent in others, and not all fields have switches, and of those that do, the switches are almost always optional (and many fields can accept multiple switches).

Unpacking that syntax further, the Field_name is an indication of which field "tool" you want to use. This must be a valid name of an existing Word field. The parameters are "variables" which tell Word what to work with.

The switches tell Word what to do with that information, mostly instructing Word in what specific manner the information is to be displayed. For example, using the field example from p. 58 ({ REF _Ref336020354 \h }) the REF portion is the Field name, and this tells Word to use the REF field, which creates a reference to another point in the document. The _Ref336020354 portion is the name of a hidden bookmark, and this is the parameter required by the REF field. Thus we are telling Word to insert a reference to the bookmark _Ref336020354, which is a special bookmark Word has inserted around Figure 33. The final portion—\h—is the switch. For the REF field, the \h switch instructs Word to create a hyperlink to the bookmark specified as the parameter, allowing the user to click on the cross-reference field and be taken to the item to which it refers. Of course you will realise that adding fields in this manner (i.e., manually) entails a fair degree of familiarity with the intricacies of each specific field (e.g., knowing the switches and their functions). You will find a number of tables (Table 8, Table 9, Table 10, Table 16, Table 24) in this book listing the field switches for specific fields. For a jump site containing links to information on all the fields in Word, go to: http://office.microsoft.com/en-za/word-help/field-codes-in-word-HA102110133.aspx. A large number of fields contain switches that allow the user to determine different kinds of formatting for the field value (e.g., numerical formatting, date/time formatting, etc.). And a large number of these make use of the \MERGEFORMAT switch to accomplish that. Since this is just a general introduction, I will not go into the details, but a very good explanation of the various formatting settings can be found here: http://office.microsoft.com/en-za/word-help/redir/HA101830917.aspx.

Instruction set 8   Inserting a field

Shortcut	Ctrl + F9 (but the field information must be added manually)
Keyboard	Alt | N | Q | F
Left click	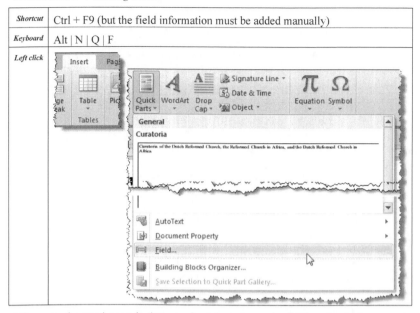

Of course, the good news is that you don't have to master field syntax before you can work with fields—Word can do all the syntax-building for you, if you add a field via the Field dialog. This is done from the Field... menu item of the Quick Parts drop list from the Text group of the Insert ribbon (Instruction set 8).

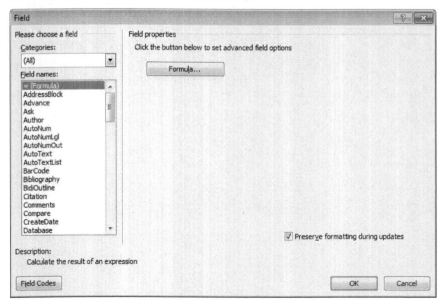

Figure 34   *Field dialog*

Once the Field dialog is open, select the field you want to use (a description of what the field does is given in the lower left corner). The remainder of the field will then show the field parameters and field switches (listed as check boxes). Thus, Figure 35 shows the parameters and switches for the Date field in the top version of the dialog. If you want to, you can switch to a higher gear by clicking on the Field Codes button at the bottom left of the dialog, which will transform it to look like the bottom portion of Figure 35. Clicking on the Options... button at the bottom left of that version of the dialog will open the Field Options dialog (Figure 36), allowing you to point and click to add the field switches for that particular field. Again a description of what each switch does is displayed. In this way, you can construct the field without any prior knowledge of the various parameters and switches, simply by reading the instruction and descriptions, and selecting what you need.

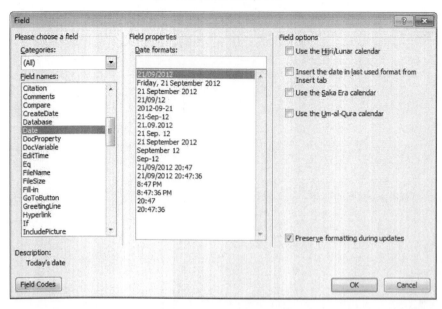

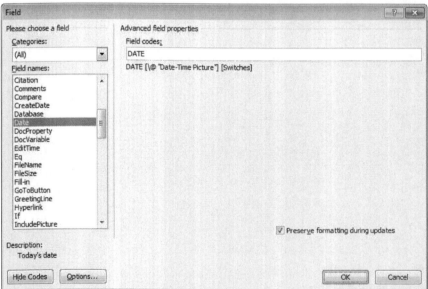

Figure 35   Field dialog: Date field

62

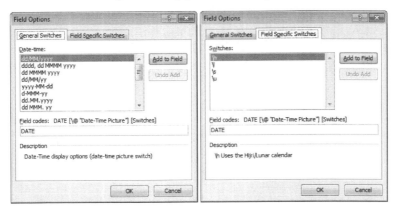

Figure 36   *Field Options dialog (Date field)*

4.2.3   Working with fields

In general, the way you will find yourself working with most fields is that you will use Word's dialogs to add the field (they are not only added from the Field dialog—the Caption dialog (Figure 119), the Cross-reference dialog (Figure 122), the Table of Contents dialog (Figure 138), the Mark Index Entry dialog (Figure 147) and the Bookmark dialog (Figure 180), to name but a few, all add fields for you. And then, only if you want the field to do something out of the ordinary, will you toggle to the field codes (**Shift + F9**) and then modify some of the switches, after which you will update the field (**F9**). I add very few fields by hand, the most common being index entries (The XE field is so elementary to use, that it can easily be done by hand, as described in section 9.3.2.3 on p. 204).

While some of these have been mentioned above, it should be noted that there are a number of keyboard shortcuts related to the use of fields, most of the important ones centred around the **F9** key. They are listed in Table 3. Be especially wary of the **Ctrl + Shift + F9** shortcut, which unlinks a field. The field value will then be displayed, but the field itself is annihilated, meaning that Word will never be able to update the field to reflect any further changes in the document.

Table 3   *Field Keyboard Shortcuts*

Access key	Key	Function
Alt+Shift	D	Insert a DATE field
Ctrl+Alt	L	Insert a LISTNUM field
Alt+Shift	P	Insert a PAGE field
Alt+Shift	T	Insert a TIME field
Ctrl	K	Insert Hyperlink
Alt+Shift	X	Insert Index entry
Ctrl	F9	Insert Field
Alt	F9	Toggle field codes in whole document
Shift	F9	Toggle field codes for selected field
	F9	Update field
Ctrl+Shift	F9	Unlink field (permanently replaces field with its current value)
	F11	Go to next field
Shift	F11	Go to previous field
Ctrl	F11	Lock field
Ctrl+Shift	F11	Unlock field

A useful tip for working with complex fields (e.g., the EQ field discussed in section 17.2.2, p. 419) is to split the screen (see section 11.8.1, p. 260) so that you can see the field code in one split, and the field result in the other.

In closing let me just make one little note about fields that should be obvious, but somehow does escape Word users who are not thinking clearly: You cannot edit the value returned by a field. It will look as if you are editing it, but when the field gets updated, the edit is lost. Thus, if you have a field that is returning the wrong value (e.g., a citation that is in the wrong format), you cannot fix this by changing the value of the field—you have to edit the field codes and switches to get it to return the right value. If this somehow cannot be done (as may sometimes be the case with citations in particular), then you would have to finalise the document, unlink (Ctrl + Shift + F9) the errant field, and then edit the resultant text.

4.3   Autocorrect and Autoformat settings

Word does a whole host of "cleaning up" whenever you type or add text. For instance, the double inverted commas in the first sentence of this paragraph were changed from what Word calls straight quotes ("") to smart quotes (""). While these features are generally useful, knowing how they work will help you distinguish when to invoke them and when not, and also allow you to better leverage their capabilities, allowing you to work faster and more accurately.

The first stop is with the actual settings, which are accessed by opening the Word Options dialog (from the File menu), then selecting the Proofing tab, and from that, clicking on the AutoCorrect Options... button (Figure 37).

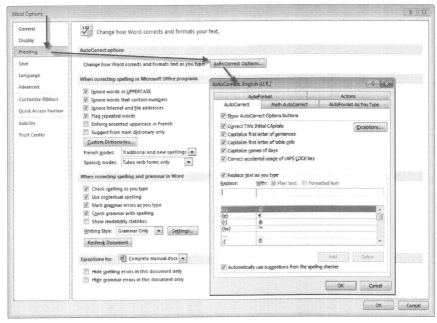

Figure 37   *Opening the AutoCorrect options*

The AutoCorrect dialog contains five different tabs which govern various aspects of auto-formatting and auto-correction. The Math AutoCorrect tab is discussed in section 17.3 (p. 425). For each of the following sections, the settings in this dialog will be discussed, before looking at how to actually make use of the feature in Word.

4.3.1   AutoCorrect

The AutoCorrect tab (Figure 38) fixes common spelling and typing errors automatically as you type. Note that it is slightly different from the others, in that there are different auto-correct text entries for different language settings (Figure 38 shows the current dictionary being used in the title bar of the dialog—this disappears for all the other tabs). Generally, you can keep most of the settings in this dialog on, although if there are words (e.g., names, such as *Theri*) that you find Word "correcting," then you can find them in the list at the bottom, and use the Delete button to remove these from the list of items which Word auto-corrects.

Of course, you can also add some of your own typical mistakes, thus "training" Word to clean up after your own sloppy typing (unfortunately, which this does help you create better quality documents, it does not make you a better typist!).

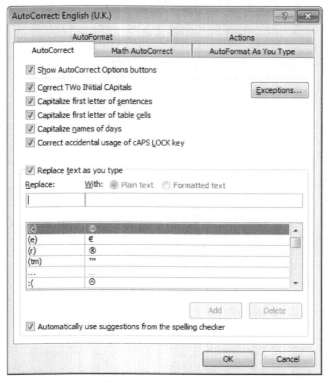

Figure 38   *AutoCorrect dialog: AutoCorrect*

Also take note of the Exceptions... button, which opens the AutoCorrect Exceptions dialog (Figure 39). Here, you can specify abbreviations after which Word should not start with a capital letter (in the First Letter tab), set which words contain two (only two) initial capital letters (in the INitial CAps tab—Figure 39 shows this being set for the word CDs), and also list other words that should not be auto-corrected (in the Other Corrections tab).

Figure 39   *AutoCorrect Exceptions dialog*

You can also use the AutoCorrect options to change text formatting (optionally while changing the text itself). For example, if there is a certain foreign language word which you would want always to appear in italics[29], or a title of a book which you refer to often and which must be italicised, etc.—then you can type the word(s), format it, select it, and then open the AutoCorrect dialog. When done in this fashion, the Plain text and Formatted text options of the Replace text as you type list will be enabled (see Figure 40–when you add entries manually, they are disabled, as in Figure 38) and the selected word(s) will be added to the With: box already. Simply type the unformatted word(s) (or even possibly misspelled words) in the Replace: box, and click on Add.

Figure 40   Adding a formatted entry to the AutoCorrect list

All that remains now, is to learn how to use the AutoCorrect options as you type. Generally, there is not much to do—just type, and wherever Word picks up something that meets the requirements, Word will correct it. However, there are some additional things that can be done to help leverage this facility. Firstly, it will happen from time to time that Word will correct something that it shouldn't. If you notice it quickly enough, you can simply undo the change (**Ctrl + Z**, or with the mouse on the QAT). However, if you were typing quickly and have already added a few more words, then undo will wipe that out too. In those instances, rather hold the mouse over the corrected word (this

---

[29] I might add that some style guides, e.g., APA (2010, p. 105), advise that this not be done for foreign phrases common in English.

applies to all AutoCorrect changes, not just typing mistakes, but also changes in capitalisation, etc.), and a small blue bar will appear below the changed word. Hold the mouse over that, and the AutoCorrect Options Action button will appear. Click on that, and some options will be supplied where you can either undo that one auto-correction, turn the auto-correction completely off (equivalent to deleting it from the list of auto-corrected words, or adding it to the list of exceptions, as the case may be), or you can open the dialog from here as well, and make further adjustments (Figure 41).

Figure 41   *AutoCorrect action button*

However, there is one more place where AutoCorrect comes into play, and it may be the most important. When you type a word incorrectly, and Word does not correct it, you can start training Word to pick up on those mistakes and correct them too. Figure 42 shows an example. I mistyped the word *typing* as *tpying*, and Word flagged it as being incorrectly spelled. When I right clicked on it, I could have selected *typing* from the top of the list and continued on my merry way. However, the next time I made the same mistake, I would have to correct it again. If, on the other hand, I were to choose *typing* from the AutoCorrect list, Word would add this to the list in the dialog (you can open the dialog after doing something like this and check), and will, from then on, automatically correct *tpying* to *typing*. You should carefully consider the likelihood of the option you are about to choose resulting from that particular mistake. Consider, as an example, the mistake of typing *typing* as *tpying*, as shown in Figure 42. I would normally not add that to the AutoCorrect list, because I could equally have wanted to type *toying*, and hit the *p* instead of the *o* (these two keys are right next to each other on the keyboard). You should only add something to the AutoCorrect list when the change you are adding is the only likely mistake from the list of suggested options.

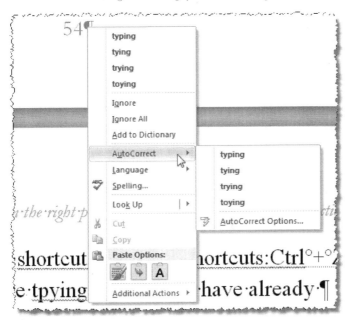

Figure 42   *Adding a word to the list of auto-corrected words*

One last thing. As you train Word to clean up your text in this manner, you will obviously build up quite a list of entries (especially if you type as poorly as I do!). When the inevitable time comes for a new computer, you would probably not want to start all over. Thus I recommend backing up your AutoCorrect entries. To do this, though, you need to make two sets of backups. This is because the formatted entries (as discussed above) are stored in the Normal template, and the unformatted entries in files called AutoCorrect List files (*.acl). Microsoft's (2008) support file on the process can be found at: http://support.microsoft.com/kb/926927. Essentially, what you want to do is go to the folder C:\Users*UserName*\AppData\Roaming\Microsoft\Office\ and back up every file that has the .acl file extension (do this periodically, in other words). Then also go to the (close by) folder C:\Users*UserName*\AppData\Roaming\Microsoft\ Templates\ and make a backup of the Normal.dotm template file (you should also do this regularly, as well as backing up any other templates that you use). When the new computer comes, after installing Office, just copy these files from your backup drive to the same location, and you're good to go.

Application 4.1   *Creating the Afrikaans 'n*

> *One common problem encountered by people typing in Afrikaans is the article 'n, which Word makes 'n. This can be fixed by going to the AutoCorrect tab, and entering 'n into the ̲Replace: box and 'n into the ̲With: box.*
>
> *Here's some hints to help you with this further:*
>
> *Word won't accept the smart quotes directly when you type them in these boxes,*

meaning the AutoCorrect entry will fail to work correctly[30]. Type and then copy ''n, and then paste into both boxes, deleting what is not needed from each.

Furthermore, you obviously will want to do this when the spelling has been set to Afrikaans, so that this works when you are typing in Afrikaans, not in other languages (see Figure 43).

Lastly, I have found that Word's auto-correct settings sometimes get the better of this process, so I have found it best to add two entries—one as above, and one without the smart quote, replacing 'n with 'n.

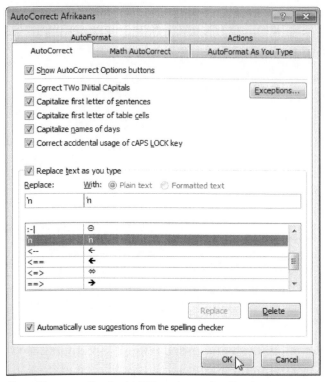

Figure 43   Creating the Afrikaans 'n as an AutoCorrect entry

---

[30] Again, excuse the pun!

4.3.2   AutoFormat

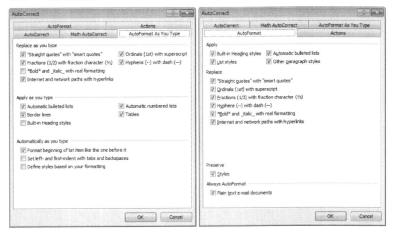

Figure 44   *AutoCorrect dialog: AutoFormat As You Type & AutoFormat*

Apart from the AutoCorrect options, Word can also automate a whole host of formatting functions, again, in theory, saving you lots of time and raising the quality of the end product of your document. How Word does this is set in the AutoFormat As You Type and AutoFormat tabs of the AutoCorrect dialog (Figure 44). You will notice that there is a large degree of similarity between the two tabs, and as such, they will be discussed together.

Most of the settings on the AutoFormat tabs are quite self-explanatory, and will thus not be discussed in detail. Rather, what I want to do is point out three setting that I prefer turning off in the AutoFormat as You Type tab:

- Built-in Heading styles: This setting tries to discern and apply heading styles as you type. But firstly, it has to do that based on formatting you provide (at the very least, a heading number you type), and it is simply quicker and less error-prone to just add the heading styles yourself, especially given the keyboard shortcuts that can be used for this (see Table 5 on p. 111).

- Set left- and first-indent with tabs and backspaces: If I type a tab or a backspace, it is because I want to add a tab, or remove the preceding character. Also, if I want to set indents, I do so explicitly, using measurements I define, not the (always incorrect) measurements Microsoft believes I want to use. Nothing irritates me more than the fact that this setting is on by default in Word.

- Define styles based on your formatting: This is an attempt by Microsoft to automate the process of working with styles, without the user having to do anything. As I mention in section 6.2 (from p. 93), this is one of the dumbest ideas ever. All it does is create a mess. Word will try to define a new style for each new formatting setting you add, but far from creating a coherent and manageable means of working with styles, it creates a mound of digital spaghetti that no person can hope to disentangle without risking their sanity. Possibly this setting irritates me just as much as the previous one.

Now that we have made sense of the settings, a quick discussion of the use of these tools is in order. Again, AutoFormat as you type works much the same as AutoCorrect—you just type, and Word does the work. Life as it was meant to be. And if Word auto-formats something that you don't want to format in that way, you can simply undo it, or follow the same procedure as demonstrated in Figure 41 above to activate the action button and reverse the formatting change (see Figure 45 for an example).

Figure 45   *AutoFormat action button*

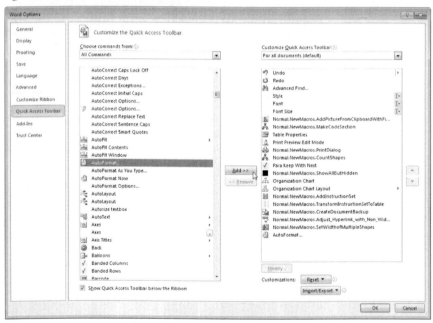

Figure 46   *Adding AutoFormat... or AutoFormat Now to the QAT*

The AutoFormat tool is actually quite well hidden. This tool does not function as you type, but is manually invoked to format (according to the rules set in the AutoFormat tab) text that you have added to your document (e.g., when copied and pasted from a web page, etc.)[31]. The first thing to decide is how you want to invoke AutoFormat. There are actually two options, AutoFormat... and AutoFormat Now. Both can be

---

[31] Of course, such text is properly indicated and referenced as coming from another source!

added to the QAT from the list of All Commands (Figure 46), but AutoFormat Now can also be invoked with the keyboard shortcut **Ctrl + Alt + K**. The difference between the two is that AutoFormat... allows you to customise the auto-formatting process, whereas AutoFormat Now just does the job, no questions ask (compare the difference between printing via the Print dialog, and via QuickPrint).

Both AutoFormat... and AutoFormat Now can be run on either a whole document (simply don't select anything), or only on a selection of text.

As an example of what auto-formatting does, consider the following paragraph copied from p. 13 of Vandenberg and Lance (2000)—Figure 47 shows the before and after auto-formatting of the text.

We maintain Byrne et al.'s (1989) distinction in Table 1 by referring to the first five of these tests as tests of aspects of measurement invariance (as they concern tests of relationships between measured variables and latent constructs) versus the next three as testing aspects of structural invariance (as they refer to tests concerning the latent variables themselves). As indicated in the body of Table 1, if an explicit order or hierarchy of tests was recommended, this order was denoted as "Step 1," "Step 2," and so forth, so that the test labeled "Step 1" occurred before "Step 2" and subsequent steps. If a particular step appears more than once, this indicates that the tests labeled in the same step appeared to be conducted simultaneously. Second (when possible), we report the name accorded for each test by the sources' authors, where quotation marks indicate at least close paraphrases for the label. Our goal was to examine consistencies and inconsistencies across published sources with respect to recommendations as to (a) how to test various aspects of ME/I, (b) which tests should be undertaken, (c) the sequencing or order in which the various tests should be evaluated, and (d) inferences accorded to each test endorsed.

We maintain Byrne et al.'s (1989) distinction in Table 1 by referring to the first five of these tests as tests of aspects of measurement invariance (as they concern tests of relationships between measured variables and latent constructs) versus the next three as testing aspects of structural invariance (as they refer to tests concerning the latent variables themselves). As indicated in the body of Table 1, if an explicit order or hierarchy of tests was recommended, this order was denoted as "Step 1," "Step 2," and so forth, so that the test labeled "Step 1" occurred before "Step 2" and subsequent steps. If a particular step appears more than once, this indicates that the tests labeled in the same step appeared to be conducted simultaneously. Second (when possible), we report the name accorded for each test by the sources' authors, where quotation marks indicate at least close paraphrases for the label. Our goal was to examine consistencies and inconsistencies across published sources with respect to recommendations as to (a) how to test various aspects of ME/I, (b) which tests should be undertaken, (c) the sequencing or order in which the various tests should be evaluated, and (d) inferences accorded to each test endorsed.

Figure 47   Text before and after AutoFormatting

If you choose to use the AutoFormat... option, the AutoFormat dialog will open, asking whether you want to AutoFormat now, or AutoFormat and review each change. (Figure 48). Obviously, if you choose AutoFormat now, Word auto-formats the text and you're done.

If, on the other hand, you choose to review the changes, Word will auto-format the text, and then present you with the next AutoFormat dialog (Figure 49), where you can either Accept All changes, Reject All changes, or Review Changes individually.

Additionally, you can open a <u>S</u>tyle Gallery (Figure 50) which will allow you to format the text according to any template Word can find in the Templates folder.

Figure 48   *AutoFormat dialog*

Figure 49   *AutoFormat Complete*

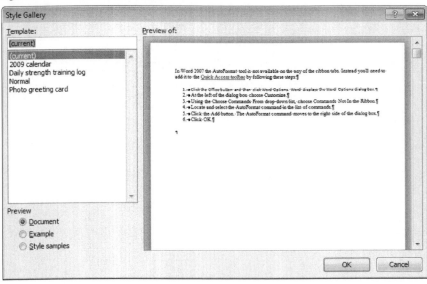

Figure 50   *AutoFormat Style Gallery*

Should you choose the review the changes individually, the last dialog to be presented is the Review AutoFormat Changes dialog (Figure 51). Here, in a fashion similar to that of working through document revisions (see section 14.5, from p. 318), you can navigate

74

between changes made with the two Find buttons, and Reject any changes you do not wish to accept.

Figure 51   *Review AutoFormat Changes dialog*

4.4   Building Blocks, Quick Parts, and Autotext

Word's AutoText functionality has a very long history. Unfortunately, with the release of Word 2007, the good people at Microsoft sought to replace something that was working perfectly well with something more "user friendly," but that, unfortunately, did not work quite as well[32]. The sought to replace AutoText with Quick Parts, and the AutoText functionality became a single component in the larger Quick Parts armoury. Fortunately, sense prevailed (presumably, irate users complained), and Word 2010, while still retaining Quick Parts, fixed the AutoText functionality.

4.4.1   AutoText

You can create two types of AutoText entries. With what I call a short entry, you create an alias that refers to the full entry (e.g., *UFS* could refer to *University of the Free State*). For a full or long entry, the AutoText title is the same as the AutoText entry itself. Of course, you could create both kinds for the same entry, but generally, shorter AutoText entries will be listed in full, and longer AutoText entries will be shortened.

To create either kind, the first step is to type out the full entry, then select it (being careful not to select anything in addition, such as paragraph end marks, etc.), and press **Alt + F3** (or add the AutoText button to the QAT[33]). This will open the Create New Building Block dialog, set to the AutoText gallery.

For a short entry, you should now give a short name (UFS for the previous example— see Figure 52), while for a long entry, you might need to type out the complete entry, or you can stand with the portion of text Microsoft has chosen to add (e.g., for *University of the Free State*, Word added only *University* to the Name box of the dialog—see Figure 53).

---

[32] Some needs to tell the people at Microsoft that "If it ain't broke, don't fix it!"

[33] The AutoText button is visible, seven items down from the selected AutoFormat item, in Figure 46.

Create New Building Block

Name:	UFS
Gallery:	AutoText ▼
Category:	General ▼
Description:	
Save in:	Normal.dotm ▼
Options:	Insert content only ▼

OK   Cancel

Figure 52   Create New Building Block dialog: Creating a Short AutoText entry

Create New Building Block

Name:	University
Gallery:	AutoText ▼
Category:	General ▼
Description:	
Save in:	Normal.dotm ▼
Options:	Insert content only ▼

OK   Cancel

Figure 53   Create New Building Block dialog: Creating a Long AutoText entry

Once the AutoText entry has been created, how you use it depends on whether you created a short or a long entry. For a short entry, type the alias, and press **F3** to have Word replace the alias with the full entry. Thus, continuing with the example, typing *ufs F3* (four characters) will insert *University of the Free State* into the document (28 characters, in this instance an 85.7% increase in efficiency). If you created a long entry, simply start typing out the long entry as usual, and Word, once it recognises the entry, will display the full entry in a tooltip, prompting you to press Enter to complete it (Figure 54). In the example, I had only to type *univ* before Word recognised it, after which I could press Enter to have it completed. Of course, this is one character more than the short entry (in this example, I must add), meaning that I had to type 125% more characters (1 character more), but still resulting in an 82.1% increase in efficiency!

Figure 54   Using a long AutoText entry

It stands to reason that you would only use AutoText for text entries that are both long, and are used often. In my dissertation, I referenced the authors Hendrick and Hendrick what seemed like countless times (but was, I just counted, 18 times). The AutoText shortcut hh F3 for 17 times (I still had to type it out at least the first time to create the AutoText entry saved me lots of typing (again it works out to an 85.7% increase in efficiency), and that is assuming that I would type *Hendrick and Hendrick* without any typing errors each time (an erroneous assumption, I can assure you). Of course, even whole pages of text could be added in this manner.

Although I consider it unnecessary, it would not be fair of me not to indicate that Microsoft has also designed it so that the AutoText entries are, for mouse-bound people, also listed in the Quick Parts gallery of the Insert ribbon (Text group), as shown in Figure 55.

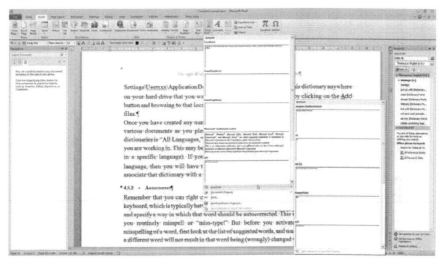

Figure 55   *AutoText entries in Quick Parts gallery*

4.4.2   Quick Parts

Although AutoText works fine, you might want to consider using the newer Quick Parts for a longer method of achieving the same result (the only advantage I can see is that the Quick Parts are visually displayed in a gallery).

To do this, again create the text you will be using, and select it—just as was done with AutoText. Then, from the Insert Ribbon (in the Text group), select Quick Parts, and at the bottom of the drop down, select Save Selection to Quick Part Gallery.... This will open the Create New Building Block dialog (see Figure 53 above), this time with the Gallery set to Quick Parts (of course, the gallery can be changed to AutoText, and it should also be noted that the Options list box gives, for both AutoText and Quick Parts, the option of just adding the selection as is, or adding it in a paragraph or page of its own).

To then use any of these entries, simply click on the Quick Parts tool to open the gallery, and then click on the item you want to have it added to your document at the insertion point, or right click on it to choose from a variety of other locations (page header or footer, beginning or end of section or document) at which to insert it.

Unfortunately, one of my biggest gripes with the Quick Parts is that they cannot be edited. Thus, if you selected a few paragraphs of text that, as an example, contained an e-mail address, and that e-mail address were to change, there would be no way to go to the entry and make that change. Rather, insert the entry into the document, change it, reselect it, and redefine the entry, replacing the old one—a rather laborious process, if you ask me.

And again, if you create a lot of these entries, you would want to preserve them, which means backing them up. They are typically found, for Word 2010, here: C:\Users\ *UserName*\AppData\Roaming\Microsoft\Document Building Blocks*1033*\14\Building Blocks.dotx[34] and some are also stored in the Normal template, found (typically) here: C:\Users*UserName*\AppData\Roaming\Microsoft\Templates\Normal.dotm.

---

[34] The number 1033 is a Locale Identifier (LCID), and may be different on your computer. See http://support.microsoft.com/kb/221435 for more information on these.

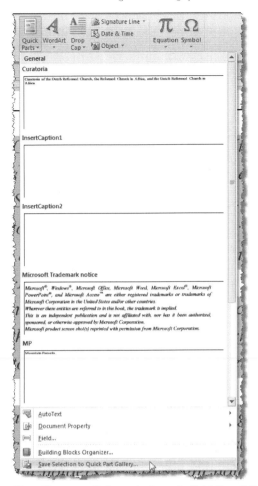

Figure 56   *Saving a selection to the Quick Parts Gallery*

4.5   Word Count

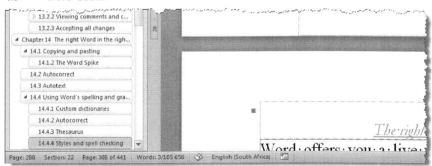

Figure 57   *Word count toolbar*

Word offers you a live word count, displayed on the status bar (Figure 57). Also, if you select only a portion of text, the toolbar will count only that portion. The Word Count dialog can be accessed almost as easily by clicking on the word count itself, or from the Review ribbon. This dialog provides some additional statistics, and allows you to set whether the foot- and endnotes should be counted or not (which will also subsequently affect the count in the toolbar).

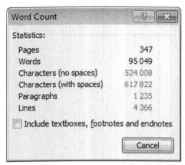

Figure 58   *Word count dialog*

A useful macro which can be used to generate a list of words in your document, together with the frequency of usage of each word, can be found here: http://word.tips.net/T000879_Determining_Word_Frequency.html.

Chapter 5
Laying a proper foundation: Learning to work with templates

Just as a house (and a life) needs a good, strong foundation, so does a dissertation. The foundation defines where the house will be, where the walls will go, and, in short, what the house will look like. The house rests on the foundation, and without it, the house will fall down. This is true also of any dissertation. While you will, of course, need a separate foundation for the *content*, you will, in Word, be concerned with not one, but two tasks: Laying a proper foundation, and building your document on that content. In Word, your foundation is understanding and using templates. Where we actually want to get to is working with styles, but styles are generally (and should be) stored in templates. Styles will be dealt with in the next chapter.

5.1 Understanding templates and how they relate to styles

Any and every document created in Word is based on a template. This may surprise you, but it normally happens quite automatically. A template is basically a container, which looks very similar to a document (documents and templates are distinguished on the basis of their respective ".docx" and ".dotx" extensions[35], and have slightly different Windows icons—see Figure 59). Templates are special Word documents that contain various settings relevant to one or a variety of document types. This includes styles, AutoText entries, macros, custom toolbars and menu settings, and shortcut keys. Templates may even contain base text or fields for text entry, which help you create the desired document quickly and easily. The important thing for the moment is styles. All text you type into Word actually looks like bland typewriter text (try using the Windows Notepad to open a Word document, and you will see what the text looks like without formatting). Styles contain guidelines instructing Word how to format the text. These include a wide array of settings, such as the various paragraph formatting settings, font settings (including "additional" font settings such as bold, underline, italics, etc.), even the language to be used in the spell checking of the text. Thus, when a style is applied to bland, unformatted text, the text quickly takes on new life. Templates, then, amongst others, are repositories for styles. They contain the information on how the text should be formatted, and can be re-used with an infinite number of documents, thus sparing us the trouble of defining that formatting anew for each document.

---

[35] These could be .docm and .dotm for the macro-containing versions, and were .doc and .dot in Word 2003 and earlier..

Doing Your
Dissertation
Microsoft Word
2010.docx

Mailing address
template.dotx

Document icon   Template icon

Figure 59   *Document icon compared to template icon*

Here it is worth realising that all the things that can be stored in a template, can also be stored in a document. Thus, even though a document is based on a certain template, it can quickly take on a life of its own. It can contain its own styles that are different to those in the template, it can contain its own AutoText entries, even toolbars and menu items, etc. This is important if you intend using the same template for a number of different documents. You need to keep your template and document aligned (see section 5.3). Let me increase your confusion even more: A template might contain ten styles. The document attached to it might contain those ten, but use only half of them, and might contain any number of additional styles which it might or might not use. Also, the styles in the document might be set to have a different appearance to their namesakes in the template (which does make you wonder why Microsoft have even bothered with templates).

The template which is used by default is the 'Normal' template (Normal.dotx), and the style which is used by default is the 'Normal' style (granted, Microsoft does not get any awards for creative names). Every time you open a new document, it is automatically linked to the Normal template, and will thus display its text in accordance with the formatting settings of the Normal template. On my Windows 7 pc, the current location for the Normal template is: c:\Users\JacquesR\AppData\Roaming\Microsoft\ Templates\Normal.dotm.

5.2   Accessing a template

In essence there are two ways in which a template can be accessed: You can either open the template, or you can base a new or existing document on the template. The former you will probably not do very frequently, whereas the latter would be the norm, especially for creating new documents based on a template.

5.2.1   Opening a template

Note that you will only want to open a template when you want to make changes to it. And even then, not always. Many of the changes you make to your templates are made from other places in Word. Also, note that any text which you type into your template, will automatically be carried over to any new documents based on it (but obviously not into existing documents which access that template). Don't add text to a template that you don't want there every time you use it—there is nothing more annoying than having to delete this unwanted text (e.g., people sometimes inadvertently save a document as the Normal template, and then all their new documents start with the text contained in that document!). This is probably the most frequent reason for wanting to physically open a template—to delete unwanted text from it.

If you like opening your Word documents from a file management program like Windows Explorer or Total Commander , note that double-clicking on a template will not open it in Word, but will open a new document based on that template. Rather, right-click on the template, and then select Open from the context menu.

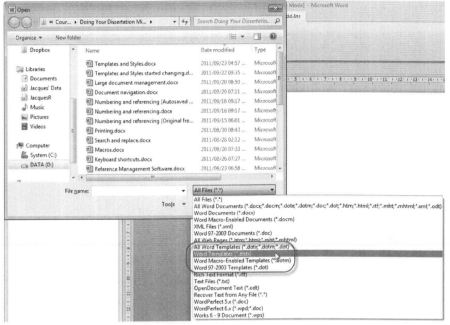

Figure 60   Selecting to open templates from the file browser

To open a template from within Word, simply select one of the "Word Templates" options in the Files of type selection bar of the File Open dialog. This might automatically take you to the Templates folder (e.g., C:\Program Files\Microsoft Office\Templates   or   c:\Users\JacquesR\AppData\Roaming\Microsoft\ Templates\Normal.dotm), where you should find most of the templates. If your template is stored elsewhere on your hard drive, you can browse to there and then open it.

Alternatively, you could select (Alt | F | N | M) My templates from the New tab of the Backstage view (File tab), as shown in Figure 61. This will open the New Document dialog (Figure 62). Here you will see, in the Personal Templates tab, all the templates listed in the directory mentioned above. You can select any template and then, with the Create New section's two option buttons, either create a new Document based on that template, or copy that template into a new Template which you can then modify and save under a new name (e.g., if you want to change a template but want to keep the existing version as a backup). To open the template itself, right click on the template you want to open, and select Open from the context menu.

You can unfortunately not browse to templates lying at other places on your hard drive from the New Document dialog, so if you cannot find a template that you know exists, and are looking for there, you must either copy it to the templates folder, or you must open a blank document and then change its attached template (see below).

Figure 61   *Backstage view: New, My templates*

You can unfortunately not browse to templates lying at other places on your hard drive from the New Document dialog box, so if you cannot find a template that you know exists, and are looking for there, you must either copy it to the templates folder, or you must open a blank document and then change its attached template (see below).

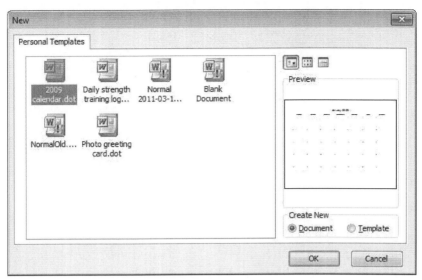

Figure 62   *New document dialog*

5.2.2   Basing a new document on a template

As was already discussed above, you can base a new document on any template of your choice from the New tab of the Backstage view (File menu). Note that choosing "Blank document" there, or pressing the keyboard shortcut **Ctrl + N** will open a new document based on the Normal template.

5.2.3   Attaching a different template to an existing document

Warning! Before changing the template to which an existing document is attached, I strongly recommend making a backup of the document. I discuss a strategy for backups in Application 12.2 (p. 267).

To see which document a template is based on, or to change the template underlying a document, you first need to activate the Developer ribbon. To do this, go to the Customize Ribbon tab of the Word Options dialog (File, Options) and activate the Developer tab there (Figure 63).

Figure 63   *Activating the Developer tab*

Next, you will find the Document Template tool in the Developer ribbon (Instruction set 3), which will open the Templates and Add-ins dialog (Figure 64).

Instruction set 9   *Document Template*

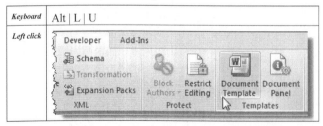

The top selection box of the Templates tab in this dialog specifies the Document template, and to its right is the Attach... button which will open the file browser, allowing you to browse to the template of your choice and attach it to the document. Take special note of the Automatically update document styles check box. I recommend that you almost never attach a new template to an existing document without making certain that this option has been activated (it is sort of defeating the purpose of attaching a new template and not activating this setting). This setting resets the styles in your document to match those of the template each time you open the document. In practice, what this means is that if you make any changes to the styles within your document, and do not carry those changes through to your template (discussed below), you will lose these changes next time you open your document! The advantage of working this way is that it forces you to keep your document and template aligned, but you may find this a bit irritating. For the changeover from the old to the new template, however, you will definitely want to make sure that this is checked, otherwise your document will retain all its old styles. Note that only existing styles in your document that have names which are found in the template, will be updated.

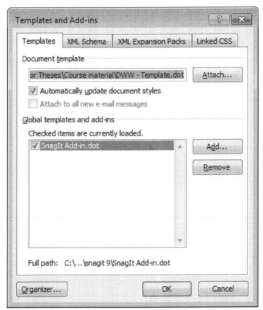

Figure 64   *Templates and Add-ins dialog*

5.3   Creating a template

One way of creating a new template has already been mentioned above. However, another way (the most common method) to create a new template is simply to open a new document, make the settings to it that you want to perpetuate in your template, and then use the Save As (F12) option to save it as a template (select Word Template from the Save as type dropdown list in the Save As dialog—Figure 65—note also the link at the top of the locations pane which will take you the default template directory on your hard drive, although you can save the template wherever you want on any of your disks).

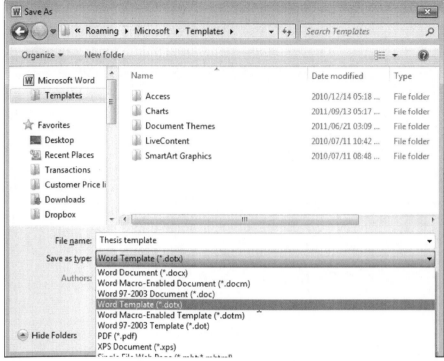

Figure 65   *Saving as a template*

Alternatively, you could select File, Save & Send, Change file type, Template, Save As[36], as is shown in Figure 66.

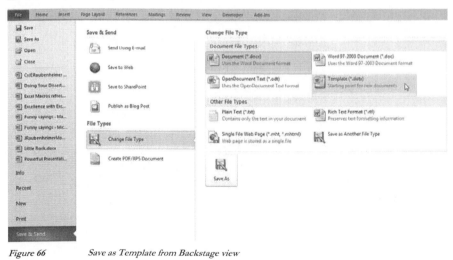

Figure 66   *Save as Template from Backstage view*

---

[36] You're right. F12 is much, much quicker.

5.4   Changing a template

There are many ways to change your template. As has already been discussed, you can open the template, make modifications, and save it. However, one of the advantages to working in Word is that you can often make modifications to a template without actually having that template open. These changes will then be propagated to all documents that access that template (provided the Automatically update document styles check box in the Templates tab of the Templates and Add-ins dialog has been selected in those documents).

5.4.1   Set as default

In a number of dialog boxes (e.g., Page Setup, Font, Language), you will see a Set as Default button. Clicking on this will allow you to carry any changes you have made through to your template (whichever template is attached to the document that you are working on). Thus the changes are made, not only to your document, but to the underlying template as well.

5.4.2   Modifying styles

Furthermore, when you access the Modify Style dialog (this will be discussed in detail in the next section), you will see a check box indicating that the changes will be applied to New documents based on this template. Checking this (and I generally recommend that you do) each time you modify a style will carry that change through to the underlying template as well. *However, this obviously means that if you want to make a change that you intend to be specific to the current document only, you should not check this.* But then you had better make sure that the Automatically update document styles check box in the Templates and Add-ins dialog is not selected, because then you will lose the changes you have made when next you open that document! Similarly, if the Automatically update document styles check box *is* selected, and you do not carry through your style changes to the template by means of the Add to template check box, you will lose those changes when next you open your document! A sure way to know that the style changes have been carried through to the template is that when you close the document, Word will ask you whether you want to save changes made to document, and Word will then next ask you whether you want to save changes made to the template. Please do, unless you are closing the document because you have messed up the styles and want to start over!

5.4.3   Organizer

A further way of changing your template is to use the Organizer (Figure 67). Click on the Organizer... button at the bottom left of the Templates and Add-ins dialog (Figure 64) or the Import/Export... button in the Manage Styles dialog (Figure 78, p. 102).

The Organizer dialog contains two tabs (Styles and Macro Project Items), both of which displays two selection list boxes (see Figure 67). Each box represents the content of a document or template, and you basically use this dialog to move or copy items across between whichever documents or templates are open in the two list boxes. You can close the document or template displayed in either window using one of the Close File buttons, in which case the button will change to Open File…, which will open the file browser with which you can open any document or template you wish in its place. Once you have the documents or templates you want to use loaded in the two list boxes, you can, in the Styles tab[37], click on any style in either list, and copy it to the other, or you can rename styles, or delete them. Please note that you may not be able to undo these changes!

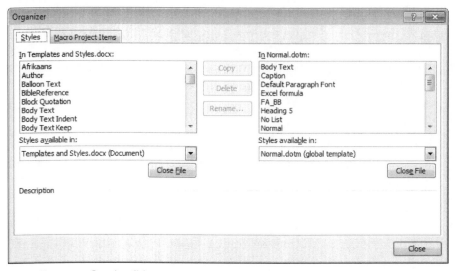

Figure 67   *Organizer dialog*

You should also note that the copying of styles with the Organizer dialog is not a perfect science. For example, you may find that you have made changes to a document, and not carried them through to the template (so that other documents based on the same template do not show the same style characteristics). To correct this, you load the document and its underlying template into the Organizer dialog, and copy the styles from the document to the template (you will be prompted to replace them), you may find that the styles in the template are still not correct (e.g., the font has changed, but numbering may still not be applied). The best thing to do then is to open the document, go to the Modify Style dialog, and then click on the New documents based on this template option (as opposed to Only in this document) without actually making any changes to the style. Then close the document, and you should be prompted to save changes to the document (which you may accept or reject), as well as changes to the template (which you should accept).

---

[37] Or code module in the Macro Project Items tab.

Chapter 6
Formatting the way it was meant to be: Using styles

All right! Now you have your template in place, and you want to start using your styles. But let's first understand the need for styles. Consider the way most people would type a dissertation, and how they would format the various elements. They type a heading. Then they select it. Then they format it. And so they go, laboriously struggling through the whole process over and over again. This is not the way to do it, for several reasons. Firstly, this is a lot of work, and secondly it is very error prone—one heading might have a slightly smaller font size than another, or numbers might get repeated or skipped. This is tantamount to trying to make a dress for yourself (guys, you'll just have to use your imagination here a bit) by holding the material against your body, and trying to cut it out and sew it together like that. We know that dresses are made by laying out the material on a table, cutting it out according to a pattern, and then sewing it under a machine. All of this, of course, requires some abstraction—we have to imagine what the end product will look like.

Working in Word should also be like this. We need to learn to separate content from formatting—something most Word users are not at all familiar with. And doing that requires some abstraction—we need to do the formatting in one place, to some extent imagining what the end product will look like. To continue the analogy I started with, imagine a little girl playing with her doll. The greatest thing about those dolls (at least, based on my own observation of girls playing) is that they can dress them up in all those different outfits. The content remains the same (it's always the same doll) bot the formatting (or the outfits) may differ. Styles allow us to do that. Styles are formatting "outfits" for our content that we can create, and even modify. And we can take the same content and "clothe" it in different "outfits"—styles.

The advantages of styles, then (if you will forgive me for stating the obvious) are basically the opposite of the disadvantages of not working with styles: Firstly, working with styles allows us to format our content with less effort, and thus also to format it quicker. But secondly, and perhaps more importantly, working with styles allows us to format our content more consistently.

6.1   Style types

The first step to learning to work with styles is to know what styles types exist.

Word contains four main kinds of styles: Paragraph, Character, Table and List, and each has its own identifying icon in the Styles pane. **Paragraph** styles (¶) define both font settings for text within a paragraph, as well as the paragraph formatting. They are the most commonly used styles. **Character** styles (a) contain settings only for character formatting (i.e., font settings), and none for paragraph formatting. They are very useful for changing the appearance of text within a paragraph in a consistent manner. Word 2007 introduced a new hybrid—called **linked** styles (¶a). These are essentially paragraph styles that can be used as character styles depending on how you apply them. Personally, while this is again an attempt by Microsoft to make things user friendly by allowing you to use tools without understanding how they work, I prefer to keep the two (paragraph and character) separate. You will have to make this choice for yourself.

Table styles define the appearance of tables, including the character and paragraph formatting of text within the tables—the use of table styles will be dealt with in section 15.3 (p. 354). However, additional paragraph and character styles can be used within formatted tables. Finally, **list** styles define the character, paragraph and bullet or numbering settings for list styles, which will be discussed in section 8.1.3 (p. 155).

6.1.1   Built-in styles

Word contains a number of built-in styles. These are special styles that may contain certain characteristics which you cannot set for styles which you create. Three of these styles deserve special mention.

First and foremost amongst Word's built-in styles is the **Normal** style. When a new document is created, especially one based on the Normal template, the default style for all text and paragraphs within that document is the Normal style. Irritatingly, Microsoft also believe that most other styles should be based on the Normal style, which is fine as long as you have absolutely no idea what you're doing in Word, but which is actually quite a bad idea. As far as possible, you should try to avoid using the Normal style in your thesis document like the plague if you want to achieve maximum consistency in your document formatting. Word attaches special significance to the Normal style (e.g., it cannot be deleted). Also, the Normal style allows you to format different bodies of text in different manners without conflicts—all of which makes for an inconsistently formatted document.

If the Normal style is to be avoided, then an alternative style is needed for most of the text in your document. Enter the **Body Text** style which is the best option for most of your plain text.

Lastly, Word has nine **Heading** styles (Heading 1–Heading 9). Although you can create your own heading styles, it is strongly recommended[38] that you use these built-in heading styles (they can be formatted differently in different templates, so there is absolutely no reason why you shouldn't use them). There are many advantages to using these styles: Word references these styles in the document map (see section 11.6.4, p. 256), in page numbers and caption numbers that include chapter numbering (see section 8.4, p. 161); Word uses these styles in creating cross-references and tables of content; and it is easy to link these styles to List styles to create complex numbering systems. If you are really serious about kicking the Normal style habit (never a bad thing), you can even instruct Word, in the Word Options dialog (Advanced tab, Edition Options group), to use the Body Text style as the default paragraph style instead of the Normal style (Figure 68).

---

[38] I would go so far as to insist, if I could!

92

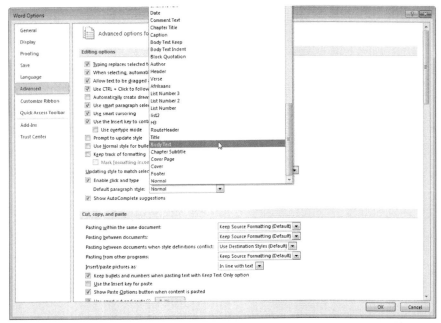

Figure 68   *Word Options: Setting Body Text (instead of Normal) as the default paragraph style*

There are a number of other styles that will be discussed at the relevant places in this book, but suffice it to note that between the Body Text style and the Heading styles (you would probably only use Heading1 to Heading5, and maybe Heading6), you will have most of your thesis covered.

6.2   Regaining control of your styles

Before we start learning how to use styles, we first need to get Word to stop treating us like idiots who have no idea what styles are, let alone how they work, and thus to stop Word from trying to operate styles on our behalf: Most Word users, sadly, don't know how to use styles properly. And so the good people at Microsoft are faced with something of a dilemma—at its most basic level, you actually must use styles (even if just the Normal style), so how do they get Word to do styles for those users who don't know how to use them? The hard, but correct, answer is: Teach them how to use styles (easier said than done, but this book is proof that I'm trying). The option Microsoft took is: Try to automate styles in the background, so that styles get applied even if people don't notice it happening. As you can imagine, if you actually do understand how to use styles, it's not very nice when the program tries to do things that you don't want it to be doing. Thus, we have to wrest back control of our styles from Word (i.e., we have to take the autopilot off, and fly this thing on our own).

To regain control over your styles, go to the AutoFormat as You Type tab of the AutoCorrect dialog (File, Options, Proofing, AutoCorrect Options...). Here, deselect the Define styles based on your formatting check box (Figure 69). This is what causes that irritating behaviour of Word where it sometimes changes the style that a certain paragraph is, simply because you formatted it manually in a different way. If you aren't actively using styles, this feature is supposed to help you. If you are actively using and applying styles to you document, this feature just gets in the way.

While you're at it, also deselect the Set left- and first-indent with tabs and backspaces setting too—if I type a tab, it's because I want a tab, not because I want to shift margins. The same goes for the Backspace.

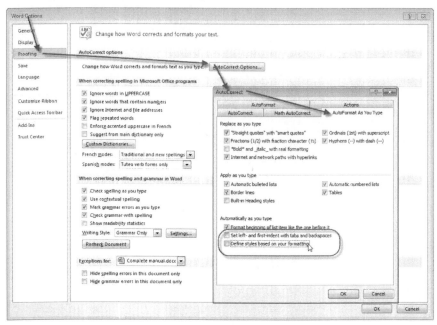

Figure 69   AutoCorrect options: Disabling Define styles based on your formatting

6.3   Style tools

Styles can be very intimidating at first, although when you realise how much time they can save you, and how much better they can let your documents be formatted, you will learn to love styles. Unfortunately, the Word team at Microsoft has seen fit to scatter style settings all across the Word interface, so that there are three places from which you access your styles (one ribbon gallery, one pane, and one dialog), and a total of three different places from which you manage your styles (one pane, and two dialogs—one of which should actually be counted twice), and this does not even take into account the organizer (section 5.4.3, p. 89).

It pays to thus first get acquainted with the various tools used to work with your styles.

6.3.1   Styles Gallery

Figure 70   Styles Gallery

The place Microsoft wants you to operate your styles from is, in my opinion, the least efficient of all the possible options: The Styles gallery on the Home ribbon. The advantages to the Styles gallery are that it takes up relatively little *extra* space (It is on the ribbon), and that it Live Previews the styles (a limited advantage). It is severely hampered by the fact that it does not show all the styles (it only displays what are known as Quick styles)—no list styles and no table styles are available, as these have been assigned to (equally hamstrung) galleries of their own. The style entries are huge (i.e., they waste space) and expanding the gallery covers vast amounts of screen space and may actually obscure the text you want to apply the style to (thus rendering Live Preview null and void). In short, I almost never use the Styles gallery itself.

6.3.2 Classic Style Gallery

Given that, as I have just described, the Word 2007/2010 Styles Gallery is actually an ill-design and wasteful tool, it is comforting to know that the Word 2003 and earlier Style Gallery (which used to reside on the Standard toolbar) is still available. It can be added to the QAT (Figure 71). Note that when modifying the QAT, you would want to choose the All commands setting in the Choose commands from list box, and that there are a total of fourteen Style tools in the list, of which a confusing seven are named Style or Styles—look at the tooltip before selecting the tool, and ensure that you have chosen StyleGalleryClassic.

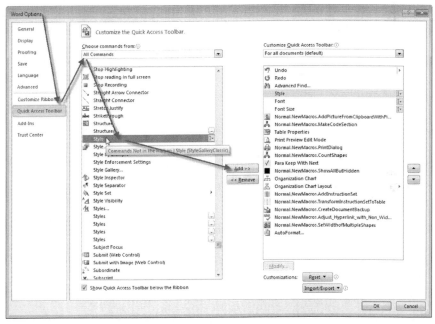

Figure 71   *Adding the Classic Style Gallery to the QAT*

Once this has been added to the QAT, you get access to a much less space-wasting list, which also lists all styles of all style types (Figure 72). Having said that, the next tool on my list is the most economical of them all (and is my favourite, although not only for its economy, but for its speed too).

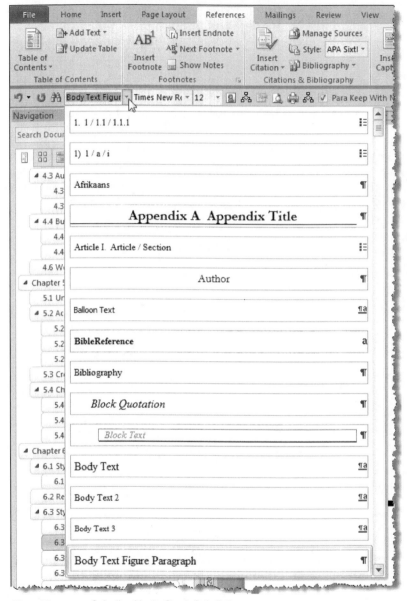

Figure 72   *Styles listed in the Classic Style Gallery*

6.3.3 Apply Styles dialog

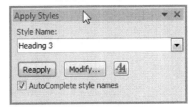

Figure 73   *Apply Styles dialog*

The Apply Styles dialog (Figure 73) is the tool I use the most for working with Styles. It is opened from the bottom list of the Styles gallery (Instruction set 10), or with the useful keyboard shortcut **Ctrl + Shift + S**. It allows you to find styles easily with its autocomplete function, it shows all styles, including table styles, and it take up almost no space on the screen. Like the Styles pane, the Apply Styles dialog can be docked to either side of the screen, although it is so small that I normally let it float over the window (although I do not keep it open all the time).

Instruction set 10   *Opening the Apply Styles dialog*

Shortcut	Ctrl + Shift + S
Keyboard	Alt | H | L | A
Left click	

6.3.4   Styles Pane

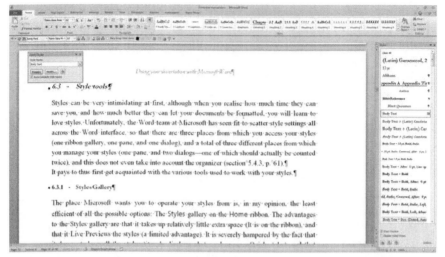

Figure 74   *Styles pane docked to right of Word window*

The Styles pane is a far more useful tool for working with Styles than the Style gallery, although I do find it less useful than the Apply Styles dialog. It is opened from the dialog launcher beneath the Styles gallery (Instruction set 11), or with the useful keyboard shortcut **Ctrl + Alt + Shift + S**. It shows a more complete list of styles, although it does not show table styles, and it shows a summarised definition of the style settings for each style, which is incredibly useful. Unfortunately, Microsoft has seen fit to hamstring the Styles pane by letting it show styles in a nonsensical order, so some more settings must be made to get it working right first.

Instruction set 11   Opening the Styles Pane

Shortcut	Ctrl + Alt + Shift + S
Keyboard	Alt | H | FY
Left click	

The Styles pane can float over your document, or it can be docked to either side of the Word window by clicking and dragging on the title bar of the pane. Figure 74 shows the pane docked to the right of the Word window, and note also the Apply Styles dialog (discussed above) floating at the top left of the window. I generally dock mine on the right of the screen. If you close it and then later reopen it, it will remember its last position.

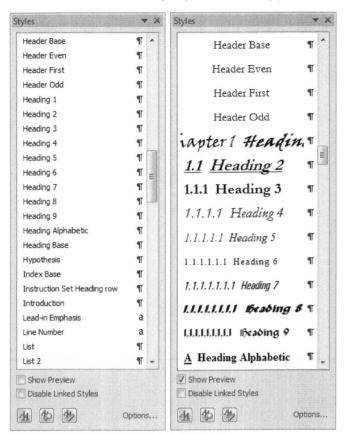

Figure 75   *Styles pane (with and without preview)*

Note the settings at the bottom of the Styles pane. You can choose to Show (or not to show) a preview of the style formatting, which formats the style name itself in a fashion reasonably similar to what has actually been defined for the style. However, I find that this generally just tends to clutter up the pane—the views with and without the preview are contrasted in Figure 75. You can also choose to Disable Linked Styles, should you want to. Furthermore, the Styles pane will summarise the style settings for you in a (rather large) tooltip which will appear when you hold your mouse over a style without clicking on it, as is shown in Figure 76.

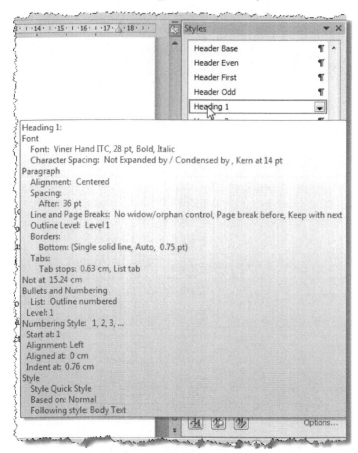

Figure 76   *Styles pane: Style information summary*

The Styles pane could potentially list all your styles, but you would need to coax it a little to do this. To accomplish this, open the associated Styles Pane Options dialog, which can, to the best of my knowledge, be opened only from the Options... link on the bottom right of the Styles pane itself (Instruction set 12). Figure 77 shows, on the left, the default settings for the Styles pane options, while the right shows the settings I recommend that you set for the best experience working with the Styles pane: Set the Select styles to show setting to All styles, and the Select how list is sorted setting to Alphabetical, as shown in Figure 77. Finally, turn off all the Select formatting to show as styles options, as these just clutter up the Styles pane with unnecessary non-style definitions (compare Figure 75 to Figure 74).

Instruction set 12   Opening the Styles Pane Options dialog

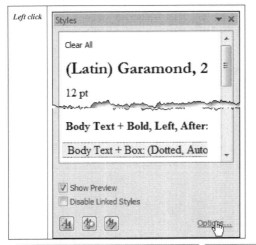

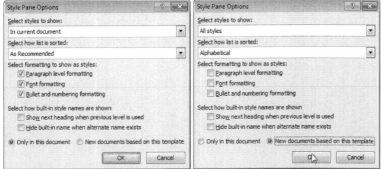

Figure 77   Style Pane Options dialog (default and recommended settings)

Apart from the Options... link on this pane, it also contains three other very important buttons, which open two more dialogs—the Manage Styles dialog and the New Style dialog—as well as the Style Inspector pane (Instruction set 13), all of which will be discussed in the following sections. Although all three of these are opened, as far as I am aware of, only from the bottom of the Styles pane, they can be added to the QAT if need be (although they are used so little that I do not consider that necessary, and for my own use, tend to access them from the Styles pane).

Instruction set 13   *Opening the New Styles dialog, Manage Styles dialog, Style Inspector pane*

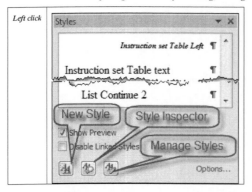

6.3.5   Manage Styles dialog

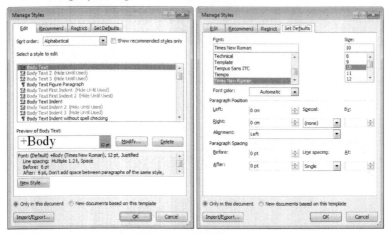

Figure 78   *Manage Styles dialog (Edit and Set Defaults tabs)*

The Manage Styles dialog (Figure 78), which is opened from the bottom of the Styles pane (Instruction set 13), is perhaps not that important, or at least, seldom used. It contains four tabs: Edit, Recommend, Restrict, and Set Defaults. These allow you to either modify existing styles or create new styles from the Edit tab (these functions acre accessed easier from other places, as will be shown), set which styles are recommended, set restrictions on the availability of styles in protected documents, or set default fonts and paragraph settings. These can be set either for the current document, or for the template on which the document is based. Lastly, the Import/Export... button opens the Organizer, which is discussed in section 5.4.3 (p. 89).

6.3.6   Style Inspector

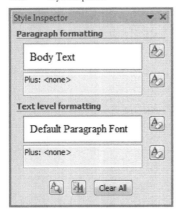

Figure 79   *Style Inspector*

The Style Inspector (Figure 79) is another floating (but dockable) small pane which is opened from the bottom of the Styles pane (Instruction set 13). It reveals the paragraph and character level formatting of the selected text, and contains buttons on the right to clear or reset each of these individually, or all together with the Clear All button. Additionally it has a New Style button, a duplicate of the one found on the bottom of the Styles pane, and, at its bottom left, a Reveal Formatting button, which in turn opens the Reveal Formatting pane[39]. The Reveal Formatting pane (Figure 80) is to formatting what the Style Inspector is to styles—it reveals all the formatting of the entire context in which the selection finds itself, from the font and paragraph formatting, to the page setup settings for the section in which the selection is found. What is very useful about this pane is that the relevant dialog for those settings can be opened by clicking on the appropriate header—for example, the mouse pointer in Figure 80 will open the Paragraph dialog if clicked.

---

[39] You are dead right—how on earth did Microsoft come up with a pane, which is opened from a pane, which is opened from a pane, which is opened from a gallery on a ribbon (or, to be fair for the latter, with a keyboard shortcut)?

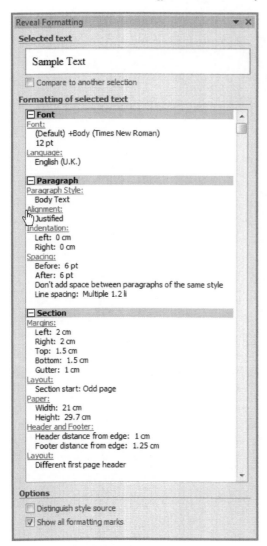

Figure 80   *Reveal Formatting pane*

6.3.7   Create New Style dialog

The last dialog we will look at here, and the most important, is the Create New Style from Formatting dialog, and it is also opened from the bottom of the Styles pane (Instruction set 13). This dialog will be discussed in greater detail in the following section.

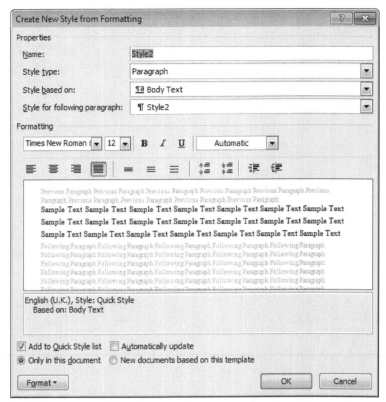

Figure 81   *Create New Style from Formatting dialog: Paragraph style*

6.4   Using styles

Now that we have surveyed the somewhat dizzying array of styles tools, we can get the actual point of learning how to use styles. Using styles entails basically two things: Creating new and modifying existing styles, on the one hand, and applying styles on the other.

6.4.1   Creating new styles

As you will have noticed from the above sections, there are a number of places from which the Create New Style from Formatting dialog can be opened. Regardless of from where the dialog was opened, the process of creating a new style is as follows:

1.   Give the style a Name that will allow you to associate it with either its intended scope of usage (e.g., "Table header") or its appearance (e.g., "Body text right aligned italics"). Where applicable, it is also useful to include the name of the style it is based on in its own name (e.g., "*Body text* block").

2.   Select the Style type from the options of Paragraph, Character, Linked, Table or List, depending on where you intend using the style (mostly this will be Paragraph). These style types were discussed on p. 91 (section 6.1).

3. For most unique styles, make sure that the style is <u>B</u>ased on No Style (you will find it at the very top of the list—press Home to get there quickly).

    Generally, it is not a good idea to leave this on Normal, although if you are avoiding the normal style like the plague anyway, you will find that this will do very   little   harm. If you do select a style here (e.g., Body text indent is based on Body text), remember that changes made to the base style will be drawn through to this style as well, unless those changes refer to specific differences between this style and the base style (in which case you will no longer be able to distinguish the base and new styles).

    Let me give an example: You have created new a style called Body text italics. Obviously, it is based on Body text, with the only difference being that it is in italics. If you were then to change the point size of Body text to 10 (from 12), Body text italics would also change from 12 to 10 pts. However, if you changed Body text to italics, Body text italics would just stay in italics, and you would then not be able to distinguish between paragraphs formatted in the two styles on the basis of their appearance only.

4. Select the <u>S</u>tyle for following paragraph (Figure 82). Generally, this will be the same as the style which you are creating (and which is the default setting), but under certain circumstances, you may want to change this (e.g., after heading styles, you would probably want to revert back to Body text). This can be a great labour-saving, as you do then not need to reset the style when a new paragraph is added.

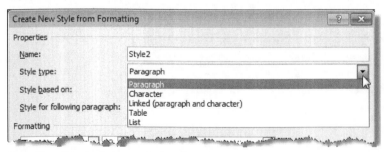

Figure 82   Selecting Style type when creating a new style

5. Click on New documents based on this template, unless you specifically want this new style to be limited to the current document only (which I generally advise against—use templates to store your styles for the least headaches).

6. Make sure that the A<u>u</u>tomatically update check box is deselected (under exceptional circumstances[40]—such as *maybe* with heading styles—you will want this on). If you leave it on, any changes you make at any single point in the

---

[40] My personal recommendation is that you *always* turn this off.

document will be carried through to all other instances of that same style in the whole document. While Microsoft certain intended this as a means of getting Word to automate the process of suing styles on your behalf, the practical implication is that you will then never be able to make exceptions to the rule for this style when this setting is turned on, as any changes will lead to the style being updated, and all instances of text formatted according to that style being shown in the new formatting.

7. If you want the style to be listed in the Styles gallery, select Add to Quick Style list.

8. Lastly, set the formatting for the style. The Formatting section of the dialog contains a number of shortcuts, or you could use the Format button (Figure 83) to access each of the Font, Paragraph, Tabs, Border, Language, Frame, Numbering, Text Effects, or Customise keyboard (from Shortcut Key) dialogs. The important thing to remember here is that even though you are using the exact same dialog which you have probably up to now used to format a specific instance of text, you are now not using the dialog to format actual text, but to set what the appearance is for all text that is using, or will use, the style being created.

9. Click on OK. The new style will be created and also be applied to the current paragraph or selected text.

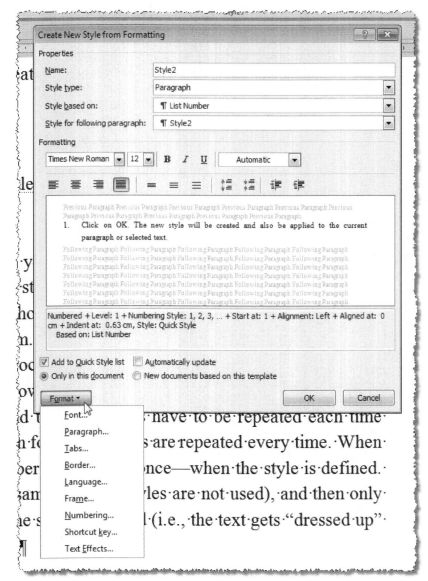

Figure 83   *Formatting options available when creating a new style*

6.4.2   Modifying existing styles

Modifying styles is a relatively simple process. There are a whole number of places from which the Modify Style dialog can be accessed—The Modify... button on the Apply Styles dialog (Figure 73) or the Manage Styles dialog (Figure 78), or by right clicking on a style in the Styles pane (Figure 84) or the Styles gallery.

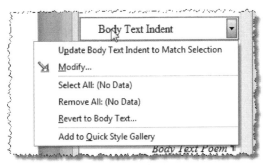

Figure 84   *Modifying a style by right clicking it in the Styles pane*

Regardless of which method is chosen, the Modify Style dialog will be opened, which, as can be seen in Figure 85, is basically the Create New Style from Formatting dialog with a different name, and the existing style pre-loaded. The process of modifying an existing style, then, is essentially the same as that of creating a new style, as was described above. Only one point needs to be emphasised, as it is not that obvious—each and every time you make a modification to an existing style, remember to select New documents based on this template, as doing this just once, and then making additional modifications will not result in the additional modifications being carried through to the template (which I confess I find quite irritating).

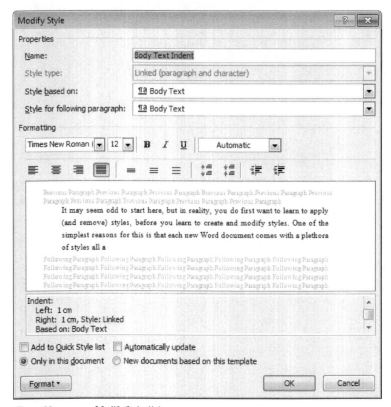

Figure 85   *Modify Style dialog*

6.4.3   Applying styles

The good news, of course, is that you need not create all the styles you will be needing—each new Word document comes with a plethora of styles all at the ready, and it is actually recommended that where a built-in style exists, you rather use that than· create your own (for each different template—or even document—these built-in styles can be formatted differently, so there is no reason not to use them).

Before we look at how to apply styles, though, it helps to again revisit the whole purpose of using styles. When you don't use styles, the process may seem simpler (Table 4). However, bear in mind that the "second" step may consist of up to ten individual formatting settings, and that both steps have to be repeated each and every time something needs to be formatted—thus all ten formatting steps are repeated every time. When styles are used, all the formatting settings are performed only once—when the style is defined. Thereafter, the text is created (exactly the same as when styles are not used), and then only one setting is performed in the third step—the style is applied (i.e., the text gets "dressed up" with the formatting as defined by the style).

Table 4   *Contrast between formatting with and without styles*

Style-less formatting	Style-ish formatting
1. Type text	1. Format style
2. Format text	2. Type text
	3. Apply style to text

So in short, the process is this: Type the text, and apply the style to the text. There are several ways in which styles can be applied. Firstly, several styles already have keyboard shortcuts assigned to them, and a keyboard shortcut can be assigned to any style (see section 6.3.7, or section 2.3.2 on p. 30 for more detail). Table 5 lists the built-in keyboard shortcuts, together with those that I prefer to create.

Table 5   *Style keyboard shortcuts*

Type	Keyboard shortcut	Style
Built-in	Ctrl + Alt + 1	Heading 1
	Ctrl + Alt + 2	Heading 2
	Ctrl + Alt + 3	Heading 3
User defined	Ctrl + Alt + 4	Heading 4
	Ctrl + Alt + 5	Heading 5
	Ctrl + Alt + 6	Heading 6
	Ctrl + Alt + B	Body Text

Styles can also be applied by selecting them from[41]: the Apply Styles dialog(6.3.3), from the Classic Style Gallery (6.3.2), from the Styles pane (6.3.4), or from the Styles gallery in the Home ribbon (6.3.1). I prefer using the latter, as it is a small floating window, and it is also very easy to select a style from this dialog—all you need to do is start typing the name of a style in this dialog, and the AutoComplete function (you should keep it turned on, then) will look it up in the list of available styles. Also, the Styles pane only shows Paragraph, Character, and Linked styles. The Apply Styles dialog, on the other hand, really shows all your styles, including the Table styles. Think of it as a more complete version of the Styles pane without all the clutter.

However, you need to take note that the way in which Word applies styles to text depends on what is selected, and which style type is used:

If you apply a character style and the I-beam is positioned within a word, then the style is applied to the whole word. If the I-beam is not positioned within a word, then it may seem as if there is no effect on the paragraph or any of the characters, but if you start typing immediately, the characters you type will assume the formatting defined by the character style. If anything, from a single character to any number of words or paragraphs is selected, then the style is applied to all that is selected. However, since character styles do not contain any paragraph-level settings, it stands to reason that none of those settings will change.

If a paragraph style is applied, then the font and paragraph settings are applied, regardless of whether something is selected or not. In short, this means that if you want

---

[41] presented in my own order of preference for usage.

to format a single paragraph, you do not need to select anything, so long as you are positioned within the paragraph. Simply apply the style, and the whole paragraph will be formatted accordingly.

If a linked style is applied, then if nothing or a whole paragraph is selected, the font and paragraph settings for the style are applied (i.e., it is applied as if it were a paragraph style). If only some characters from the paragraph are selected, then only the font settings of the style, but not the paragraph settings, are applied (i.e., it is applied as if it were a character style).

The right-click context menu (see Instruction set 14 below) also contains the Quick styles from the Styles gallery, as well as a button to open the Apply Styles dialog.

A final method of applying styles is by copying and pasting them. Of course, when text from a paragraph (but not the whole paragraph—i.e., the paragraph end mark has not been selected) is copied, only the font formatting for that text is included. If the text was formatted using a character style, that style will be copied too. If a paragraph or linked style was applied, that style's paragraph-level formatting is not copied and pasted. If a whole paragraph is copied and pasted, obviously the paragraph-level style settings accompany it. However, it is possible to copy only character style formatting or only paragraph style formatting using the format painter. This means that, if you want to apply a certain style at regular intervals in one session (e.g., a certain heading level), you can copy the correct style to the format painter (**Ctrl + Shift + C**), and then, as you go along, paste that formatting when needed (**Ctrl + Shift + V**). Just remember that this appears to be a more powerful means of applying a style. For example, if I have a paragraph of text in the Normal style, and one word is formatted in a red font colour, the following difference will be noticed: When I make the paragraph Body text from the Styles pane, the whole paragraph is formatted as body text, including the red word, but the red word retains is red font colour, even though the Body text style is not in red. This happens regardless of whether I simply place my insertion point within the paragraph, or select the entire paragraph. But when I copy the Body text style the format painter, and then paste it onto my paragraph, if the insertion point is within the paragraph, but not in the red word, then my word retains its red font colour. But if my insertion point is in the red word, or I select the whole paragraph, the word loses its red font colour. Now this is relevant, because sometimes you want to apply a style to a whole number of paragraphs at a time. The only practical way to do this is to select those paragraphs. But if you do that, any outstanding formatting will be lost—rather use the Styles pane to do it if this is not what you want.

6.4.4 Rehabilitating styles

Sometimes, especially when you are still learning how to use styles, things can go wrong. You may find that even though a certain style has been applied to a text or a paragraph, the settings for the style do not seem to have been applied. This is because normally, text can be formatted over and above the formatting already applied by the applied style. In this instance, the first recourse is to reapply the style. Simply select the offending text, and select the style from the Styles gallery or the Styles pane, or use the

Reapply button in the Apply Styles dialog. If this fails, you may have to strip away all the extraneous formatting manually (Instruction set 14).

Instruction set 14   Removing extraneous formatting

Shortcut	**Ctrl + Space bar** to remove character formatting **Ctrl + Q** to remove paragraph formatting
Keyboard	Alt H | E
Left click	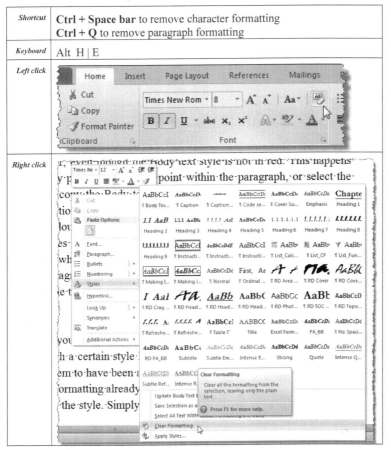
Right click	

A last desperate measure is to select the text, copy or cut it, and then to use Paste Special... (Instruction set 15), to paste Unformatted Text (in the Paste As: list box)to get raw text. Now reapply the style you want, and this time it should be right.

Instruction set 15   Paste Special

Shortcut	Ctrl + Alt + V
Keyboard	Alt │ H │ V │ S
Left click	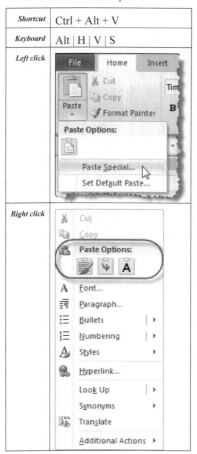
Right click	

6.4.5   Selecting styles

It should also be noted that when you right click on a style in the Styles gallery or the Styles pane, you also have the option of selecting all instances of that style in your document. This is useful if you would want to either copy that text, change the style from one style to another, or even just see how many instances of that style exist in your document—as Figure 86 shows, if you right click on the style again after the selection has been made, Word will give you a count of the number of instances of that style found in your document.

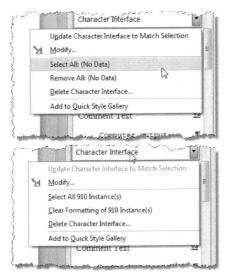

Figure 86   *Selecting all instances of a style*

6.5   *Style roundup*

Some last pointers about styles. All this talk of styles, and creating styles may seem daunting. The good news is that you will find yourself using chiefly only a few styles. The Heading styles and the Body text style will make up the large majority of the styles you will use manually. Word also invokes the Caption style and the TOC styles each time you invoke one of those—see section 8.4 (Caption numbering) on p. 161 and section 9.1 (Tables of content) on p. 183. Some other built-in styles that you might encounter if you use some of the techniques in this book are the Index styles (see section 9.3, p. 194), the Footnote- and Endnote Reference and Footnote- and Endnote Text styles (see section 8.6, p. 171), the header and footer styles (Header, Header Even, Header First, Header Odd, and the same for Footer)—see section 7.5, p. 136—and the Table of Figures style (see section 9.2, p. 190).

Here and there, you might want to create a style for a specific piece of text, but these are the minority.

Some examples of styles that you will see used in this book are the use of a character style I created (called *Character Interface*) to indicate the parts of the interface referred to in the Segoe UI font (I mentioned this in section 1.7 on p. 6). I also created a paragraph font (called *Making it Practical*) which I used to create the boxed italic effect of the various Application entries and one called *Code Section*s for the various macro listings. You will also notice that I use several different kinds of bulleted lists in the book, each of these is a List style of its own (e.g., *List Book* for the lists that use the book icon as a bullet) and the tables in this book are formatted with a Table style called *Table Training Materials light*.

Finally, you will recall that there are four main types of styles. Paragraph and Character styles have been the main topic of discussion in this chapter, although much of what was discussed here (e.g., how to create new styles), also applies to List styles and Table styles. Nonetheless, in their unique contexts, the remaining two style types will each receive a more detailed discussion—List styles in section 8.1.3 (p. 155) and Table styles in section 15.3 (p. 354).

Chapter 7
Planning for the printed page: Page Setup

A simple fact of the 21st century is that ever fewer books are being printed on paper, so much so that some books never see the light of day as text on paper, but live entirely as e-books. However, a dissertation is still a beast that can slay many trees, and, despite the fact that it is entirely possible for a dissertation to be written by a student and reviewed by multiple promoters entirely electronically (the whole of Chapter 14 is devoted to this), the reality is that, from start to finish, drafts of your dissertation will probably be printed out multiple times, and the final product is still required to be submitted in hard copy by most universities (in fact, all universities in my limited sphere of experience)—Chapter 19 is devoted to the actual printing of the dissertation.

What this chapter will focus on is those factors that you would do well to take into consideration if you do plan on actually printing your dissertation on paper. Also note that, since my focus is on theses and dissertations, which are printed in simplex (i.e., only on one side of the folio), I do not discuss some issues which are relevant to the layout of a duplex document, such as this book.

7.1   Understanding Sections

The foundational concept to all the material dealt with in this book is that of the section. The first thing you will want to do is make sure that you can actually *see* the section information, which Word does not display by default. To get this information, right click on the status bar, and make sure that Formatted Page Number, Section, and Page Number are all activated (Figure 87).

Next, what is a section? It helps to think of this in terms of an analogy. Let's try to get a grip on how Word itself sees the structure of a document (Please do not quote what I am about to say here, as it is an oversimplification that omits some facts). To Word, each document must consist of at least one section. A section, to Word, does not consist of pages, but paragraphs. And Paragraphs do not consist of lines, but sentences, which again consist of words. So, for example, in VBA, this is one way in which I could refer to the first word of the first sentence of the first paragraph of the first section of this very document (that word, by the way, is *Doing*): Activedocument.Sections(1).Range .Paragraphs(1).Range.Sentences(1).Words(1). Now that may seem Greek to you, but to Word, it makes perfect sense (I also understand it, barely!). Now let's put that into an analogy. Think of words to your document as bricks to a house. Those bricks get built together into walls, just as words make sentences. Then those walls add up to make rooms, just as sentences make paragraphs. And paragraphs make sections, just as rooms make a floor level, and floor levels make a building, just as sections make a document. Now firstly, the implications of the fact that Word does not really take pages into account are discussed in more detail in Chapter 19 (from p. 467). However, consider the following: A building must have at least one floor level to be a building. And a floor level must consist of at least one room. And a room must consist of at least one wall (a round room!). So also, each document has at least one section, and at least one paragraph, which consists of at least one sentence[42].

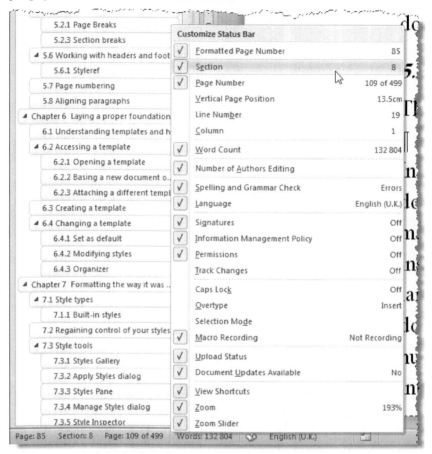

Customize Status Bar

√	Formatted Page Number	85
√	Section	8
√	Page Number	109 of 499
	Vertical Page Position	13.5cm
	Line Number	19
	Column	1
√	Word Count	132 804
√	Number of Authors Editing	
√	Spelling and Grammar Check	Errors
√	Language	English (U.K.)
√	Signatures	Off
√	Information Management Policy	Off
√	Permissions	Off
	Track Changes	Off
	Caps Lock	Off
	Overtype	Insert
	Selection Mode	
√	Macro Recording	Not Recording
√	Upload Status	
√	Document Updates Available	No
√	View Shortcuts	
√	Zoom	193%
√	Zoom Slider	

Page: 85   Section: 8   Page: 109 of 499   Words: 132 804   English (U.K.)

Figure 87   *Displaying section and page count information in the Status bar*

So you can see that a section is an integral part of each and every Word document. But, just as most buildings are single-story buildings, it is entirely possible to have multi-story buildings as well (and now we even have the Burj Khalifa[43] in Dubai that has 163 floors). And just as the complexity of constructing a building with many stories increases exponentially, so also for a document with many sections, although having multiple sections often becomes inevitable. Some advice, then, is to use sections wisely—do not unnecessarily add section breaks to your document. But *do* use sections, as there are many things that require them.

---

[42] And so my little VBA statement above even applies to a blank document.

[43] http://www.burjkhalifa.ae/

Ok. But that actually still does not reveal to use what a section is, except that it is a foundational component of a document. A section, then, is a part of the document which contains all the information required for the page layout of all the paragraphs (not pages) contained within that section. Thus, if I want to set the width between paragraphs, or the spacing between the lines of a paragraph, or even the alignment of the paragraph relative to the page margins, I can do all of that from the Paragraph dialog. But the minute I want to set the page margins themselves, or the vertical positioning of the paragraphs on the page, or the page orientation for the pages on which those paragraphs will be printed, then I am working with section-level settings. And, just as you can have different room layouts on different levels of a building, but not on the same level, so also I can have different page-layout settings on the same page (because pages don't really exist to Word), but not in the same section. If, thus, you want different section level settings for different parts of your document, you need to chop the document up into different sections.

These, then, are the section-level settings you can set for each section:

- Page margins (top, bottom, left, right, as well as gutter)
- Page orientation
- Page size
- Pages in document printed per sheet of paper in printer
- Paper source (thus allowing pages from different sections to be printed from different printer trays)
- Section start
- Headers and footers
- Vertical alignment of text on the page
- Line numbering
- Page borders (not text or paragraph borders and also not page colour which, as far as I can tell, is set for the document as a whole)
- Columns

Not all of these will be discussed, since they are not all relevant to the typing of a thesis or dissertation. However, note that, in your document, all of this information is stored in section breaks. Thus, our discussion will start there.

7.1.1 Section start and section breaks

Each section in your document is defined by a section break. These are invisible if the display of non-printing characters has been turned off, thus the first secret to working with sections is to turn the display of non-printing characters on (see section 3.2.1, p. 38). However, note that, depending on their position, they can, at times, even be difficult to see when visible in Print Layout view, although they are impossible to miss in Draft view. Figure 88 shows what the section break at the end of p. 80 in this book looks like. Generally, section breaks as displayed as two parallel dotted lines *on the outside* of a paragraph end mark (remember that sections contain paragraphs, not the other way around), and then, if space permits (it all depends on how close that paragraph end mark is to the page margin) the words Section Break with, in parenthesis, an indication of the kind of section break.

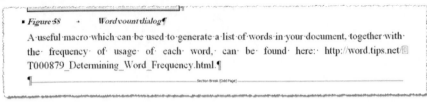

Figure 88   Section break displayed in document

Oddly, the section break contains the page layout settings for the pages above it, but the section start setting for the section following it (it may be better to think of this, then, as a kind of section *end* setting, but that is not what Microsoft calls it). The implication of this will become apparent soon.

7.1.1.1   Adding section breaks

Section breaks are added from the Breaks tool in the Page Setup group of the Page Layout ribbon (Instruction set 16—in Application 2.2 (p. 32) I demonstrate a keyboard shortcut well worth creating for adding a section break).

Word allows four kinds of section breaks:

- Next Page (the kind that you should use whenever possible)
- Even Page
- Odd Page
- Continuous

Next Page section breaks basically combine a section break and a page break—i.e., the new section always starts on a new page. Since sections contain section-level settings that determine how the text is laid out on the pages of that section, it stands to reason that this is the kind of section break you would want to (and should) add most often.

Even Page and **Odd Page** section breaks function similar to Next Page section breaks, in that they force a new page, barring that the new page (i.e., the page directly after the section break) will always be either an even- or odd-numbered page, depending on which is chosen. Thus, if the current page is page 20, and an Even Page section break is inserted, a blank page is added after the current text (the page may or may not be displayed, depending on whether you are in Print Layout view or not), and the next page after the section break will be page 22. If an Odd Page or a Next Page section break were inserted, no blank page would be inserted, and the next page would be page 21. If, with the Even Page section break, you were to add more text at the end of page 20, so that it overflowed onto the next page, that next page would become page 21, and nothing would change for page 22. If, however, you added even more text, such that it again overflowed onto the next page, that next page would become page 22, and page 22 would become page 24 (again creating an intervening blank page, page 23). The good news is that for a thesis printed simplex (i.e., on only one side of the folio), as most theses are, Even- and Odd Page section breaks are moot—you should not use them. Only with books where printing is duplex do they come into play. For example, you will notice that each chapter starts on a facing page (known as the recto)—this is accomplished through the use of Odd Page section breaks at the end of each chapter (or is that, before the start of each chapter?).

Instruction set 16   Adding a section break

Shortcut	None, but Alt + Shift + Enter can be created—see Application 2.2, p. 32)
Keyboard	Alt | P | B N (Next page) Alt | P | B O (Continuous) Alt | P | B E (Even page) Alt | P | B D (Odd page)
Left click	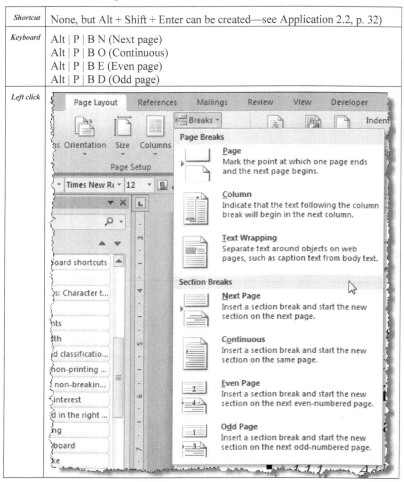

Continuous section breaks leave out the page break—the new section starts on the current page, immediately after the text. Generally, Continuous section breaks are not used that much, and should be avoided wherever possible. Common uses for Continuous section breaks are where portion of a page's content should be displayed in a different number of columns than the rest (section 15.5, p. 363 discusses another option), or with table notes, as is described in Application 8.6 (p. 181), or where a portion of the text must show line numbers. The problem with Continuous section breaks, and the reason they should be avoided, is that each and every section in a Word document contains at least one (sometimes more) section headers and footers.

Unfortunately, unlike programs like Excel, you cannot access the Word Headers and Footers through a dialog, but only in Print layout view. This makes it practically impossible for Word to show all the headers and/or footers when many continuous section breaks are used (Word cannot show three headers in the space for one header) and this is a recipe for disaster when page numbering or other header or footer settings start going wrong.

As we shall see in a moment, deleting section breaks is no simple matter. Fortunately, if you have a section break that is of the wrong sort, you can change it without having to delete and re-insert it—the Layout tab of the Page Setup dialog contains a Section start list box (Figure 89) which allows you to set the section start setting for the section break *above* the current section (i.e., make sure that you have positioned the insertion point *below* the section break whose section start you want to change before opening the dialog).

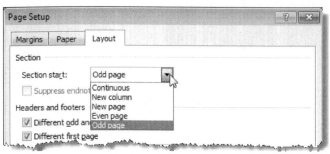

Figure 89   *Setting section start in the Page Setup dialog*

7.1.1.2   *Working with section breaks*

The most important thing when working with section breaks is just the remember the golden rule that the section break itself stores all the section-level settings for the pages above it (until the next section break). This has several implications.

Firstly, if you add a section break, it will assume most of the section-level settings of the section it has just split into two—i.e., you will now have two sections, one above and one below that section break, that have, until you change them, the same section level settings.

Second, there is an implicit section break in the very last paragraph mark of a document. Copying that paragraph mark (again, a motivation for displaying non-printing characters) results in the section-level settings also being copied (this is only relevant when you are pasting into a different document).

Third, deleting section breaks results in behaviour that baffles many Word users who do not keep that principle in mind. Consider Figure 90. This represents an imaginary document which consists of 6 pages. The image on the left shows two section breaks as the black line (the second section break, we could say, is the implicit section break in the last paragraph mark of the document). The upward-pointing arrows show that the section-level settings stored in the section breaks apply to all the pages above the section break. If the section break between pages 3 and 4 were to be deleted, most Word users would expect pages 4 to 6 to become portrait, just as pages 1 to 3, but instead, pages 1 to 3 become landscape, just as pages 4 to 6. This is because, once the section break has been deleted, the section-level settings of the lower section break now apply to all the pages (now 1 to 6) above it (until the next higher section break or the start of the document).

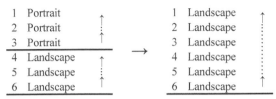

1 Portrait		1 Landscape	
2 Portrait		2 Landscape	
3 Portrait	→	3 Landscape	
4 Landscape		4 Landscape	
5 Landscape		5 Landscape	
6 Landscape		6 Landscape	

Figure 90   *Demonstrating the influence of section-level settings stored in a section break*

Fourth, remember that section breaks can be copied or cut and pasted. This can be done together with text (and is sometimes done unknowingly by people who do not have their non-printing characters displayed), or even on their own—it is possible to select only a section break, and then copy or cut that. It stands to reason that when a section break is pasted, the section into which it is pasted breaks into two, with the lower of the two new sections retaining the section-level settings of the original section, and the upper of the two sections now assuming the section-level settings of the pasted section break.

The fifth point to remember is that when you make changes to section-level settings (i.e., those items listed on p. 119), you are often given the choice (see Figure 91 for an example) to determine whether those settings must be applied to the Whole document (i.e., all sections), This section (i.e., only the current section, or currently selected sections), or This point forward (i.e., all sections, including the current section, right through to the last section of the document—the one governed by the implicit section break in the last paragraph mark of the document). It is actually best to change this setting first, before changing anything else in the dialog. Word will then hide any settings that are different for the various sections, as is described and illustrated below for when you have selected multiple sections and then want to change section-level settings.

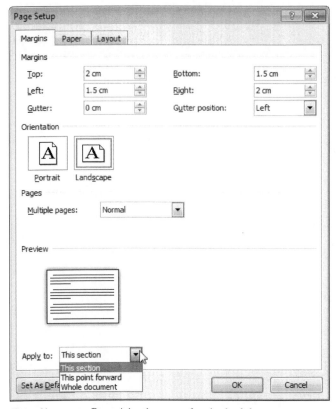

Figure 91   *Determining the extent of section-level changes*

It should also be noted that you can set section-level settings for multiple sections simultaneously by selecting all the sections you want to work on (this is similar to the setting discussed above, but allows more options). When you open the relevant dialog (e.g., the Page Setup dialog, or the Columns dialog, etc.), the settings that are the same for all the applied sections will be displayed, and those that are different for the various sections will be hidden. Changing any of those will result in them being standardised across the various sections. As an example, Figure 92 shows the Margins tab of the Page Setup dialog, and it can be seen that, for the sections selected, the Top and Bottom margins are the same, but the sections have, at present, different Left and Right margins.

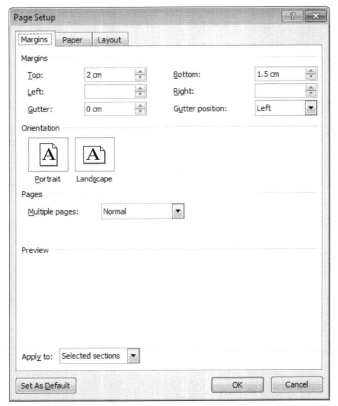

Figure 92 · Page Setup dialog with multiple sections selected

Lastly, when Continuous section breaks are inserted, Word continues with the page layout of the current section until it is able to switch to the page layout of the new section (if that is different). Thus, the section-level formatting of the new section that can be applied immediately (e.g., columns), is, and the section-level formatting that cannot be applied immediately (e.g., page orientation), will only start on the next page. It would be better, though, to only use continuous section breaks where those kinds of discrepancies do not occur, and to rather use the other three (and preferably Next page) where they do.

7.2   Page Setup

Page setup settings are, then, defined, at the very least, at the section level. This does not mean that different sections, or even all sections, in one document cannot have the same page setup settings, but it does mean that no smaller unit of a document than a section can contain different page setup settings. Many of the Page Setup settings can be set from the various tools in the Page Setup group of the Page Layout ribbon, but to avoid duplication, I will just discuss the various settings as found in the Page Setup dialog itself, which is also opened from the same place (Instruction set 17).

Instruction set 17   Opening the Page setup dialog

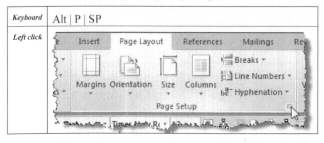

Keyboard	Alt	P	SP

7.2.1   Page margins

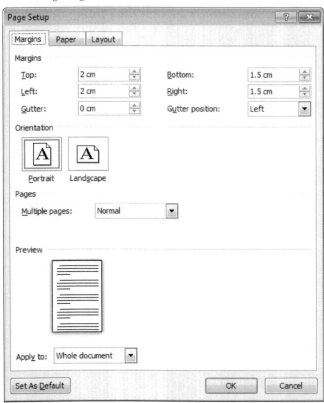

Figure 93   Page Setup dialog: Margins tab

The Margins tab of the Page Layout dialog (Figure 93) allows you to set margins for each section (or all). Choose margins that are practical and visually appealing, although your institution may have guidelines in this regard. Some promoters insist that their students use huge margins (e.g., 3 cm all around), which I suspect may be in an attempt to make the dissertation look thicker, but which I just think just wastes space and paper. I generally tend to think that about 2 cm on the right and 3 cm (or 2 cm with a 1 cm gutter) on the left is quite broad enough.

Note that the ruler also displays the page margins (Figure 94).

Figure 94   *Page margins displayed on the ruler*

Word also allows you to set a page Gutter. Basically, this is a non-printable space provided on either the left (normally), right or top of the page for printing. If your document has both portrait and landscape sections, Word will adjust the gutter position accordingly, should it be applied to the whole document (i.e., portrait sections will, for example, have the gutter on the left, and landscape pages will have it on the top).

The gutter is useful in that it provides extra space needed for binding the pages into a book (by whatever means). If your book is printed on only one side of the page, then this is not actually necessary, as the space can simply be added to the left margin. However, even then, if you have both portrait and landscape sections, the gutter becomes useful, because you then don't need to figure out the margins of each section individually. Remember, though, that the gutter reduces the size of your printable page, and will thus result in a re-arranging of your document's layout. Also, if you do use a gutter, remember that you may actually not want to make your left margin on portrait sections, and perhaps also your top margin on landscape sections, too big, as the "printed" margin is equals to the sum of the left (or top) margin and the gutter. Thus using a 2cm gutter and a 2cm left margin, actually means that you are not using the left 4cm of your page, although the binding commonly used for dissertations actually requires a very small gutter—1cm should be plenty.

The Multiple pages list box on this tab of the dialog allows you to choose between Normal, Mirror margins, 2 pages per sheet, or Book fold. For simplex printing, as with a thesis or dissertation, this setting should not be set to anything other than Normal. As such, the operation of the other modes will not be discussed here.

7.2.2   Page orientation

In all likelihood, most of your thesis will be in Portrait, but you may, for some portions which are too broad to fit in the narrower width of the portrait page, switch to Landscape (see, for example, Appendix A, p. 497). Note that this generally entails adding two section breaks, one before, and one after the portion of text that is to be "rotated" to Landscape, then positioning yourself in between those two new section breaks, and then changing the page orientation.

7.2.3   Paper size

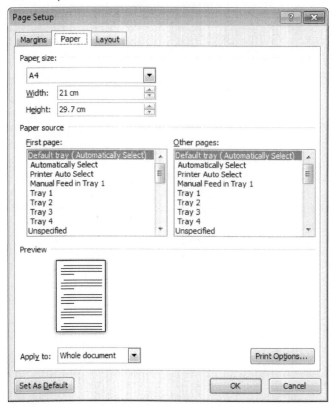

Figure 95   *Page Setup dialog: Paper tab*

The Paper tab of Page setup dialog (Figure 95) allows you to set the paper size, and even which tray the printer should use for the pages of that section (e.g., if a printer has card stock in one tray, and standard paper in another). Not much needs to be said here, apart from the fact that you should ensure that your paper size is correction for the region of the world you find yourself in[44].

Application 7.1   Pages are not printing out as they appear on the screen

I go into a lot of detail discussing printing from Word in Chapter 19, also discussing the fact that Word is a WYSIWYG program. One problem that students sometimes encounter is that they see certain content being displayed on page x, *but when the document is printed, it appears on page* y, *or, in exceptional circumstances, gets dropped (e.g., a line is visible on screen, but is not on page* x, *and not on page* y *either). The first thing to check in these instances is the paper size. Although there is a setting to rescale paper to fit a different size (Figure 96), this does not necessarily resolve the*

---

[44] You can read more at: http://en.wikipedia.org/wiki/Paper_size or http://www.paper-sizes.com.

problem. Prevention is better than cure, so make sure that the paper size is set correctly for your whole document.

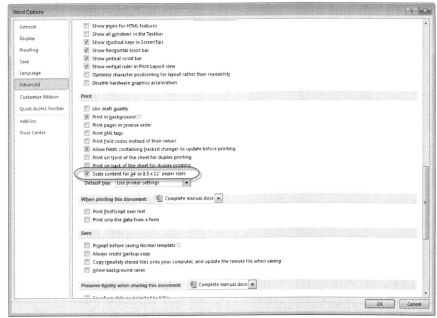

Figure 96   *Word Options: Scale content for A4 or Letter size*

7.2.4   Page layout settings

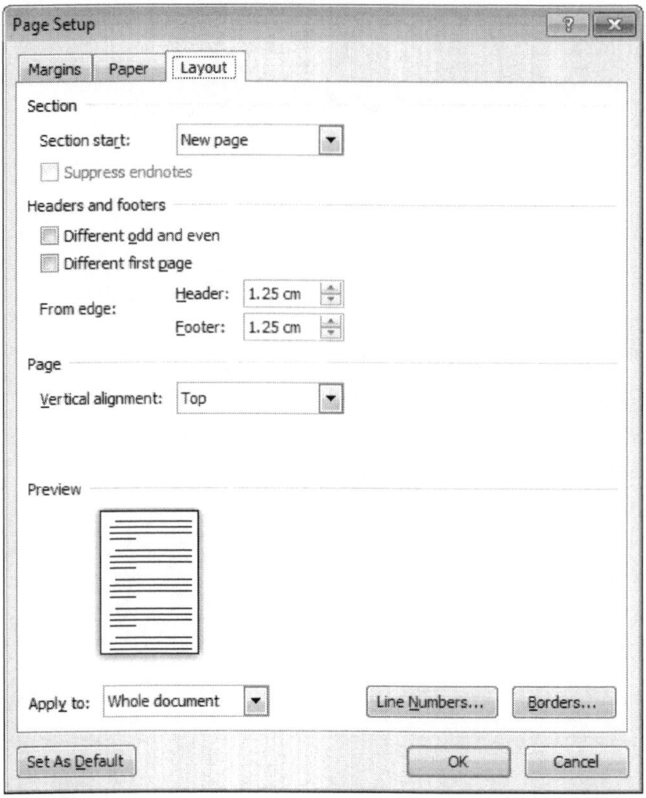

Figure 97   Page Setup dialog: Layout tab

The Layout tab of the Page Setup dialog contains a mixed variety of settings. Section start has already been discussed above, Headers and Footers will be discussed below, and suppress endnotes will be discussed on p. 175 (Application 8.4).

This tab of the dialog also allows you to set the Vertical alignment of the text:

- Top is the default setting, and fills the page from the top, with text extending downwards as you type.
- Center fills the page from the middle, with text expanding towards the top and bottom of the page simultaneously as you type. This is often used for title pages.
- Justified fills the pages from the top and bottom, with text "converging" towards the middle of the page. This setting is not used often.
- Bottom fills the page from the bottom, with text extending upwards as you type. This setting is not used often.

Furthermore, you can select the Line Numbers... button to open the Line Numbers dialog (Figure 98). Since line numbers are set for an entire section, it is common to insert two continuous section breaks, one before, and one after, the text that must show the numbering, and then to add the line numbers for that section. Figure 99 shows an example of the use of line numbers from a book I am working on concerning the writing of VBA macros in Excel. Note the two continuous section breaks.

Figure 98   *Line Numbers dialog*

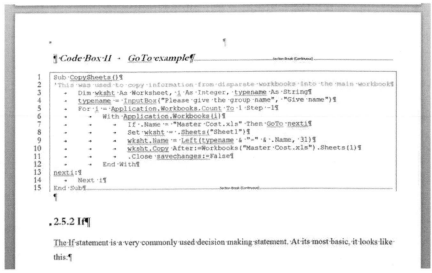

Figure 99   *Demonstration of the use of line numbers*

Lastly, on this tab, the Borders... button will open the Borders and Shading dialog to the Page Border tab (the other two tabs in this dialog are not relevant to section-level settings). Although this dialog is displayed in Figure 100, I will be assuming that the settings here will be familiar enough, or self-explanatory enough, to not have to go into an extensive discussion of setting page borders here.

131

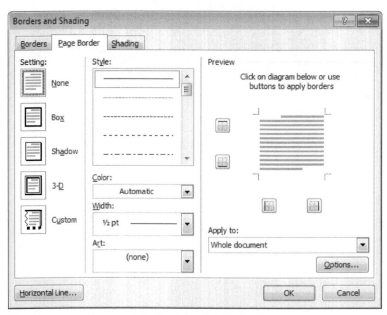

Figure 100   *Borders and Shading dialog: Page Border tab*

7.3   Columns

It should be evident that continuous section breaks are not used often. In fact, the only time when it makes sense to use them is when the formatting desired is formatting which is applied at the section level, and is different from the current section formatting, but which is also not different to the general page layout (page orientation, margins, headers and footers) of the current section. One such instance is the introduction of columns.

It should be noted that for small amounts of text that need to be arranged in adjacent columns, a table (with two or three or however many columns are desired) can be inserted. For a proper "columnar" look, the table borders can be set to invisible. The advantages are that there are fewer sections in your document, and there is no need to hassle with multiple section breaks. However, the disadvantage of this workaround is that the text cannot flow over from one "column" (table cell) to the next. If this feature is needed (e.g., you may want to make changes to the text, or there is a larger amount of text that has to be arranged in adjacent columns, or you are not certain how much text there will be), then you will need to use actual columns.

If you want the text to flow naturally with the rest of your text, then insert two continuous section breaks and format the intervening section to multiple columns. A shortcut is to select the text which you want to appear in columns, and then use the column tool. Word will automatically insert both continuous section breaks for you.

The Columns tool in the Page Setup group of the Page Layout ribbon (Instruction set 18) allows for the easy setting of one, two or three columns, or two unbalanced columns (to the left or the right). Also, the Columns dialog can be opened from it.

Instruction set 18   Setting columns

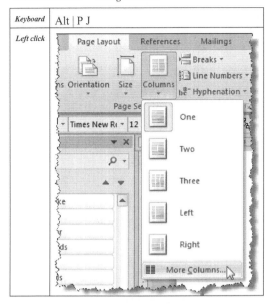

The Columns dialog (Figure 101) contains all of the above-mentioned presets, as well as allowing for full customisation of the number of columns, the width of each individual column, and the amount of space in between columns. A column divider (as is sometimes used in news print) can be added with the Line between check box.

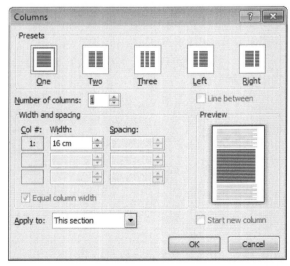

Figure 101   Columns dialog

If you have multiple columns in a section, the text will "snake" from one column to the next, basically trying to fill all of the columns more or less equally. However, you can force a different distribution of text amongst the columns by adding column breaks (Instruction set 19). Column breaks are also visible only if non-printing characters are displayed, and look similar to section breaks, barring that they are single lines (not the parallel lines), and, of course, they contain the word Column Break, not Section Break (and only if space permits). As with section breaks, column breaks can be selected, cut, copied and pasted.

Instruction set 19   Adding a column break

Shortcut	Ctrl + Shift + Enter
Keyboard	Alt | P | B | C
Left click	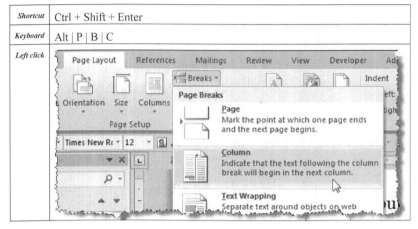

7.4   Page Breaks

Instruction set 20   Adding a page break

Shortcut	Ctrl + Enter
Keyboard	Alt | P | B | P Alt | N | B (alternate)
Left click	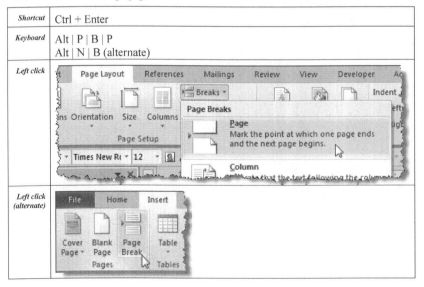
Left click (alternate)	

I remain astounded[45] by the number of people who believe that the only way to get text onto the next page when the current page is not yet full is by pressing Enter until they reach the next page, leaving a string of empty paragraphs (of course, these are invisible to them, since these people invariable also do not work with non-printing characters visible). This is always a bad idea, as any changes to the document text (and there *will* be changes) will result in the text that was thought to be at the top of the page, no longer being at the top of the page. As a side note, I believe that in a well-constructed document, there should be almost no instances of two paragraph marks directly after each other (i.e., no empty paragraphs at all), not even for adjusting the spacing of various elements (this should be done with paragraph spacing).

Of course, the correct way to do it is to add a page break, which can be done from either the Insert ribbon (Pages group) or the Breaks tool in the Page Setup group of the Page Layout ribbon, or, ideally, with **Ctrl + Enter** (there really are some keyboard shortcuts you just must learn, and this is one of them). Simply put, page breaks force whatever follows to appear on a new page, regardless of how much text is on the current page. This should warn you to use them with discretion, as changes to your document could result in pages with very little text (and a succeeding page break) on them. Having said that, page breaks are a better way to guarantee that a certain section of text begins on a new page than multiple carriage returns, which, after changes, may result in that section beginning at the middle of the page, instead of the top.

Lastly, note that page breaks can be set to paragraph styles. Thus you may want to set your top heading level (i.e., the Heading 1 style) to start on a new page by selecting the Page break before option from the Line and Page Breaks tab of the Paragraphs dialog (Figure 102). Remember to do this, not from the menu, but from the Modify Style dialog, so that the setting is applied to the style, and not only that one paragraph (see section 6.4.2, p. 108).

---

[45] This is why I am including this topic, which I consider elementary, in a book on advanced Word techniques.

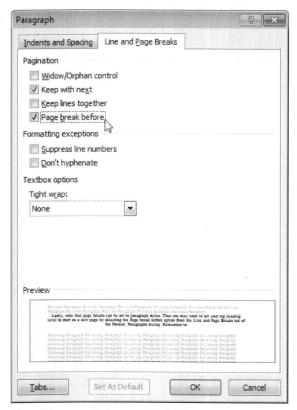

Figure 102   *Setting a page break before a paragraph*

7.5   Headers and Footers

Headers and footers do not form part of the actual document content, but they contain information that will appear on every page eventually printed. Headers and footers are set by section, meaning that every section can have a different header and/or footer, although headers and footers can also be shared between sections. For example, in this book, every facing page (called the recto) contains the chapter title at the top of the page. Every back page (called the verso) lists the book title at the top of the page. All the pages show the page number at the bottom of the page. All of this is done with headers and footers. Also note that to Word, headers and footers are pretty much the same thing, one is just on the top of the page, and the other at the bottom (you will see that a common set of tools govern both). As such, I will also discuss them together—whatever I say about a header, also applies to a footer, and vice versa.

7.5.1   Types of headers and footers

For every section, you can specify any of four different kinds of headers and footers, although the maximum you could have per section is three, as will be explained.

The simplest is the section header or footer, which are just called the header or footer (no surprises there!). But in addition, we can specify a first page header or footer. This footer can contain different information to the other headers. For example, I have mentioned that the recto pages (which are the odd numbered pages) in this book show the chapter title. However, because I also start each chapter on a recto (using Odd page section breaks), this means that it would look quite odd to have the chapter title appear on the top of the page on which the actual chapter title appears. Thus I have used first page headers and footers to suppress that information for the first page. Often it may also be the case that your institution does not want a page number to appear on the first page of a section such as a chapter, and in this case, first page headers and footers are your solution. Lastly, we can instruct Word to provide different headers and footers for odd and even pages, thus giving us an odd page header and footer, and an even page header and footer. However, it stands to reason that turning on different odd and even page headers and footers will suppress the standard header and footer. This also means that the most headers and footers a section can have is three: First page, odd page, even page. Note that, as has been mentioned in the piece on section breaks, since most theses and dissertations are printed in simplex , this means that you need not, in typing your dissertation or thesis, concern yourself with different odd and even page headers and footers.

7.5.2   Adding headers and footers

Strictly speaking, adding a header or footer is a bit of a misnomer, since every section in a Word document (and, as I have described, each document has at least one section) has at least one header and footer. So in actual fact, we are not adding a previously non-existent header or footer, but are rather adding something to an empty header or footer. Thus even just going into the header or footer area will allow you to edit headers and footers.

Since Word 2007, Word contains headers and footers in a gallery of building blocks. There are actually six such galleries, all found in the Header & Footer group of the Insert ribbon (Figure 103): One for Headers, one for Footers, and, under Page Number, four more galleries (for Headers, listed as Top of Page, for Footers, listed as Bottom of Page, and Page Margins (actually, still in either the header or footer), and finally Current Position (which can be used, again, in either the header or footer).

Figure 103   *Header and Footer tools on the Insert ribbon*

If you select one of the abovementioned building block items from the gallery (Instruction set 21), it is added to the header or footer, and you are taken to the header or footer region to edit that header or footer further. Also note the very useful Remove Header/Footer item near the bottom of the list, which allows you to easily empty the header or footer. There is also an option to create a header or footer of your liking, and then to select it and use the Save selection to header/Footer gallery... option. Admittedly, while this is a nice feature, it will probably not be used that often. However, if you are doing your thesis or dissertation by typing each chapter in a separate document (a strategy I will advise against in Chapter 12), then this is a useful way of ensuring that all the documents have a standardised header and footer.

Instruction set 21   Adding or editing headers and footers

Shortcut	Double click in header or footer area
Keyboard	Alt | N | H | E (Header) Alt | N | O | E (Footer)
Left click	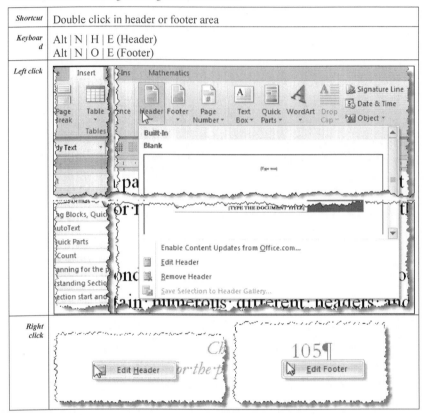
Right click	

7.5.3   Editing headers and footers

When you edit headers and footers, you enter a special mode in which the header and footer areas are activated, and the Header & Footer Tools ribbon is displayed (Figure 104). Note in Figure 104 how the header area is indicated on the ruler, and the two indicators on the left and right of the header area line, indicating that this is the Odd Page Header -Section 8-, and that this header is set to Same As Previous.

Figure 104   *Editing headers and footers*

Looking closer at the Header & Footer Tools ribbon (Figure 105), some general pointers can be made. Firstly, the three galleries from the Insert ribbon are repeated here, for the sake of convenience (remember that you can start editing the headers and footers by double clicking on the header or footer area). Furthermore, some other pertinent tools from the Insert ribbon are also duplicated here in the Insert group. While I will not discuss in detail the process of adding something like a picture to the header or footer, it should be noted that adding anything to the header or footer does not mean that it has to remain in the header or footer area—merely that it will appear on all pages for that section. Thus the watermarks added with the Watermark tool (Page Layout ribbon, Page Background group) are added to the header (mostly), but appear behind the main text. The secret is that these items are anchored in the header area (the object anchor and how it works is discussed in section 18.4.1.1, p. 445).

Figure 105   *Header & Footer Tools ribbon*

I will focus my discussion, then, on the next three groups of this ribbon. Note that the last group (Close) consists of only one tool, which closes the ribbon and takes you back to editing the main text of the document. While you are editing the main text, you cannot edit the headers and footers, and while you are editing the headers and footers you cannot edit the main text. You can also return to the main text by double clicking on the main text area.

The Position group in the Header & Footer Tools ribbon is quite self-explanatory. It allows you to add tabs for alignment of items in the header or footer, and allows you to set the distance of the top of the header from the top of the page, and the bottom of the footer from the bottom of the page (these settings are also available in the Layout tab of the Page Setup dialog—see Figure 97, p. 130). Note, though, that the top and bottom page margins also set the distance of the main body text from the top and bottom of the page respectively. However, Word helps you deal with this, so that you cannot accidentally place your document text over the header or footer text. If, for example, my header is set 1 cm form the top of the page, but is several lines long, so that its total height is 2 cm, that would mean that the bottom of my header is 3 cm below the top of the page. If I were to set my top margin to 2 cm, that would mean that Word might let the top 1 cm of my main text fall over the bottom 1 com of my header text. However, in those instances, Word cleverly overrides the top margin setting, moving my main text down (of course, this does not apply to objects anchored in the header but set to float behind the text). The same, naturally, applies for footers. Nonetheless, you would do well to ensure that the top and bottom margins are set to a little more than the top and bottom of the header and footer plus the height of the header and footer, as a little bit of space to create a natural separation is needed.

The Options group of the Header & Footer Tools ribbon is very important, as this is where you specify, for the current section, which if the header and footer kinds you want to use in that section. Note that you choose to have, for example, different odd and even headers *and* footers—you cannot have different odd and even headers, but only a standard footer.

This group also has a setting to Sho<u>w</u> Document Text. While it may be useful to suppress the display of document text temporarily of you have an object that is floating behind the text, I generally recommend that you display the document text so that you can see the header or footer in relation to the main text.

The Navigation group in the Header & Footer Tools ribbon is also extremely important. The P<u>r</u>evious and Ne<u>x</u>t buttons allow you to move between headers and footers from one section to the next. If a section contains multiple headers and footers, then the Next tool moves you through these in the following order: First page header/footer→Even page header/footer→Odd page header/footer→First page header/footer of next section, etc[46]. It may take a little concentration to keep track of where you are, but it is not that difficult. Where it does start getting difficult is when you have added multiple continuous section breaks. These sections will then be assigned, by Word, headers and footers that you will not be able to access.

The Navigation group also contains two handy buttons that allow you to jump between the header and footer areas.

The last tool in the Navigation group: Lin<u>k</u> to Previous is vitally important. Up to this point, you may be forgiven for not remembering what I casually mentioned on p. 136— headers and footers can be shared across sections. This design feature is incredibly useful, as it allows you to set up one header or footer which will then be used across all the various sections of your document, minimising the amount of work needed, and improving the chances of success. If you look back at Figure 104, you will see that Link to Previous is activated in the ribbon, and that the Same as Previous tag is displayed on the bottom of the Header line. Note that the Same as Previous (or Link to Previous) setting actually means that the relevant sections share the *same* header/footer (not that they have different headers and footers that just look the same). What this means is that changes to any header or footer will carry through to all other headers and footers in

---

[46] This is assuming you have an Odd page section break. For an Even page section break, the order of odd and even headers and footers would be switched.

both preceding and succeeding sections throughout the "same as previous" chain. Thus, if you delete the page number from the last section of a document, and that section was set as "same as previous" to the preceding section, which was also set as "same as previous" to the section preceding it, then the page numbers will be removed from all three those sections.

Some other things related to this setting are perhaps not that apparent. For example, if you are using all the possible kinds of headers and footers, then they are linked by kind. That means that, for example, the first page header and footer of section 2 are linked to the first page header and footer of section 1 (bypassing the odd and even page header and footer), and so also the odd page header and footer of section 2 are linked to the odd page header and footer of section 1, and the even page header and footer of section 2 are linked to the even page header and footer of section 1. Now you really have to start keeping your wits about you! Furthermore, if you are using these different kinds of headers and footers, and they are linked, and you turn one of the kinds off (e.g., different odd and even page headers and footers) in one of the sections, then it gets turned off in all of the linked sections. If this was not what you had wanted, then you first need to break the links, and then turn off the headers and footers you don't want.

Furthermore, while you are must have the same kinds of headers and footers in a section, you can link and unlink headers and footers independently. This means that you can have totally independent headers throughout all of the sections of your document, while all the footers of all the sections of your document are linked. In essence, the tool is very flexible, which allows it to do a lot, but at the same time, it does require some concentration to use.

In essence, then, the best way to use this tool is to link as many headers and footers as you can, creating a chain of linked headers and/or footers. Wherever you need different information displayed in a header or footer, simply break the chain by deactivating Link to Previous on the ribbon. For example, if you need no page numbers on the title and acknowledgements page of your thesis, Roman numbering on the table of contents pages, and Arabic numbering on the pages of the main text, then you need two (next page) section breaks to separate those three elements, and the link to previous setting must be off for the second and third sections. Then the different page numbers can be added to the second and third sections successfully.

7.6   Page numbering

Page numbering is essentially a part of the process of working with headers and footers, but since it is such an important topic, I will elaborate on it here. The most important thing to remember is that page numbering is set by section. This means that you cannot have different types of page numberings in the same section (but see below), although you can have different types of page numbering within the same document. In fact, you can have as many different kinds of page numbering as you have sections. This, of course, means that if you have mastered working with sections (as dealt with previously), you should have almost no problems dealing with page numbers.

There is a bit of an exception to this rule: As we saw in the previous section, Word allows you to have a different header and footer for the first page of each section in your document. When you make use of a first page header and footer, you can supress the page number on the first page of the section. I have opted not to use that setting in this book, but many books do not show a page number on the first page of each new chapter.

7.6.1   Adding page numbers

The first decision is, again, to decide where you would want to place your page numbers (if your institution has not already prescribed it). By convention, there are six possible positions—top (header) or bottom (footer), left (although page numbers are seldom placed on the left), centre or right. You will see all of these options in the galleries of the Page Number tool (Instruction set 22).

Generally, I tend to be reasonably old-fashioned when I add page numbering, first editing my header or footer, and then positioning myself where I want the page number to be, and then using the Current Position option to add the number. Note that all of the options from the first three galleries of the Page Number tool actually add complete formatted headers or footers, while the Current Position gallery just adds the page number as an element of its own.

Instruction set 22   Adding page numbers

The Page Number tool also contains an option at the bottom of its menu to Remove Page Numbers.

7.6.2   Formatting page numbers

Once page numbers have been added, you may need to format them to get what you need. To do this, select the Format Page Numbers... option from the menu of the Page Number tool to open the Page Number Format dialog. This dialog is quite simple, allowing you to choose, from the Number format list, Arabic, upper- and lowercase alphabetic, and upper- and lowercase Roman numbers. You can also choose to include the chapter number, ideally when you are using the built-in heading styles (see section 6.1.1, p 92), as well as specify the separator between the chapter and page numbers. Lastly, you can specify where the page numbering should start—either continuing from the previous section, or starting at a point specified by you. Interestingly, if you are using Arabic numbers, the numbering can even start at 0 (allowing you to suppress the number on the first page of the section, and letting the second page be numbered as page 1).

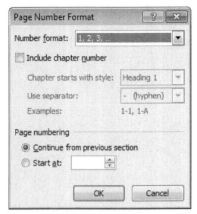

Figure 106   *Page Number Format dialog*

Note also that when section headers and/or footers in Word have the Same as Previous setting on, this actually means that all the sections in the chain (i.e., however many of them have the setting on) actually share the same header and/or footer. Thus, changes made to one of these sections (such as formatting or deleting the page numbers) will affect all the sections in the chain, both forward and backward. Also, when this setting is off for a specific section, it can cause problems with page numbering, especially with the page numbering starting again from 1 in the next section. The simple solution to this is to open the Page Number Format dialog (even if numbers already exist in the section) and select the Continue from previous section option button to "pick up the trail again," as it were.

Chapter 8
Safety in numbers: Getting Word to number for you

I see a fair amount of theses and dissertations in the line of my work (not as many as some others, though). It is normally painfully evident when students have tried to number all their dissertation elements themselves—they would either skip a number somewhere, or repeat a number somewhere, or both. Only the most perfectionist of students would get this right if doing it manually, and by that I mean the top 1% of students in the perfectionist scale. There are several problems associated with trying to do the numbering yourself. Firstly, remember that this is a document normally set up over a few years. When you work on such a large thing, for such a long time, the probability of a mistake creeping in increases the further you go. If you can get Word to take control of the numbering, you can rest assured that your numbering will be right. Secondly, the document is changed multiple times over its development life—if you do your numbering manually, you would have to renumber all changed parts of the document each time. If Word does the numbering it renumbers for you each time. Third, if you number manually, you often have to duplicate that numbering in a manual content list, such as a table of contents, or a list of tables or figures. When Word does the numbering, you can then generate these lists automatically for you. Fourth, numbering manually wastes huge amounts of time. Getting Word to take charge of the numbering means you can focus your time on more important things, like the content of your dissertation.

This chapter will help you get all the different elements of your dissertation numbered right. There are a wide variety of ways that you can number things, and each will be examined in turn.

8.1   Multilevel numbering—How to number your headings

To grasp the need for multilevel lists, think of the function of numbering. In a simple numbered list, the numbers indicate only sequence—i.e., "this numbered item comes before that one, but after this other one." However, in a multilevel list, the numbers indicate not only sequence, but also membership—i.e., "apart from its current position before this numbered item and after that one, this item here belongs to, or is a part of, that larger grouping level." Simply looking at the table of contents of this book will show that the book is organised into main structural units—chapters. Each chapter is then broken into subsections, each of which can be broken down into sub-sub sections, and so on. Word offers you nine such levels, indicating that any particular heading could have, at maximum, eight possible higher level groups to which it can belong. Of course, please note that nine levels are available, not because you would ever need them, but rather because it is more than you would ever need, thus meaning that Word's tool is up to the worst you could ever want to throw at it. The general consensus amongst the academics I speak to seems to be that about five is the most you would ever need, and perhaps, in very exceptional circumstances, six. More than that fragments your document so badly that your readers would probably not be able to follow your line of thought—you don't need more levels, you need a writing coach!

8.1.1   Word's changes are numbered

Warning! If you want to hear me gripe a lot about the changes Microsoft has made, or if you are working in an older version of Word (Word 2003 or earlier), or you are interested in background knowledge, then read on. If you just want to learn the best way to do multilevel numbering in Word 2007 or 2010, then skip ahead to section 8.1.3 on p. 155.

Microsoft made some major changes to the way numbering is handled from Word 2003 to Word 2007. They have motivated it as an improvement, and I am certain that, in terms of what happens behind the scenes, it may very well be (many people have managed to "break" Word's numbering because they did not understand how it works). Nonetheless, I do feel that they have made the process of adding numbering slightly more cumbersome. I have been working with Word since the days of Word 5 for DOS and I have lost count of the times that I see Microsoft trying to "dumb down" things that work perfectly well, just so that users who haven't gone to the trouble of learning how the tool works, can have the tool work for them while still not understanding how it works. This seems to be another of those cases. But some things, of course, we just have to live with. At least the numbering still works, which we can be thankful for.

It does help to understand, though, how the numbering was changed, as that will allow you to better grasp how to use the new numbering method. However, to really get a grip on Word's numbering, you need to understand how the program deals with numbering in documents, which is too technical for the scope of this book. In summary, though, Word has traditionally had three numbering systems: Field-based numbering, List numbering (bulleted lists and numbered lists are essentially the same thing), and outline numbering (allowing you to create a hierarchical numbering structure). Then Word 2002 (aka Word XP) introduced List styles[47], where various levels of numbering could be associated with a single style. In Word 2007, the Outline numbering was renamed Multilevel lists," and incorporated in the interface with list styles. This last move I find very ambiguous, since one the one hand, Microsoft is encouraging people to not use the multilevel lists, but rather the list styles—Stuart J Stuple (2007) of the Word Team writes: "When creating new lists, I recommend using list styles rather than multilevel lists (formerly known as Outline Lists) because while both share the same functionality, list styles have the added advantage that they can be named and then modified." However, on the other, the single Multilevel list button on the Home ribbon houses both, and pride of place in its gallery is given to multilevel lists. Of course, for me, the big change was that now you could no longer access the Outline Numbering dialog from the Modify Style dialog—essentially separating styles from outline numbering in a certain sense. You now need to create an outline numbering list (now called a multilevel list), and then explicitly assign certain styles to it—making what was

---

[47] Interestingly, one of the Microsoft Word team members even claims that "List styles were introduced in Office 2007" (Microsoft Word Team, 2009) when, of course, List styles existed two versions before that. For example, (Figure 103) shows the List style dialogs from Word 2003—you will notice a high degree of similarity between this and the Word 2007/2010 versions shown later.

once one step, now two distinct steps, and hence, as I have said, much more cumbersome.

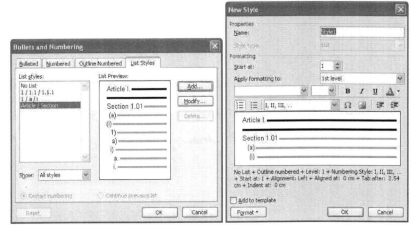

Figure 107   List Styles as part of Word 2003

All right, that's enough griping, so in the remainder of this section I will deal with how to use the tool.

8.1.2   Multilevel lists (a.k.a. Outline numbering)

I will deal here with Multilevel lists simply for the reason that it is the current incarnation of what was once known as Outline numbering, which used to be the only way you could create multilevel numbering in Word. It is still included for compatibility reasons, so that Word can open documents created in older versions and successfully deal with the numbering found there. You can still very successfully create multilevel numbered lists in Word using this tool. However, Microsoft seems intent on half-heartedly coercing its users, in new documents, to use list styles instead, which are discussed in section 8.1.3.

8.1.2.1   *Accessing Multilevel lists*

The new method of creating multilevel lists means that you can create any such number of independent lists in a document, although I would strongly warn against that. You only need one such list. It also means that these lists can exist quite independently of styles, since you are never even rally prompted for these, but again, this is simply looking for trouble—as your multilevel list and styles could then get out of sync, inviting all sorts of numbering chaos. Thus, the process now involves two steps: Firstly, set up your heading styles, as was discussed in Chapter 6. These heading styles will, at this stage, be unnumbered, as the Modify Style dialog now does not allow for anything but simple numbered lists for paragraph styles, such as your heading styles will be. Secondly, create a multilevel numbering list, and in the process, associate it with your heading styles. Now you will have created a numbering list, and you will actually never need to invoke it again, as your heading styles will do all the work for you.

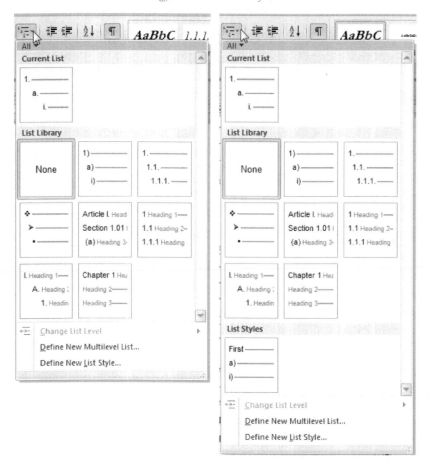

Figure 108   *Multilevel list*

Since we have already discussed the creation of styles, we can now jump right in with the second part of the process. The Multilevel list tool is in the Paragraph group of the Home ribbon (Figure 108, or Alt | H | M). Note that Figure 108 shows two different versions—each time you click on this list, you can expect slightly different contents, as the list shows what is relevant to, and available in, your document. Thus, simply copying numbered items from another document and pasting them into your document without pasting only the text, can result in a new numbering list being silently smuggled into your document. Note that the second example shows not only the multilevel lists, but also the list styles—you can see now why I said that pride of place is still given to multilevel lists.

The two tools you will be most interested in appear at the bottom of the gallery— Define New Multilevel List and Define New List Style (the latter will be dealt with in the next section). If you look at the numbering structure used in this book, which I believe will be similar to what you would want to use for your thesis, then you will notice that it is not immediately available from Word's built-in multilevel lists. Specifically, you would want to look at something that is a combination of the sixth and eighth items in the gallery, albeit even then with a little further tweaking. Although you could build this desired multilevel list from the ground up using the Define New Multilevel List, I have found from experience that it is slightly less work to start with one of Word's lists, and then just to modify it (and then also the sixth one would be the best to start from). To incorporate it into your document (I recommend doing this with your template—cf. Chapter 5), simply click on it in the gallery—the currently selected paragraph will then be numbered, but once you have made your modifications, you can reset the style of that paragraph to Body Text, and then still have the numbering list available in your document.

The next thing you need to do, then, is modify that Multilevel list. In an omission that I find more careless than curious, you cannot right click on the Multilevel list and select Modify from the context menu, while you can do that for both List Styles in the same gallery, and all Styles in the Styles gallery (Figure 109). This has, peculiarly, been the case in both Word 2007 and Word 2010.

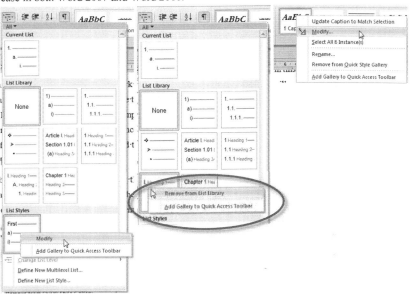

Figure 109   *Why can List styles and other styles be modified from the context menu, but not Multilevel lists?*

There are two ways to modify an existing multilevel list, both of which I find somewhat obscure: The first is to right click on any of the members belonging to that list (i.e., any paragraph formatted with this numbering) and then to select Adjust List Indents (Instruction set 23—note the grey number, indicating a field, and also indicating that you need to actually right click on the number itself, not anywhere else in the paragraph). The second is to go to the Multilevel list tool on the Home ribbon and then to select <u>D</u>efine New Multilevel List. Both of these methods will then open the Define new Multilevel list dialog (Figure 111), which may make you think you are creating a new list, but actually, if you examine it carefully, you will see that all the settings for the current list are what is loaded in the dialog—you are actually modifying the existing list. Both of these methods are equally valid, so long as you have only one multilevel list in your document. If you have more than one (which you shouldn't), then please use the first method, as you will not be able to guarantee that the second method actually opens the list you want to edit.

Instruction set 23   Adjust List Indents

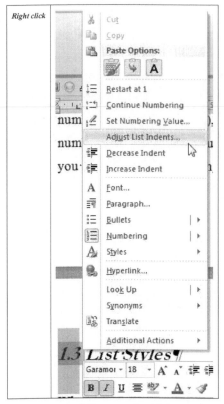

I know I sound like a spoilt child with all my complaining, but this situation is, quite simply, just dumb. It comes down to the simple fact that you are never actually sure which Multilevel list you are modifying, other than that it is the list which applies to the current paragraph in question. If you mistakenly (and this can happen very easily when you copy numbered items from another document into yours) have more than one multilevel list in your document, you might not know which one you are working on, and your numbering can go awry. Of course, if you do modify the list in a discernible manner, then by implication all paragraphs that reflect that change will also be members of that list, but checking that in a large document is well-nigh impossible. To make things even more confusing, if you have several documents open, and they contain different Multilevel lists, then the Multilevel list tool shows a new section reflecting all of those lists (Figure 110). Surely the intent is good—to make life easy for you by allowing you, with the click of a button, to import a list from another open document into the current document. But at the same time, this is anathema to your document—allowing you to totally wreck the numbering of the current document with a single mouse click. In other words, in the name of user friendliness, Microsoft has now made it even easier for you to accomplish something you should be trying to avoid at all costs—having different multilevel lists in the same document.

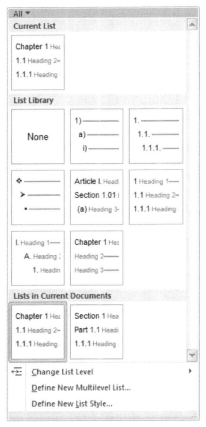

Figure 110   *Multilevel lists in all documents*

8.1.2.2   Defining Multilevel lists

Figure 111 shows the Define new Multilevel list dialog. Note that the More/Less button at the bottom left has been selected so as to show the entire dialog. There is a lot that you can set via this dialog, and we will devote quite some time to it.

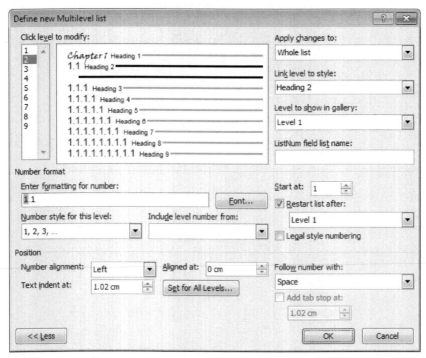

Figure 111   *Define new Multilevel list dialog*

The first thing to note about this dialog is that it is essentially nine dialogs all folded into one. The Click level to modify list contains a number for each of the nine levels of a Multilevel list. All the other settings in the dialog are for that level selected in that list. Thus, you *could* set each of the other settings in the dialog nine times, once for each level. Right next to this list is a small preview box, which gives you an idea of what the nine levels look like, as set in the dialog.

At the top right is the Apply changes to list box, where you can make the changes as set in the dialog apply to the whole list, only the current paragraph, or all paragraphs from the current position to the end of the document. It would, of course, be very unwise to change this to anything other than whole list (i.e., leave this setting alone!), as doing so will essentially case Word to create a second Multilevel list in your document, something you want to avoid at all costs.

The next setting is Link level to style. I strongly recommend that when you create a multilevel list, you *do* link the levels you use to styles, and mostly, to the built-in Word heading styles (Heading 1–Heading 9). This means that whenever you apply the style, Word also automatically applies the numbering from the corresponding linked level of the multilevel list. It also goes without saying that the style number must correspond to the level number.

The next two settings are also best left alone—you do want to show the top level in the multilevel list gallery, and you generally do not want to mix up your ListNum fields (discussed in section 8.2 below) with multilevel lists.

The bottom half of the dialog concerns the actual appearance (formatting) of the numbers for the different levels. The place to start is with the Start at combo box. Generally, you would want the numbering to start at one (or whatever the first indicator is in the numbering style you will select in the Number style for this level list box), but if, for some obscure reason (superstition?), you do not want this to be the case, you could change that here. Furthermore, you would generally want each level to "reset" itself when an instance of the immediately preceding (i.e., higher) level, occurs, but again, you could change this (and again, you probably shouldn't) in the Restart list after list box.

After having determined how your numbers for that level will behave, you then determine what they will look like. The first thing to do is to choose a numbering style from the Number style for this level list box. Word gives you a wide variety of choices, including Arabic, Roman, written, ordinal, and a variety of bulleted or picture bulleted options. Whichever option you choose will be reflected in the Enter formatting for number text box. This box is also used to build "compound" numbers. For example, if a heading 3 number is 1.1.1, then the first 1 is from the heading 1 level, the second 1 is from the heading 2 level, and the third 1 is from the heading 3 level. If you do not want higher levels to be included, you can delete them from this list box—just make sure that you delete the right one. If they have been removed, you can re-insert them by first making sure that the I-beam is in the correct position in the numbering structure, and then selecting the level you wish to insert from the Include level number from list box. Note that you cannot type those in, but must use this list box—you will see in this text box that the numbers appear as fields (with the grey shading), which is, of course, exactly what they are. What you can type in is both the separators (e.g., periods, right parentheses, hyphens, etc.) between numbers from the different levels, as well as any words that should appear in that level. Thus, if you want your first level to be "Chapter x", then type, in front of the number for the top level, "Chapter " (note the space). Lastly, the Font button opens the Font dialog, where you can set the font of the number. Note that this font setting could be different to the font settings you have made for the corresponding heading level, which will mean that the number will appear with a different font to the rest of the heading. Generally, this is not advised, although in certain circumstances a small deviation can be allowed (e.g., using the same font for the number as for the heading, but in a slightly larger point size). Unfortunately Word has never been able to show the text in the Enter formatting for number text box without the font settings, and the box is not resizable, which means that if you choose a relatively large point size, you will not actually be able to see your number here. Thus, first make all the desired changes for the particular level, and then set the font last.

Legal style numbering forces Arabic numbering, even when Roman numbering has been indicated (this appears to be an option not used by many people).

The last thing to set is the position of the number. You can set the number alignment, the number indentation (Aligned at) and the text indentation for each level. The text indent less the numbering indent indicates how much space is allotted for the numbers, although if the number is wider than the allotted space, it will overflow that, resulting in your numbers and headings not all being equally aligned. Also remember that if your heading should run over the line, then the text indent will serve as the alignment point for a hanging indent (i.e., all lines of the heading will start at the text indent)—all the more reason to ensure that this indent is wide enough for your number.

An easier (and probably better) approach is to use the Set for All Levels... button, which opens (you guessed it!) the Set for All Levels dialog (Figure 112). Here, you can set the numbering and text indents for the first level, and then choose an additional measurement by which both of those settings are incremented for each of the successive nine levels. If you want all your numbers to stay at the same alignment point, then simply set the increment to zero.

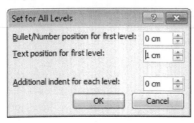

Figure 112   *Set for All Levels dialog*

Application 8.1   *Getting the numbering and text indents right*

> *There is a fundamental problem in aligning the numbers and text for the different levels. Essentially, what you would want is for all your numbers to be left aligned (this is easy—in Set for All Levels, just set the number position to zero). But then also each heading must start close enough to the number that it does not appear as if there is a chasm between them, but not so close that there is too little space for the number. And herein lies the problem. As you move down the levels, you have to make space for more and more numbers (compare 1.2 to 1.2.1.4.3 for a level 2 to level 5 width comparison).In other words, what we would want is to be able to increment the text indent, but not the number indent. Unfortunately, Word cannot do this for you with Set for All Levels. However, this does not mean that you have to do all the indents for all the levels manually. Rather, still use Set for All Levels but with a zero increment. Then all you need to do is go to the levels where you feel an extra indent for the text is needed, and set that manually.*

The last setting is to decide what the number should be followed with: A space, a tab, or nothing. If you choose a tab, then you should also indicate the width of that tab stop, although if you leave the Add tab stop at check box unselected, Word will default to the text indent setting. The tab stop should be the same as the text indent. Remember that the first line of the heading will start at the tab stop and the second line of the heading (if there is any) will start at the text indent. If the tab stop is less than the text indent, then the first line of the heading will start further left than the second line of the heading. If the converse is true, then the first line of the heading will start further right than the second line of the heading. If they are the same, then the first and second lines will be perfectly aligned.

8.1.3   List Styles

In contrast to multilevel lists, where each level of the numbering structure may or may not be associated with a *different* style, with the "new" list styles, each level of the numbering structure may be contained in a single style, or be associated with different styles (if this sounds confusing, it's because it is).

When Word numbers heading styles, each style represents a different level of numbering. Thus "Heading 1" is the first (highest) heading level, and will only have a single number (e.g., 1, 2, etc.) in its numbering. "Heading 2" is the Second heading level, and will have two numbers (e.g., 1.1, 1.2, etc.) in its numbering. By contrast, when a list is numbered, the different numbering levels are set *within* that single list style. This is, for example, a nice way of automating the numbering of questions in a test (although this is not quite relevant to the typing of a dissertation).

To create a list style, select the Define New List Style... tool from the Multilevel List gallery on the Home ribbon (Figure 113).

Figure 113   *Defining a new list style*

This opens the Define New List Style dialog (Figure 114). This dialog contains many settings that make it seem a hybrid between the Modify Style dialog and the Define New Multilevel list dialog. Note again that the Apply formatting to list box again transforms this dialog into one dialog which represents nine levels, the same as the Define New Multilevel List dialog. Essentially, though, there are only two[48] settings that you will want to make in this dialog. Firstly, give your List style a very good name. This is because you will be accessing this List style either from the Multilevel list gallery or the Organizer dialog (section 5.4.3, p. 89), and the name will be your only identifier. The second thing you will want to do (most of the time) is take this List style through to your underlying template by selecting that the Style be defined in New documents based on this template. Thirdly, you will want to make the actual numbering settings in the Modify Multilevel list dialog (Figure 115), which you can access by

---

[48] Actually three, but we'll get there in a moment....

selecting the F<u>o</u>rmat button and choosing <u>N</u>umbering... (see the second image in Figure 114).

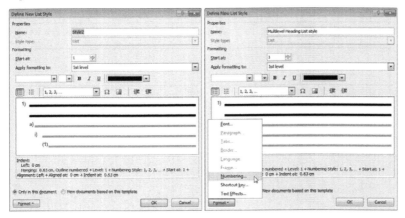

Figure 114   *Define New List Style dialog*

If you're perceptive, you will realise that you are now doing exactly the same as before with a multilevel list (apart from the title and some settings which have been fixed, this is the same dialog), and in order to eliminate repetition, I will not explain the whole process again.

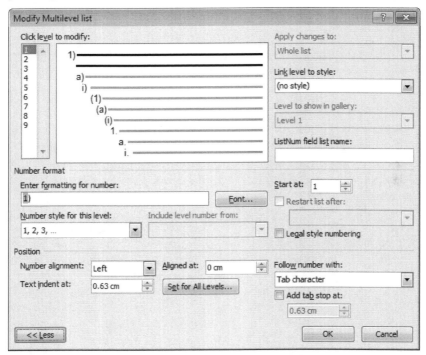

Figure 115   *Modify Multilevel list dialog*

8.1.4 Multilevel numbering—quo vadis?

So now what? Microsoft recommends using List styles, but as you will have seen, they are more work to get the same results, from the same dialog, as Multilevel lists. Even Microsoft Word MVP Shauna Kelly (2010) notes, after a lengthy explanation of how to create a list style, that the Multilevel lists from the list library "may be just the thing" for "quick 'n dirty work." The truth is that if you store that multilevel list in your template, and if you consistently access that list, it will work fine. If it's any consolation, the numbering in this book was done, not with a list style, but with a multilevel list. And it seems to me to be working quite fine.

8.1.5 Adjusting numbered levels

Regardless of whether you created your multilevel numbered list using multilevel lists or list styles, you may later want to adjust the numbering of some or other section. We will return to this topic when we deal with Outline view (section 12.1, p. 266), but for the moment, the simple adjustments will be covered.

Once you have created an outline numbered list, you can apply that numbering at any position in the document. If you want to change the hierarchy level (e.g., use a higher level—i.e., closer to level 1—in the hierarchy), simply right click on the numbering, and select "Increase indent" to lower the level, or "Decrease indent" to raise it. In this way you can have multiple numbering levels (up to 9), with various higher and lower levels. These tools can be seen in the context menu of Instruction set 23 and are also in the Paragraph group of the Home ribbon.

However, there is an even easier way to apply the numbering scheme. Because each level was linked to a heading style, the simple implication is that once created, you actually never again have to apply or adjust your numbering list/style. All you need to do is apply or change the associated heading style, and the numbering level will change in unison.

8.2 *LISTNUM fields*

The Listnum field can be set using the Define New Multilevel List dialog, or it can be inserted directly, which is much to be preferred. The advantage of the Listnum field is that it can be used to generate numbered lists independent of styles. These numbered lists can be continued consecutively at various points in the document. Each list is identified by its list identifier. Also, the Listnum field can be used to create multiple instances of consecutive numbering within a single paragraph.

To insert a Listnum field, press **Ctrl + F9** to insert field braces. Then type the name of the list you want to work with (this need not be identified anywhere prior to this), and any switches you want to use. Each different list identifier is thus numbered consecutively. For example, you could enter a field such as **{LISTNUM Hypothesis}** to number your hypotheses consecutively. The switches are used as follows: The \l switch set the numbering level, and the \s switch sets the starting point, and both are represented by integer numbers. Thus **{LISTNUM Hypothesis \l 2}** will set the field to the second numbering level; **{LISTNUM Hypothesis \s 4}** with start the numbering at 4 (or the corresponding element in one of the other numbering formats—e.g., d; iv; four,

4th; etc.); and **{LISTNUM Hypothesis \l 3 \s 2}** with format the field as having the third heading level, and starting at 2.

You should note that the LISTNUM field is affected by heading styles when its switches are not used. Thus, if a heading style is applied to a paragraph above a LISTNUM field which is not set to a specific level with the \l switch, that field item will be automatically demoted by one level. This means that you will have to manually reset the level, or use switches. The nice thing about the LISTNUM field is that once it has been created, you can merely copy the whole field and paste it wherever you need it, and Word will sort out its numbering automatically. This means that you might as well go to the trouble of including the switch the first time round, and then just copy and paste as needed.

8.3   SEQ field numbering

The SEQ(uence) field is a very old, but very stable single level numbering system. The big advantage to SEQ fields is that they can appear anywhere in your document and will all follow in sequence, and you can create as many of them as you would want to, all with different identifiers, and all fields that share the same identifier will then share the same numbering sequence. SEQ fields could be inserted in much the same way as the LISTNUM fields described above, in fact, some would say that the example I used there should best be done with SEQ fields rather than LISTNUM. And for simple numbering lists, manually inserting the field braces (**Ctrl + F9**) and typing something like **{SEQ Hypothesis}** will suffice. However, the SEQ field is much, much more powerful than that. And perhaps the best way to display what it can all do is to examine the "automated" method of adding it. From the Insert ribbon, select the Field... option from the Quick Parts tool in the Text group (Instruction set 24). This will open the Field dialog, from where you can choose the SEQ field (Figure 116).

Instruction set 24   Opening the field dialog

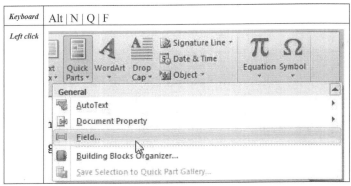

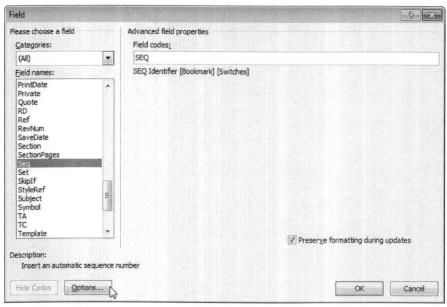

Figure 116   *Field dialog*

From this dialog, after selecting the SEQ field, click on the Options... button to open the Field Options dialog. Figure 117 shows the General switches for the SEQ field. You will see that you can set a very wide array of sequential numbering and even other numeric formats to the SEQ field.

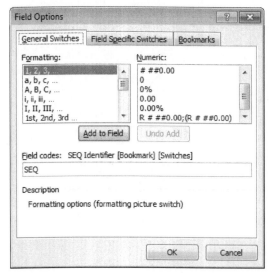

Figure 117   *Field Options dialog, General Switches tab—SEQ field*

Figure 118 shows the field-specific switches for the SEQ field, which you can use to adjust how the numbering is applied.

Figure 118   *Field Options dialog, Field Specific Switches tab—SEQ field*

8.4   Caption numbering

Captions can be used for a variety of functions. Each separate function will be numbered independently (captions use SEQ numbering in the background), and will allow you to generate a separate list (as with tables of content) to which we will return later.

8.4.1   Captions and the caption style

Captions are literally numbered list items, where the number is prefixed with the caption title. These can be used at various places throughout the document (unlike normal list items, which follow each other directly), and Word will number them consecutively throughout the document. Word comes with three Caption functions loaded (Equation, Figure, Table), and additional ones can be created (e.g., Slide, Box, etc.). Some of the captions used in this book are: Instruction set and Application.

Word also has a pre-defined style, the Caption style, which it uses for all of its different caption types. This means that all your captions will look the same[49], which should generally not be problematic. If you want your various captions to look different, you will have to create separate styles for each (I recommend, in this instance, basing them on the original caption style, although this is not a necessity), and apply that style each time you insert a caption. But only do that as a last resort, because you will only be

---

[49] This does not, of course, mean that they have to be used in the same way. For example, APA style dictates that Table headings must be above the table, and must have all major words capitalized, while Figures must have their labels below them, and must have only the first word capitalized. What it does mean is that they will have the same formatting (font, paragraph alignment, etc.)

making life difficult for yourself in the long run. Note that when you insert a caption, Word automatically changes the style of the paragraph to the Caption style.

8.4.2   Inserting captions

The Insert Caption tool from the Captions group of the References ribbon (Instruction set 25) opens the Caption dialog (Figure 119).

Instruction set 25   Insert Caption

Keyboard	Alt | S | P
Left click	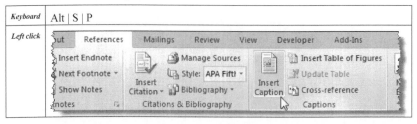

The Caption box shows you what the formatted caption will look like (as Figure 119 shows, this is not as successful as Microsoft had hoped), and allows you to add any succeeding text (which you normally won't) to the caption number. The Label list box allows you to choose the relevant label (as I have mentioned, you will start with Figure, Equation and Table, but any you add will appear here).

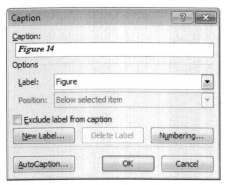

Figure 119   Caption dialog

Thirdly, if you want to create a label of your own, click on the New Label... button and enter the new label's name (Figure 120). It will then appear in the Label list box whenever you work in Word.

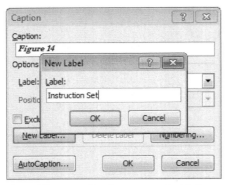

Figure 120   *Creating a new caption label*

By clicking on the N<u>u</u>mbering... button, you can adjust the numbering settings for the label (Figure 121). <u>F</u>ormat will allow you to choose the number format, and then you have the choice between sequential numbering (i.e., each caption with that label is numbered sequentially, regardless of which chapter it is in) or Chapter-based numbering, where each caption with that label is preceded by the chapter number and the numbering restarts with each new chapter. The only sensible style to link the caption number to is Heading 1. Furthermore, you can choose form one of five delimiters (period, hyphen, colon, em dash, en dash). To see the effect of these two types of numbering, note that the Figures, Tables and Instruction sets in this book are numbered sequentially, and the Application boxes are numbered with chapter-based captions.

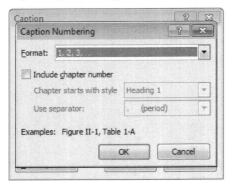

Figure 121   *Setting Caption numbering*

8.4.3   Using AutoCaption

In the Caption dialog, you can click on <u>A</u>utoCaption... and then select the item(s) from the list that you want Word to automatically insert captions for. For example, if you select Microsoft Word Table, then each time you insert a table, Word will automatically insert a paragraph above the table, insert the Table caption in that paragraph, and change the paragraph style to Caption. This can save a lot of time if you are working with many tables, as you do not have to follow the normal procedure explained above. Of course, if you insert many tables and only want some of them to be captioned, then this can become annoying, as you would always have to delete the automatically added caption. Thus you would use this setting only where it genuinely does save time.

Application 8.2   *Keeping a Caption with its Referent Object*

> *One of the mysteries of Microsoft is that they seem to never have, in all the years, realised the basic problem with caption positioning: Whether the caption label is above or below the thing to which it refers, it must always stay with that thing. This is actually such a basic problem that I simply cannot believe they have not solved it yet. Nonetheless, we may have to wait a very long time if we have to wait for Microsoft to fix this (I've been waiting for seventeen years for a fix from Microsoft to this one, and I think others maybe even longer). So here's what to do.*
>
> *The simple fix, you might think, would be to set the* Keep with Ne<u>x</u>t *paragraph setting to true for the caption style. That is a solution, but it will only work if all your captions precede the objects to which they refer. However, if you have different captions that must be placed differently (e.g., Table captions above tables, and Figure captions below figures), then this will work for all the captions above the object (the Table captions), but will backfire for all the captions below the object (the Figure captions)—it will actually pull those captions away from their objects when the paragraph below the caption goes to the next page. Basically, what I do is to set the* Keep with Ne<u>x</u>t *paragraph setting to true for the caption style, as I suggested above. But then, when I insert the caption below, I do two things: Firstly, I manually set the* Keep with Ne<u>x</u>t *paragraph setting to TRUE for the Body Text paragraph in which the object is placed, and then I manually set the* Keep with Ne<u>x</u>t *paragraph setting to FALSE for the caption paragraph. Of course, this actually involves a number of repetitive steps, so I have created a simple macro to do the work for me each time—see Macro Listing 1. On p. 484 ff. I explain how to add and use a macro in the context of Reclaiming the Print dialog and Print preview.*
>
> *This technique obviously works best when the object has been inserted inline (see section 18.4.1, p. 445), but even if the object is a floating object and it has a caption, all you need to do is make sure that the object is anchored in the paragraph directly before the caption, and that the paragraph formatting for that paragraph is set to Keep with Next.*

Macro Listing 1   *AddPictureFromClipboardWithFigureCaption*

```
Sub AddPictureFromClipboardWithFigureCaption()
' Created by J. Raubenheimer
'Adds a figure already copied to the clipboard and then adds a figure
caption
' as well as setting the necessary Keep with Next settings
    With Selection
        .Paste
        .ParagraphFormat.KeepWithNext = True
        .TypeParagraph
        .InsertCaption Label:="Figure",
TitleAutoText:="InsertCaption1", _
            Title:="", Position:=wdCaptionPositionBelow,
ExcludeLabel:=0
        .TypeText Text:=vbTab
        .ParagraphFormat.KeepWithNext = False
```

```
      End With
End Sub
```

Application 8.3   *Placing a captioned item at the top of a page*

*Generally, I recommend not using too many page breaks in your document, but rather to use the paragraph settings (*Keep with ne<u>x</u>t *and* <u>K</u>eep lines together*) to "stick" multiple paragraphs together, and then to let Word handle the flow of text. If, however, you have finalised the document and are going through the layout (as I discuss in section 19.6, p. 490) and you decide that, for example, a table and its caption must move over to the top of the next page, the question arises as to what would be the best way to do it.*

Generally, I would recommend using manual page breaks, but this gives rise to the problem of the page break being swallowed up into the caption bookmark (I discuss this, with an explanation of how to deal with the problem, in Application 11.2, p. 245). The advantage to this is that the page breaks can later be removed easily (e.g., with a search and replace (see section 10.4, p. 225), but it does mean some extra work to deal with the bookmark.

The other method would be to use the Page <u>b</u>reak before *paragraph setting. This is less work, as you do not need to worry about the page break being swallowed into the bookmark, but it is less visible and harder to remove (not impossible, and can also be "reset" with a slightly more complex search and replace—see Figure 173, p. 225).*

8.5   Cross-references

All your automatic numbering in Word is pretty much useless without the ability to reference those numbers in a way which changes as the numbers do. If you had to manually type in a reference to a numbered item in your thesis, and changes you made to the document then caused that number to change, then your manually typed reference would refer to the wrong item, or, worse yet, an item that no longer exists. However, Word has a tool which enables you to create dynamic cross-references. These will always refer to the same item (i.e., the one you pointed it to), but will dynamically update as the item itself changes, with the end result that, no matter what structural changes you make to your document (deleting sections as the only exception), all your references will remain in sync.

Instruction set 26   Inserting a cross-reference

Keyboard	Alt | N | RF Alt | S | RF
Left click	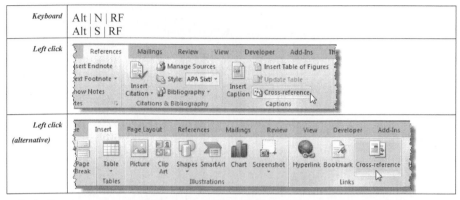
Left click *(alternative)*	

Word allows you to cross-reference to a whole number of different items. The basic procedure is to select the Cross-reference tool—either from the Links group of the Insert ribbon, or from the Captions group of the References ribbon (Instruction set 26). This will bring up the Cross-reference dialog (Figure 122).

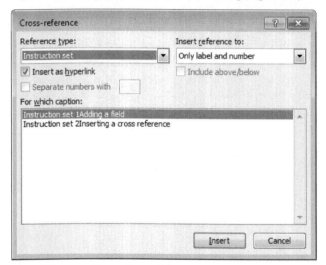

Figure 122   Cross-reference dialog

The Cross-reference dialog can create cross-references to any numbered item (including numbered lists, or headings), headings, bookmarks, foot- and endnotes, and any caption labels in your document—these are all available in the Reference type list box (Figure 123). This list is, thus, very comprehensive. Perhaps a little elaboration on this list is in order. For Numbered item, any numbered paragraph is included. This thus includes your use of the built-in heading styles, as well as numbering added through any other means. Heading, by contrast, displays only the built-in headings—one reason why I insisted (on p. 92) that you use the built-in heading styles. After these two options come Bookmark and Foot- and Endnote. The last items in the list reflect all the caption labels you have created (see section 8.4 above), listed alphabetically. All of these, being all captions, are given the same treatment in the Cross-reference dialog.

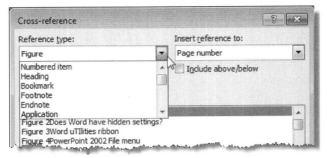

Figure 123   *Cross-reference dialog: Reference types*

Note that the Insert reference to list box contains a slightly different list of options for different items selected in the Reference type list box (Figure 124 shows the options for inserting a reference to a heading). You can, for example, refer to the number of the item, to its page, even to the text it contains.

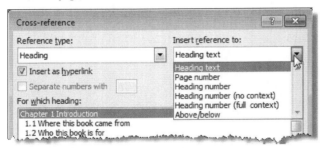

Figure 124   *Cross-reference dialog: Insert reference to*

Table 6 summarises the various options available depending on what reference type has been chosen. Note that the Include above/below check box is not available for all kinds of references—those for which it can be used are indicated with the asterisks in the last column. Also, its operation does vary slightly depending on what is select, and the context. Normally (i.e., when the numbered paragraph or heading or bookmark or foot/endnote number is selected for the reference type), it will add either the word *above* or the word *below* (with a preceding space) to the cross-reference, depending on whether the item referred to is above or below the reference point in the text (e.g., *123 above*). However, when a reference is inserted to the page number on which the numbered paragraph or heading or bookmark or foot/endnote number or caption is found, Word will add the reference *on page xx*, instead of *xx above*, as one might expect (e.g., *on page 123*).

The next consideration is the difference between adding a reference to a paragraph number, or the paragraph number showing no or full context. When full context is selected, note that the Separate numbers with option becomes available, where a separator of your choice can be specified. The good news is that, for the paragraph numbering used in a thesis or dissertation, you need not concern yourself with these options, and use only (typically) the Heading number option. If these different options are used for numbering that is applied to whole paragraphs, the result will be the same for all three. The latter two options (no context and full context) only really come into play when an outline numbering scheme is used that combines several levels of numbering in the same paragraph (such as in a contract or a constitution, etc.). You can find a fuller explanation of the different results they will produce in that context here: http://office.microsoft.com/en-za/word-help/paragraph-number-options-in-cross-references-HP005189543.aspx.

Table 6   *Summary of Cross-reference Dialog Options*

Reference type	Insert reference to	Can include Above/below?
Numbered items	Paragraph number	*
(Also Headings)	Paragraph text	
(Also Bookmarks)	Paragraph number (no context)	*
	Paragraph number (full context)	*
	Page number	*
	Above/Below	
Footnotes	Footnote number	*
(also Endnotes)	Footnote number (formatted)	*
	Page number	*
	Above/Below	
Captions	Entire caption	
	Only caption text	
	Only label and number	
	Page number	*
	Above/Below	

A further nice feature of this dialog is that it is a modeless dialog—meaning it can stay open as you work in Word. This is especially useful if you have two monitors, where you can position the Cross-reference dialog on one, and the Word window on the other. Each time you click on the dialog, it does a quick update of its contents, so if you have added extra items (e.g., extra headings or extra caption labels), they will be displayed as soon as you click on the dialog (there is thus no need to close and open it to get the full contents).

Once you have made your selections from this dialog and you insert the cross-reference, Word inserts a REF field in the document which contains the cross-reference information. If you have the "Insert as hyperlink" setting on, which is recommended, you can jump to the referred items by pressing Ctrl and clicking on the cross-reference marker—this is because Word will then add the \h switch to the REF field. The various REF field switches are shown in Table 7.

Table 7   *REF field switches*[50]

Switch	Usage
\d	Specifies the characters that separate sequence numbers (such as chapter numbers) and page numbers.
\f	Increments footnote, endnote, or annotation numbers that are marked by the bookmark and inserts the corresponding note or comment text. For example, the bookmark "Note1" marks the reference mark of footnote 1. The field { REF Note1 \f } is inserted after footnote 2. The field result displays the footnote reference mark "3" in the document text and inserts the text of footnote 1 into the footnote window.
\h	Creates a hyperlink to the bookmarked paragraph.
\n	Causes the field to display the entire paragraph number for a referenced paragraph without trailing periods. No information about prior levels is displayed unless it is included as part of the current level.
\p	Causes the field to display its position relative to the source bookmark using the word "above" or "below." If the REF field appears in the document before the bookmark, it evaluates to "below." If the REF field appears after the bookmark, it evaluates to "above." If the REF field appears within the bookmark, an error is returned. This switch can also be used in conjunction with the \n, \r, and \w switches. When this is done, "above" or "below" is appended to the end of the field result.
\r	Inserts the entire paragraph number of the bookmarked paragraph in relative context—or relative to its position in the numbering scheme—without trailing periods.
\t	Causes the REF field to suppress non-delimiter or non-numerical text when used in conjunction with the \n, \r, or \w switch. With this switch, for example, you can reference "Section 1.01," and only "1.01" is displayed in the result.
\w	Inserts the paragraph number of the bookmarked paragraph in full context from anywhere in the document. For example, when referencing paragraph "ii.," a REF field with the \w switch would return "1.a.ii" as a result.

Please note, though, that it is far more economical to insert cross-references using the Cross-reference dialog than manually adding REF fields. This is because the dialog actually performs two steps when you add a cross-reference. First, it creates a hidden bookmark to the item being cross-referenced (if none such exists, and sometimes, I have noticed, even when such exists). Then secondly it adds the REF field using that bookmark name just created. To do it manually, you would have to first go to the item (which may be quite far away in your document), add the bookmark, then return and add the cross-reference.

Because the reference is created with a field, if the referent changes, the cross-reference changes with it. When the referent is deleted, the field will (when updated) give the following message: "Error! Reference source not found." This means that Word can no longer find the item to which the cross-reference points. This may seem irritating, but it is a useful means of error trapping, as, had you not used Word's cross-referencing, you

[50] Adapted from the Microsoft Word help files (2012): http://office.microsoft.com/en-us/word-help/field-codes-ref-field-HA102017423.aspx.

may never have noticed the problem, and would have had a manually typed cross-reference to something which no longer exists.

Note that cross-references do not update automatically, which is quite sensible, as a long document can contain hundreds, if not thousands of cross-references. You can set Word to update fields before a document is printed in the Word Options dialog, Display tab, Printing options group (Figure 107). However, it may be simpler to just periodically update your fields manually. This is easily done with **Ctrl + A, F9**—the former selects the whole document, and the latter updates fields.

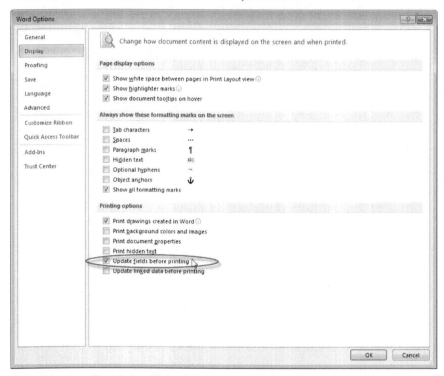

Figure 125   *Word Options: Update fields before printing*

Problems can sometimes occur when you move referents around. For example, Figure 126 shows how, after Table 1 was copied from a different location and pasted above Table 2, the cross-reference to Table 2 suddenly included the whole of Table 1, including its caption (note the grey selection of the field showing where the cross-reference should be). This cross-reference had to be deleted and re-inserted. If you ever see a large field containing lots of text, the culprit is normally a cross-reference gone wrong. The actual reference will almost always be right at the end of the field ("Table 2" at the end of the grey area in Figure 126). Simply delete the cross-reference (nothing will be lost, since all the text included in the field is referenced from somewhere else) and then reinsert the cross-reference. The exact nature of the problem (it actually concerns the hidden bookmark created by the cross-reference dialog), and a more comprehensive solution, is discussed in in Application 11.2 (p. 245).

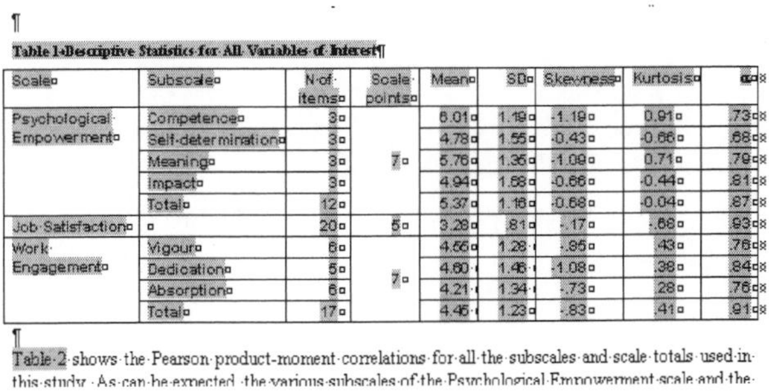

Table 1·Descriptive Statistics for All Variables of Interest¶

Scale¤	Subscale¤	N·of·items¤	Scale·points¤	Mean¤	SD¤	Skewness¤	Kurtosis¤	α¤
Psychological·Empowerment¤	Competence¤	3¤	7¤	6.01¤	1.19¤	-1.19¤	0.91¤	.73¤
	Self·determination¤	3¤		4.78¤	1.55¤	-0.43¤	-0.66¤	.68¤
	Meaning¤	3¤		5.76¤	1.35¤	-1.09¤	0.71¤	.79¤
	Impact¤	3¤		4.94¤	1.68¤	-0.66¤	-0.44¤	.81¤
	Total¤	12¤		5.37¤	1.16¤	-0.68¤	-0.04¤	.87¤
Job·Satisfaction¤	¤	20¤	5¤	3.28¤	.81¤	-.17¤	.68¤	.93¤
Work·Engagement¤	Vigour¤	6¤	7¤	4.56¤	1.28	.95¤	.43¤	.76¤
	Dedication¤	5¤		4.60	1.46	-1.08¤	.36¤	.84¤
	Absorption¤	6¤		4.21	1.34	-.73¤	.28¤	.76¤
	Total¤	17¤		4.46	1.23¤	.83¤	.41¤	.91¤

¶
Table·2·shows·the·Pearson·product-moment·correlations·for·all·the·subscales·and·scale·totals·used·in·this·study.·As·can·be·expected, the·various·subscales·of·the·Psychological·Empowerment·scale·and·the·

Figure 126   *Referent included in cross-reference*

Multiple cross-references can be used to great effect (but don't overkill…) when you refer to an item (e.g. a table) with one cross-reference, and its page number with another cross-reference, such as the reference to Application 11.2 (p. 245) in the preceding paragraph, which consists of two cross-references—one to the caption label and number, and a second to the page number.

8.6   Footnotes and Endnotes

Footnotes and endnotes are essentially the same devices, only with different placements—footnotes at the bottom of the page to which they are added, and endnotes to the end of the section in which they have been added. A footnote or endnote consists of a superscripted mark (typically a number) in the text, and then a repetition of that mark either at the bottom of the page (footnote) or at the end of the chapter or book (endnote). Bear in mind that the discipline you are studying in will determine, to an extent, the stylistic guidelines you might want to follow, and thus whether you should be using footnotes, endnotes, or neither (e.g., the APA style guide (American Psychological Association, 2010) generally discourages the use of footnotes).

8.6.1   Adding footnotes or endnotes

Instruction set 27   Inserting footnotes and endnotes

Shortcut	Ctrl + Alt + F (footnote)
	Ctrl + Alt + D (endnote)
Keyboard	Alt | S | F (footnote) Alt | S | E (endnote)
Left click	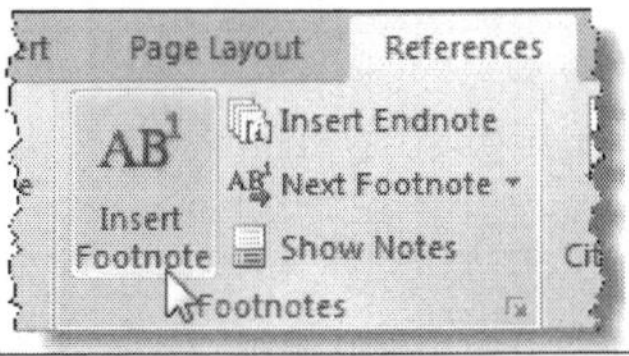

Footnotes and endnotes are added from the Footnotes group of the References ribbon (Instruction set 27), although they each have handy keyboard shortcuts. When they are added in Print Layout view, Word immediately takes you to the footnote or endnote area where you can type your note. Word also uses two dedicated styles (Footnote Text and Endnote Text for the text in these areas.

Once you have typed your footnote or endnote, you will want to get back to where you were working in the main document text. If it was a simple note with little correction, the **Shift + F5** keyboard shortcut should get you back there, and if that doesn't then take up your mouse and double click on the footnote or endnote marker to take you to its position in the main document text (alternatively, the Show Notes tool—Alt S | H, see Instruction set 29 below—will also toggle you between the main text and the footnote/endnote area).

Using the Insert Footnote or Insert Endnote tools from the References ribbon lets Word add what can best be described as "default" foot- or endnotes, which is, of course, what you would want most of the time, and thus also proves to be the quickest method of operation. If, however, you want to add more complex footnotes or endnotes, the Footnote and Endnote dialog will give you that functionality. This is opened from the dialog launcher in the Footnotes group of the References ribbon (Instruction set 28).

Instruction set 28   Opening the Footnote and Endnote dialog

Keyboard	Alt | S | Q
Left click	

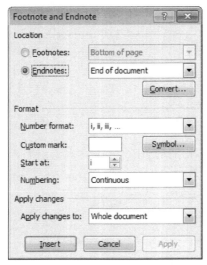

Figure 127   *Footnote and Endnote dialog*

Here a large amount of customisation can be done. Footnotes can be added either to the Bottom of the page, or Below the text. Endnotes can be added to the end of the document or the end of the section.

The Convert... button will open the Convert Notes dialog (Figure 128), which allows you to convert all footnotes in the document to endnotes, or vice versa, or to switch footnotes and endnotes.

Figure 128   *Convert Notes dialog*

Furthermore, you can choose from a variety of Number formats (Arabic, upper- and lowercase alphabetic, upper- and lowercase Roman, and symbols), as shown in Figure 129. If the succession of symbols in the Number format list box is not sufficient, the Symbol... button will open the Symbol dialog, allowing you to specify any symbol of your choice in the Custom mark box.

Figure 129   *Footnote and Endnote dialog: Number formats*

The Footnote and Endnote dialog also allows you to specify details concerning the numbering, so that you can specify the starting number/value, and also specify whether, for footnotes, numbering should run continuously throughout the document or section, or restart at each section or each page (Figure 130). For endnotes, numbering can be set to run continuously throughout the document or section, or restart at each section (but not each page).

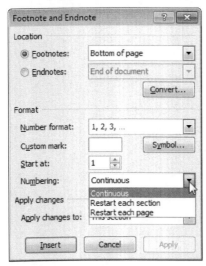

Figure 130   *Footnote and Endnote dialog: Number start*

And lastly, the Apply changes to list box allows you to set different numbering schemes for different sections of the document, or to set a uniform numbering scheme for the whole document. Remember also that once you have made your adjustments in the Footnote and Endnote dialog, you can then continue, while in the same section or document (depending on your settings), to add your foot- or endnotes in the normal way without the dialog, and they will confirm to the scheme you have specified.

Application 8.4   *Suppressing endnotes*

A common situation when using endnotes is to position the endnotes at the end of each chapter. This is easily done in Word, where the specification is to add the endnotes to the end of each section, and a section break (see section 7.1.1.1, p. 120) is added between each chapter.

However, a problem arises when additional section breaks are added within a chapter (e.g., when some landscape pages need to be added).

Word does, however, allow for this situation. Simply make sure that the insertion point is placed within the section where the notes should not *be displayed, and open the* Page Setup *dialog. There, in the* Layout *tab, select* Suppress endnotes *to essentially "move" the endnotes to the end of the next section. Of course, this can be done for any number of sections in a row—the endnotes will be displayed at the end of the first section whose endnotes are not suppressed (unless, of course, that last section whose endnotes* are *suppressed also happens to be the last section in the document, in which case this setting will have no effect[51]).*

---

[51] To my mind, Microsoft should have disabled this setting if the insertion point is in the last section of the document.

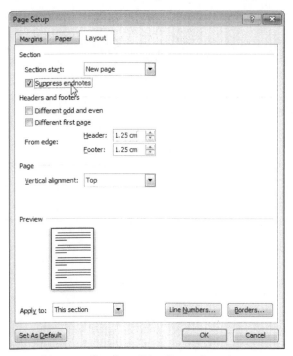

Figure 131   *Page Setup dialog: Suppressing endnotes*

8.6.2   Viewing and navigating between notes

Instruction set 29   Show Notes

Keyboard	Alt | S | H
Left click	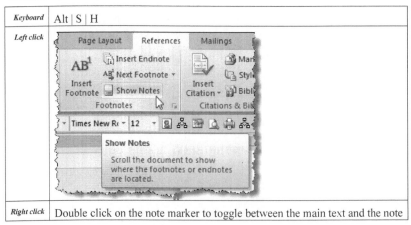
Right click	Double click on the note marker to toggle between the main text and the note

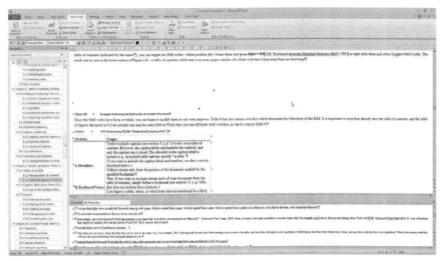

Figure 132　　　*Footnotes frame in Draft View*

When footnotes or endnotes are added in Draft view (the old Normal view), Word will open the Footnote or Endnote frame (these look the same)—Figure 132. Here you can again type the note, and click close or press **Alt + Shift + C** to return to the text. This pane can also be opened or closed in Draft View using the Show Notes (Alt S | H) tool (see Instruction set 29).

You can also view the contents of a foot- or endnote by holding the mouse over the note marker in the main text. Word will then display a tooltip showing the content of the note (or most of it, if it is a very long note). Figure 133 shows this for what is currently footnote 44 of this book (footnote 52 on p. 188).

Remember also that you can jump between the footnote or endnote marker in the main text and the notes area (and back again) by double clicking on the note marker.

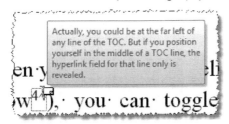

Figure 133　　　*Footnote tooltip*

The Footnotes group of the References ribbon also contains tools for navigating backwards and forwards between the various notes of your document (Instruction set 30). The Go To dialog (section 11.3, p. 247) and the Object Browser (section 11.4, p. 248) also allow you to move between footnotes and endnotes.

Instruction set 30   Navigating between foot- and endnotes

Keyboard	Alt | S | O | N (Next footnote)
	Alt | S | O | P (Previous footnote)
	Alt | S | O | X (Next endnote)
	Alt | S | O | V (Previous endnote)
Left click	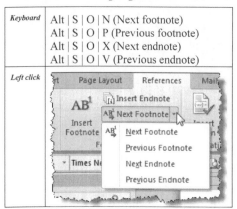

8.6.3   Note-area separators

Word has special components that define the foot- and endnote areas where these appear. In total, there are three of these, viz. the Footnote Separator, the Footnote Continuation Separator, and the Footnote Continuation Notice (of course, endnote areas have the equivalent three components: the Endnote Separator, the Endnote Continuation Separator, and the Endnote Continuation Notice). Figure 134 shows the Footnote Separator.

- 45. Actually, you could be at the far left of any l hyperlink field for that line only is revealed.¶
- 46. Adapted from the Microsoft Word help files (http://office.microsoft.com/en-gb/word-help/redir/HP005186201.aspx?queryid=e445

Figure 134   Footnote separator

While it will probably not be necessary to modify these for most theses or dissertations, they can, in fact, be modified. To do this, first switch to Draft View (**Ctrl + Alt + N**, or Vie<u>w</u> ribbon, Draft vi<u>e</u>w), and then show the notes area (Instruction set 29 above).

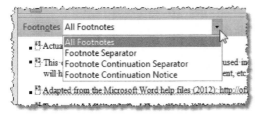

Figure 135   *Notes frame: Switching between various notes area components*

The Notes frame contains a list box (Figure 135) which you can use to switch between viewing the notes themselves, or the Separator (which demarcates the notes area on the printed page), the Continuation Separator (which is used when the note is so long that the notes area on one page is not big enough, and the note flows over to the second page), and the Continuation notice (when a note overflows to the next page, this indicates that the note continues on the next page). You can then modify these to suit, or use the Reset button to convert these back to the Word defaults (a short solid line for the Separator, a long solid line for the Continuation Separator, and nothing for the Continuation Notice). For example, you could type *continued over...* for the Continuation Notice).

8.6.4   Further Footnote and Endnote tips

Foot- and endnotes can easily be moved. Simply select the marker in the main text, cut it, and paste it in the new location. The text of the note is moved with the marker to its new relative position.

Also remember that while right clicking on a foot- or endnote marker in the main text provides no useful shortcuts in the context menu, right clicking in the notes area (Figure 136) does: You can (in the order shown in Figure 136) go back to the note marker in the main text, or open the Footnote and Endnote dialog, or convert footnotes to endnotes or vice versa.

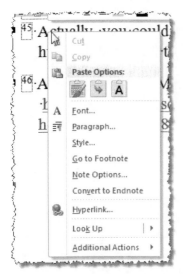

Figure 136   *Right clicking in the notes area*

Remember that normally, footnotes and endnotes are not included in the word count, although the Word Count dialog can be set to Include textboxes, footnotes and endnotes (see Figure 58 on p. 80).

You can also use the Find and Replace dialog (discussed extensively in Chapter 10, form p. 215), to search for foot- and endnote markers (and even, for example, replace them with something else)—^f is the tag for a footnote marker, and ^e the tag for endnote markers (but when using wildcard searches—discussed in section 10.5, p. 229—Word makes no distinction between foot- and endnote markers, using instead the ^2 tag for both). Example 10 of Application 10.3 (p. 236) gives an example of a foot- or endnote wildcard search and replace.

Remember also that Word uses two dedicated styles (Footnote Text and Endnote Text for foot- and endnote text respectively. This means that it is relatively easy to set the appearance of your foot- and/or endnotes—simply modify the relevant style, as described in section 5.4.2 (p. 89). Word also uses a further two styles for foot- and endnote markers: Footnote Reference and Endnote Reference. Obviously, these two styles can also be modified to suite your requirements, although bear in mind that Word uses this style for both markers—the one in the main text, and the corresponding one in the notes area. As an example, this means that, if you are using footnotes and endnotes in the same document (which I would generally not recommend), you can format them differently to help your readers tell them apart. Furthermore, if you want to use footnotes and endnotes within the same document, Word will by default change the numbering style of the footnotes and endnotes. Of course, it doesn't make sense to change this back so that your footnotes and endnotes are numbered in the same way! You can also use symbols as your footnote markers.

Application 8.5   *Multiple references to the same footnote or endnote*

If you want to insert multiple references to one footnote or endnote, there is no easy way to achieve this, as each note must have its own corresponding marker, and each marker its own note. What you can do, however, is to position the I-beam in the main text, where you would want your second marker to be, and then insert a cross-reference (cf. 8.5) to that note, using the Formatted *option. This results in a cross-reference with the same marker, and the same formatting, as the note. This way, it will automatically update along with your actual note marker, saving you the trouble. An example of this is footnote 25 on p. 43.*

Application 8.6   *Table notes*

If you have to add notes to a table, the general requirement is that those notes be displayed directly underneath the table. Generally, because these are used so infrequently, the simplest is to do them manually—type the marker, superscript it, and then type the note underneath the table with its own marker.

However, if you have many such notes, and want to use Word's foot- and endnote feature for this, you can—within limits.

Firstly, if you are using footnotes in your document text, then use endnotes for the table, and vice versa. If you are already using foot- and endnotes in your document (which I have already advised against), then you are pretty much out of luck.

Now, add the table, and ensure that the table is followed immediately by a continuous section break. Then use the Footnote and Endnote *dialog to add the footnote or endnote (as the case may be), and ensure that, if it is footnote, it is placed* Below the text*, and if an endnote, then at the* End of *the section. This will ensure that the note ends up below the table.*

Chapter 9
Reader navigation: Tables of content, Tables of Figures, Indexes, and Tables of Authorities

One of the most time-saving tools Word offers you is its ability to generate tables of content and indexes for your document. The tools are age-old in Word, but remain faithfully efficient.

Traditionally, you accessed the Index and Tables dialog to add indexes, tables of content, tables of figures (a bit of a misnomer), and tables of authorities. As of Word 2007, the dialog had been redesigned a bit. You still get the same dialog, but you now access it from four different locations (instead of one), and each location you access it from determines which tab you get access to—all the other tabs are disabled, as is shown in Figure 137.

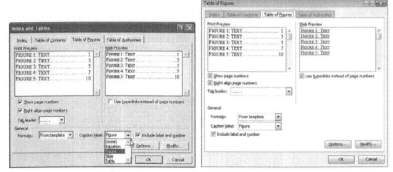

Figure 137   *Index and Tables dialog: Word 2003 vs Word 2010*

9.1   Tables of content

Instruction set 31   Inserting a Table of Figures

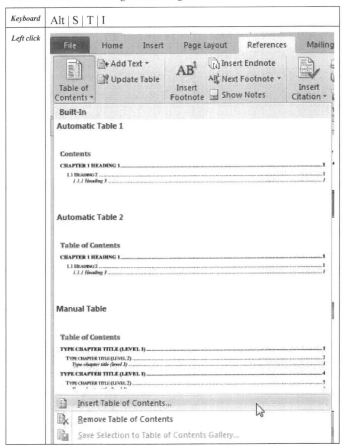

Keyboard	Alt	S	T	I
Left click	

Word has some custom tables of content built into the gallery, but I generally prefer using the Table of Contents dialog (Figure 138)—perhaps it just because I'm so used to using it from previous versions of Word, or perhaps I'm a control freak. Having said that, note that you can create your own Tables of Content using the dialog, and then save them to the gallery (bottom option in the list), thus getting the best of both worlds.

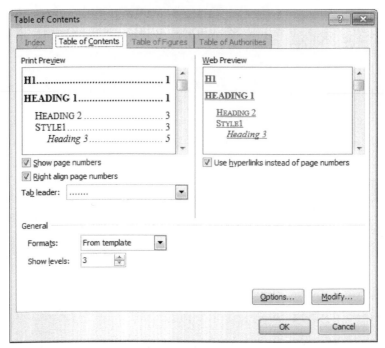

Figure 138   *Table of Contents dialog*

The most important setting here is how many heading levels you would want to show. Word scans your document for the built-in heading styles, and uses those corresponding to the levels you specify to build the table of contents. Word only includes the levels you have in the table of contents, so if you have only six levels, and choose nine here, then Word will still only show those six levels. On the other hand, if you chose three, Word would not display levels four to six. In other words, it is always better to play it safe and select more than you think you have if you are not certain about the number of heading levels in your document. The nice thing about this feature is that it allows you to present summarised Tables of Content as well—you insert two tables of content at different places in your document, one showing only the main heading levels, and one showing all the heading levels.

Note furthermore that each of the nine heading levels in your document has its own corresponding Table of Content style, (TOC1–TOC9). You can format each one as you would any other style, and these styles apply only to table of content entries appearing at that particular level.

Next, still in the General section, choose from one of the six built in styles for the table of contents, or stay with the "From template" option, which allows you to customise your own style, should you choose. When you choose this option, you can then modify each of the corresponding nine TOC styles in your document or document template. You can access these styles by clicking on the Modify... button, which opens a style dialog showing only this list of styles (Figure 139). Clicking on Modify... again will open the Modify Style dialog (Figure 139). This means that you can control the appearance of every single aspect of the table, including the font, line spacing, tabs, etc., for all nine levels.

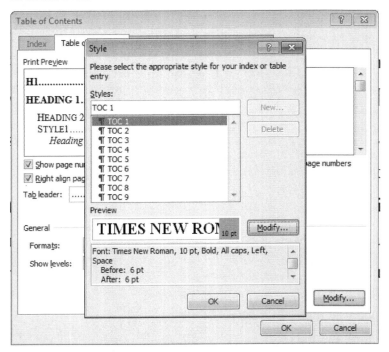

Figure 139   *Modifying the TOC Styles*

From the top left of the dialog, decide whether you want to Show page numbers (this is on by default, and should probably be left on in most instances). If you are showing the page numbers, it is also best to Right align page numbers. Next choose the Tab leader of your preference (this will appear between the title of your caption and the page number). Generally, I almost never have to change anything here.

When you are done, you can click on OK, and Word will do its magic—it runs through your document, and finds all your headings, building your table of contents from that information.

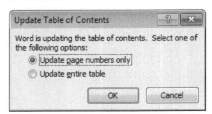

Figure 140   *Update Table of Contents dialog*

185

Once the table has been generated, you can update it at any time by selecting it and pressing F9 (there is also an Update Table button in the Table of Contents group of the References ribbon, if you must use the mouse). Sometimes the small dialog shown in Figure 140 will appear—it is merely a time-saving device, as the option of updating page numbers only is much quicker. It assumes that the structure of the document (and thus the table of contents) has not changed, and only checks the page numbers of the items already in the table. The second option rebuilds the entire table, and is best selected when you want to be absolutely sure that no mistakes are made, or, of course, after you have made structural changes to your document (like adding a new heading).

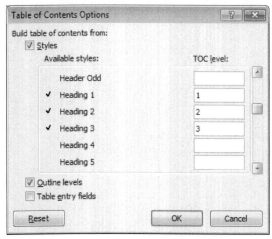

Figure 141   *Table of Contents Options dialog*

The Options... button in this dialog is quite important. Word customizes it by default based on the number of heading levels you choose. For example, when you have selected to show only the top three heading levels, then the dialog will show only tick marks across Heading 1 to Heading 3 as in Figure 141. Note that you can have your heading levels be formatted with different TOC styles by modifying the numbers in the TOC level section of this dialog.

The reason these options are so important is twofold. Firstly, you sometimes find certain parts of your document being pulled into the table of contents, when they should not. Simply go to this dialog, and clear the number from the TOC level section across the relevant style(s) (the tick mark next to this style will also disappear). When you now update the table of contents, the errant entries will disappear.

Furthermore, you may sometimes want certain entries to be added to your table of contents, even though you did not use the built-in heading styles for them. Simply find the corresponding style in the Table of Contents Options dialog, and in the TOC level section, just type in the level number you want your entry to appear at. Word will now include it in your table of contents.

9.1.1   Manual tables of contents

If you did not use the built-in heading styles, or you want to add other entries that utilise other styles, you can mark these manually (generally, it is simply much less work to just use the built-in heading styles). This is done by selecting the relevant paragraph (or at least just positioning yourself within it), and then opening the Paragraph dialog (Figure 142). There, set the Outline level to the level you want the entry to appear at in the table of contents. Then, in the Table of Contents Options dialog, make sure that Outline levels is selected. Word will now include all such marked paragraphs into the table of contents.

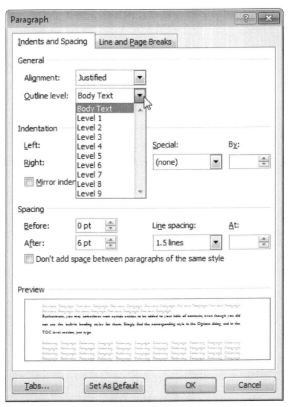

Figure 142   Paragraph dialog: Setting the outline level

You will also notice in the Table of Contents Options dialog that you can use Table entry fields. This is the old way in which tables of contents were built in prehistoric versions of Word, and these are discussed below in the context of tables of figures (section 9.2.1)—their functioning is exactly the same when used for tables of content (the TOC field which builds a table of contents can use the TC field information listed in Table 9).

9.1.2   Advanced tables of contents

A table of contents is nothing more than a field. As such, its field codes can be revealed and, if desired, modified. Figure 143 shows the first few lines of a four-page table of contents. When you position yourself to the left of the first line of the table of contents (indicated by the arrow[52]), you can toggle the field codes—either position the I-beam there and press **Shift + F9** or right click there and select Toggle Field Codes. The result can be seen in the lower section of Figure 143—a table of contents which runs over many pages consists of a field code that is just more than one line long!

Table·of ·Contents¶

CHAPTER·1·INTRODUCTION ....→..7¶
   1.1 PROBLEM STATEMENT ....→...7¶
   1.2 AIM OF THIS STUDY ....→...8¶
   1.3 LAYOUT OF THIS STUDY ....→...8¶
CHAPTER·2·PROBLEM·STATEMENT ....→...9¶

Table·of ·Contents¶

{ TOC ·o "3-3" ·h ·z ·t "Heading 1,1,Heading 2,2,Heading 4,4,Heading 5,5,,Introduction,1,Reference List Title,1" }¶

Figure 143   *Example of showing the field codes for a table of contents*

Once the field codes have been revealed, you can begin to modify them to suit your purposes. Table 8 lists the various switches which determine the behaviour of the field. It is important to note here already that the table of contents, and the table of figures discussed in 9.2 are actually one and the same field in Word, they just use different field switches, as can be seen in Table 8.

---

[52] Actually, you could be at the far left of any line of the TOC. But if you position yourself in the middle of a TOC line, the hyperlink field for that line only is revealed.

Table 8 *TOC field switches*[53]

Switch	Usage
\a *Identifier*	Used to include captions (see section 8.4, p. 161) into your table of contents. However, the caption labels and numbers are omitted, and only the caption text is listed. The *Identifier* is the caption label to include (e.g., to include table captions specify "\a table." If you want to include the caption labels and numbers, use the \c switch described below.
\b *BookmarkName*	Collects entries only from the portion of the document marked by the specified bookmark. Thus, if you want to exclude certain parts of your document from the table of contents, simply define a bookmark (see section 11.2, p. 240) that does not include those portions.
\c *"SEQIdentifier"*	Lists figures, tables, charts, or other items that are numbered by a SEQ (Sequence) field. Word uses SEQ fields to number items captioned with the Caption command (see section 8.4, p. 161). *SEQIdentifier*, which corresponds to the caption label, must match the identifier in the SEQ field. For example, { TOC \c tables } lists all numbered tables.
\f *EntryIdentifier*	Builds a table from TC fields. If *EntryIdentifier* is specified, the table is built only from TC fields with the same identifier (typically a letter). For example, { TOC \f t } builds a table of contents from TC fields such as { TC "Entry Text" \f t }. See section 9.2.1 for how to set up these TC fields.
\h *Hyperlinks*	Inserts TOC entries as hyperlinks.
\l *Levels*	Builds a table of contents from TC fields that assign entries to one of the specified levels. For example, { TOC \l 1-4 } builds a table of contents from TC fields that assign entries to levels 1-4 in the table of contents. TC fields that assign entries to lower levels are skipped.
\n *Levels*	Omits page numbers from the table of contents. Page numbers are omitted from all levels unless a range of entry levels is specified. For example, { TOC \n 3-4 } omits page numbers from levels 3 and 4. Delete this switch to include page numbers.
\o *"Headings"*	Builds a table of contents from paragraphs formatted with built-in heading styles. For example, { TOC \o "1-3" } lists only headings formatted with the styles Heading 1 through Heading 3. If no heading range is specified, all heading levels used in the document are listed. Enclose the range numbers in quotation marks.
\p *"Separators"*	Specifies the characters that separate an entry and its page number. For example, the field { TOC \p "---" } displays a result such as "Selecting Text---53." The default is a tab with leader dots. You can use up to five characters, which must be enclosed in quotation marks.

---

[53] Adapted from the Microsoft Word help files (Microsoft): http://office.microsoft.com/en-gb/word-help/redir/HP005186201.aspx.

Switch	Usage
\s *Identifier*	Includes a number such as a chapter number before the page number. The chapter or other item must be numbered with a SEQ field. Identifier must match the identifier in the SEQ field. For example, if you insert { SEQ chapter } before each chapter heading, { TOC \o "1-3" \s chapter } displays page numbers as 2-14, where "2" is the chapter number.
\d "*Separator*"	When used with the \s switch, specifies the number of characters that separate the sequence numbers and page numbers. Enclose the characters in quotation marks. Word uses a hyphen (-) if no \d switch is specified. In the table of contents generated by { TOC \o "1-3" \s chapter \d ":" }, a colon (:) separates chapter numbers and page numbers — for example, "2:14."
\t "*Style, Level, Style, Level,...*"	Builds a table of contents from paragraphs formatted with styles other than the built-in heading styles. For example, { TOC \t "chaptertitle,1, chapterhead,2" } builds a table of contents from paragraphs formatted with the styles "chaptertitle" and "chapterhead." The number after each style name indicates the table of contents entry level that corresponds to that style. You can use both the \o switch and the \t switch to build a table of contents from built-in heading styles and other styles.
\u	Builds a table of contents by using the applied paragraph outline level
\w	Preserves tab entries within table entries.
\x	Preserves newline characters within table entries.
\z	Hides tab leader and page numbers in Web Layout view.

9.2 Caption tables (a.k.a. Table of Figures)

This tab in the dialog is titled Table of Figures. As I mentioned, this is a bit of a misnomer, as it is actually the tool that you use to create a list of any caption label (section 8.4, p. 161) you have used in your document.

Instruction set 32   Inserting a Table of Figures

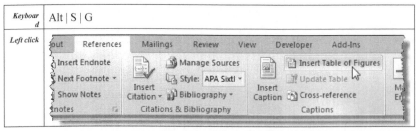

Keyboard	Alt	S	G

To create a table of figures, or any table listing *any* caption you have created, simply navigate in your document to where you want the list to be. The tool is accessed from the Captions group of the References ribbon (Instruction set 32).

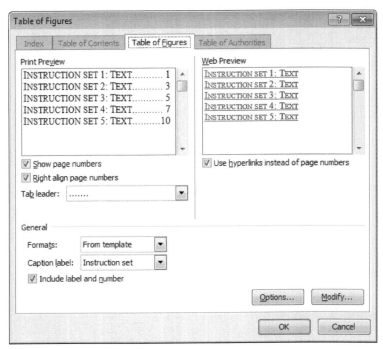

Figure 144   *Table of Figures dialog*

In the Table of Figures dialog (Figure 144), I will ignore the Web Preview section. In fact, you will notice that in normal use, there is almost nothing that you need to set.

The most important choice you need to make is to select the Caption label for your need in the Caption label list box—this list box will display all captions that you have created, together with the three Word defaults. Note that this means that it will display caption types which might not have been used in your document, although I don't find this a particularly bothersome problem at all.

Next, still in the General section, choose from one of the five built in styles for the table of figures listed in the Formats list box, or stay with the From template option, which allows you to customise your own style, should you choose. The secret to this is that Word uses a particular style to format your table of figures. This style is named (no surprises) the Table of Figures style. A shortcut to this style can be access by clicking on the Modify... button, which opens a Style dialog showing only this style (Figure 145). Clicking on Modify... again will open the Modify Style dialog (Figure 145). This means that you can control the appearance of every single aspect of the table, including the font, line spacing, tabs, etc., using the techniques discussed elsewhere in this book.

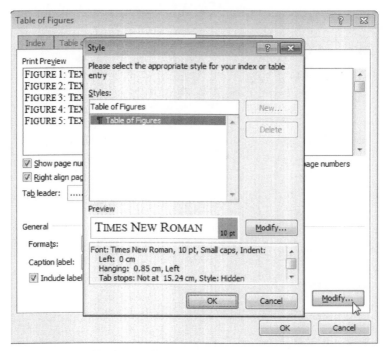

Figure 145   *Modifying the Table of Figures Style*

The last setting in the General section is whether you want to Include the label and number for the caption or not. Generally, I recommend that you do.

From the top left of the dialog, decide whether you want to Show page numbers (this is on by default, and should probably be left on in most instances). If you are showing the page numbers, it is also best to Right align those page numbers. Next choose the Tab leader of your preference (this will appear between the title of your caption and the page number). In short, you will notice that you almost never have to change anything in this dialog.

When you are done, you can click on OK, and Word will do its magic—it runs through your document, and finds all your captions using the label you selected in the dialog, building your table from that information.

Once the table has been generated, you can update it at any time by selecting it and pressing F9.

Remember as well that this is one tool, but you can use it to create separate "Tables of Figures" for each and every caption style you use in your thesis. See the front of this book for examples of how this is done—there is a List of Tables, a List of Figures, a List of Application entries, and a List of Instruction Sets, all created using this same tool.

9.2.1 Out of the ordinary tables of figures

Lastly, if you have to do something out of the ordinary (i.e., if you did your captions right, this won't be necessary), you can select the Options... button to open the Table of Figures Options dialog (Figure 146). There are two other ways that Word can find what you want to have included in the table (and these can be used together as well). The first is to use styles. By activating the Style check box, and then selecting a different style than the Caption style, you can use that to build your table of figures. Note, though, that that style may only then have been used for those entries you want in this table—or, alternatively put, every single place you have used that style in your document will appear in this table.

If you want to use table entry fields for your table of figures (remember that you can use these in addition to a style), activate the Table entry fields check box. You will then have had to mark the relevant labels in your document using TC fields and the \f switch. The value you used in the \f switch of the TC fields is what you select in the Table identifier list box—Word will then search through your document and find the relevant entries for your table.

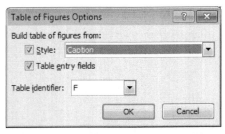

Figure 146   *Table of Figures Options dialog*

Note, though, that this is a hold-over from the very, very early versions of Word, where you first had to mark all your table of contents entries with Table of Contents Entry (TC) fields, and then build the table of contents. This is how the TC field works:

Identify the text that you want to have included. Position the I-beam directly to the left of the first character of this text. Typically, this will be at the start of the paragraph containing the label. Next, press **Ctrl + F9** to add the Field braces. Type TC followed by the text you want to appear in your table, followed by any switches you want to add. The switches are explained in Table 9. All of these elements are separated by single spaces.

Table 9 　　　　*TC field switches*[54]

Switch	Name	Usage	If omitted
\f	Type	TOC identifier. Typically, just use alphabetic letters (this is not case sensitive). All TC fields sharing the same \f identifier will be used in creating the table. For example, all TC fields with a "\f A" switch will wind up in a table of figures specifying the "A" Table identifier in the Table of Figures Options dialog.	If the \f switch is omitted, the field will appear in all tables of content and tables of figures. If you're only using this to manually create one list, you could skip this, but Murphy says that you will later want a second, separate list, and will have to go back and modify all of these, so rather use it.
\l	Level	Allows you to place your table entries at different hierarchical levels (i.e., 1 to 9). Word will use the TOC style corresponding to the level number you specify for the formatting.	If omitted, TOC1 (i.e., level 1) is used.
\n	Suppress page number	Allows you to selectively show and not show page numbers for entries in your table.	Page numbers are shown for all entries by default.

As an example, you could do something like this: { TC "Appendix 1" \f A \l 1 }. This would tell Word to create a TC entry with the text "Appendix 1" (note that Word does not automatically number these). These entries can be corralled into a Table of Figures using the "A" table identifier, and this entry will appear at level 1, showing the relevant page number (because the \n switch is not used).

Application 9.1 　　*A Separate Table of Figures*

> **Problem:**
> *You want to have all your appendices appear separately in a List of Appendices. However, you want them to be formatted differently from the normal table/figure captions in your document, so you can't use caption numbering. Also, you don't want your appendices to form part of the normal table of contents.*
>
> **Solution:**
> *Simply create a style for your appendix headings, and then use that in the List of Tables tools, options dialog. Easy as that.*
>
> *Of course, if you were a glutton for punishment, you could always get the same effect with the TC fields...!*

9.3   Indexes

Word allows you to build reasonably professional indexes to your dissertation. Although the process is somewhat labour-intensive, you can make it less tedious by getting into the habit of doing it automatically as you type the dissertation. I will discuss

---

[54] Adapted from the Microsoft Word help files: http://office.microsoft.com/en-gb/word-help/redir/HP005186197.aspx (Microsoft).

this later. Also remember that most universities now require you to submit the thesis in hard and electronic copy (the latter usually in pdf format). An electronic copy can be searched, and this, to a certain extent, means that a reader can cope even if there is no index—these searches do tend to deliver a large number of "false positives," and they also cannot account for subject discussions in which certain terms are not used (i.e., text searches also miss some things), but at least they do find the text the reader is interested in.

As a side note, remember that indexing is a professional occupation. There is a Society of Indexers, and even a (very well indexed) journal devoted to indexing (see www.theindexer.org). Many, many books have been written on the subject, such as Knight (1988), Mulvany (2005), Wellisch (1996), Booth (2001). Of these, Knight is a book recommended by many different indexers. Having said that, it costs a lot of money to have a book indexed, and since you would just be doing a thesis, that, in all likelihood, might not get published, chances are slim that you would have the desire or the budget for a professional indexer. But you might want an index. The alternative, then, is to do it yourself. Indexers often debate about whether an author should index their own books, and it is so that authors often lack the necessary skills as indexers for the job, and also that authors are too often too subjectively involved in their own books to do the work with the necessary objectivity. If you need a quick introduction to the techniques underlying indexing, consult Carey (1951) or Spiker (1964)[55].

Lastly, by way of introduction, be aware that Word is not a perfect, nor even professional, indexing tool. Word cannot indicate things like index entry markers in footnotes, passim, etc. Word will not always sort all kinds of strange names and surnames correctly in the index. Word cannot sort index subheadings chronologically instead of alphabetically, etc. In other words, word may suffice for your thesis, but you may have to be willing to live with some measure of error. If all else fails, you can generate the index, and then convert it to text by copying it and using Paste Special to paste the formatted text (rtf), and then do the final editing by hand.

After all that, here follows an introduction to using Word for DIY indexing.

9.3.1 Indexing principles

The first step to a good index is to figure out how you want to organise it[56]. For this, you need a good knowledge of your subject matter (which you should have, considering you are doing a thesis on it!). Which topics are subtopics of others, which are stand-alone, which belong together, etc. Remember also that the index is organised according to words, which may represent actual terms (typically jargon terms) or concepts. This means that your actual thesis text may deal with a topic, without ever using the word which represents that topic in the index.

---

[55] Spiker's book is germane, since it assumes you will be indexing a work you have authored. Take note, though, that some indexers might take issue with some of her recommendations, and that her book dates from the pen-paper-typewriter era, meaning that certain portions will not be relevant to what we are doing with Word.

[56] There is even an ISO standard for this: "ISO 999:1996 Guidelines for the Content, Organization, and Presentation of Indexes."

Here are some guidelines to help you get your index right:

- Do not mark every occurrence of a word you want to include in your index, but only at those places in your document where the concept is explained or discussed. Definitely not those where it is merely mentioned in passing. The bane of automatically generated indexes (discussed in 9.3.2.2) is that they mark all occurrences (granted, only one per paragraph) of the terms you supply—that includes in your headings, your list of references, etc.
- Also, do not mark all topics, but only those that are relevant to finding specific information in the thesis. It helps to distance yourself, and ask yourself what kinds of information would a reader want to find in the index.

  One of the most common faux pas is to reference the main topic of the book. For example, if I were to list every occurrence of thesis, or Word, in this document, the index would become quite unwieldy (Carey, 1951, p. 6; Carey, 1961; Knight, 1988, p. 53).
- Decide how to list multiple-word entries. For example, Knight's book is (tongue-in-cheek) "Indexing, the art of" while it could, in an index, also be "The art of Indexing." Indexers normally use the former, as it allows the main term in the phrase to be highlighted by its place in the index. But whichever you choose, you need to apply it consistently, lest your readers become confused, thoroughly!
- If numbers (e.g., dates, important scientific constants, etc.) need to be listed, decide whether you will list them as Arabic/Roman numbers, or written out.
- Decide whether you will use cross-referencing in your index or not—this is discussed on p. 200.
- Decide also whether you would want to link (but not directly cross-reference) related topics. The difference is that with a cross-reference, the referring index entry has no page numbers of its own, but simply refers to another index entry, from which the reader must glean the relevant page numbers (i.e., when you cross-reference in the index, the terms being cross-referenced are synonymous). The referring term usually has "*See* x" in the place of page numbers.

  Linked topics, on the other hand, are not synonymous, but related (i.e., if readers are interested in topic A, they would most likely also want to read about topic B). For linked topics, each term would have its own page numbers in the index. These would also be created by using the cross-reference method discussed on p. 200, although you would only need to add one such cross-reference somewhere in your document. The related topic is often indicated by "*See* also x" at the end of the list of page numbers.
- Apart from cross-referencing, don't forget that some topics might get referenced under multiple headings in the index. There is nothing wrong with adding multiple index entry marks right next to (but not within!) each other—Word will resolve them quite correctly.
- Decide whether you want only one index, or multiple indexes—the most common example of this is having an author index and a subject index. Perhaps I should put it this way: The decision is actually about whether you really *need* more than one index—separating indexes may just be unnecessary work if your document does

not really warrant it. Most indexers recommend one index for most works, which may distinguish between different kinds of topics through formatting (e.g., making names italicised). Generally, only when you have a second extensive list of topics (e.g., a long list of scripture references in a theological work or a long list of dates in a historical work) in addition to your main list, should you consider a separate index for each. Adding such font formatting to index entries is discussed on page 201.

📖 Finally, take heed to Carey's (1951, p. 8) advice: "It is anyhow a pity to be completely dominated by hard-and-fast rules in matters which call supremely for common sense."

9.3.2 Marking index entries

The second step is to mark the index entries. This basically means that you have to read through the document, and mark all the relevant items. As you can imagine, this is quite a big job, which explains why it is better to use the divide-and-conquer strategy of marking the index entries as you type—this is just a good habit to cultivate.

We will first look at manual marking, and then discuss some alternatives for (supposedly) speeding the process up.

9.3.2.1 *Manually marking index entries*

Instruction set 33 Marking an Index Entry

Shortcut	Alt + Shift + X
Keyboard	Alt	S	N
Left click	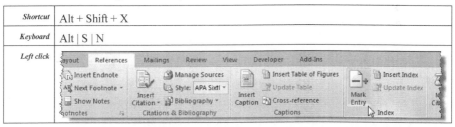

Marking the index entries themselves is relatively easy (Instruction set 33). You can either select a word or phrase (typically, the word or phrase to which the index entry refers), or insert the index entry at a single point (typically, when you are referring to a concept under discussion, not necessarily identified by a keyword in the discussion). Then press **Alt + Shift + X**. The Mark Index Entry dialog (Figure 147) will come up.

Figure 147   *Mark Index Entry Dialog*

If you have selected a word or a phrase, that selection will appear in the Main entry text box—you may or may not want to change that. The main entry is the word or phrase under which the item you are marking will appear in the index. Word also allows you to create subentries and sub-subentries in the Subentry text box. For example, you may want a main entry called "SI Units," with sub entries "Base units; Prefixes." Under the subentry "Base units," you might want these sub-subentries: "Length; Mass; Time; Electric current; Thermodynamic temperature; Luminous intensity; Substance amount." The generated index is shown in Figure 148. To create this, you would, for example, enter "SI Units" in the Main entry text box, and "Base units:Mass" in the Subentry text box.

There are some things you should note about this whole process.

Firstly, and quite obviously, spelling counts—every misspelled entry will appear as an entry on its own (in its correct alphabetical order, as misspelled) in the index.

Secondly, and less obviously, case counts too—the index entries are case sensitive. If I were, in different places, to create these two subentries: "Base units:Mass" and "Base units:mass" they would appear as separate subentries in the index (the lowercase "mass" would appear first).

Third, beware of phantom spaces. "Base units:Mass" and "Base units: Mass" will create two separate entries in the index[57].

Fourth, it should be evident from the example that you indicate sub-subentries with the colon. You can create a total of six levels of subentries (i.e., a main entry with six levels of subentries) using these colons. This means that Word allows your index to have a

---

[57] Interestingly, the latter will appear in the index sans the space. Remember this when you start debugging your index (see 9.3.4) and you find inexplicable duplicate entries.

maximum of seven levels[58]. However, just because you can do this, doesn't mean you should. About a sub-subentry (i.e., going down to the third level) should be sufficient in almost all circumstances, and a sub-sub-subentry (i.e., going down to the fourth level) in only very, very extreme cases. You could, by the way, use the colons in the Main entry text box, and skip the Subentry text box entirely (e.g., "SI Units:Base units:Mass" in the Main entry text box).

If you want to index symbol (e.g., % $ # @, etc.), enter the symbol in the Main entry text box and follow it immediately with ;# (semicolon followed by the hash). These symbols will appear at the beginning of the index, and if an index style is chosen which uses headings for each letter of the alphabet, then the heading assigned to the symbols will be the hash (#). Microsoft recommends replacing this with any text you want (e.g., "Symbols"), but of course each time you update the field, this change will be lost. I think a better solution would be to anchor a text box in the same paragraph as the start of the index, and to position it directly over the errant hash, of course floating with its text-wrapping position set to in front of text.

SI Units
   Base units
      Electric current, 16
      Length, 14
      Luminous intensity, 19
      Mass, 14
      Substance amount, 20
      Thermodynamic temperature, 18
      Time, 15
   Prefixes
      deca-, 40
      exa-, 42
      giga-, 41
      hecto-, 40
      kilo-, 41
      mega-, 41
      peta-, 42
      tera-, 42
      yotta-, 43
      zetta-, 42

Figure 148   *Example of an entry with subentries in an index*

In the Options section of the dialog, you can decide how you want the reference to be made. The most commonly used setting, which is also the one selected by default, is the second—Current page. Quite understandably, the index will reference the page on which the mark is made.

---

[58] I find it interesting that Word has nine Index level styles, but for the life of me, in all my testing, I could not get it go lower than the seventh level. I am not too concerned about that, though—from a stylistic perspective, seven levels is already way too much.

The first option in the dialog, Cross-reference, allows you to create cross-references in your index. This is actually a bit more complex than the Word help files seem to indicate. To create a cross-reference entry (e.g., "Current, *see* Electricity"), you have to create two index entry marks[59]. For the first one, create a standard index entry referencing the current page for the item under which you want to see the page number listed (i.e., the item to which the cross-reference points—"Electricity" in my example). Next, create a second index entry mark, this time putting the referring item ("Current" in my example) in the Main entry text box. Then select the Cross-reference option button, and type "Electricity" after the "*See* " in the adjacent text box. You can, of course, replace the "*See* " bit with anything of your choice (e.g., "*Cf.* "), although the standard practice in English indexes is to use *See*. For a fuller discussion of cross-referencing in indexes, see Knight (1988, pp. 109–114). It almost goes without saying that you should, as directed by Knight, check all cross-references carefully.

If an entry runs over a very long section, even several pages (this is typically when you are using a concept as your index marker), you first need to create a bookmark spanning that range (see section 11.2, p. 240), and then under Options in the Mark Index Entry dialog, click on Page range and then select the bookmark from the list (Figure 149). Ironically, these entries can be added almost anywhere in your document, as their location is not referenced, but the bookmark is. I recommend that you follow one of these two strategies to maintain some sense of order: Either try to insert these entries just before the start of the bookmark to which they refer, or insert them all in a central location in your document (e.g., near the end of your document, just before the actual index itself) from where you can access all of them at the same time. I prefer the former, but the latter will also work, and has its own advantages. A tip for actually creating these bookmarks (see section 11.2.3 on p. 241) is to use the name *XEBookmarkName*, so that all bookmarks used for Index references will be found in one place, and then near the bottom of the list in the Bookmark dialog.

---

[59] I find this surprising, unless I totally blew the application of this tool.

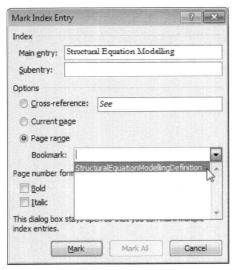

Figure 149   *Adding an index entry to a bookmark*

It should also be noted that when Word finds the same index entry on successive pages, it will not conflate those pages into a single range. Thus, if you want a page range, you must use the bookmark method. The bookmark method also allows the flexibility of having the intervening content change, and having your index reference adapt accordingly.

Some of the settings for your final index can be controlled from the Mark Index Entry dialog as well:

- You can add Bold and/or Italic formatting to the page numbers for the entry you are currently marking. This is typically done to emphasise one of the page references (the one you are currently marking) in the index. You can decide how to apply this, but generally this kind of emphasis (and generally it is using bold text) is done to mark the main or most important reference for that index entry. See Knight (1988, pp. 108–109) for more on this.[60]

- You can right click on the main or sub entry boxes and select Font... (Figure 150) to control their appearance in the final index. Don't do this without good reason, though, as it disrupts the uniform formatting of the index. One instance where you might want to do it is where you would want names to be differentiated by making them italicised. Also note that if you have index entry markers to the same term on various pages, they must all be formatted in the same way for the formatting to be pulled through to the index.

---

[60] I do not think (or could not figure out how to get Word to) that Word can indicate extraordinary references, such as references contained in footnotes (n.) or to illustrations or figures, etc.

Figure 150   *Changing the font of an Index entry*

When you are done with all of these setting we have discussed, click on M̲ark to actually mark your entry. Also note that the Mark Index Entry dialog is a modeless dialog—it stays open, and you can select different words in your text and mark them. This means that you can read through sections of your document, marking things for the index as you read.

9.3.2.2   *Automatically Marking Index Entries*

Before you consider automatically marking your index entries, a word of warning: the idea behind indexing is to mark those pages in which the topic found in the index is discussed and/or explained, not those in which it is merely mentioned. Word, of course, has no way of being able to make this distinction—it just searches for the words you provide. Thus, if you do use any method of automatically marking your index entries, you *must* go through them (cf. 9.3.4) and check that the correct entries only have been marked. You might find it more work to check automatically marked index entries than just to do them by hand.

9.3.2.2.1   Mark All

There are two strategies to speeding up the marking process. The first is found in the Mark Index Entry dialog (Figure 147). If you have a word or phrase that is very clearly a unique jargon term (i.e., it is in only one context, with only one meaning), and that word does not form part of other words (e.g., class forming part of classification), then you can ask Word to find all instances of that word or phrase, and mark it. An example of such a phrase would be "Structural Equation Modelling."

The first step to doing this is to find the term, and to select it (this option does not work of you have not actually selected the term). Open the Mark Index Entry dialog and, after having completed the necessary fields in the dialog (at the very least, the Main e̲ntry text box), instead of clicking on M̲ark, click on Mark A̲ll. Word will then search through your entire document for the phrase, and mark each occurrence for you. Remember again, that this is a case-sensitive search (which means that you just might run into problems if your term is not normally capitalised, but is somewhere used—such as at the start of a sentence—where it is capitalised).

9.3.2.2.2 AutoMark

The second approach to speeding things up is to use an Index Concordance File. But beware, these files are often not worth the effort—they cannot capture concepts, only keywords, and can only be used in contexts where the keyword is absolutely and entirely unambiguous: in other words, most only for jargon terms that have only one meaning, or in exceptional circumstances, words that are used in only one context in your thesis. An Index Concordance File is a simple Word document that contains *only* a two-column table (an example is shown in Figure 151). The first column contains the index entry triggers (i.e., the text you would normally have selected to mark as an index entry). You will have to be very thorough and yet also very specific in creating these entries. For example, you want to find all forms of a word, but you don't want unwanted triggers making it into your index either. Note that these entries are, as in the Mark Index Entry dialog, case sensitive (i.e., for certain words, you would want two rows, one with the capitalised and one with the non-capitalised versions[61]. Word does whole-word searches for these trigger words, so you need not be concerned about that.

The second column of the table contains the text which will appear in the index (i.e., the actual index entry). If you want to enter a subentry in the second column, separate it from the main entry by a colon. To mark your document with the concordance file, open the Index dialog (Instruction set 34, below), and click on the AutoMark... button. Word will then load the File Open dialog, where you can select your concordance file. Word will search for each trigger entry in your document, and mark all the occurrences it finds. As with the Mark All option, it only searches each paragraph until it finds a reference, and then jumps to the next paragraph.

---

[61] Be careful that Word's automatic capitalisation of the first word in a sentence not do you in here.

Love¤	Love¤	¤
Love·style¤	Love:Love·styles¤	¤
Love·styles¤	Love:Love·styles¤	¤
Agape¤	Love:·Love·styles:Agape¤	¤
Eros¤	Love:·Love·styles:Eros¤	¤
Ludus¤	Love:·Love·styles:Ludus¤	¤
Pragma¤	Love:·Love·styles:Pragma¤	¤
Structural·Equation·Modeling¤	Structural·Equation·Modeling¤	¤
Path·Analysis¤	Structural·Equation·Modeling:Path·Analysis¤	¤
Confirmatory·Factor·Analysis¤	Structural·Equation·Modeling:·Confirmatory·Factor·Analysis¤	¤
Fit·Index¤	Structural·Equation·Modeling:Fit·Indices¤	¤
Fit·Indeces¤	Structural·Equation·Modeling:Fit·Indices¤	¤
RMSEA¤	Structural·Equation·Modeling:Fit·Indices:RMSEA¤	¤

Figure 151   *Example of entries in an Index Concordance File*

9.3.2.3   Manually Typing Index Entries

Probably the fastest way to add index entries is just to type them yourself. If you understand the XE field switches (and mostly even if you don't), you can consider adding your index entry fields without the Mark Index Entry dialog. To type an index entry, simply press **Ctrl + F9** to insert the Field braces, and then inside the field braces, type: XE[62] "index main entry:index subentry" followed by any switches you might want to add (mostly no switches are needed, but you can quickly learn the most important one, and if you want to start adding all sorts of options, the dialog might be the better choice). The field switches are summarised in Table 10.

Table 10   **XE Field Switches[63]**

Switch	Usage
\b	Applies bold formatting to the entry's page number in the index, but the switch removes bold formatting if the index style for the entry is bold.
\f "Type"	Defines an entry type ("Type" typically being a single letter), allowing different indexes to be created (e.g., an author index and a subject index). Indexes inserted by using the field { INDEX \f "Type" } (whatever type was defined as) will include only index entries marked for that type. The default entry type is "i."
\i	Applies italic formatting to the entry's page number in the index, but the switch removes italic formatting if the index style for the entry is italic.
\r Bookmark	Lists the range of pages marked by the specified bookmark as the entry's page numbers in the index.
\t "Text"	Inserts the text in place of a page number for that entry in the index. This is typically used for index cross-references.

This technique of manually typing index entries is especially useful if you add your index entries as you type your document, as you can quickly copy a term, add the field,

---

[62] You will notice that as soon as you have typed XE, Word will change the field to hidden text.

[63] Adapted from the Microsoft Word help files http://office.microsoft.com/en-gb/word-help/field-codes-xe-index-entry-field-HP005186216.aspx (Microsoft).

and then paste the term as the index entry in the XE field, without having to worry too much about dialogs. You can then also copy the entire field and paste it elsewhere. If you do this, and even when using the Mark Index Entry dialog, remember not to include a space before the XE field, as the net effect will be that, when the field is hidden, there will still be a space before and after the field, meaning you will have two spaces between the preceding and succeeding words. If you're a stickler for keeping things neat, you could format that preceding space to hidden (easily done with the **Ctrl + Shift +H** keyboard shortcut), but I consider that too much work, and the chances of your missing some increase dramatically.

Application 9.2   ***Keeping Track of Your Index***

Regardless of how you add your index entries, you have to keep the whole thing more or less in your mind, so that you don't, as you progress, have a change of heart concerning a specific topic and inadvertently index it in two or more different places. This can easily happen when you work on a dissertation for two or three years. What you need is a system to keep track of your index as you build it.

Generally, this is how professional indexers do their work: They receive a proof copy of the finalised document, and read through it. Whenever they find a new term that has to be indexed, they write it on an index card, together with the page number. These cards are placed in a sorted container. When a term recurs, they simply add the new page number to the card. When they have worked through the book, the cards, which are already sorted, simply get typed. Of course, there are professional indexing software programs that allow them do to this same process, without the pen and the cards.

Since you will find that most students tend to hand in their thesis right on the very last day of submission, you might not have the time for this. If you want to index, then budget about a week for it.

Alternatively, you could cultivate the disciple of building your index as you type your thesis—it's not perfect, but if you work at it, you can actually make it part of your practice.

Nevertheless, here's a tip for the process: Since you don't have fancy indexing software, building the index as you type the thesis means you need a method of keeping track of the index as it develops. One way of doing this is to periodically generate and update the index (this works best of you are typing the whole dissertation in one document, which I recommend—see section 12.2, p. 270) and then also just scan through it to make sure that everything is still in order.

An alternative is that you could easily duplicate the index in an Excel file, with columns for each level. As the index develops, your Excel file will grow, but you will still be able to see your index in a structured way. Figure 152 shows two such examples, using the same entries shown in Figure 148. Note that I have used Excel's Freeze Panes to lock the column titles in place. There are two examples, the first is structured more like an index, and the second (my preference) uses full entries for each line. This is not actually much more typing work, as Excel's autocomplete feature makes filling in the higher levels a cinch. Also, this structure is more compact, and allows me to sort and filter the index as I want, which is very useful as it grows.

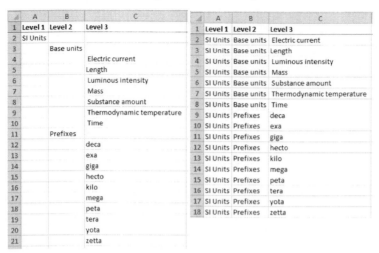

	A	B	C
1	Level 1	Level 2	Level 3
2	SI Units		
3		Base units	
4			Electric current
5			Length
6			Luminous intensity
7			Mass
8			Substance amount
9			Thermodynamic temperature
10			Time
11		Prefixes	
12			deca
13			exa
14			giga
15			hecto
16			kilo
17			mega
18			peta
19			tera
20			yota
21			zetta

	A	B	C
1	Level 1	Level 2	Level 3
2	SI Units	Base units	Electric current
3	SI Units	Base units	Length
4	SI Units	Base units	Luminous intensity
5	SI Units	Base units	Mass
6	SI Units	Base units	Substance amount
7	SI Units	Base units	Thermodynamic temperature
8	SI Units	Base units	Time
9	SI Units	Prefixes	deca
10	SI Units	Prefixes	exa
11	SI Units	Prefixes	giga
12	SI Units	Prefixes	hecto
13	SI Units	Prefixes	kilo
14	SI Units	Prefixes	mega
15	SI Units	Prefixes	peta
16	SI Units	Prefixes	tera
17	SI Units	Prefixes	yota
18	SI Units	Prefixes	zetta

Figure 152   *Tracking an index in Excel*

9.3.3   Creating the index

Instruction set 34   *Opening the Index Dialog*

Keyboard	Alt | S | X
Left click	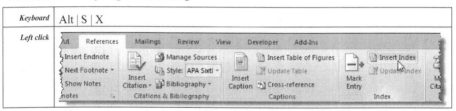

When you want to create the index, simply go to the point where it is to be inserted, and select the Insert Index tool from the Index group of the References ribbon (Instruction set 34). This will display the Index dialog (Figure 153).

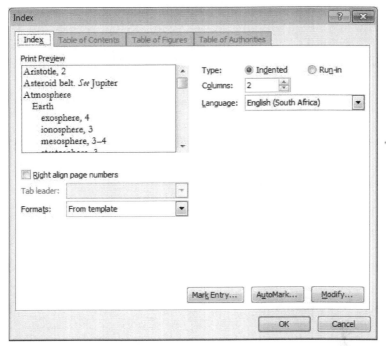

Figure 153   *Index dialog*

The Index dialog is reasonably intuitive to use. Most of the settings relate to the appearance of the final index. You can choose from an Indented or a Run-in index (compared in Figure 154). Further examples of these can be seen in Knight (1988, p. 55). Basically, in the indented index, each sublevel entry is in a line of its own, appropriately indented. In the run-in index, each main entry forms a "paragraph" of its own, with subentries following each other, separated by semicolons. The indented index (my preference) is not nearly as compact as the run-in index, but at the same time it is cleaner and easier to read.

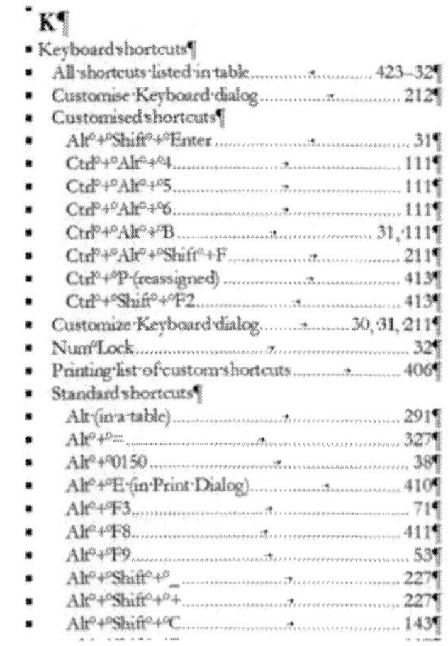

K
- Keyboard shortcuts
  - All shortcuts listed in table 423–32
  - Customise Keyboard dialog 212
  - Customised shortcuts
    - Alt + Shift + Enter 31
    - Ctrl + Alt + 4 111
    - Ctrl + Alt + 5 111
    - Ctrl + Alt + 6 111
    - Ctrl + Alt + B 31, 111
    - Ctrl + Alt + Shift + F 211
    - Ctrl + P (reassigned) 413
    - Ctrl + Shift + F2 413
  - Customize Keyboard dialog 30, 31, 211
  - Num Lock 32
  - Printing list of custom shortcuts 406
  - Standard shortcuts
    - Alt (in a table) 291
    - Alt + = ... 327
    - Alt + 0150 38
    - Alt + E (in Print Dialog) 410
    - Alt + F3 71
    - Alt + F8 411
    - Alt + F9 53
    - Alt + Shift + _ 227
    - Alt + Shift + + ... 227
    - Alt + Shift + C 143

Indented Index

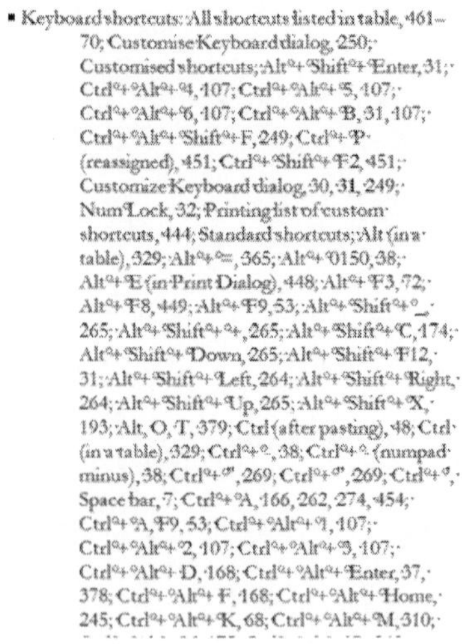

- Keyboard shortcuts: All shortcuts listed in table, 461–70; Customise Keyboard dialog, 250; Customised shortcuts; Alt + Shift + Enter, 31; Ctrl + Alt + 4, 107; Ctrl + Alt + 5, 107; Ctrl + Alt + 6, 107; Ctrl + Alt + B, 31, 107; Ctrl + Alt + Shift + F, 249; Ctrl + P (reassigned), 451; Ctrl + Shift + F2, 451; Customize Keyboard dialog, 30, 31, 249; Num Lock, 32; Printing list of custom shortcuts, 444; Standard shortcuts; Alt (in a table), 329; Alt + =, 365; Alt + 0150, 38; Alt + E (in Print Dialog), 448; Alt + F3, 72; Alt + F8, 449; Alt + F9, 53; Alt + Shift + _, 265; Alt + Shift + +, 265; Alt + Shift + C, 174; Alt + Shift + Down, 265; Alt + Shift + F12, 31; Alt + Shift + Left, 264; Alt + Shift + Right, 264; Alt + Shift + Up, 265; Alt + Shift + X, 193; Alt, O, T, 379; Ctrl (after pasting), 48; Ctrl (in a table), 329; Ctrl + -, 38; Ctrl + - (numpad minus), 38; Ctrl + ", 269; Ctrl + ", 269; Ctrl + ', Space bar, 7; Ctrl + A, 166, 262, 274, 454; Ctrl + A, F9, 53; Ctrl + Alt + 1, 107; Ctrl + Alt + 2, 107; Ctrl + Alt + 3, 107; Ctrl + Alt + D, 168; Ctrl + Alt + Enter, 37, 378; Ctrl + Alt + F, 168; Ctrl + Alt + Home, 245; Ctrl + Alt + K, 68; Ctrl + Alt + M, 310;

Run-in Index

Figure 154 *Indented vs Run-in indexes*

You can also have your index listed in any number of Columns from one to four, or set it to Auto to let Word decide based on the length of the index entries and the width of the page.

Next, in the Formats list box you can choose from one of six predefined index styles or use the nine (three!) Index styles from your document or template. All of the predefined styles, with the exception of the Simple style, include section headings (typically, the first letter of the alphabet). You can also choose whether to allow the page numbers to immediately follow the index entry, or be right aligned, and if right aligned, what tab leader (if any) to use.

If you do use the Index styles, you can again click on Modify to modify the nine Index styles (Figure 155).

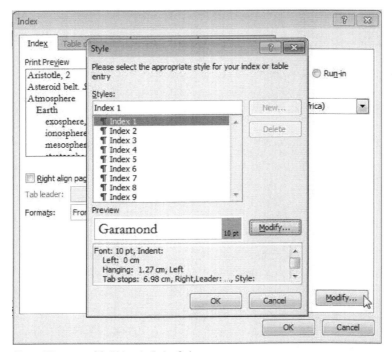

Figure 155   Modifying the Index Styles

Lastly, the Mar<u>k</u> Entry dialog and A<u>u</u>toMark dialogs, which have already been discussed, can be launched from here.

Once you have made the settings you wish, you can click on OK to have the index inserted. The Index can be updated at any time in the same way as any field is updated (**F9** or right click and selected <u>U</u>pdate Field). You can also relaunch the Index dialog from anywhere in your document, and Word will determine that your document has an index already, and will then ask you whether you want to create a new index or replace the existing index (Figure 156).

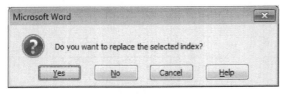

Figure 156   Replace an existing index

If you select <u>Y</u>es, Word will find the existing index and replace it. Of course, if you are creating multiple indexes, then select <u>N</u>o.

9.3.4   Debugging your index

Even the pros rarely get it right the first time. Once you have generated your index, check it carefully to make sure that the entries are in the right order, with the right structure (i.e., levels). If you find any mistakes, it means you made a mistake with the marking[64].

To generally check your index entry marks, you can browse (see Chapter 11) through them by field. First, of course, you have to make sure that your non-printing characters are displayed (see section 3.2.1, p. 38). Then, the simplest method to navigate is to use the Go To dialog (Figure 157) to find the first XE field. Then cancel the dialog, and use Page Up and Page Down (or the browser buttons) to move backwards and forwards between XE entries.

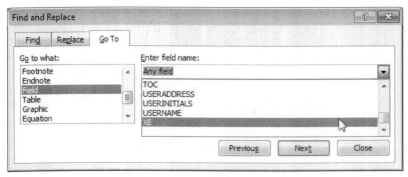

Figure 157   *Go To XE fields*

You could also use the Find dialog to find your index entries (search for "^d XE") and then also browse up and down after the first find. If you know exactly what index entry it is you want to find, you could, for example, search for "^d XE "SI Units:Base units:Mass"" but you can imagine that this might not work if you are looking for an errant entry (e.g., one that has a phantom space in front of, or after, one of the colons). A quicker method might be to go to the page (again, Go To is useful), and then either Go To the XE fields from the top of the page, or turn on field shading (Figure 158) to easily see all the fields on your page, which will allow you to spot the XE entry very quickly.

---

[64] Word, of course, *never* makes mistakes!

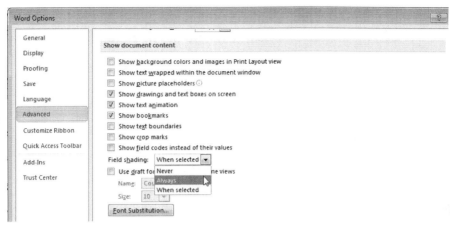

Figure 158   *Word Options: Turning on field shading*

Once the errant XE entry has been found, you can simply edit the XE field (e.g., by deleting the phantom space, changing the case, etc.) to correct it. Then simply update your Index, and the mistake should disappear.

Further customisation of the index (e.g., to create separate author and subject indexes) is possible by using the Index field switches (Table 11).

Table 11   *Index Field Switches*[65]

Switch	Usage
\b Bookmark	Builds an index for the portion of the document marked by the specified bookmark.
\c Columns	Creates an index with more than one column (maximum: four columns) on a page.
\d "Separators"	Used with the \s switch, specifies the characters (up to five) that separate sequence numbers and page numbers. The field { INDEX \s chapter \d ":" } displays page numbers in the format "2:14." A hyphen (-) is used if you omit the \d switch. Enclose the characters in quotation marks.
\e "Separators"	Specifies the characters (up to five) that separate an index entry and its page number. The { INDEX \e "; " } field displays a result such as "Inserting text; 3" in the index. A comma and space (,) are used if you omit the \e switch. Enclose the characters in quotation marks.
\f "Identifier"	Creates an index using only the specified entry type. The index generated by { INDEX \f "a" } includes only entries marked with XE fields such as { XE "Selecting Text" \f "a" }. The default entry type is "I".
\g "Separators"	Specifies the characters (up to five) that separate a range of pages. Enclose the characters in quotation marks. The default is an en dash (–). The field { INDEX \g " to " } displays page ranges as "Finding text, 3 to 4".
\h "Heading"	Inserts text formatted with the Index Heading style between alphabetic groups in the index. Enclose the text in quotation marks. The field { INDEX \h "—A—" } displays the appropriate letter before each alphabetic group in the index. To insert a blank line between groups, use empty quotation marks: \h "".
\k "Separators"	Specifies the characters that separate an index entry and its cross reference. The { INDEX \k ": " } field displays a result such as "Inserting text: See Editing" in the index. A period and space (.) are used if you omit the \k switch. Enclose the characters in quotation marks.
\l "Separators"	Specifies the characters that separate multiple-page references. The default characters are a comma and a space (,). You can use up to five characters, which must be enclosed in quotation marks. The field { INDEX \l " or " } displays entries such as "Inserting text, 23 or 45 or 66" in the index.
\p "Range"	Compiles an index for the specified letters. The field { INDEX \p a-m } generates an index for only the letters A through M. To include entries that begin with characters other than letters, use an exclamation point (!). The index generated by { INDEX \p !--t } includes any special characters, as well as the letters A through T.
\r	Runs subentries into the same line as the main entry. Colons (:) separate main entries from subentries; semicolons (;) separate subentries. The field { INDEX \r } displays entries such as "Text: inserting 5, 9; selecting 2; deleting 15".
\s	When followed by a sequence name, includes the sequence number with the page number. Use the \d switch to specify a separator character other than the default, which is a hyphen (-).
\y	Enables the use of yomi text for index entries.
\z	Defines the language ID that Microsoft Word uses to generate the index.

[65] Copied from the Microsoft Word help files (2012): http://office.microsoft.com/en-za/word-help/field-codes-index-field-HA102017394.aspx.

9.3.5 Formatting the index

When the index is inserted (cf. Figure 153, p. 207), the Formats option allows you to choose from any of the built-in Word Index styles. However, these many not be to your liking. You can create your own format for the index by modifying the different Index styles (Index 1 to Index 9, and Index Heading, if used). This was alluded to in the discussion of Figure 155.

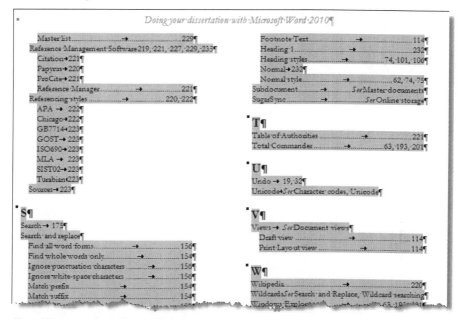

Figure 159   Poorly formatted index

However, it might be useful to see this in action. Figure 159 shows an early draft of the index used for this book. Note that for very short items, the page numbers are not correctly aligned (this is because of a silly default ½ inch (1.27cm) tab stop added by Word. I modified two groups of settings for each of the styles Index 1 to Index 3: I set the paragraph to keep its lines together, and to have, successively, 0cm, 0.5cm, and 1cm left indents, and always to have a 1cm hanging indent. I also formatted the Index Heading style. The I reinserted the index, using the template styles for the formatting. Next, I edited the field codes (Figure 160) to add the heading (working from the template, the option to add a heading is not available in the dialog).

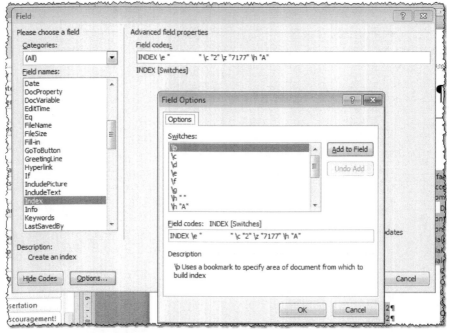

Figure 160   *Editing field codes for the Index field*

The end result can be seen in Figure 161, where the effect is much more organised and legible.

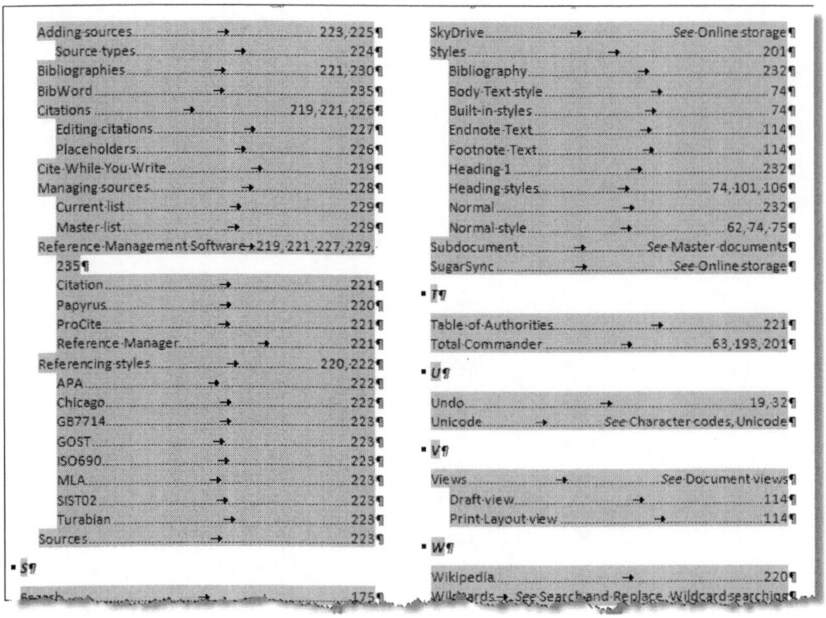

Figure 161   *Properly formatted index*

214

Chapter 10
Lost and Found: Search and replace

It is difficult to separate the Search and Replace functioning of Word from Word's document navigation, as the two are so integrally linked. What I want to do here is elaborate on the Search functioning, without repeating what was said there. I hope you will realise that Word's search functionality is far more powerful than you could have imagined. Many people specify far too uncomplicated search criteria, with the result that they have to wade through a whole litany of false positives before they find what they are actually looking for, which can waste hours of time, when accumulated. Creating complex search criteria does take a little time (you actually have to think), but will probably save time overall by cutting down on the false positives, and is also a mentally stimulating activity (did I mention that you actually have to think?).

10.1   Replacing

Note that in most of this chapter, the focus will be on searching, but remember that replacing just takes the concept one step further—instead of just searching for something (which, of course, is often a suitable goal in and of itself), now we are searching for something, and replacing it with something else. More specific focus will be given to the replace part of the equation in the sections discussed after Standard searching.

Some simple things can be briefly said about replacing, though. The dialog (Figure 162) allows three options when being used. Firstly, you can select Replace All to scan through the whole document, finding all instances of whatever you have specified in the Find what text box with whatever you have specified in the Replace with text box. This can be dangerous if you are not certain that you have specified the search exactly right, but is, conversely, an extremely powerful and efficient way of executing the task. If you are not certain, you can step through each instance where Word finds what you have specified, and decide for yourself whether to do the replacement (by selecting Replace) or pass it over (by selecting Find Next).

Figure 162   *Replace dialog*

A last tip to remember before discussing the specifics of searching is that Word's replace actions can, generally, be undone. If you see that your search and replace has made a mess of things, you can either undo the changes (Word will let you undo them one at a time with the **Ctrl + Z** keyboard shortcut or from the Undo button or Undo stack on the QAT. Note that you can undo replaces one by one if you did them one by one, but if you used Replace All, then all that you can undo is the Replace All. Alternatively, for very complex searches, you can save the document before doing the replace (generally a good idea), and can then simply close the document without saving, and then re-open it and start again.

10.2   Standard searching

Instruction set 35   Accessing the Find and Replace dialog (Advanced Find)

Shortcut	No direct keyboard shortcut any more, but can be created (see section 2.3.2, p. 30), or use Ctrl + H for Replace, or Ctrl + G for Go To
Keyboard	Alt | H | FD | A
Left click	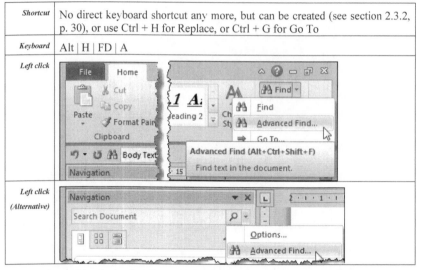
Left click (Alternative)	

Standard searching is the function most Word users are familiar with. Word can search for certain things, and replace them with others. So far so good. As was discussed in the previous chapter, the Find and Replace dialog now needs to be accessed in a more round-about manner (Instruction set 41), although I did present alternatives to getting hold of it quicker.

Figure 163   Find and Replace dialog

To understand standard searching, it helps to understand the Find and Replace dialog (Figure 163). In its simplest form, the dialog asks what you want to search for, and then offers some basic options for where or how to find it. Firstly, the F<u>i</u>nd In button allows you to decide whether you want to search in the main document text, or in the document's footnotes and/or endnotes (which options you see will depend on which of these exist in the document).

The F<u>i</u>nd Next button allows you to move to each successive instance of what it is you entered in the Fi<u>n</u>d what text box.

<u>R</u>eading Highlight allows you to highlight all instances of the search term entered in the Fi<u>n</u>d what text box, as can be seen in Figure 164, with the result shown in Figure 165. Word will indicate how many instances were found, and will highlight them all. You can still navigate between them with the F<u>i</u>nd Next button, but the fact that they are highlighted makes them easier to spot as you move through the document. As was discussed in Chapter 11, you can also dispense with the dialog and navigate through the found instances with the object browser or **Ctrl + Page Up** and **Ctrl + Page Down**— Word will keep all found instances highlighted until such time as you make an edit to the document.

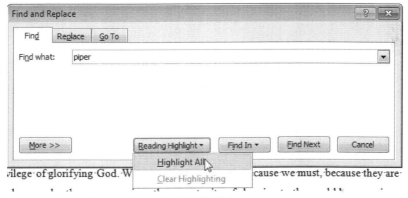

Figure 164 *Find and Replace: Reading Highlight*

to demonstrate? John Piper, in his profound book *Don't waste your life,* (2007:53) asks "Can work and leisure and relationships and eating and lovemaking and ministry all really flow from a single passion? Can sex and cars and work and war and changing diapers and doing taxes really have a God-exalting, soul-satisfying unity?" Then he answers, "Now we see that every experience in life is designed to magnify the cross of Christ, or… to magnify Christ and him crucified."¶

Paul, on whose writings much of Piper's argument is based, shows that (as was already alluded to in section 4.15.2),

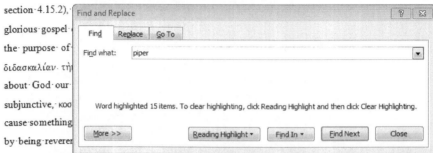

are given the privilege of glorifying God. We do not do these things because we must, because they are commanded, but because by them we are given the opportunity of showing to the world how precious God is to us. Piper (2007:31), again, explains "God created me—and you—to live with a single, all-embracing, all-transforming passion—namely, a passion to glorify God by enjoying and displaying his supreme excellence in all the spheres of life." When we live the way God has called us to, we show to

Figure 165   *Find and Replace: Reading Highlight result*

However, note that Word's Find and Replace can do much (much!) more. To discover some of these options, click on the More button at the bottom left of the dialog to expand the dialog (the dialog can be collapsed again with the same button, which will have changed to Less). This reveals a host of additional options (Figure 166) which can be used to refine your search.

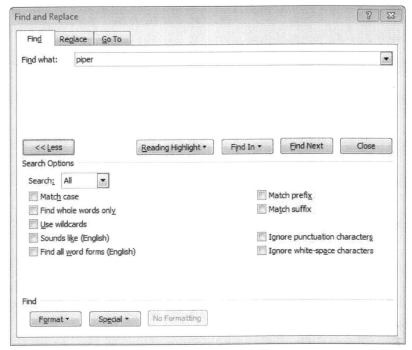

Figure 166   *Find and Replace dialog showing all options*

First, you can specify the search direction in the Search: list box. All is the default, and you can specify in addition to either search Up or Down. Note that whenever you perform a search, Word records the point at which the I-Beam is situated (if you have made a selection, the search is restricted to the selected area). Word will then search from that point to the end or beginning of the document (depending on the search direction you specify), and will then ask you whether you would like to continue search from the beginning (or end, as the case may be) of the document (Figure 167). If you select Yes, Word will then resume the search from the beginning (or end, as the case may be) of the document until it reaches the I-beam position it recorded.

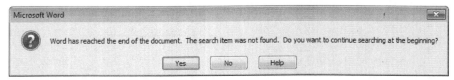

Figure 167   *Search has reached document end*

The slight semantic difference between setting the search direction to All (the default) and Up or Down is that generally, All will work the same as Down, but if you were to search for something that does not exist in the document, All will search through to the end of the document and will then automatically resume at the beginning, until it reaches the recorded I-beam position. Down, by contrast, will first ask you whether you want to resume at the beginning of the document. In either instance, Word will eventually report to you that it could not find the item you are looking for (Figure 169).

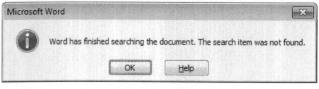

Figure 168   *Search has reached document end*

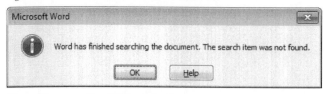

Figure 169   *Search item not found*

Second, you can indicate whether the item you are searching for must match on case. This is useful when, for example, someone has a name that also functions as a regular word (Joe Soap and John Doe both having such surnames), or when an acronym (which would be capitalised) could also be a regular word. Note that when the Match case option is not selected, Word intelligently searches for, and replaces your search item. For example, if you enter a term as lower case (or upper case) and enter the replacement term in lower or upper case, and Word finds the word and it is not capitalised, it will replace it with an uncapitalised version, and if it is capitalised, it will replace it with a capitalised version.

Third, the Find whole words only option allows you to limit the search to instances where the word you typed exists as a whole word (thus, for example, if you searched for "fill," it would not find it in "filled," etc.). This option is only available when the search term you have entered contains no spaces or other punctuation (i.e., it really must be a single word—not even hyphenated words are allowed).

Fourth, across from this option are a further two settings that can actually be seen to work in conjunction with this. The Match prefix and Match suffix options search for your search term as either the start of a word (prefix) or the end of a word (suffix). These options should thus rather be read as "Match start of word" and "Match end of word" as they do not search for prefixes and suffixes in the grammatical sense. Interestingly, these two options are available for multiple-word search terms. And furthermore, note that you can select either or both of these, but that when you select both, it is not an OR operation, but an AND operation—i.e., selecting both is the same as selecting Find whole words only, with the exception that it is a way of specifying a sort of "Find multiple whole words only" (e.g., if you want to find "and it," but not "hand it66" and not "and its" nor "and it's"). These three options (Find whole words

---

[66] For example, in the sentence "Hand it over."

220

only and Match prefix and Match suffix) are useful in the sense that you can exclude a lot of unnecessary finds through using them, thus saving a fair amount of time. To give you a bit more of a feel for how they actually work, Table 12 provides a comparison of what will and will not be found in certain conditions when these options are activated.

Table 12   *Comparison of Whole Word, Prefix and Suffix Matching*

Search for	Mail				Male		
In	mail	mailman	mailbox	blackmail	male	malevolent	female
Whole word only	Yes	No	No	No	Yes	No	No
Match prefix	Yes	Yes	Yes	No	Yes	Yes	No
Match suffix	Yes	No	No	Yes	Yes	No	Yes
Match prefix and suffix	Yes	No	No	No	Yes	No	No

Application 10.1   *Matching whole words*

There are, of course, many instances where you do not want to turn the Match whole words only option on, but the only result from having it on when you should have it off is that you might not find all the instances you were looking for (this should not be considered an insignificant problem, though!). However, forgetting to turn it on when you should actually have it on can lead to more serious problems:

I once had a group of students who had to submit a research protocol. They consistently used the word "we" when referring to themselves. Then their study leader (correctly) told them that they should use a more formal style, and refer to themselves as "the researchers." They thought the solution would be easy—search for "we" and replace with "the researchers." However, they forgot to turn the Match whole word only option on. And so, apart from (correctly) changing "we" to "the researchers," other words were incorrectly changed—words like "between" became "betthe researchersen," "week" became "the researchersek," and many other such confounding errors!

A friend also told me that in a document he was working on, he had to change the word "class" to "subject" and also omitted the Match whole word only option, thus inadvertently also changing "classification to "subjectification" (and the original word "classification" had appeared in a whole number of places in his document!).

Fifth, and while on the topic of delimiting your search to whole words, or the beginning or ending of words, it is worth examining the next two options together. Ignore punctuation characters allows you to ignore punctuation in words. Sometimes, you wrote a word, and can't recall whether you spelled it as a compound word or whether hyphenated (e.g., is it "world-wide" or "worldwide"?). You can enter "worldwide" in the Find what box, and select Ignore punctuation characters to find both. You could also, if you wanted to replace all instances of world-wide with "worldwide," type the same word "worldwide" into both the Find what and Replace with boxes, and activate this option. You might wonder why not just search for "world-wide" and replace with "worldwide," but that will not find "world¬wide" (i.e., "world[optional hyphen]wide").

Furthermore, this option allows you to skip over a whole range of punctuation characters67: . , / ? ! : ; ' " - – - ¬. Then, note that it will ignore any number of punctuation characters, whether repetitions of the same character or even combinations of the different characters. Thus, a search for "11" with this setting activated will also find, for example, "1.,/?!:;'"—1."

The Ignore white-space characters allows you to skip spaces, tabs, and ¼ em spaces (but, interestingly, not em spaces, en spaces, or nonbreaking spaces).

Also, note that these two options (Ignore punctuation characters and Ignore white-space characters) can be used together. You may, for example, want to find places where two words occur after each other, even if one is at the end of a sentence and the other at the start of the next sentence. It may seem odd, but typing those two words immediately after each other, with no space separating them, and activating both of these options, will find them.

Sixth, Word offers you two options for, for want of a better term, "grammatical" searches, but only (currently) in English. Note, though, that the two options are mutually exclusive—you cannot activate both at the same time. The Sounds like option allows you to search for homophones. The words "mail" and "male" in Table 12 are an example. Searching for either, and activating this option, will find both.

The Find all word forms will search for different conjugations of a word. But note that it does not search for others words based on the same root. Thus, searching for all word forms of "love" will find love[68], loving, loved, and loves, but none of lover, lovely, lovingly, lovable, loveless, or lovelorn. So be very certain of what you expect it to find. A simple search for "lov" would, of course, find all of those, but for a word like find which conjugates to found in the past tense, this option can be very useful.

Seventh, and last, the Use wildcards option deserves its own treatise, and will be discussed in section 10.4 below.

10.3 Formatted searching

Apart from all the different criteria you can use for searching, Word also allows you to further refine the search, or empower the replacement, by adding formatting to the mix. In fact, by leaving the Find what box empty, you can search for any text with the specified formatting.

The formatting settings are accessed from the Format button at the lower left of the expanded Find and Replace dialog (Figure 170).

---

[67] The full list is: Period, comma, forward slash, question mark, exclamation mark, colon, semicolon, single inverted comma, double inverted comma, hyphen, en dash, nonbreaking hyphen and optional hyphen. Interestingly, em dashes are not included.

[68] Obviously!

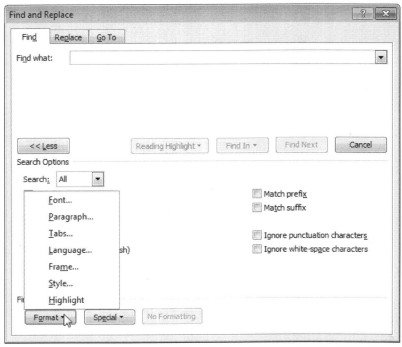

Figure 170   *Search and Replace: Formatting*

As is evident from this list, a whole gamut of formatting options can be searched for:

☐ Font   ☐ Tabs   ☐ Frame   ☐ Highlight
☐ Paragraph   ☐ Language   ☐ Style

Each option from the menu opens the corresponding dialog, which you can then use to set the formatting you want to search for. Note that when you do this, the dialogs will be opened "empty," meaning that all the settings have been deactivated. This can be seen in Figure 171, where the Font dialog was opened from this menu. Firstly, note that the dialog title reflects the context: Find Font. Secondly, note that the Font, Font style, and all the other settings are empty. What this means is that, for example, if the Font list box left unchanged, you would be searching for text with any font. However, the minute you choose a font, you will be searching only for text formatted in that font. Furthermore, the check boxes are blocked out. What this means is that they will be ignored. If, however, you check them, you will search for text formatted like that, and if you uncheck them, you will search for text not formatted like that. To make this concrete, let's use the Strikethrough setting. If left in the state it is in in Figure 171, Word will find text that both is or is not struck through. However, if the option is clicked, the check box will be marked, and Word will find text which is struck through, but not text which is not struck through. If the option is clicked a third time, the check box will be unmarked, meaning that Word will find text which not struck through, but not text which is struck through. Thus, you effectively have three choices for these options: Ignore, with, or without.

Figure 171   *Setting font formatting for a search*

This simply means that you can search for things formatted according to some or other specification, which you set from one or more of the dialogs. Note that you can also replace whatever it is you are searching for with something else which can, optionally, be formatted differently. For example, Figure 172 shows how any text, regardless of what it is, that is formatted in the Times New Roman font, Bold, 12pt, Left aligned, in US English, is replaced with the same text (i.e., because both Find what and Replace with are blank, the text itself stays unchanged), but now in the Body Text style, and with South African English (this last language setting is actually superfluous, as language is also set under the style, but is done here for the sake of the example).

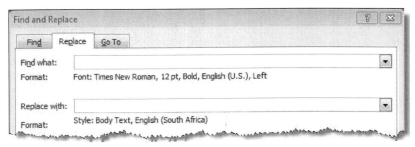

Figure 172   Finding and replacing formatting

This ability to search for text according to how it is formatted is very useful. As a simple practical example, if you have hidden text in your document, you can later search for it using this method (just leave Find what blank and set the font formatting to Hidden). This, combined with the ability to navigate between finds as discussed in section 11.1 (p. 239), makes this extremely effective.

As a further example that uses paragraph formatting, Figure 173 shows how the search and replace mentioned in Application 8.3 (p. 165) can be done.

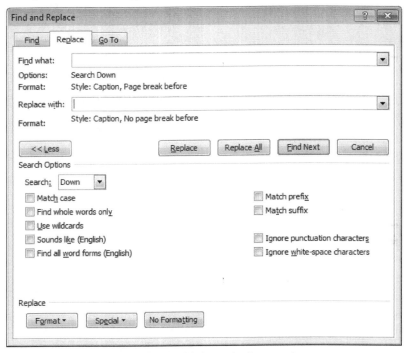

Figure 173   Removing the Page break before setting from a caption

10.4   Special characters

Word has a list of special characters that you can search for, and replace with. These are very useful, as they add yet another dimension to Word's search and replace capabilities. These can be typed manually (if you know them), or selected from the Special button in the lower portion of the extended Find and Replace dialog (Figure 174).

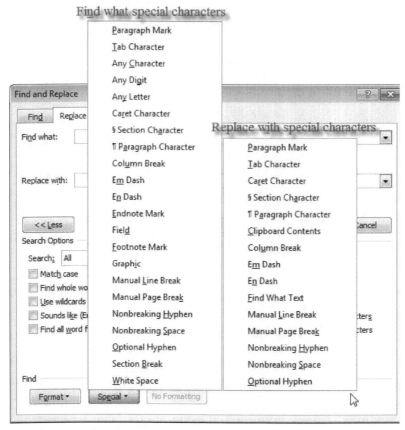

Figure 174   *Special characters for find and replace*

I will not discuss the use of each special character, as once you have understood the principle, you should be able to extend it to each different character. Using this, you can, for example easily remove manual page breaks, multiple instances of hard-carriage returns (e.g., Search for "^p^p" and replace with "^p"), nonbreaking characters, etc. Or you may have pasted information from a statistical package's output into Word, and find that the text is tab separated, but that an unequal number of tabs separates information on various lines. You can then use this to trim down unnecessary tabs. You could, as another example, replace section breaks with page breaks. In short, the possibilities with this are legion. You should note that some of these can be used to simulate Go To functions, although, if a Go To function exists, it would be better to use that (e.g., instead of using Find to find section breaks, simply use Go To to move to sections). Figure 175 shows one final example, where output from a statistical package has been pasted into Word. The idea is to convert this into a table, but Word will not be able to do this accurately with the differing amounts of spaces. However, searching for white space (^w), and replacing with tabs (^t), will leave the data with exactly one tab between each element, which will result in a very easy format for Word to then convert into a table.

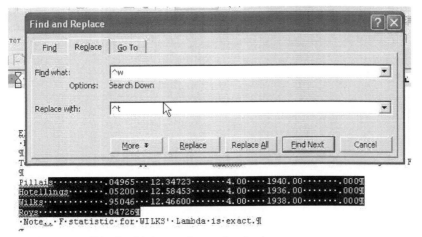

Figure 175   *Using Special characters in a search and replace*

It sometimes speeds things up to know the codes that Word uses for special characters (instead of having to select them with the mouse from the Special list each time). Below is a list of the most common codes (Table 13), modified (and quoted) from information provided by Microsoft (). Note that the items in the table have been re-organised into conceptual groups (thus they do not reflect the exact order from Word's list as shown in Figure 174). The Item column refers to what you would be searching for or replacing with. The Code column shows you the code you would type in, or the code Word inserts when you select the item from the Special list. The Find and Replace columns indicate whether the item may be used in the "Find What" and "Replace with" text boxes (some may be used in both, some in only one of the two). The Wildcards column indicates whether the code will work with pattern matching (aka wildcard searching—cf. 10.4). This means, by implication, that all of these codes can be used for string matching (i.e., standard searches). Where codes cannot be used with pattern matching, and alternatives exist, they are given in the last column. It should be noted here that pattern matching makes no distinction between manual page breaks and section breaks, and between footnote and endnote markers. Additional comments are given at the end of the table. Also note that some of the items in Table 13 are not in the list shown from the Special button.

Word can also search for characters by their character code. If you know the ANSI, ASCII or Unicode codes for a certain character (these can be found in the Symbol dialog, for example), then you can search for, and/or replace with, these characters by specifying their codes.

Table 13   Special Character Codes for Search and Replace

Item	Code	Find	Replace	Wildcards	(Wildcard) alternative
Paragraph Mark	^p	Yes	Yes	No	^13
Tab Character	^t	Yes	Yes	Yes	^9
White Space[a]	^w	Yes	No	No	" {1,}" or " @"
Nonbreaking Space	^s	Yes	Yes	Yes	
Nonbreaking Hyphen	^~	Yes	Yes	Yes	
Optional Hyphen[b]	^-	Yes	Yes	Yes	
Em Dash	^+	Yes	Yes	Yes	
En Dash	^=	Yes	Yes	Yes	
Any Character[c]	^?	Yes	No	Yes	?
Any Digit	^#	Yes	No	No	
Any Letter	^$	Yes	No	No	
Caret Character	^^	Yes	Yes	Yes	
§Section Character	^%	Yes	Yes	No	
¶Paragraph Character	^v	Yes	Yes	No	
Column Break	^n	Yes	Yes	Yes	^14
Manual Line Break	^l	Yes	Yes	Yes	^11
Manual Page Break	^m	Yes	Yes	Yes	^12[d]
Section Break	^b	Yes	No	No	^12
Endnote Mark	^e	Yes	No	No	^2
Footnote Mark	^f	Yes	No	No	^2
Graphic[e]	^g	Yes	No	Yes	^1
Field[f]	^d	Yes	No	No	
Opening field brace[f]	^19	Yes	Yes		
Closing field brace[f]	^21	Yes	Yes		
Comment	^a	Yes	Yes		^5
Clipboard Contents	^c	No	Yes	Yes	
Find What Text[g]	^&	No	Yes	Yes	\n[h]
ANSI characters	^0nnn[i]	Yes	Yes	Yes	
ASCII characters	^nnn[i]	Yes	Yes	Yes	
Unicode characters	^Unnnn[i]	Yes	Yes		
Em Space (Unicode)	^u8195	Yes	Yes	Yes	
En Space (Unicode)	^u8194	Yes	Yes	Yes	

b: Any combination of regular and nonbreaking spaces, and tab characters.

c: If you include the optional hyphen code, Word finds only text with optional hyphens in the position you specified.
   If you omit the optional hyphen code, Word finds all matching text, including text with optional hyphens.

d: I.e., letters and digits.

e: Also finds or replaces section breaks when wildcards are on.

f: If you're searching for graphics, Word finds only inline graphics; Word does not find floating graphics (by default, Word inserts imported graphics as inline graphics, but you can change a floating graphic to an inline graphic). Go To–Graphic locates both inline and floating graphics.

g: If you're searching for fields, you must display field codes. To switch between displaying field codes and field results, click the field, and press SHIFT+F9. To show or hide field codes for all fields in the document, press ALT+F9. Go To–Field locates all fields, regardless of whether field codes are displayed or not.

h: I.e., the contents of the Find What text box.

i: Where n is the grouping number (see 10.5 below).

j: Where nnn is the character code.

Application 10.2   Special characters not in the list

If there is a character that is not on the list (e.g., a symbol added with the Symbol dialog, such as ▢), you can copy it from the text, and paste it in the relevant window. A tip in this regard is to copy both characters (e.g., if you want to replace ® with ™, then type ®™ *(Ctrl + Alt + R, Ctrl + Alt + T) copy it, open the Find and Replace dialog, paste into the Find what box and delete the ™, then paste into the Replace with box and delete the ®). Note that this exact example is actually a bit spurious, as Word actually allows you to type the keyboard shortcuts into the Find what and Replace with boxes, although the Insert Symbol dialog is not accessible there.*

10.5   Wildcard searching

What most people do not know is that Word actually has two distinct "search engines." The one that has been described up to now is the string search engine. However, in the Search Options of the Find and Replace dialog (Figure 166), you will see the check box Use wildcards. This option actually tells Word to switch to its other search engine, the pattern search engine, which is much, much more powerful.

The pattern matching process works as follows:

- You may use normal text and characters as with string searching, but all characters are case sensitive (i.e., searching for A is not the same as searching for a)—thus, the Match case options is not available when you have selected to use wildcard searching. Also, in normal searching, Word ignores "smart" formatting—e.g., " and " and " are all equivalent. In wildcard searching, they are all unique. If you want to include and "smart" character formatting, you need to copy those characters from the text, and paste them into the Find dialog.

- Word uses special placeholders as well. Thus ? represents any single character and * represents any number of characters, even none. So a search for "n?d" (without the quotes, of course) would find "nod" but not "need," and a search for "n*d" would find both of them, as well as "end," "knowledge," and even an "n" and a "d" separated by a few words, such as "... knew it was bad."

- Word allows you to search for variable characters (i.e., any one of a set of characters), when they are placed within brackets. Note that Word will search for any one of the characters included in one set of brackets. Thus [A] will search for only an uppercase A, [a] will search for only a lowercase a (both of these are superfluous, since the brackets can be omitted for the same effect), and [Aa] will search, not for two As, but for an A regardless of case. [ABC] will find "A," "B" or "C" but only in upper case.

- You may include ranges inside the square brackets. Thus [A-C] will search for upper case A or B or C, and [3-5] will search for 3, 4 or 5, and [A-C3-5] will search for upper case A, B, C as well as 3, 4 or 5. Also, [A-Z] searches for any capital letter, and [0-9] searches for any single digit number.

- To search for multiple instances of a character, a set of characters, or a list of variable characters, follow the specification with the number of instances in braces. Thus "[A]" finds only a single uppercase "A," while "[A]{3}" will find only "AAA" and "[A]{1,3}" will find "A," "AA" or "AAA," and "[A]{1,}" (no upper limit specification) will find "A," "AA," "AAA," "AAAA" or any number of uppercase As, as no upper limit is given. This could be useful when you are searching for characters (such as spaces) which could appear in any number. The lower limit need not, of course, be 1, but the largest number that may be used for either the lower or the upper limit is 255. Thus, just to illustrate (the search itself is meaningless, as it will find anything), searching for any 256 characters like this: "?{256}" will result in an error, but "?{255}" will not.

📖 @ represents {1,} (i.e., any number of the preceding character), but it does not represent {2,} (i.e., two or more of the preceding character) or any other specification with a lower limit other than 1.

📖 Quantity specifications—{*lower limit,upper limit*}—should be used with care after other special wildcard characters, as the results may not be what was expected. For example, "n?{2}d" is not understood by Word as "n??d" but rather as "n*d". The correct specification for a n followed by any two characters, and then a d, is: "(n)(?){2}(d)".

📖 You can use the square brackets together with the exclamation point (as the first character in the brackets) to create exclusions. Thus [!A-C] will search for any characters except upper case A, B or C.

When special characters are used in exclusions, they need not be preceded by the backslash (see below).

📖 < allows you to search for strings beginning a word. Thus "<n*d" will find "need" but not "knowledge," whereas "n*d" would find both.

📖 > allows you to search for strings ending a word. Thus "es>" will find "searches" but not "escape," whereas "es" would find both.

📖 < and > can be used together (but obviously not directly after each other). If, for example, you were looking for the date of a reference that started with 198 (i.e., only references in the 1980s), you could specify it as "<198[0-9]>" This would prevent you from finding numbers in other places (e.g., in your statistical results), as this search specifies a four digit number, beginning with "1", followed directly by "98" and ending with a single digit. Thus "<198[0-9]>" would find "1989" but not "198934," and not "11989," whereas "198[0-9]" would find all three.

📖 You can use parentheses to group your search items, so as to specify the order of evaluation or to re-arrange them in the replacing process (where they are referred to without the parentheses). For evaluation, "<re*ing>" will search for a word beginning with an "r", followed by an "e" with any number of characters in between, and ending with a "g" (but preceded by "in"). "<(re)*(ing)>" will search for any word beginning with "re" and ending with "ing," and with any number of characters in between (although these will be functionally equivalent, it is important to understand the difference).

📖 To search for special wildcard characters—!@*()-[]{}\<>?—precede the character with a backslash. Thus \\ will search for a single backslash. A search for any punctuation marks at the end of sentences will thus look as follows: "[.\!\?]"

📖 For re-ordering in replacement, you first need to group your search items with parentheses, as just discussed, and then use the numeric index of the group preceded by a backslash, to reorder the items. For example, you could search for "(Stone)(,)([0-9]{4})" (i.e., Stone followed by a comma and a space, and then any four digit number—a date reference), and then replace it with "\1:\3 (i.e., Stone followed by a colon and then the date (the four-digit number) found together with Stone). Thus "Stone, 1986" would be replaced with "Stone:1986" and "Stone, 2002" would be replaced with "Stone:2002."

Please note that a bug exists in Word—this re-ordering sometimes fails when you have track changes (discussed in Chapter 14) turned on. For example, when I tried to replace "(.)([A-Z])" with ". \2" Word reversed it, and put my group 2 in first, and then the period and two spaces. Changing the specification to replacing "(.)( )([A-Z])" with "\1 \2" resulted in Word replacing my period, single space and character with a period, two spaces, and no character! Turning Track changes off resulted in the correct search and replace. Similarly, a search to replace "([!])('n [A-Z])"—not a space, followed by a space, 'n, another space, and any upper case character—with "\1 \2"—Group 1, a space, and then Group 2, results in Group 1 and Group 2 being added directly, and then the space after Group 2. Yet another failed Search and Replace was "([0-9])(-)([0-9])" with "\1–\3." In essence, Word is tracking the change even as the search and replace function is executing it, which is what leads to this incorrect change. Generally, I don't think it is a good idea to do wildcard search and replace with track changes on.

However, taking this further, the simple fact is that when you are doing these kind of search and replaces, you shouldn't necessarily select the Replace All option unless you are very sure, from experience, that you will get the desired result. It's better to first replace a couple individually, until you are certain that you are going to get what you want, before going for the Replace All option. When I saw Word doing this, I used the search specification to find the first instance, then cancelled the dialog, and used the **Ctrl + Page Down** shortcut to find each occurrence, and changed them manually—tedious, unnecessary, but still better than searching by hand! Alternatively, do the search and replace with Track Changes off, if you can.

📖 Finally, a limitation of wildcard searching is that it makes no distinction between manual page breaks and section breaks (when the ^12 code is used in the Replace with box, Word replaces with page breaks), and between footnote and endnote markers.

Figure 176 shows one example of a wildcard search and replace. In a document in which two spaces are used after the period, the writer has accidentally placed two spaces in between some other words mid-sentence. A search and replace is used to find two spaces, and the specification—using the ! for "not"—excludes two spaces found after a period, a question mark, an exclamation mark, a colon, and a right double quote (note that the smart quote is copied from the document text and pasted in, as wildcard searching distinguishes between plain and smart quotes, and thus also between left and right smart quotes). Also note that the replace specification is followed by a single space, which is, understandably, not visible in Figure 176.

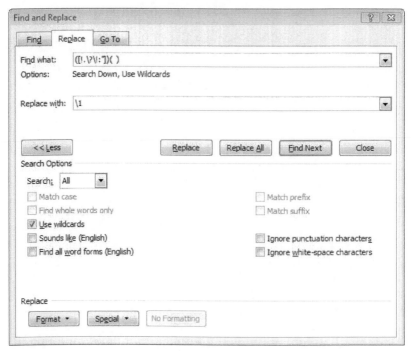

Figure 176   *Wildcard Search and Replace example*

Note that a limited number of special characters can also be accessed when doing wildcard searching, as can be seen in Figure 177. These were discussed in Table 13, which also shows some alternatives that can be used for certain characters.

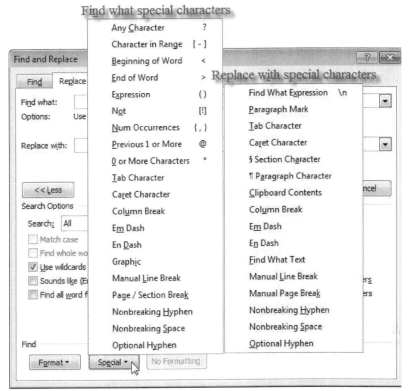

Figure 177   *Special characters for find and replace when using Wildcards*

Application 10.3   *Practical wildcard searches*

Because wildcard searching can be so intimidating, I have decided to show some practical examples, and if you work through these examples, you may learn better how to do it yourself. I will start with easy examples, and gradually make it more complex. Bear in mind that for many of these examples, you would have to select the block of text in question (and these are not shown) before performing the search and replace.

Example 1:

A numbered list has been pasted into Word, and the writer wants to strip away the numbers. The search specification is [0-9]{1,2}. {1,} which is any 1- or 2-digit number, followed by a period, and one or more spaces. The replace with box is left empty, and so the numbers, together with their following periods and spaces, are removed.

Example 2:

A table of numbers has been pasted into Word, and the numbers use the commas as the thousands separator, which the student wants removed. The search criterion is: ([1-9]{1,2})(,)([0-9]{3}) which consists of three groups: The first group is any 1- or 2-digit

233

number (the student knows the largest value is less than one hundred thousand). The second group is just the comma, and the third is a 3-digit number (which it must be if the total number is greater than a thousand). The replacement criterion is \1\3 which is simply the first part of the number, and the next part of the number, skipping the comma.

Example 3:

A section of text pasted into Word from a website has a paragraph mark at the end of each line (and thus two at the end of each paragraph). Replacing every paragraph mark with nothing will result in one huge block of text, and the original "paragraphs" will have been completely lost. By specifying (^13)([!^13]) in the Find what box, and \2 in the replace with box, the job is done. The search specification creates two groups: A paragraph mark, followed immediately by anything but a paragraph mark. The replacement is with only the second group—whatever it is that was found, and this strips away the paragraph mark, but only where it is not immediately followed by another paragraph mark.

Example 4:

The writer capitalised the word "biblical" throughout his document, only to discover, in a style guide, that it should not be capitalised. He needs to change all instances of "Biblical" to "biblical" except, understandably, those at the beginning of a sentence. By searching for ([!.\?\!"])(Biblical), and replacing with \1 biblical, the problem is easily solved. The search criterion contains two groups. Firstly, any character except a period, a question mark, an exclamation mark, or a Quotation mark, and secondly a space, an upper case B, and the remaining letters of the word. The replace with specification is simply the first group (i.e., whatever characters were found) and then the uncapitalised word "biblical."

Example 5:

A student typed spaces instead of tabs after his figure caption labels, resulting in misaligned figure captions. He wants to correct all such instances with a search and replace. The search criterion is (Figure [0-9]{1,2}:)( )@ with, additionally, a formatting setting (see section 10.3 above): Style: Caption. There are two groups here. The first consists of the word Figure, followed by a space, then any 1- or 2-digit number, and lastly a colon. The second group is quite simply one or more spaces. The replace with specification is simple: \1^t, which means substitute the first group and then a tab.

Example 6:

A style guide says that when the names of biblical books are used in parentheses, they should be abbreviated, but when used in the text, they should be written in full. The writer has already completed his thesis with all such references abbreviated. He will have a lot of search and replacing to do (69 book titles), but at least those books that are numbered can be dealt with together using wildcard searching, reducing the total considerably. For example, searching for ([!(])([1-2]^s)(Thess) *and replacing with* \1\2Thesselonians *will cover that book. The search criteria specifies three groups (the parentheses). The first group is any character but a left parenthesis (this could also, in reality, have been just a space). The second group is either the numbers 1 or 2, followed by a non-breaking space (the writer consistently used these). The third group is the word "Thess." The replacement inserts group 1 (whatever the character was that was found), then group 2 (the number 1 or 2 and the non-breaking space), and then the word "Thesselonians."*

Example 7:

A student typed her references with commas between the author name and the date, and now needs to remove those commas. She knows that no author name she references is longer than 30 characters, and all the references she has to change are from the 21st century. The search criterion is: (\([A-Z][A-Za-z]{1,30})(,)(20[0-9][0-9]) *which is explained as follows: There are three groups. The first group starts with a left parenthesis (indicating that it is a reference), then any capitalized letter, then any combination of thirty or less (upper or lower case) letters and spaces (for multiple-part surnames). For emphasis, take special note of the space after the lowercase z. The second group is just the comma, and the third group is the year, which starts with a space (after the comma), then the digits 20, and then any two digits between zero and nine (this part could also have been specified* [0-9]{2}*). The closing right parenthesis is not included, as multiple references from the same year are indicated by a suffix letter (a, b, c...), but if she wanted to (it would make the search even more precise), she could include that as follows:* [a-d]{0,1}\) *(this assumes no more than four suffixes, thus the d).The replace with specification is just* \1\3 *which reinserts the first and third groups, thus omitting the comma in the second group.*

Example 8:

A table pasted into Word has columns in which some values are less than one, and are indicated only as a period and a digit; and some values larger than one, where the values are a digit, a period, and then another digit. Those values smaller than one must be found, and a zero added before (to the left of) the period. This one is slightly more complicated. First all the periods are replaced with an x (or any other letter of your choice)—this need not be done with a wildcard search and replace. The reason for this is that Word does not recognise the period as being able to start a word. The second step is to search for (<x)([0-9]) *which means any "word" starting with an x and then followed by any digit, and then to replace it with* 0^& *which is a zero and the Find what contents. You may wonder why not* 0.\2 *which would replace the x with a period, but remember that the numbers larger than one still include an x instead of a period. The third step is then to replace x with a period.*

Example 9:

Students have manually numbered and formatted their thesis before learning about the principles taught in this book which allows Word to do their numbering for them. They want to start using this system (e.g., so as to still be able to use Word to create their table of contents), but cannot simply apply the heading styles, as all the old numbers still have to be deleted manually, and in any case it would be great if Word could actually find all their headings and update them to the styles automatically, without the students having to apply the style to each heading.

The secret is to start with the lowest heading level (the principle is the same, so I will only do levels three and higher). Also note that this assumes that the students very consistently did their numbering, missing no separating periods, no formatting mistakes, etc. For heading three, the search specification is ([1-6].[1-9].[1-9])(*^13) *which assumes that the students did not ever use more than nine third level subheadings to a single second level heading, the same for second to first level headings, and that the student has six chapters in the thesis. In addition, the formatting for the Find what box should be set to the formatting used for the third level heading. The search specification consists of two groups: The number, which is a digit between 1 and 6 for the chapter, followed by a period, a digit between 1 and 9 for the second level heading, followed by a period, and a digit between 1 and 9 for the third level heading, followed by a space. The second group is any text (in this case, the heading text) up to a paragraph mark. The replace with criteria is simply* \2 *with the formatting specification of* Style: Heading 3. *Thus the number is stripped away, and the style applied, all at the same time.*

The process can then be repeated, with ([1-6].[1-9])(*^13) *for the second level heading, and exactly the same replace with specification, except that now the formatting is set to* Style: Heading 2, *and of course the appropriate formatting for the Find what box too.*

For the Chapter titles, again the appropriate formatting for the Find what box is set, and then the specification is (Chapter [1-6])(*^13) *with exactly the same replace with criteria and with the formatting specification of* Style: Heading 1. *In this way, an entire manually numbered thesis can be transformed into an automatically numbered thesis in a matter of minutes.*

Example 10:

A student placed footnote markers before punctuation marks, and then discovers that his university wants them placed after the punctuation marks. The student uses (^2)([,.?!]) *for the search specification, and* \2\1 *for the replace with specification, essentially swapping the marker and the punctuation marks around.*

10.6   Search tips

You would have noticed that wildcard searching (and even Word's string searching) is extremely powerful. When making dramatic or sweeping changes via search and replace (such as those shown in Application 10.3), I recommend first making a backup of your document, and then doing the change. This way, if things go wrong, you should still be able to go back and undo most of the harm, even if it is only discovered months later.

Also be very careful of replacing entire paragraphs, but not including the hard carriage return at the end of the paragraph. If this is included in the "Search for" text box, but not in the "Replace with" text box, you could end up merging paragraphs, with sometimes astounding consequences (e.g., the inclusion of entire tables or figures in in-text cross-references—cf. Figure 126, p. 171).

A final note should be made about the order in which you search for and replace items. Sometimes, search and replace should be done in a process of three steps, especially where two "values" must be swapped. Obviously, with pattern matching, it is possible to search for and replace multiple items or groups of items simultaneously. However, sometimes unforeseen problems can be encountered, especially when you are using string matching. For example, let's say that you mistakenly confused two very similar references (obviously, this example assumes that you are not using Reference Management Software, see Chapter 13). Stone, 1989 should have been Stones, 1998, and Stones, 1998 should have been Stone, 1989. If you change all the instances of Stone, 1989 to Stones, 1998, then, when you change all the Stones, 1998 references to Stone, 1989, you will be undoing your first change, and all the references in your document that you thought you had changed will now be Stone, 1989. The best way to solve this problem, is to add something to the first result so that it is distinguished from the other search criterion (e.g., by adding a font colour to the replacement text). Remember to choose a colour not already part of your marking colour scheme (cf. Application 11.1, p. 239). The second search will then search for only that text that does not have that characteristic, and a third search will then remove that distinguishing characteristic from the first search's results.

First Search		Second Search		Third Search	
Find What	Replace with	Find What	Replace with	Find What	Replace with
Stone, 1989	Stones, 1998, formatted Pink	Stones, 1998, formatted Black	Stone, 1989	Stones, 1998, formatted Pink	Stones, 1998, formatted Black

Chapter 11
Finding your way: Document navigation

Finding your way around a two page letter in Word is one thing, but finding your way around the 300 page behemoth your dissertation has become is quite another. This short chapter will show you those time saving tips that will keep you from wasting unnecessary time looking for things, freeing your time up to focus on the important task of writing.

11.1 Searching

Note that one way of quickly going to a certain point in your document is by doing a search for it. This is, however, such a broad topic, that it deserves a chapter of its own (Chapter 10, p. 215). Notwithstanding that, if you know the text you are looking for (e.g., a name), you can do a search for it and go there quickly.

But Word has one more very useful feature that is also a great aid in document navigation, as it applies to both the sections following in this chapter (Go To and the Object browser), as well as the next on searching: Word remembers what you were looking for last. Thus, if you performed a Go To or a search (even if it was a search and replace), then, even without the dialog open, you can still employ that action again. With the keyboard, simply press **Ctrl + Page Down** to go to the next instance of whatever you were looking for, and **Ctrl + Page Up** to go to the previous instance of whatever you were looking for. In fact, when I am looking for something (i.e., I do not intend performing a replace), I often prefer doing only a first search, and then cancelling the Find dialog completely. I then simply use **Ctrl + Page Down** (or **Page Up**, as the case may be) to jump between instances in my document until I have found what I am looking for. This is extremely useful in all manner of contexts, including normal searches, formatted searches, and wildcard searches (all of these will be discussed in the next chapter).

If you don't want to use the keyboard for this, the Object browser (below) will also "remember" your previous search or Go To.

Application 11.1   Marking text

*Another quick way to move to specific points in your document is to mark them. Bookmarks (see section 11.2, p. 240), are very useful in this regard. By judiciously using bookmarks, you can quickly jump to key points in your document. A different strategy is to colour-code text. You can define your own code, for example red can indicate things that need to be checked (for accuracy, etc.), blue to indicate things that you still want to elaborate on, green for things you still need to find sources for, etc. You can then quickly browse through all the different colour-coded sections of your document by using the Search function. All you need to do is specify a search with no search text, and only the formatting for that colour specified. You can then either keep clicking on "Find Next" until you have found what you are looking for, or you can find the first item, then press Esc, and then use **Ctrl + Page Up** and **Ctrl + Page Down** to move between your colour-coded text. When you want to search for something else*

> *apart from formatting, simply click on the* No Forma<u>tt</u>ing *button to remove the formatting options from the search.*

11.2   Bookmarks

Before we discuss further navigation tools, we need to learn to use the Bookmark feature of Word. Just as you can use bookmarks in a real paper book, Word allows you to add any number of bookmarks to a document.

11.2.1   Various uses for bookmarks

I tend to use bookmarks for two different purposes. Firstly, they can be moved as you work (as with a real bookmark in a paper book). I normally name one such bookmark AA, since this will always appear right at the top of the list, and is thus easy to set and reset. This provides a more permanent alternative to the **Shift + F5** method discussed in section 11.5 below, although it does require the slight effort of moving it along with you as you work. You can thus easily move to these bookmarks using the <u>G</u>o To button in the Bookmark dialog (see below), or by selecting the Bookmark option in the Go To dialog (see section 11.3 below).

The other purpose of bookmarks is to serve as fixed markers, marking out places in your document that cannot be identified easily by other means such as headings, figures, tables, etc. These bookmarks can then serve as targets for navigation, but more importantly, also as targets for cross-references (section 8.5, p. 165), and index entries (section 9.3, p. 194)—footnote 71 on p. 244 is one such example in this book.

11.2.2   Displaying bookmarks

Before you start using bookmarks, you will want to change the Word settings so that you can actually see them. To do this, open the Word Options dialog, go to the Advanced tab, Show document content group, and activate the Show bookmar<u>k</u>s setting (Figure 178).

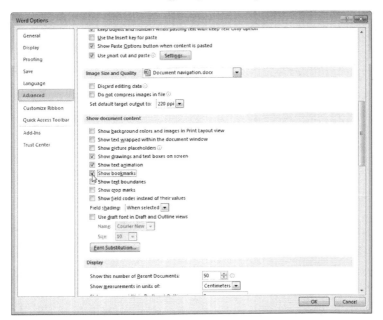

Figure 178   Showing bookmarks

Once you have done this, bookmarks will appear as a set of faint grey brackets in your document (Figure 179). When the bookmark is inserted at a single point[69], the vertical parts of the brackets are superimposed on each other, such that the horizontal tops and bottoms actually point past each other, looking something like an I (Figure 179).

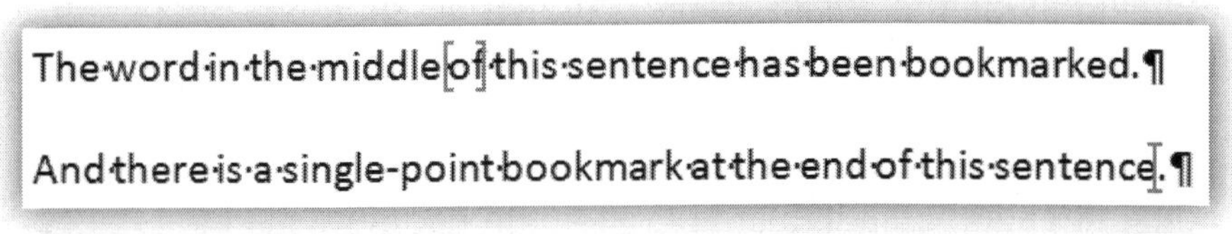

> The·word·in·the·middle[of]this·sentence·has·been·bookmarked.¶
>
> And·there·is·a·single-point·bookmark·at·the·end·of·this·sentence.¶

Figure 179   Examples of a bookmark displayed in a document

11.2.3   Adding and moving bookmarks

Now you can start using bookmarks. All the bookmark functions are controlled from the Bookmark dialog, which is found on the Insert ribbon, or with **Ctrl + Shift + F5** (Instruction set 41).

---

[69] These bookmarks are known as empty bookmarks.

Instruction set 36   Accessing the Bookmark dialog

Shortcut	Ctrl + Shift + F5
Keyboard	Alt | N | K
Left click	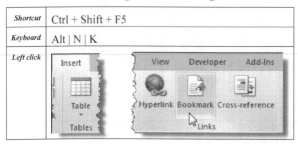

The Bookmark dialog (Figure 180) is quite simple to use. To create a bookmark, select either the point where you want it to be inserted, or the text around which you want it to be created (this may even span a whole number of pages). Then open the dialog, type the name for your bookmark, and select Add. Choose a name that defines either the positioning of the bookmark (especially when the bookmark is intended never to be moved), or its purpose. The requirements that bookmark names must comply with are:

    📖 Bookmark names may contain no spaces or special characters (! @ # $ % ^ & * ( ) { } [ ] - + = | \ / : ; " ' < > . ? , etc.)—i.e., basically only the normal set of alphanumeric characters (some diacritical marks—e.g., é—as only one example are allowed, but generally not advised).

    📖 Bookmark names may not start with a number or underscore (i.e. bookmarks names must start with an alphabetic character).

    📖 Bookmark names must be no longer than 40 characters.

Bearing this in mind, you can make your bookmark names easier to read by replacing spaces with underscores, or using what is known as camel case, where each successive word is capitalised (e.g., BookmarkName).

To move an existing bookmark, select the new position, open the dialog, select the name of the bookmark, and again click on Add.

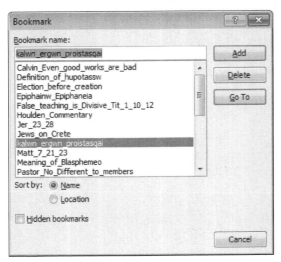

Figure 180   *Bookmark dialog*

The Bookmark dialog also allows you to navigate to your various bookmarks using the Go To button. You can use the Delete button to delete bookmarks (only the bookmark itself is deleted—the text around which it was placed remains unaffected). The Sort by option group allows you to sort the bookmarks either alphabetically (Name) or in the order in which they occur in the document (Location).

Finally, you can also use the dialog to reveal Hidden bookmarks—these are bookmarks added by other applications or processes working in the Word environment (e.g., third-party Reference Management Software programs add these, Word itself uses these to keep track of certain entries such as heading entries for a table of contents, cross-references, etc.). You need not really bother with showing hidden bookmarks unless you are a pro seeking to resolve issues in "broken" documents, in which case they can become quite useful. Of course, remember that a hidden bookmark is, well, hidden—in other words, even though you can see it in the dialog, the bookmark indicator (Figure 179) is not shown for these. The only way you can access them is through the dialog, or through a VBA macro.

11.2.4 Understanding bookmarks

Like so many of Word's tools, bookmarks have their own idiosyncrasies. Understand these can help avoid some common bookmark problems.

11.2.4.1 Bookmark positioning

First, it is important to understand that bookmarks are placed around a selection, although, oddly, that selection can be nothing—this was illustrated in Figure 179. Nonetheless, Word keeps track of the start and end of that selection (so that when the selection is nothing, the start and end are the same). However, the implication of this is that anything that is added to that selection will become part of the bookmark's selection. Thus, referring back to Figure 179, positioning the insertion point exactly on the left of the o of "of," and adding text, will cause the added text to be included into the selection of the bookmark. However, position the insertion point to the right of the f of "of" will not change the selection. Also, when the bookmark refers to a collapsed section of text (as with the second bookmark in Figure 179), adding text on either side makes no change to the bookmark. To better understand this, remember that Word keeps track of the start and end of the bookmark by counting the number of characters from the beginning of the document to that point. Thus, if the start of the first bookmark in Figure 179 is, say, at character 100, then the end would be at 102. Typing to the right of the f of "of" would not change the end, thus the selection for the bookmark remains unaltered. Typing to the left of the "o" (i.e., at character 100), adds characters that will, counting from the start of the document, come *after* the start of the bookmark (i.e., at character 100, moving the current characters 100 and 101 on). This is important, for, as we shall see in Application 11.2 below this can sometimes cause some unintended problems.

A further point to remember is that bookmarks can overlap (leading to difficulty in discerning where each bookmark begins and ends), and that multiple bookmarks may even be created for exactly the same range (although this is obviously not to be recommended).

11.2.4.2   Hidden or automatic bookmarks

A number of programs, foremost of which is Word itself, can create a special kind of bookmark, known as a hidden, or automatic, bookmark. When the Bookmark dialog (Figure 180) is open, the Hidden bookmarks checkbox allows these bookmarks to be displayed[70]. Figure 181 shows some hidden bookmarks in the bookmark dialog. These bookmarks can easily distinguished by the fact that they start with an underscore—you will recall from p. 242[71] that bookmark names may contain, but may not begin with, underscore characters. However, when a bookmark is created programmatically, the first character can be set to an underscore, and that bookmark will then be considered a hidden bookmark.

---

[70] In what I can only assume to be a definite Word bug, this dialog sometimes opens with this checkbox marked, but without the hidden bookmarks displayed. If you suspect that the hidden bookmarks are not actually being displayed, just uncheck and recheck the check box, and they will be displayed.

[71] Take note that this particular cross-reference was created by bookmarking the paragraph in question, and then inserting a cross-reference to the page on which that bookmark is found.

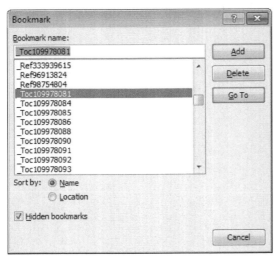

Figure 181   Bookmark dialog showing hidden bookmarks

The reason for bringing all of this up is that Word uses bookmark internally for a whole number of tasks, such as for tables of contents, cross-references, etc. Word will create these bookmarks as and when needed. For example, whenever you insert a cross-reference to a certain object, Word first creates a hidden bookmark around that object, and then it creates the reference to that bookmark (using the REF field). Thus, the multiple references to Figure 179 above look like this when the field codes are displayed: { REF _Ref300768504 \h }. Normally, once this bookmark has been created, Word will use this same bookmark for all future cross-references to that item, but I have seen instances where Word has created multiple hidden bookmarks all referring to the same text range (I have not attempted to discover under what circumstances this occurred)[72]. This will all come together now in Application 11.2 where a particularly insidious Word problem will be solved.

Application 11.2   Avoiding Problems with Cross-references to Captions

A whole new class of problems crops up when you start to create references to captions (either with a list of figures, tables, or other types of captions, or with in-text cross-references to those captions). Here's how to prevent those problems right from the start:

There must be a hard carriage return between the caption paragraph and the object it refers to. This means, to use the two most common examples, that there must be a hard carriage return after the figure and before the caption (as an example of an item where the caption is placed below), and after the caption and before the table (as an example

---

[72] As an example, my Bookmark Manager shows that the Application entry here (Application 11.2) is the target of three different hidden bookmarks, all created by Word: _Ref315768544 refers to just the text "Application 11.2", while both _Ref315768544 (used for a cross-reference) and _Toc329804594 (used for the table of contents) refer to "Application 11.2 Avoiding Problems with Cross-references to Captions" (and both exclude the paragraph end mark).

of an item where the caption is placed above). Simply put, caption paragraphs must be preceded and succeeded by hard carriage returns. The absence of the hard carriage return could cause the cross-reference in the text to include the entire table or figure! This is, obviously, also very important to remember when searching and replacing. Understanding how Word creates its hidden bookmarks helps explain this phenomenon. A further extension of this problem is found when you want an above-captioned item (e.g., a table) to start on a new page, and innocently add a manual page break before the caption. Word will include the page break in all references to that caption (i.e., in all your cross-references, as well as in your list of tables, to continue with the example). The reason for this has already been explained—when you add something to the start of a selection of text encapsulated in a bookmark, that bookmark then expands to incorporate the newly added text—in this case the manual page break.

Initially, before learning about how Word's hidden bookmarks, I thought that the secret to resolving this problem was the little-known Style Separator (see section 3.2.3.2, p. 40). However, I found that the Style Separator works for page breaks, but does not work for section breaks.

However, understanding what Word does with its hidden bookmarks, the process become easily resolvable, even if it involves some degree of drudgery.

Basically, add the page break. Then find a cross-reference to that caption. Select it, and press Ctrl + F9 to reveal the field codes. Copy the name of the bookmark. Now select just the caption, not the page break, and then use the Bookmark dialog to reset the bookmark (paste the bookmark name in the dialog[73]) to the smaller selection.

All this may seem daunting, which is why I created my Bookmark Manager (as part of the Word uTIlities). Using this tool, simply select from the paragraph before, to the paragraph after the caption, and launch the manager. It will reveal to you the name of the bookmark. You can then also reselect the caption while the dialog is open, excluding the page break, and then use the reposition button to exclude the page break from the bookmark. This is illustrated in Figure 182.

However, because people working with numbered mathematical equations (see section 17.1.7, p. 412) may run up against this problem a lot, I have taken the liberty of adding another little tool that resets a bookmark by one character (which should normally be enough). Simply select the field with the cross-reference which you want to adjust, and then launch this tool, and it should do its magic for you. Note that this will not work for errant Table of Contents bookmarks, but only for cross-reference bookmarks. The TOC bookmarks you will have to adjust using the uTIlities Bookmark Manager.

---

[73] This is a very interesting case, as the Word Bookmark dialog does not allow you to create hidden bookmarks—as soon as you type the underscore as the first character of a bookmark name, the Add button is diabled. However, pasting the hidden bookmark name does not disable the Add button!

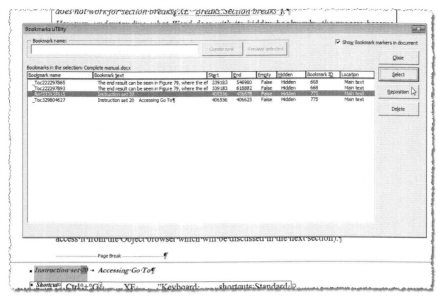

Figure 182   Using the uTIlities Bookmark Manager to reposition a bookmark

11.3   Go To

The Go To tool is obscurely hidden with the Find tool (Instruction set 33) but is easily accessed with **Ctrl + G** (you can also access it from the Object browser which will be discussed in the next section).

Instruction set 37   Accessing Go To

Shortcut	Ctrl + G
Keyboard	Alt | H | FD | G
Left click	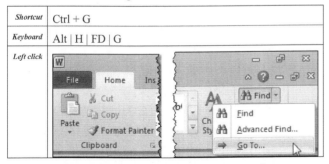

Once you have the dialog, you can easily use it to navigate to any number of document "landmarks." The dialog is shown in Figure 183, and is discussed below.

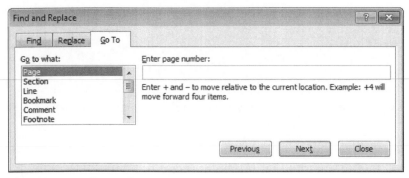

Figure 183   *Find and Replace dialog: Go To*

The first thing to do with the Go To dialog is to decide *what* to go to. You can choose between:

- Pages
- Lines
- Comments
- Endnotes
- Tables
- Sections
- Bookmarks
- Footnotes
- Fields
- Headings

- Graphics (i.e., any kind of image inserted into the document)
- Objects (i.e., any non-Word or even other Word document item inserted using the Insert Object tool)

Then, decide "how" to move. Firstly, if you know the exact number (e.g., page 3 or Table 7 or the name of a reviewer or bookmark), then type it in in the Enter text box (whatever follows the word Enter will depend on what you have selected). Alternatively, you can move by "units." For example, to go to every second page or table or whatever, type "+2". Obviously, typing "-2" will take you back two of whatever you want to navigate to. To simply go to the next instance, leave the box blank (if you like doing unnecessary work, type "+1").

After that, it is simply a matter of pressing Go To and you will move to that item (if you leave the Enter text box blank, the buttons are Next and Previous. As I mentioned before, it is wonderful to be able to navigate to the first instance, dispense with the dialog, and then use the **Ctrl + Page Up** and **Page Down** keyboard shortcuts to move backwards and forwards through the document.

11.4   Object browser

The Object browser is a small tool situated at the bottom right of the Word window (Figure 184). It consists of only three buttons, the first and last of which are the same as the **Ctrl + Page Up** and **Ctrl + Page Down** keyboard shortcuts—they repeat the last search or Go To action.

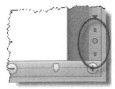

Figure 184   *Object Browser*

When the middle button is clicked (or the keyboard shortcut **Ctrl + Alt + Home** is pressed), a small pane of options to which you can go to is revealed. These are essentially the same as some of the Go To options listed above (Objects, Bookmarks, and Lines are not included). If you hold your mouse over the relevant icon, a text description of that item appears in the lower section (which reads "Cancel" in Figure 185). Note also that the three icons at the bottom left are slightly different in their functions. The first two will open the Go To and Find tabs of the Find and Replace dialog, while the third will browse between your last edits (see section 11.5 following).

Figure 185   *Object browser options*

11.5   *Browsing by edits*

This function was hinted at with the discussion of the Object browser. Although it can be accessed from there, I prefer the keyboard shortcut: **Shift + F5**. Word continually monitors and remembers yours last five editing points. Sometimes, of course, these are all in the same paragraph, and this keyboard shortcut doesn't mean much then. But at other times, you may be typing something, then have to move to another place in your document (e.g., to read something, or to copy something), and then want to return to the place where you were busy typing—simply press **Shift + F5** and you will be back there. Of course, you may have moved somewhere to quickly add something, in which case **Shift + F5** will take you to the starting point for that edit (this is in itself a useful little shortcut), but remember that **Shift + F5** stores your last five editing points, so just press it again and you will eventually end up where you want to be (most of the time!). You can actually just keep pressing the shortcut and continue cycling through those last five editing points.

There is one last use for this keyboard shortcut that makes it one of my all-time favourites. I was sorely disappointed to discover that Microsoft had broken it with Word 2007 (it doesn't work there) and overjoyed to discover that they had fixed it in Word 2010.

Let me first set the scenario. You are working hard on your dissertation, and eventually you just have to shut down and go to bed (or work!). Tomorrow morning (or evening!) you start up again, and open your dissertation document. Now, wouldn't it be nice if you could immediately to exactly that point where you left off, and start typing there? You can—when you close the document, Word stores your very last (not five, in this instance) editing point. Simply press **Shift + F5**, and you will end up there, even if it was hundreds of pages into the document. Now you are set to go, and can continue typing. This single shortcut alone has probably saved me scores of hours of time over the years!

11.6 Navigation pane

Word allows you one further tool with which to facilitate your navigation: The Navigation pane, which is turned on from the View ribbon (Instruction set 38).

Instruction set 38   Showing the Navigation pane

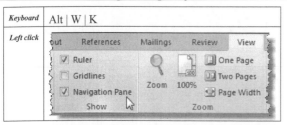

The Navigation pane is displayed to the left of the document window, as will be displayed in the figures in the following sections. The Word 2010 Navigation pane incorporates three tools: The Document map, the Thumbnail view (which was introduced in Word 2003) and a new search list.

11.6.1   Thumbnail view

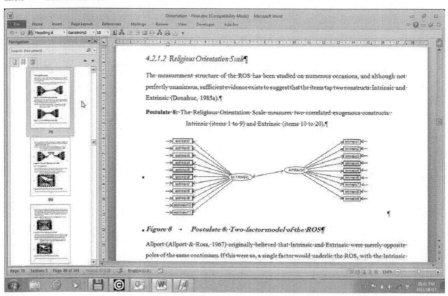

Figure 186   Navigation pane: Thumbnail view

The thumbnail view is not my personal favourite, as it shows very little information per screen (i.e., it has a low data density, which is of limited use for large navigation). For example, Figure 186 shows that on my laptop screen, with the ribbon minimised to give me more space on the screen, I can only see the equivalent of three pages. By contrast, the first and last items on the Document map shown in Figure 193, shown on the same screen but with the ribbon maximised, spans 17 pages from the top item in the map to the bottom item (this will vary depending on how many headings you have and how much text is covered under each heading (it could potentially be hundreds of pages). Having said that, the thumbnail view is useful in those exceptional circumstances where you want to navigate to some point which is not close to a particular heading (or you don't know under exactly which heading it is), and it is recognisable in miniature. For example, Figure 186 shows statistical models (Structural Equation Modelling diagrams, of you must know), which can be recognised quite easily even though they are so small. All you need to do is click on the page in the Navigation pane, and you are taken there.

11.6.2   Search list

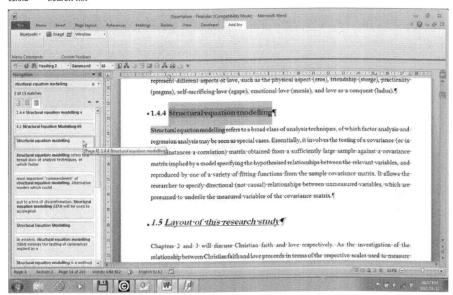

Figure 187   Navigation pane: Search list

More will be said about doing searches in the next chapter (much more!), but a new feature introduced with Word 2010 is the search list in the Navigation pane (Word 2007 added the thumbnail view to the document map). Personally, I'm not a big fan of this, although it does have its uses. Figure 187 shows the results of a search using this feature. Its usefulness lies in the fact that it shows all the instances in which the thing searched for has been found, together with the immediate context in which those items were found. Holding the mouse over one of these without clicking shows a tooltip with the page number on which the item was found, together with the heading under which it resorts.

Note, though, that the search function is not impotent. Firstly, there is a drop-down next to the search button (Figure 188). From this, you can also access some of the Go to options as with the Object browser (Graphics, Tables, Equations, Footnotes/Endnotes, and Comments). Furthermore, the Advanced find..., Replace..., and Go To options all open the relevant tabs of the Find and Replace dialog.

251

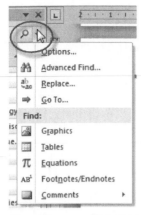

Figure 188   *Navigation pane search options*

The Options... item opens a new dialog (Figure 189) that allows you to set various options for the search you want to conduct from the Navigation pane. Most of these options are from the traditional Find and Replace dialog, and these will be discussed in that context below. All that is worth nothing for the moment is that the standard setting for search from the Navigation pane (visible at the bottom left of the dialog) are that all finds are highlighted and that an incremental find is used (that is the one option not available from the standard find dialog). Any options you set here can also be made permanent through the Set As Default button. The Incremental find setting deserves a brief mention. It is only available when Highlight all is selected (this is the same as Reading Highlight in the standard Find and Replace dialog) and simply means that Word will search as you type. Thus, if you were to type "Word," Word would first search for all Ws in the document, then all Wo, then all Wor, and finally for all instances of "Word." Turning off Incremental find means that you will have to manually click on the search button after having entered your search criterion, but at the same time may speed up the process of searching from the Navigation pane in a very large document.

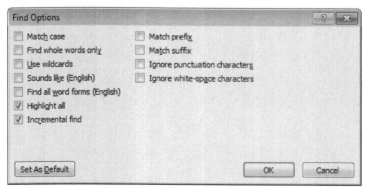

Figure 189   *Navigation pain search—Find options*

11.6.3   Reclaiming the Find and Replace dialog

I think what irritates me about this feature is that Microsoft has not offered it as an additional option, but rather pretty much foisted it on us—the old **Ctrl + F** keyboard shortcut which always used to open the Find and Replace dialog, now opens the Navigation pane search list[74]. I still prefer to use the Find and Replace dialog for most of my searching, as I still find the process quicker to use (this will be described in more detail in the next chapter, and is especially fast when combined with the techniques just described in section 11.5).

I can offer you one of two solutions for this: Firstly, you can assign a new keyboard shortcut to the old Find and Replace dialog (which is now called Advanced Find). To do this, go to the Customize Ribbon tab of the Word Options dialog, and click on the Keyboard shortcuts: Customize button. This will bring up the Customize Keyboard dialog (Figure 190). Here you can go to the Home Tab in the Categories list box, then EditFind in the Commands and then in the Press new shortcut key box, create a shortcut—I suggest using **Ctrl + Alt + Shift + F** as it modifies the **Ctrl + F** from the old shortcut, and is not assigned to any other Word function, although you may not find it that easy to press. You could, of course, always reclaim **Ctrl + F** which is assigned by default to NavPaneSearch as shown in Figure 191 (you could then give NavPaneSeach the **Ctrl + Alt + Shift + F** keyboard shortcut). The last thing to do then is click on the Assign button to complete the task. Personally, I followed the latter suggestion, giving my old find dialog the **Ctrl + F** keyboard shortcut back, and assigning **Ctrl + Alt + Shift +F** to the Navigation pane.

---

[74] Note to Microsoft (as if they'll listen to me!): Why not let Ctrl + F open the find dialog when the Navigation pane is not displayed, and default to the search list when the Navigation pane is open?

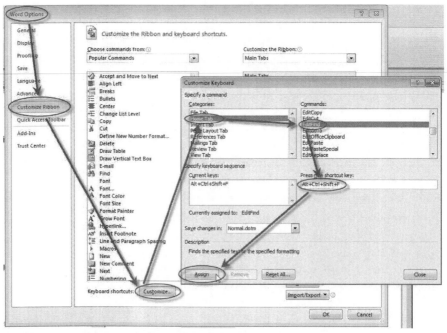

Figure 190   *Customise Keyboard dialog: Setting Ctrl + Alt + Shift + F*

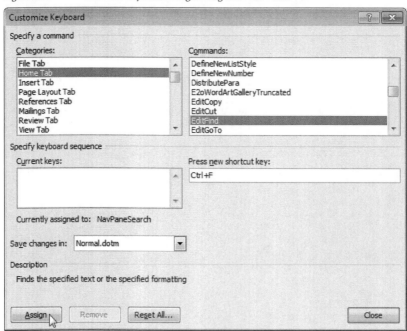

Figure 191   *Customise Keyboard dialog: Resetting Ctrl + F*

The second option is to add it to the QAT as shown in Figure 192.

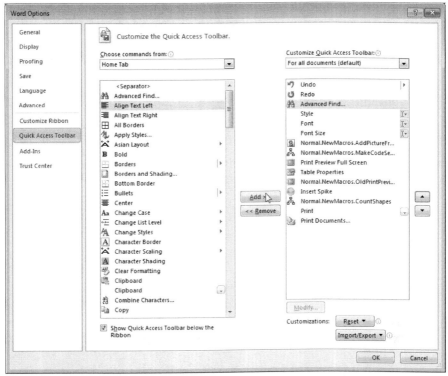

Figure 192   Adding Advanced Find to the QAT

After all of that, I should perhaps add that the dialog, of course, consists of three tabs, and while **Ctrl + F** no longer opens the dialog anymore, **Ctrl + H** (for Replace) and **Ctrl + G** (for Go To) still do. You could always just cultivate a new habit of opening the dialog that way, and then switching to the Fin<u>d</u> tab (I wouldn't recommend just learning to do searches from the Re<u>p</u>lace tab when you don't intend replacing, as somewhere along the line you are going to do some unintended damage...). But still, I personally think it was unfair of Microsoft to foist this on us.

11.6.4 Document map

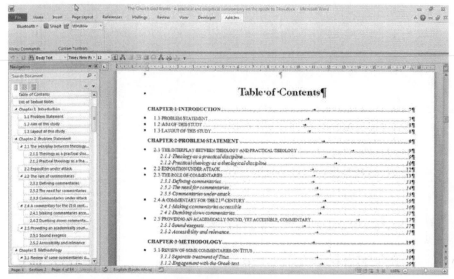

Figure 193   *Navigation pane: Document map*

The Document map is a great navigation tool. Note, though, that to use it, you ideally need to have set up your document using appropriate styles (e.g., the Heading1–Heading9 styles), as discussed in (Chapter 6). The reason for this is that the Document map picks up on the outline levels associated with your various document paragraphs, and builds a browsable index from it. Note how, in Figure 193, the Document map reflects the document's table of contents. You can use this to navigate through your document. Simply click on any heading, and you will be taken to that page immediately. You can also aid this navigation by collapsing or expanding sections. For example, in Figure 194, Chapter 1 has been collapsed, as is evident from the ▷ icon, and Chapter 2 is expanded, as can be seen from the ◢ icon. The search box can also be used to find a certain heading, which will be highlighted, as is also shown in Figure 194.

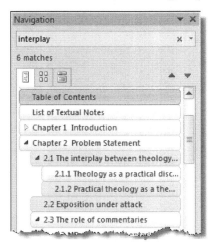

Figure 194   *Navigation pane: Document map showing collapsed section*

However, in Word 2010 Microsoft introduced new capabilities into the Document map. Essentially, you can now make structural changes to your document, as you have always been able to do through Outline View (section 12.1, p. 266) . I will make an argument below (11.6.5) for rather doing this in Outline View, though. There are several ways that this can be done. Firstly, you can click and drag a heading, and it and all subheadings and all associated text will be moved to the new location where you drop it.

Furthermore, you can right click on an item to either promote or demote it (i.e., move it up or down the heading hierarchy levels); add new headings of the same level before or after it (thus you can populate the structure of your document before adding the text); add a new subheading to the item; or delete the item and all subheadings and all associated text under them. You can also select the heading item together with all its subheadings and all associated text, or print the same. Finally, you can expand or collapse the entire Document map or you can display the entire document map to certain level (i.e., expanded for that level and above, but collapsed for all levels below that). All of this is shown in Figure 195.

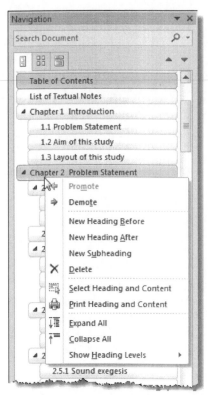

Figure 195   *Navigation pane: Document map—making structural changes*

11.6.5   A word of warning about the Word 2010 Document map

Word has, for far more than a decade, had the Document map (I think it was introduced with Word 95). This has always worked well, until Microsoft started toying with it by introducing thumbnail view in Word 2007. When I first read about the changes to this tool in late 2009 (when the Word 2010 Public Beta was released) that allow you to use it to rearrange your document, I simply couldn't believe that the people at Microsoft could be so naive. They leave me with the impression that they don't seem to have much contact with computer users in the outside world (they probably spend too much time in their cubicles)—or at least, they don't seem to have contact with the kinds of people who come to me for help when their computers lose or otherwise destroy things.

Let me explain the problem first. Has this ever happened to you: In Outlook (or whatever e-mail program you use), you want to drag a mail to a folder, and accidentally drop it into the wrong folder. If, for example, you want to switch the order of two chapters, and you drag a chapter up in the Document map and drop it below the preceding chapter, then whatever was left of that preceding chapter will now become part of the chapter you dragged—not at all what you had intended (this can be avoided by collapsing the chapters before you move them, or by correctly using Outline view).

Or in Windows Explorer (or whatever file management program you use—I hate Explorer and swear by Total Commander) you move the mouse over a file or folder, and in the process accidentally click the file in the moving process, resulting in your having dragged and dropped it into a folder, and you aren't even certain which folder? This is especially wont to happen if you are working on a laptop touchpad (for example, when it is hot and humid and your fingertips are sweaty, touchpads easily "misinterpret" a touch as a click). All of this means that the "helpful" feature Microsoft has introduced in the new document map in Word 2010 is a sure-fire way to mess up your document accidentally. And as we all know (and the insurance companies love reminding us, accidents do happen). I know that somewhere, sometime, someone is going to click and drag parts of their document into oblivion without even knowing that they have done that. And Microsoft hasn't even provided its loyal users with any checks (e.g., a little dialog popping up saying "Do you really want to do that?") or even the option of disabling this feature. Please note that I am not against innovation and new features. But this functionality is not new. As we will see in section 12.1 (p. 266), Word has allowed you to do this kind of manipulation with Outline view for what seems like eons. But there the process is very well controlled, and you have almost no chance of doing it by mistake. Here, you have a very good chance of rearranging your document purely by accident, and I think it is simply irresponsible of Microsoft to facilitate that without putting any checks or balances in place.

There, now you've been warned. Used this tool with care, and always concentrate very hard when you move your mouse over the document map. I will add that I have used this tool when I wanted to do a quick rearrangement, but for the serious stuff, I still prefer Outline view.

11.7   Navigating with the Table of contents

Another way of navigating to specific sections of your document is to use the Table of Contents (this is especially useful when you open the document and Word seems to have forgotten your last editing point—cf. 11.5). Basically, by holding down the Ctrl[75] Key and clicking on the page number of any item in your table of contents (see section 9.1, p. 183), you will be taken there immediately.

11.8   Working with multiple windows

One last topic needs to be touched on, and while it does not relate directly to moving around within a document, it is still relevant. You may often find yourself wanting to work in two different places in your document at the same time (it could be more than two as well, although two is the most realistic you can expect to work successfully). Examples of this could be when you want to type at one point in the document while reading what you typed at an earlier point. Or you might want to copy some things (e.g., some values from a table) and paste them somewhere else (although note that the Office clipboard might provide you with a better tool for this than jumping backwards and forwards between windows).

---

[75] This behaviour (requiring the Ctrl key or not) can be set under Tools, Options, Edit, Use Ctrl + Click to follow Hyperlink.

Word offers several tools for this kind of work, and which you will choose depends on what you want to do.

11.8.1   Splitting the window

My favourite method is splitting the window (Instruction set 39), although this method only works for two points in your document.

Instruction set 39   Splitting the window

Shortcut	Ctrl + Alt + S
Keyboard	Alt | W | S
Left click	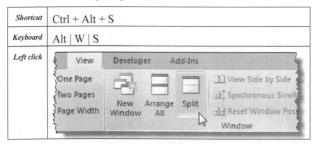

Once you activate the split (whether with the keyboard shortcut, or with the ribbon), a split bar appears across the screen (Figure 196), splitting it exactly in half, and the mouse is automatically repositioned on the split bar. You can then use the mouse (or, with the keyboard, the up and down arrows) to resize the split if you want to. For example, if I want to read what I have written in one place, and type in another, I prefer making the top part larger for reading, as I generally don't need a large area at the bottom for typing. When you have the split sized as you want, you can simply click with the mouse or press enter with the keyboard, and the split is made (Figure 196). Note that, as can be seen in Figure 196, the split can be resized at any time by grabbing it with the mouse and dragging it. Once the split has been made, you can navigate in each window independently, and you can jump between the two windows and work in either. The big advantage of the split is that it wastes minimal space (the ribbon, etc., is not repeated), and you can maximise your use of the screen space by temporarily minimising the ribbon (**Ctrl + F1**).

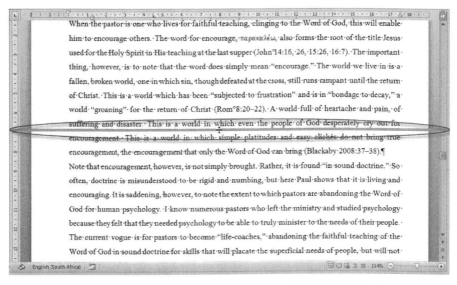

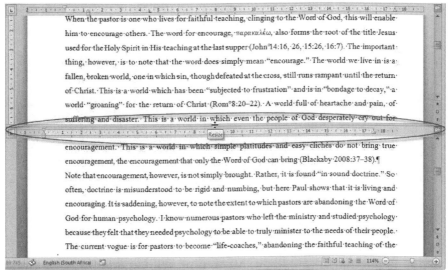

Figure 196   *Splitting the window*

The split is easily removed in exactly the same way it is added (it is thus a toggle), whether from the ribbon or with the **Ctrl + Alt + S** keyboard shortcut (you can also double click on it to remove it).

11.8.2   Multiple windows

Another option, although one that I use less, is to open a second document window (Instruction set 40).

Instruction set 40   Opening a new document window

Keyboard	Alt	W	N
Left click	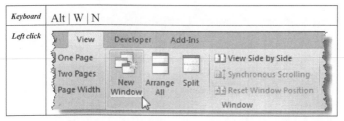

Once you have a second window open, you will notice that each window's title in the title bar is suffixed with a colon and the window number. Now, you can use either the View Side by Side tool or the Arrange All tool from the same ribbon group to position your windows. You can also resize each separate window individually with the mouse. This is a more cumbersome process, and it duplicates the ribbon, and hence I prefer the split. But if you have a nice wide screen, or if you are working on two monitors, then this tool becomes extremely useful—you can resize Word across both monitors, and then have each document window fill up one monitor, giving you lots of space to work in. Again, the time spent creating this setup mitigates against using it often, but for those big jobs, it can actually save time.

Working with the View Side by Side tool is discussed in section 14.6.1 (p. 327).

11.9   Using zoom

Sometimes you just cannot seem to remember where that thing is that you wanted to work on (and thus the headings are of no use to you, although this probably means that either the conceptual ordering of your dissertation is lacking, or your heading titles are no good). But if it is near some recognisable object (e.g., a table, drawing or graph), you can (in Print Layout View) reduce the zoom to 10%. This will show multiple pages of your document at a time, and you can easily search for that "landmark" object, click on it, increase your zoom, and go from there. Figure 197 shows an example of this. Of course, this technique is not only useful when the headings are no good as reference points—sometimes this may just be the quickest way of getting to where you want to be.

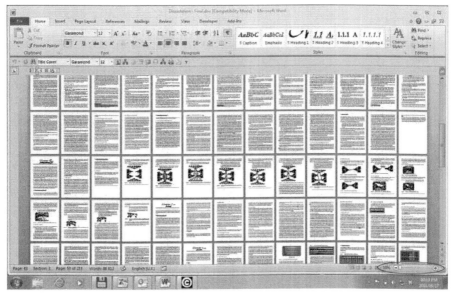

Figure 197   *Using zoom to get a bird's eye view of your document*

11.10   Increasing navigation speed

Something that will be discussed in greater detail in Chapter 19 is the way Word displays your document. In Print Layout View, Word is constantly checking to see that your document is displayed (apart from non-printing characters that are being shown) as it will print (and it needs to query the printer driver continuously to do this). This, of course, slows down your computer (you may often see the message "Word is repaginating "your document.doc" page xxx Press Esc to cancel," followed by a long wait before Word actually shows you what you want to see). And this problem is further exacerbated by graphic objects (be it graphs, pictures, equations, Word Art objects, even tables, etc.), which are very memory-intensive. The simple solution to this is to switch to Draft view (in versions of Word up to Word 2003, this was known as Normal View). You now no longer have the WYSIWYG[76] view of your document (most importantly, some images are not shown—inline images display as empty placeholders, but floating images are not seen at all), but it will speed up your navigation through the document considerably.

---

[76] What You See Is What You Get

Chapter 12
Getting a grip: Managing documents

A thesis or dissertation is a big document, and that means that it can become a big file very quickly, especially if it contains a lot of images or charts or other such objects. There are several strategies for dealing with this, one of which is to do each chapter in a separate Word document. Note, however, that Word is quite adept at handling large documents—you can quite easily create documents which run into thousands of pages, and, provided your PC has enough disk space and memory, Word should handle it quite smoothly. Microsoft notes that a single word document can contain a maximum of 32Mb of text, and images and charts and other such objects can further inflate the file size to a maximum of 512Mb.

Word is so good with large documents, in fact, that I actually recommend that you do your thesis or dissertation in one single document. This is easier to manage (e.g., when making backups), and elements from the larger file (e.g., individual chapters) can very quickly and easily be copied into new documents (e.g., if you want to send a specific chapter to your supervisor). I have done two masters theses and one PhD dissertation (which is quite enough, thank you!), and all three of those were each done in a single document. In fact, the last masters thesis document was 167 pages in total, and the file (Word 2007 docx) was only ±365Kb, although it should be noted that this particular document had only two tables and no images or charts.

It wouldn't be fair of me not to mention the liabilities of storing your whole thesis in a single document. Firstly, if your document should become corrupt (something which, thankfully, does not happen too often if you follow the basic rules, and the impact of which can be limited through a good backup system), you could, of course, stand to lose a lot more. Furthermore, there is a limit to how many spelling errors Word can keep track of, and thus, in a large document, you might find that warning shown in Figure 198, which means that the Check Spelling as you type option will be disabled—you can, of course, still do a manual spell check.

Figure 198   *Too many language errors*

Some things, though, might seem to be liabilities of working in one document, but actually aren't. For example, if you feel that navigation through a large document of hundreds of pages is too difficult, then I hope that Chapter 11 (Finding your way: Document navigation) will have assuaged that fear.

There are, of course, disadvantages to working in separate documents too. Foremost is co-ordinating all your styles amongst the various different documents (not too hard if you keep your wits about you). Also, you cannot cross-reference (see section 8.5, p. 165) between chapters. Building a coherent index for your document is also much harder with index entries scattered across a number of documents, although in the section on building an index, I did discuss a strategy that will help you keep track of your index, even if it is scattered across several documents (see Application 9.2, p. 205). The largest liability to separate documents, though, is having to stitch them all together at the end.

Application 12.1   ***Keeping file size down***

> *Sometimes Word documents can become extremely large. Although there may be a myriad of causes for this, there are, unfortunately, only a few solutions. And even in today's world of flash disks, CDs, and DVDs, large file sizes can cause problems (e.g., when you have to e-mail the document to someone).*
>
> *One option which has already been dealt with is to manage your graphs properly, so that they cause the minimum inflation in document size. If you find that your document has suddenly ballooned, one trick that sometimes (only sometimes...) works, is to copy the whole document (**Ctrl + A**, **Ctrl + C**) and paste (**Ctrl + V**) it into a new document (obviously also based on the same template as the existing document), and then save this. The results are not consistent, but sometimes it does work. Of course, don't delete the old document until you have checked, and are happy with, the new one.*

12.1   *Working with document structure (Outline view)*

Before we examine the ways in which numerous documents can be "merged," we need to deal with a vital strategy—how to work with your document on a structural level. Word's Outline view is a tool which shows, and allows you to work with, your document on the structural level.

Instruction set 41   *Accessing Outline view*

Shortcut	Ctrl + Alt + O
Keyboard	Alt | W | U
Left click	

Before we examine the tools, two things need to be noted. Firstly, Outline view only really works properly if you have been using styles to format your document, and best when you used the built in heading styles and body text. Secondly, these tools are extremely simple to use and extremely powerful, let me warn you—tools as powerful as this will also allow you to do near-irreparable damage to your document. When I am confident that my document is properly structured, I will readily use Outline view without too much concern. But if I am at all concerned about the structural integrity of a document, I first make a backup before making changes with Outline view, and then check through the document very carefully after having made my changes.

Application 12.2   How to back up your thesis or dissertation

I have seen students with all manner of stored versions of their files. Then you get directories filled with file names like thesis version 1.docx, ... thesis version 3a.docx, thesis version 3b.docx, thesis version 3b revised.docx, thesis version 4 after supervisor Joe Blogs commented.docx, *etc. And sometimes they come to me, and don't actually know which is the most recent version of the document. Then we would have to open several of these files, so that we would have to open a whole number of them so that they can see what is actually in the file to figure out which one is the newest. Firstly, this wastes time unnecessarily, and secondly can lead to all sorts of problems—imagine you send the wrong version of your thesis to the printers, the one containing that critical fault!*

Here is a better system for backing up your files. Choose a simple name for the file you will always be working on (i.e., the file that should always represent the most recent version)—something like thesis.docx *will do quite fine. Then, when you want to back it up, copy the file in Windows Explorer, or whatever file management program you use— I prefer Total Commander (I don't recommend doing a Save As from Word, because you might just have made some change that has not been saved in the primary document). Rename the copied file in this manner:* file name yyyy-mm-dd.docx *(e.g.,* thesis 2011-04-01.docx*). The advantages to this system are that you can immediately distinguish your backups from your primary file, you can immediately see when a particular backup was made, and even when you sort your files by name, they are also sorted in the order in which the backups have been made.*

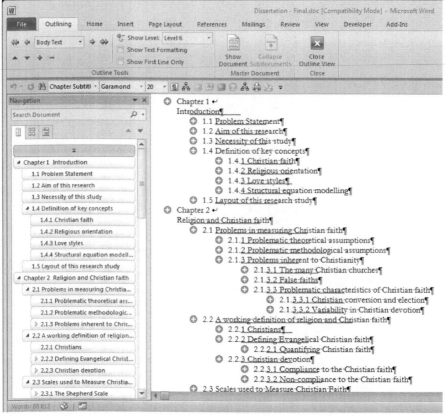

Figure 199   *Outline view of a document sans formatting*

Figure 199 shows the outline view of a document. Note the similarity between the outline and the document map. Also note that Outline view has its own ribbon, which appears to the left of the Home ribbon. The ribbon can be closed, and your document returned to Print Layout view, with the Close button on the far right of the ribbon, or you can close the ribbon by simply switching to Print Layout view (e.g., **Ctrl + Alt + P**. Lastly, note that the Show Text Formatting option has been deselected. When this option is on, all the headings (actually, all the text) will be displayed with its native formatting, which can be bothersome, as this formatting may waste a fair amount of space, or can be useful, as it will allow you to visually recognise heading levels based on their formatting. Which setting you choose to use, then, will be very much a matter of personal preference.

If you have very long headings, or if you are showing the body text as well, you can also again save space by turning on the Show First Line Only option. This will show only the first line of every paragraph.

Each heading item in the outline has, to its left, a grey circle with a plus in it (body text paragraphs will have a smaller grey circle without the plus). You can click on these circles to select all the text that falls under that level in the outline (e.g., clicking on the circle for a chapter will select the entire chapter). Double clicking these circles with either collapse or expand all the text which falls under that level in the outline.

However, the real power of Outline view lies in the remaining tools. Firstly, note that the Show Level tool (Figure 200) allows you to show your document at various structural levels. If you choose any of the levels from 1 to 9, then all headings above or at that level will be shown, but no body text will be shown. If you select All Levels, then the entire document, including all the body text, is shown. If you are not certain how many heading levels a document contains, you can always select Level 9 to exclude all body text and include all headings. Note that in Figure 199, the level was set to Level 6.

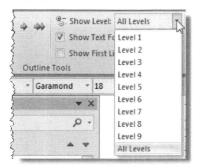

Figure 200   *Outlining tools: Show Level*

The set of tools on the left allows you, not to *view* the structure of your document, but to *alter* it. The top (green) tools allow you to adjust the level of any text you have selected in the outline. I dislike the two outermost tools, which change everything selected, regardless of initial level, to either Heading 1 or Body text. The inner two tools (**Alt + Shift + Left** and **Alt + Shift + Right** on the keyboard respectively[77]), allow you to variably move each level up or down one (e.g., Heading 2 in the selected text becomes Heading 1, Heading 3 becomes Heading 2, etc.). The list box in the middle allows you to choose a level, but again the same level is applied to everything that is selected.

The lower (blue) tools allow you, not to alter the levels of your outline, but to reorder parts of your document in the outline. Oddly, the Plus (**Alt + Shift + +**) and Minus (**Alt + Shift + _**) tools do not actually change anything, but also relate to how you view the outline—they either expand or collapse parts of the outline. What does make them nice is that they do it by level, unlike the grey circle icons in the outline. Thus, if I have an expanded outline, clicking the minus (or **Alt + Shift + _**) will, for that part of the outline that is selected only, collapse to the next highest level, and the plus (**Alt + Shift + +**) will expand that selected part of the outline by one level more.

The last two tools (at the bottom left of the group) are the really powerful ones. They allow you to reorder items in the outline. However, the way to use them effectively is

---

[77] These keyboard shortcuts work even when you are not in Outline view, although in Outline view it is easier to select large bodies of text and then apply the keyboard shortcuts.

slightly cryptic. First, let me point out that if you like living dangerously, you could click and drag items in the outline to reorder them. I explained on p. 258 why I think that is a bad idea—I am far too scared to do that, and always rather revert to these two tools. The up arrow (**Alt + Shift + Up**) allows you to move what you have selected up (i.e., forward in the outline), and the down arrow (**Alt + Shift + Down**) allows you to move what you have selected down (i.e., further on in the outline). However, the two tools do not move items at their same level, but rather in the outline, regardless of level. Thus, if I have expanded to all available heading levels, and I position myself on a Heading 1 item (e.g., Chapter 2), and the item above it is a Heading 2 item (e.g., 1.5), and I use the Move up tool, then two things should be noted. Firstly, the whole of Chapter 2 is not moved up (if I had used the grey circle to first select it, it would have been). Secondly, Chapter 2 and Chapter 1 are not switched, rather, Chapter 2 now becomes part of Chapter 1, and specifically, it now finds itself in the position 1.4. In other words, the tool did not just reorder items, but it also changed their level in the process. You might recall that when I spoke earlier of the power of the remaining tools, the first tool I discussed was the Show Level tool. I find it best to use this tool in conjunction with the move tools. Thus, if I want to switch two chapters, which are obviously at the Heading 1 level, then I first use the Show Level tool collapse to Level 1. Then I can position myself in one of the chapters, and move it. Now, because all the levels and text underneath it have been collapsed, they are all moved together, and because the other chapter has also been collapsed, the two chapters literally switch places.

Application 12.3   ***Reorganising your thesis or dissertation***

It is a relatively common thing for supervisors to ask their students to switch parts of chapters, or even whole chapters around. This has happened to me with the theses and dissertations I wrote, and I often see students struggle with these demands when they write their own theses or dissertations. This Outline tool can literally save, not just hours of time, but whole days of work. Do make a backup, but do learn how to use these tools. And remember also that the outline view is a great writing tool, as it allows you to see the flow of your thinking and a bird's eye view of the organisation of your material.

12.2   Combining smaller documents into one larger document

If you find that your document is too big, and you would prefer to break it up into smaller individual documents, or if you have in any case decided to do your chapters individually, then you will need, at the very end, to bring it all together again. There are two strategies for this. The low tech, but tried and tested method is actually very simple: Create a new document based on your base template, and then sequentially copy and paste each of your document chapters into it. When you are done, the result will be one document containing all the basic components.

Warning: If you are using the Citations & Bibliography tool (see Chapter 13, p. 281), then copying a document's text into another document does not also copy the sources. You will have to copy the sources across from the master list into the new document as described in section 13.2.5, p. 290).

The other strategy is to consider using master documents.

12.2.1   Using master documents

Master documents is the feature of word used to stitch together smaller documents into a coherent whole. The theory is that you can edit and work on the individual documents, or at any time revert to the larger document. However, using master documents is not for the faint-hearted. Any number of things can, and usually will, go wrong. In fact, the Word MVPs (Most Valued Professionals) generally advise against using master documents, as all the documents used (i.e., the master and its subdocuments) will all tend to become corrupted over time.

Basically, a master document is one in which "contains" a number of smaller documents (sub-documents). Each sub-document thus contains only a section of the larger document, and all the sub-documents are brought together in the master document. You can open the master and work on any of the individual documents, and if you save it, those individual documents that have been altered will be saved. You can also open and edit any subdocument on its own, and if you later open the master, those changes will obviously be reflected there.

There are essentially two approaches to working with master documents. One is to break a larger document up into a number of subdocuments, and the other is to start each document individually and then later merge them into a master document. Before we discuss those, though, it will help to understand the way a master document and its subdocuments are structured.

12.2.1.1   What is a master document?

Figure 201 attempts to explain the structure of a master document with its subdocuments. A master document is, at its most basic level, still just a Word document. It can (but need not) contain text, just like any other document. Importantly, it is also based on a template, and this is very important, since the first thing to make sure that your master document is working properly is to ensure that both the master and all the subdocuments are based on the same underlying template. Get this wrong, and a nightmare is awaiting you in your future. However, in addition to the fact that a master document can contain text, any number of subdocuments can be inserted into it at any number of position. Wherever the subdocument is inserted, it will contribute all of its text to the master.

Figure 201   *Master document structure*

The final thing to note is that Word maintains the distinction between the master and its subdocuments by inserting section breaks: A continuous section break is added to the master document just before the point at which the subdocument is added, and a next page section break is inserted at the very end of the subdocument. Thus, if you don't want to work with a document that is broken into many different sections, you had best avoid working with a master document. Also, it would not be wise to try to delete the section breaks that Word inserts.

Because working with the master document is essentially a way of working with the document structure, the tools are accessed from Outline view (section 12.1). If you select the Show Document button on this ribbon, the Master Document tools are expanded on the ribbon (Figure 202).

Figure 202   *Outlining ribbon showing Master Document tools*

12.2.1.2   *Breaking a document into subdocuments*

Instruction set 42   Creating a subdocument

Keyboard	Alt │ U │ A
Left click	

If you have an existing document and want to break up the document into subdocuments, all you need to do is switch to Outline view, select the text that you want to break away into the subdocument, and then (Instruction set 42) select the Create (subdocument) button in the Master Document tools group of the Outlining ribbon

(Word will complain if the section does not contain any headings, and the ideal is to select a whole chapter at a time). Word will automatically save the subdocument to the disk using the first line of text in that section as the file name. Also, importantly, if your original document is based on a template, then the subdocument will be based on the same template.

Word will also save the subdocument in the same directory as the original (now master) document. Although it may not look like it, Word inserts the sub-document into the master document with relative referencing—i.e., the sub-document's location on the hard drive is stored relative to the location of the master document. When the master- and sub-documents are in the same directory, they can be moved from disk to disk or directory to directory without Word losing the link between them.

12.2.1.3   Adding subdocuments to a master document

Instruction set 43   *Inserting a subdocument*

Keyboard	Alt | U | N
Left click	

The opposite approach is to create the subdocuments individually (this gives you the advantage of giving each document its own name[78]). Please note that each document *must* be associated with the same template as the master document, and the Automatically <u>up</u>date document styles *must* be activated[79]. Next, in the master document, switch to Outline view, and then go to the position where you would want each subdocument inserted, and select the Insert (subdocument) tool (Instruction set 43). Word will open the file browser, and you can choose the subdocument you want, and Word will insert it into that position in the master document.

However, beware of the common error of creating or inserting one sub-document within another sub-document, instead of just before or after it in the master document.

12.2.1.4   Working with the master document

Obviously, you can open each subdocument individually and work on it. You can also print and e-mail each subdocument individually.

However, there are a number of times when you would want to open the master and work with it (e.g., if you want to add a cross-reference from one subdocument to another, or if you want to print out the larger document, etc.). To do this, open the

---

[78] Make sure that the names you choose help you to identify the document contents—names could be as simple as "Chapter 1," etc. The master document's title should reflect its status (again, even a simple name such as "Dissertation" will do).

[79] Sure, you can ignore this advice, and it will still work, until the styles start breaking!

master document. You will see that each subdocument appears as a link inside the master document (Figure 203).

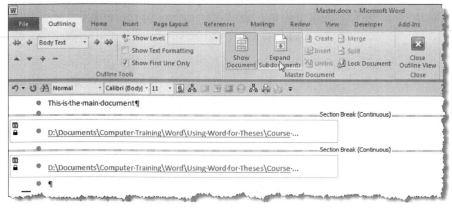

Figure 203   *Master document containing subdocuments*

You can then expand the subdocuments (either with the **Ctrl + ** keyboard shortcut, even in Print Layout view), or with the Expand subdocuments tool in the Outlining ribbon (Instruction set 44). This will then display the text of all the subdocuments within the master document. You can also double click on any individual link for a subdocument to have Word open that document in a separate document window. Note that each subdocument is enclosed in a feint grey rectangle. If you want to do some work on the master (e.g., I will be discussing page numbering briefly for a master document below), then make sure that you click outside of the grey rectangle. This is especially important when you add successive subdocuments to the master—make sure that you position yourself outside of the rectangle before you insert a subdocument, or else you will insert a subdocument into a subdocument—anathema for working with master documents!

When you close the master, Word will ask you whether you want to save each of the subdocuments in which anything was changed.

Instruction set 44   *Expanding subdocuments*

Shortcut	Ctrl + \\
Keyboard	Alt	U	N
Left click	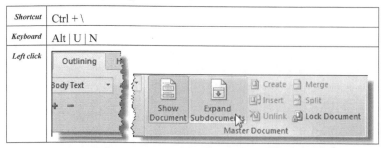

I will not show separate instruction sets for the remaining tools, but will rather discuss them briefly in turn. All of these tools can be seen in any of the preceding Instruction sets or figures. However, take note that even though the tools are there, the general consensus amongst Word MVPs is that not all of these tools should actually be used. I will discuss a strategy for working with master documents after the explanation of the tools.

If you select the Unlink (Remove subdocument) tool (Alt | U | I), the subdocument text will be copied into the master document, and the link to it will be removed. This is, then, essentially the reverse of creating subdocuments.

You can also use the Split (subdocument) tool (Alt | U | S) to break a single subdocument up into two different subdocuments. The reverse of this can be done with the Merge (subdocument) tool (Alt | U | G)—multiple subdocuments can be merged into a single subdocument (all the text from each subdocument is merged into the first subdocument). Simply select the entirety of the documents in Outline view, and then merge them together.

Lastly, the Lock (subdocument) tool allows you to lock a subdocument so that it cannot be changed from the master. I generally advise against this, though, as locking subdocuments is often the first step down the slippery slope of failed master documents.

12.2.1.5 *A strategy for using master documents*

After all of this, perhaps a strategy should be devised for how to work with master documents while incurring the minimum trouble.

Perhaps the first thing to remember about using masters is that you generally shouldn't. When considering the typical page count for a dissertation, Word can handle that number of pages easily. What if your supervisor wants you to send just a single chapter? Well, with Outline view, it is the easiest thing on earth to select the entire chapter, and then to paste it to a new document. Just remember to first base that document on the same template, and to Automatically update styles in the process. The Word uTIlity Copy to New automates this process for you.

If you do work with separate documents, then you need to make sure that you do the following:

1. Ensure that all of the separate documents are based on the same template, and that all of them are set to Automatically update document styles in the process. The Word uTIlity Share Template automates this process for you.

2. If you want to combine the separate documents, consider not combining them as subdocuments into a master, but rather just copy their content, sequentially, from the individual documents into a new document that contains all the text. This is especially effective if you have ensured that all the documents, and the new document, are all based on the same template. The Word uTIlity Combine Documents automates this process for you.

3. Only merge the subdocuments into the master when you need to work on the whole, and preferably leave that right to the end. The process of inserting subdocuments is so quick that you can really take your documents (see the next point first, though), merge them into a master, use that master, and then delete it again.

4. Check and work through all changes and revisions in the separate documents before you start merging them into your master. There should be absolutely no revisions outstanding.

5. Before you insert your subdocuments into your master, first make a backup of the unmerged documents (zip them into an archive). Then work with the files to merge them into the master, knowing that if they do become corrupt, you will still have the unadulterated originals at your disposal. This, of course, explains why it is best to only merge the documents at the end. Please note that the master itself should also be backed up in this way before any of the subdocuments are merged into it. This is because, as we shall see in the next point, your master itself will probably contain some text already.

6. Despite the fact that the master document can contain large amounts of text, interspersed in between the various subdocuments, this is again an invitation to corruption. The master should only contain the "preliminary" pages of your thesis or dissertation (i.e., title page, acknowledgements, etc., up to the table of contents) and then the closing reference list. All appendices, and all chapter, should be inserted as subdocuments. The table of contents and the reference list, of course, cannot be subdocuments, because they need to access all the information from all the subdocuments for their information. In short, keep the text in the master to the minimum. I normally create everything that needs to be in the master, up to and including the titles and a blank paragraph for the table of contents, list of tables and/or figures, and the reference list. Then this gets saved, the subdocuments get inserted, and the table of contents and reference list generated in the master.

7. Set the page numbering (actually, all the header and footer information) of the entire document from within the master. If you find yourself having problems in this regard, then delete the page numbering from all the documents (master and all subdocuments—in the subdocuments, delete all the headers and footers), and then re-insert the page numbering only in the master document.

Some don'ts should also probably be mentioned. You may notice that there is a similarity between some of these and some of the points just mentioned, but that is intentional, I can assure you.

1. Never insert a subdocument into an existing subdocument—Word will let you do it, but this is just inviting ruin and destruction into your documents. There should also be no need to do this. If you do find the need to do something like this, then it means that you have made a mistake in how you have divided up your subdocuments—you should rather rethink how you have divided your text into the different subdocuments than fall into the temptation of inserting a subdocument into another subdocument. Note, though, that this is actually easy to do accidentally if you aren't concentrating when you are inserting your subdocuments into the master—all you need to do is position yourself somewhere within another subdocument.

2. Don't set page numbering in a subdocument. If you do, delete it before merging it into your master. In fact, don't add anything to the headers or footers of your

subdocuments, and if you do, delete them in entirety before adding them to the master.

3. Don't adjust the numbering so that each subdocument's numbering will start at the "right" number for that chapter. Your supervisor will have to get used to chapter five being printed out as chapter 1—assure them that it will come out right in the end (or, if they are very immovable, copy the whole lot to a new document, adjust the numbering there before printing/e-mailing, and then keep your original unadjusted).

4. Do not use different numbering lists in your different subdocuments. Always make sure that the lists you use are stored in, and accessed from, the template, which should be the same underlying template for all documents.

5. Do not use track changes in the master or in any of the subdocuments from the master. Do not work with the master while there are any unresolved revisions in any of the subdocuments.

6. If you read up about master documents on the Internet, you will see that many word MVPs recommend deleting all section breaks in the master and the subdocuments. The reasoning behind this is that section breaks, in and of themselves, invite document corruption, and master documents are full of section breaks. I recommended on p. 272 that you not delete the section breaks. The simple reason for this is that some of your separate documents may have very different section settings (e.g., some of them might be landscape, which is precisely why they are in a separate document). You could wipe out many of these settings in this way, and create even more of a mess. However, if you do want to delete section breaks in an attempt to recover a master document that is failing (if you followed some of my previous recommendations, you would probably be able to just start over with a new master, rather than struggling with the current one), then I advise against using a Find and Replace to remove all section breaks. Rather, use Find or GoTo to navigate to the next section (this was discussed in section 11.3, p. 247). Then go to the end of the document (**Ctrl + End**). Then use the object browser (**Ctrl + Page Up** to go to the last visible section break in the document (technically, the second to last section break in the document), and work your way up from there, deleting the section breaks you don't want manually, and in reverse. If you are doing this, save often.

In closing, you may have read this whole section, and come to the conclusion: "If master documents are so much trouble to work with, why bother?" Precisely!

12.3   Opening corrupted documents

Chances are, the day will come when a document you open consistently causes Word to crash. Or, Word will tell you that the document is corrupted and cannot be opened. Normally, this is the time for the "I told you so" speech about having good backups, etc. And perhaps it would be good to mention that there are several good online backup facilities available at little or no cost. Microsoft's Windows Live SkyDrive (http://get.live.com) is available to registered users of Office (that's you, since you're typing your dissertation in Word). You could also look at services like DropBox (www.dropbox.com) or SugarSync (www.sugarsync.com). I even know of one guy who just e-mails his important documents to himself, so that they will be stored in his Gmail inbox (my Gmail inbox at present is standing at 7Gb—that's plenty of space for backing up some important files). You could even create a filtering rule to move all your mails with the subject line "Backup from Me" or something similar to a dedicated backups folder, and then just delete older versions there, if you have to manage your space.

All right, now that I've berated you for your carelessness, is there anything that can be done to rescue the situation? Fortunately, yes. Microsoft have become quite adept at recovering documents, and much of this functionality is built into Word. Firstly, note that Word 2010 keeps track of several versions of your document as you work. Figure 204 shows the various autosaved versions of a document from the Info Tab of the Backstage (File) view. You can click on any of those to open that version.

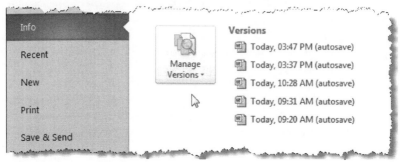

Figure 204   *Previous versions of a document*

Furthermore, Word can attempt to recover information from corrupted documents. When opening a file, instead of clicking on Open in the File browser, select the drop-down portion of the Open button (Figure 205). You will see some useful options there, such as the ability to open a copy of a document (leaving the original intact), and the last option is the one you want—Open and Repair. Word will them attempt to extract as much of the text formatting from the document as is possible, and even to repair many of the other settings. At worst, you will lose all your formatting but still have your text. If you had mainly text to start with, that wouldn't be so bad, as the formatting can quickly be restored using styles. If you have a lot of tables, and that is lost, you may have a lot more work to do. But, considering that you had no backup, it may still be less work than doing the whole thing over.

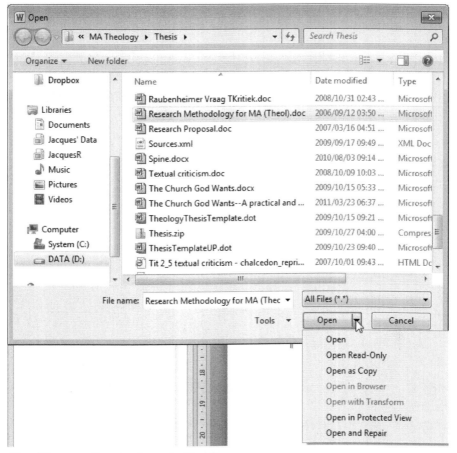

Figure 205   Alternatives for opening Word documents

If you do recover something from a document, I recommend selecting the whole document except the last paragraph mark (**Ctrl + Home**, **Ctrl + Shift + End**, **Shift + Left**). Then copy this, and paste it into a new document that has been based on your thesis template. The reason that you want to exclude the last paragraph mark is that it contains the implicit last section break, and selecting this is the same as pressing **Ctrl + A**, which selects the document with all its metadata, including the possible information which corrupted it in the first place. It's quite unlikely that that data would have survived the Open and Repair process, but since the document has become corrupted once, it won't hurt to be careful.

Chapter 13
Going to the Source: Citations and References

Academic writing means engaging the scientific literature of your chosen field in a responsible and critical manner. This means that you need to reference your sources—the bane of a disorganised post graduate student's existence.

13.1   Reference Management Software

A not-so-recent development in the world of computers is the use of Reference Management Software (RMS), sometimes also referred to as Reference Management Systems. Surprisingly, very few academics (at least in South Africa) are even aware of the existence of such programs, let alone make use of them. It is not my intention here to explain in detail how to use this kind of software program—each of them could require a course on their own. Far rather, allow me to quickly list the advantages of these programs:

First, they store all your references in a database. This means that you will never have to go searching through a dusty old file cabinet, or paging through countless of your articles to find a reference you once used. Also, references can be stored in a single or multiple databases—this means that if you do work in a variety of unrelated fields, you can create databases for each one, and thus introduce order into your references. References can also be copied from one database to another, and can be sorted within databases according to a number of keywords. This makes it very easy to share references with colleagues. Also, having a reference in a database means that you will never have to type in that reference again—you type it in once, and it is always there (provided you make backups, of course).

Second, good RMS programs allow you to insert citations from your database into Word (e.g., EndNote/ProCite/Reference Manager's Cite While You Write/CWYW™) . Thus you don't need to jump up and down continuously to get the reference details right. You can insert the reference without ever having to leave Word. And, obviously, if the citations can be inserted into a Word document then it stands to reason that good RMS programs can generate a reference list or bibliography for you, saving you countless hours of work.

A big problem with large documents such as dissertations (much more so than small articles) is that they may contain hundreds of references (a typical well-researched dissertation would have in the order of 400 or more references—one person I know had over 900!). It is no small feat to get the reference list on such a large document right. For instance, just getting the references in alphabetical order is harder than it seems (not even Word's Sort feature can always handle all the intricacies of ordering some surnames!). Furthermore, you promoter may ask you to delete a section which may contain your only reference to a certain source. It is not always easy to ensure that your reference list contains *all* the references it should, on the one hand, and *only* the references it should, on the other. The database features of RMS programs allow you to check very clearly which references have been used, and which have not.

Allow me to also list one caveat to using RMS programs: They do the work for you, but they don't (can't) think for you. Many people, when they first hear of RMS programs, think that they now no longer need to learn how referencing styles work. This is simply not true. RMS programs increase the accuracy of your referencing, and they vastly reduce the amount of work required in referencing, but to get it all right, you still do need to learn the referencing style(s) that you are using. Many RMS programs come with predefined styles, and this is often touted as an advantage. My own experience is that these predefined styles do not match the style guides they claim to represent, and unwary users who rely on the programs to do all the thinking, may end up with incorrectly formatted references and/or reference lists. Fortunately, most good RMS programs allow users to modify their styles, and even create their own styles, although this is often a complex process, and can be frustrating until you get the hang of it. The advantage, of course, is that this has to be done only once (provided you back up all the styles that you have created). Having said that, the ability to have and define styles is still a big plus. The customisation of existing styles is still much better than sorting it all out from scratch.

Some (but not all) of the most popular RMS programs on the market are shown in Table 14. You can also find an elementary reference on Wikipedia (http://en.wikipedia.org/wiki/Reference_management_software), and an internet search for "Reference Management Software" (include the quotation marks) will take you to numerous websites discussing these systems, and also comparing their features.

Finally, referencing tools are now also being built into word processors. OpenOffice has basic bibliographic tools included. In Word 2007, Microsoft introduced its own attempt at this, and these features were slightly tweaked in Word 2010. Word's referencing tools are, however, very basic (as will be pointed out), and might suffice for a pregraduate assignment, but would barely be sufficient for a full-blown dissertation. As an example, they come with very limited style sets, and style sets can also not be customised.

Table 14   *Selected Reference Management Systems*

Program	Website	License
Papyrus	http://www.researchsoftwaredesign.com	Unsupported Free
Citation	http://www.citationonline.net	Commercial
EndNote	http://www.endnote.com	Commercial
Reference Manager	http://www.referencemanager.com	Commercial
RefWorks	http://www.refworks.com	Commercial
Zotero	http://www.zotero.org	Open source

13.2   Citations and Bibliographies in Word

Since Word 2007, Word now contains a new set of tools to help with citations and bibliographies. These tools reside in the Citations & Bibliography group on the References ribbon. Please do not confuse them with the Table of Authorities tools (also on the References ribbon), which have to do with legal style referencing.

Figure 206   *References ribbon: Citations & Bibliography group*

13.2.1   Setting referencing style

The first step to using Word's bibliographic tool is to choose the referencing style you will be using (Instruction set 45). This is important, because both the way the sources are captured and the way they are inserted depends on the style you are using. The problem, of course, is that to date Word only has a total of ten main different styles[80] (listed in Table 10), whereas good RMS programs have hundreds or even thousands of different styles, including the main styles used around the world, as well as specific styles for specific scientific journals[81]. Furthermore, good RMS programs have the ability to add new styles through a customised GUI (i.e., you can pretty much point and click to define your style), which Word does not. Only if you are willing to take on the vagaries of XML programming, can you create your own customised styles in Word[82].

A further problem is that the styles that come with RMS programs (and that probably includes Word) almost never match the precise definition that your institution might be using. Good RMS programs also have the ability to customise all of your existing styles, whereas Word does not easily allow this[82].

A little caveat is that you want to download the Service Packs for Word 2010 (SP1[83]) or Word 2007 (SP3[84]) which contain updates to the styles, although, as can be seen in Instruction set 45, all Microsoft did was a cosmetic upgrade of the styles, instead of a proper expansion of the styles—I remain bitterly disappointed by their efforts in this regard.

---

[80] There are some variations (e.g., different editions) of the main styles, but you would typically only use the latest edition.

[81] If you intend publishing in a certain journal, you can often download a style template of programs like EndNote for that journal from their website.

[82] See http://blogs.office.com/b/microsoft-word/archive/2009/04/29/bibliography-citations-102-building-custom-styles.aspx for an introduction.

[83] http://office.microsoft.com/en-za/word-help/redir/XT102653134.aspx

[84] http://office.microsoft.com/en-za/word-help/redir/XT102843954.aspx

Instruction set 45   Setting the Referencing Style

Keyboard	Alt	S	L
Left click	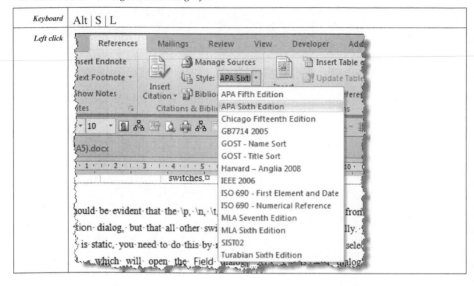

Table 15   *Referencing Styles in Word 2010SP1*

MSWord style name	Responsible organisation	Institutional Website	File name
APA	American Psychological Association	http://apastyle.org/	APA.XSL APASixthEditionOfficeOnline.xsl
Chicago	The Chicago Manual of Style	http://www.chicagomanualofstyle.org/tools_citationguide.html	CHICAGO.XSL
GB7714	Standardization Administration of China		GB.XSL
GOST - Name Sort	The Federal Agency of the Russian Federation on Technical Regulating and Metrology	http://www.gost.ru	GostName.XSL
GOST - Title Sort	The Federal Agency of the Russian Federation on Technical Regulating and Metrology		GostTitle.XSL
Hardvard[85]—Anglia IEEE 2006	Anglia Ruskin University Institute of Electrical and Electronics Engineers	http://libweb.anglia.ac.uk/referencing/harvard.htm http://www.ieee.org/documents/stylemanual.pdf	HarvardAnglia2008OfficeOnline.xsl IEEE2006OfficeOnline.xsl
ISO 690 - First Element and Date	International Organization for Standardization	http://www.iso.org/iso/iso_catalogue/catalogue_tc/catalogue_detail.htm?csnumber=43320	ISO690.XSL
ISO 690 - Numerical Reference	International Organization for Standardization		ISO690Nmerical.XSL
MLA	Modern Language Association	http://www.mla.org/style	MLA.XSL MLASeventhEditionOfficeOnline.xsl
SIST02	Standards for Information of Science and Technology by Japan Science and Technology Agency	http://sist-jst.jp/handbook/sist02_2007/main.htm	SIST02.XSL
Turabian	Turabian Style (University of Chicago)	http://www.press.uchicago.edu/books/turabian/index.html	TURABIAN.XSL

[85] ⑧There are several "variants" of the Harvard style, notably Anglia, Leeds, and Exeter, as well as the South African version.

13.2.2 Adding sources

The next step to using Word's bibliographic tool is to add your sources to a database. If you have a whole bunch of sources to add, you can open the Manage Sources dialog, and click on the New... button repeatedly to add them. Alternatively, you can add them one at a time, from the Insert Citation menu's Add New Source... option (Instruction set 46).

Instruction set 46   Adding a New Citation Source

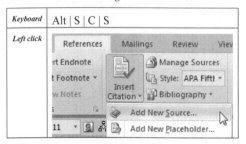

This will bring up the Create Source dialog (Figure 207). Word allows you to add 17 different types of sources, which at least cover the most common types of sources (with some important omissions like computer programs[86], personal communications, etc.). The seventeenth source type is "Miscellaneous," which is meant to cover all those that are not in the list, but might not quite meet your needs. The fields presented for you to complete will, of course, depend on which source type and which referencing style you have chosen (hence the importance of setting the referencing style first, and of choosing the right source type).

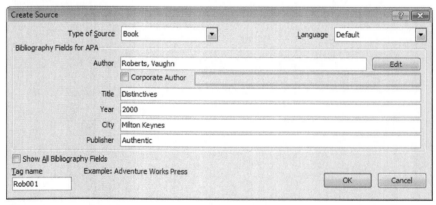

Figure 207   Create Source dialog

If you find that you need to add certain information which is not in the list of fields given to you (e.g., the volume number of a book), you can select the Show All

---

[86] One would really have thought a company like Microsoft, which creates computer programs, would not miss that one!

Bibliography Fields button to have more fields displayed (Figure 208), although these will again be source type specific. It is also a good idea to set the language being used for the reference in the Language list box at the top right. You will also notice that Word assigns a tag to your source. This is used to distinguish sources from each other, and as Word automatically assigns a unique tag to each source, you need actually not worry about changing this (in fact, it is best not to fiddle with this, because if you create duplicate tags, you will be messing up your referencing).

In contrast to adding sources via the Manage Sources dialog, if you added the source via the Insert Citation tool, it will, when you are done, be added automatically at the current working position—this is nice, since it means that you can add your sources as you are working.

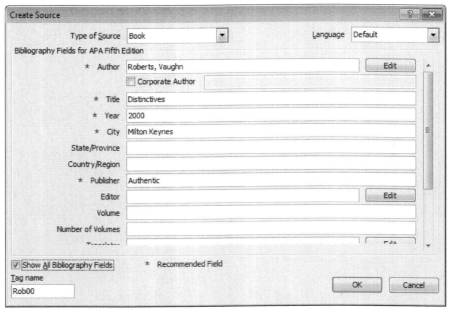

Figure 208　　　*Create Source dialog showing more fields (compare Figure 207)*

Application 13.1　　*Adding source details*

Even though Word guides you through the process of adding information about a source with an example for each field displayed near the bottom of the Create Source dialog, some tips for entering information into the Create Source dialog might help.

Firstly, add all the information you have available. Sometimes you might not have some information about your source—add it anyway, and edit it later to add whatever is missing. Sometimes you might have information that you think you might not need—add it anyway. The little time lost adding information now that you end up not using pales in comparison to the time lost trying to find information about a source when you later discover you need it. An example of this is to add the author's full names, if you have them. Some (very few) journals, for example, might want full names. But it's a lot easier to abbreviate full names in your references and bibliography, than what it is to later go and find all those full names again.

Secondly, while we are on the topic of author names, if you don't have a full name, just add the initial, without a period, and separate multiple initials with spaces. Also, if you have more than one author, separate their names with a semicolon and a space.

Third, use proper capitalisation in the titles of sources (i.e., the first word of the title and all proper nouns get capitalised, all else is not capitalised).

Fourth, remember that en dashes (see section 3.2.3.3.4, p. 41) are used for number ranges, thus, when you add the page numbers, use the en dash (the dialog accepts it).

13.2.3   Inserting a citation

Once the source has been added, it will appear in a list under Insert Citation. Thus, if you did not add a citation "on the fly" by using the Add New Source... option, you can insert the citation from the list of sources in this tool (Figure 209). Note that, since you will only be adding a source once, most of your citations will be added in this fashion.

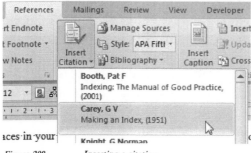

Figure 209   Inserting a citation

If you don't have a source, you could also just insert a placeholder from the Insert Citation tool (see Instruction set 46 again). You can then later return and add the source to the placeholder by selecting Edit Source (see the list of options in Figure 211), and adding the source details in the Edit Source dialog (which is, apart from the title, exactly the same as the Create Source dialog). You can also search for a source using the Search Libraries tool, which will open up the Research pane.

While the citation will look like standard text, it is actually a Word Citation field, as you will discover if you were to hold your mouse over it (see the shading shown in Figure 213), or click on it (see the citation box shown in Figure 211).

Remember that one often references multiple sources for a single point (especially if you have done your reading well). Word will allow you to reference as many sources as you want, and will combine them in the citation. If you want to do this, make sure that you position yourself within the citation field (the simplest is just to press ← once as soon as the citation has been added). When you then add another source, it is added to the same citation field. Figure 210 shows a citation with two sources, and a third about to be added.

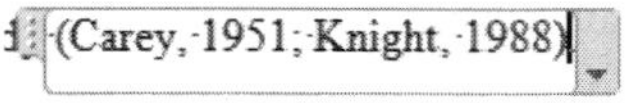

(Carey, 1951; Knight, 1988)

Figure 210   *Adding multiple sources to a single citation*

13.2.4   Editing citations

Once the citation has been added, you can then modify it (I must admit, I find this a bit laborious—proper Reference Management Software applications allow you to add the reference and do the modification in a single step). If you do click on it, you will see the citation box, with an arrow on its right. Selecting this arrow (Figure 211), or right clicking anywhere on the citation, will allow you to edit the citation, edit its source (e.g., if you see that you misspelled the author's name), convert the citation to text87, or update your bibliography (see 13.2.6 below), and so include your new reference, without having to go there first.

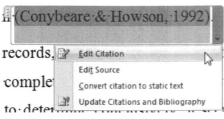

Figure 211   *Selecting Edit Citation*

The Edit Citation dialog will allow you to enter page numbers for your reference, or to suppress the author, year or title information (Figure 212).

Figure 212   *Edit Citation dialog*

For example, Figure 213 shows the same citation from Figure 211, just with the page numbers added. If you want to suppress the author name, Word may, depending on which referencing style you are using, replace it with the title[88], so you may need to actually suppress the author name *and* title to get only the date displayed. As was mentioned before, en dashes (section 3.2.3.3.4, p. 41) are used for number ranges, thus, when you add the page numbers, use the en dash (the dialog accepts it).

---

[87] Note that the field is then removed, which means that this reference will no longer be updated if you were to edit it (e.g., in the Source Manager dialog), and will not be included in the bibliography.

[88] Microsoft reports this as a known bug.

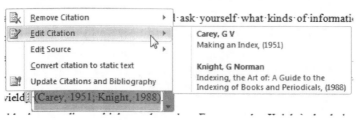

in (Conybeare·&·Howson,·1992,·pp.·832–834).¶

Figure 213   *Citation with page numbers added*

If you have referenced multiple sources in a single citation, you can then edit every source in a citation individually (e.g., to add page numbers, or suppress one of the information fields)—the Edit Source option will change to a sub-menu title, and holding your mouse over it will display all the sources cited in its sub-menu (Figure 214). Similarly, you can remove any of the sources, or edit any of the sources.

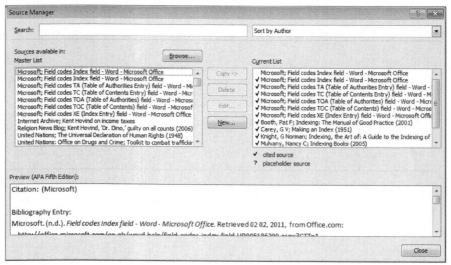

Figure 214   *Working with multiple sources in a single citation*

13.2.5   Managing sources

When you have a large number of sources, you will want to manage them. This is done with the Source Manager dialog (Figure 215), which is launched from the Manage Sources tool in the Citations & Bibliography group on the References ribbon (Alt | S | M).

Figure 215   *Source Manager dialog*

This tool will allow you to sort your sources by Author, Title, Year or Tag (good RMS programs allow you to sort on any number of fields, which is essential for managing really large numbers of sources). You can also search for a source using the <u>S</u>earch tool, and Word will preview the bibliographic entry for the source based on the referencing style you have chosen (see 13.2.1).

It's important also to understand how Word handles sources that you add to it. Whenever a source is added (as described in 13.2.2), it is added to what Word calls the Master List of sources (stored in C:\Users*UserName*\AppData\Roaming\Microsoft\ Bibliography\Sources.xml), regardless of which document you are working in. In other words, Word collects all the sources that you ever use. If you want to use a source that you have already added at an earlier stage, you need to load it to the Current List for that document. Simply select the source (you can select multiple sources at a time) and click on <u>C</u>opy. The source will now appear on the list of sources on the Insert Citation tool (as shown in Figure 209). You can also <u>D</u>elete, <u>E</u>dit, and add <u>N</u>ew sources (the latter was mentioned on p. 286). Lastly, the sources already cited in the document will have tick marks next to them—this will come into play again when we examine creating a bibliography in the next section.

Sadly, all this tool does is show you your sources in your master list and in your document—in reality it does very little to actually help you *manage* your sources. Good RMS programs help you manage your sources by allowing you to easily identify duplicates (in Figure 215, Word gives no indication that the two sources at the top of the list are duplicates), by allowing you to filter, group, and classify your sources, and by allowing you to easily index your sources with keywords. If you have only a few sources, that's not a major problem, but if you do large amounts of work, over lengthy periods of time, where your sources might run into the thousands, this is not just a problem, it is a major shortcoming.

13.2.6   Creating a bibliography

When you are ready, Word can create a bibliography for your document. Simply position yourself in the document at the place where you want the bibliography to be added, and select the Bibliography tool in the Citations & Bibliography group on the References ribbon (Alt | S | B). As Instruction set 47 shows, Word has two options built in, and you can create your own using the <u>S</u>ave Selection to Bibliography Gallery... tool.

Instruction set 47   Inserting a bibliography

Keyboard	Alt | S | B | B
Left click	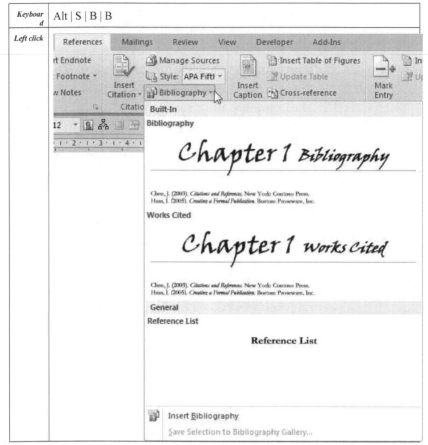

Unfortunately, the two options provided by Word (Bibliography and Works Cited) provide exactly the same result: a bibliography, just with two different titles. In academia, a bibliography is a list of all sources consulted in the course of your work, both those referenced in your thesis and those not referenced. A reference list, by contrast, is a list of only those sources which are directly referenced in your thesis (Neville, 2007, pp. 13–14, 87). Most disciplines require reference lists, although some may want bibliographies. Word cannot, automatically, give you a reference list.

The distinction between the two titles also reflects a misunderstanding of the terms (i.e., Microsoft's Wunderkinds got it wrong—they may be clever programmers, but they show little experience of having done academic work): Most styles would distinguish between a "Bibliography" and a "Reference list," whereas the MLA style distinguishes, respectively, between a list of "Works consulted" and a list of "Works cited" (and hence, presumably, Microsoft's two different titles). In other words, the options you should have seen should have been "Bibliography" and "Works consulted" (not "Works cited"), since both options provide you with a bibliography only. Now what we would have *wanted* to see[89] would have been these two options: "Bibliography/Works consulted" and "Reference list/Works cited" (And depending on whether you have chosen MLA or one of the other styles, Word should have named it appropriately).

Getting back to what Word does offer, The two options differ only with regards to their titles ("Bibliography" or "Works Cited"), and both will insert a bibliography field into a box, but will use all the sources in the current list for the document (see the Source Manager dialog in Figure 215) into that bibliography. The top of the box (Figure 216) will have options to switch from one title to the other, or to convert the bibliography into static text, and will allow you to update the bibliography at any time.

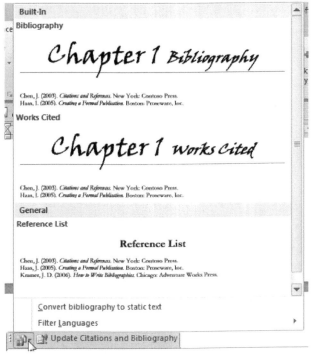

Figure 216   *Bibliography options*

Note that Word uses the Heading 1 style for the title (you may want to change that) and also the Bibliography style for the bibliography (you should probably not change that, but you may want to customise it, as it is based on the Normal style—see Chapter 6 for a discussion of these styles).

How, then, can a reference list be created? The first thing to do is to create the necessary title: Add a bibliography as already described. Then rename the title to "Reference List" and make sure that it is in the style you prefer (note the different style shown in the gallery in Instruction set 47 and Figure 216). Then select the new title and the entire

---

[89] If anyone from Microsoft is reading this book, please take note!

bibliography. Next, click on <u>S</u>ave Selection to Bibliography Gallery... in the Bibliography tool in the Citations & Bibliography group on the References ribbon (Alt | S | B | S, cf. Instruction set 47).

All that remains is to make sure that no sources appear in the list that are not cited. To do this, use the Source Manager dialog discussed above, and make sure that there are no sources in the current list of your document (the list on the right) which do not have tick marks next to them by deleting them from the current list (see the top duplicated reference in Figure 215). This is a real hassle, as it means that you have to manually check that the document source list contains no unreferenced sources, but until Microsoft comes up with a better solution, this is what you will have to do.

13.2.7 Doing more with citations

The Citation field which is inserted when you use the tool described above results in a static field—you cannot display the field codes and change it. If you select the <u>E</u>dit Citation option (cf. Figure 211 and Figure 212) you can change a few things, such as adding page numbers, and suppressing the author, title and date. But what if you need to do more (e.g., when using a secondary source, adding the prefix "in " to your citation)?

The important thing to note is that adding citations via the tool on the References ribbon just adds a field. You can add the citation field manually as well. It has the basic format   { CITATION Tag [Optional switches] }.   The Citation field switches are explained in Table 16.

Table 16   *Citation field switches*[90]

Switch	Name	Explanation
Tag	Citation identifier	This case sensitive code uniquely identifies each source in the list of sources. This is not optional (it is not a switch per se), and must form part of the citation.
\p	Page	Add page numbers to the citation.
\n	Name	Suppress the author name.
\t	Title	Suppress the title.
\y	Year	Suppress the year (actually, date) of publication.
\l	Locale ID	Used to set the language in which the citation must be displayed. Can safely be ignored most of the time, but if you want to use this, read the Word help files for more information.
\v	Volume number	Add a volume number to the citation.
\f	Prefix	Add a prefix to the citation. Must be followed by text in quotation marks, which will be prefixed to the citation.
\s	Suffix	Add a suffix to the citation. Must be followed by text in quotation marks, which will be suffixed to the citation.
\m	More	Add more sources to the current citation. Must be followed by the tag name of the next citation, with its switches.

It should be evident that the \p, \n, \t, \y switches can be controlled from the Edit Citation dialog, but that all other switches need to be added manually. Since the field is

---

[90] Adapted from: http://office.microsoft.com/en-za/word-help/field-codes-citation-field-HA010215707.aspx

static, you need to do this by right clicking on the field, and selecting Edit Field...,
which will open the Field dialog, where you can add the switches you want. Figure 217
shows the Field dialog with a citation field showing the \f (prefix) switch, and the
resultant citation (using the Harvard - SA style) is shown just above this.

·the·people·of·Christ·must·learn·to·"do·*good·works.*"·Fee·(in·Stott·1996:207)·

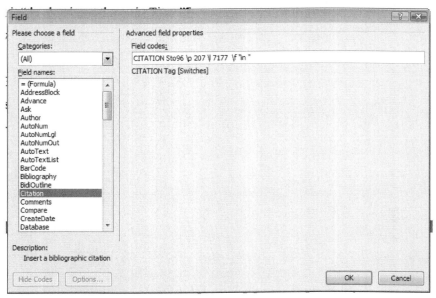

Figure 217　　　　*Field dialog: Edit citation field*

Application 13.2　　　*Those pesky hyperlinks*

*The problem with hyperlinks, which now occur very often in references, is that Word
treats them as one long word, often causing all manner of paragraph alignment
problems. One solution is to add a zero-width space after each slash (which can be
done with search and replace), or just after the slash where you want the break to
occur. If you want the hyperlink to be live, then first create the link. After that, position
the I-beam where you want the break, and then open the Insert Symbol dialog. On the
Special characters tab, you will find, second from the bottom "No width optional
break." The result, when non-printing characters are displayed, looks like a small
frame added to the text. In practice, this character allows the line to break there, and
yet itself remains unprinted.*

*My Word uTIlities (see section 1.9, p. 7) contains a macro, Fit Hyperlink, which will
scan a whole hyperlink and add no-width optional breaks (see section 1.9, p. 7) to every
forward slash (except the first double slash). Unfortunately, though, this will not work
in references inserted with the Bibliography tool. Your only option there will to convert
the reference list to static text, and then modify the hyperlinks with the tool.*

13.3   The shortcomings of Word's citation tool

I have, throughout this chapter, pointed out several shortcomings of the Word Citations and Bibliography tool. Students doing pre-graduate studies may find the tool useful, but it may start running out of steam when it comes to handling the needs of postgraduate students. Some pointers are in order here too.

Firstly, the tool can be used fruitfully for a thesis. The thesis which can be downloaded from my website (see section 1.9, p. 7) shows that this tool can be used for a smallish thesis. It is also the example used in this chapter. I have, thus, proved that at least a mini-thesis for a Master's degree can be done with this tool. I do, however, think that a full PhD dissertation with many hundreds of reference sources will really become problematic using this tool. Also, I seriously doubt that the tool will work well enough for an academic pursuing a career in which the norm should be the publishing of many articles in a certain field over a course of what may possibly be several decades.

In short, commercial RMS programs may be expensive, but considering the power of these programs and the full feature set, both of which are still very lacking in Word's citation tool, I still consider these to be a worthwhile investment for people doing "heavy" referencing work.

13.4   BibWord

What, then, is the postgraduate student to do? Buy an "expensive" RMS program? Consider an open source alternative? Is there a middle ground in which Word's citation tool might still make the grade[91] for a thesis or dissertation?

Enter BibWord. BibWord was developed by Yves Dhondt of MIT in an attempt to overcome some of these limitations to the Word Citations & Bibliography tool. It is downloadable freely from the website (http://bibword.codeplex.com).

Essentially, BibWord allows you to "hotwire" Word's citation styles and add styles of your own. The tool basically consists of two parts: Firstly, the "end user" tools are for students who just want to use the tools, you will find some extra styles which Yves created on the site. These can be copied to the Bibliography Styles folder on your pc. Also, there is the BibWord Extender which allows for the creation of numerically ordered in-text citations (e.g., when referencing according to the Vancouver referencing style). Secondly, there are the "developer" tools, the BibWord template and the BibType tool, for more advanced users, who wish to develop their own styles. I have, for example, used the BibWord template to develop a (relatively complete) South African Harvard style for Word.

If you want to use the developer set of tools, details can be found on the BibWord site. I will briefly show how to use the BibWord *end user* tools here.

The first thing to do is to copy the BibWord styles to the Style folder of your Word installation (typically, for Word 2010, C:\Program Files\Microsoft Office\Office14\ Bibliography\Style, **and   not**   C:\Users*UserName*\AppData\Roaming\Microsoft\ Bibliography\Style)—you may need administrator access to do this. Figure 218 shows

---

[91] Please excuse the pun!

this folder on my PC, before the BibWord styles were added (i.e., these are the styles provided by Microsoft with Word 2010 SP1 or Word 2007 SP3).

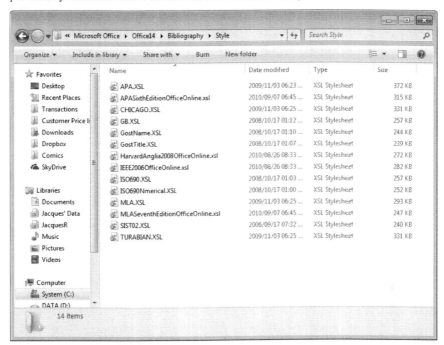

Figure 218   Word Citation Styles folder

The styles that are available from the BibWord web page (as at September 2012) are listed in Table 17. One more style—HarvardSA.XSL—which I created using the BibWord template, can be downloaded from my own website (search for it on www.insight.trueinsight.za.com/word).

Table 17   *Referencing Styles Available via BibWord*

Style	File names
Associação Brasileira de Normas Técnicas (ABNT)	ABNT_Author.XSL
	ABNT_Num.XSL
	ABNT_Num_Alt.XSL
Association for Computing Machinery (ACM)	ACMCitSeq.XSL
	ACMNameSeq.XSL
American Medical Society (ACS)	ACSCitSeq.xsl
	ACSCitSeq2.xsl
American Medical Association (AMA)	AMA.XSL
American Sociological Association (ASA)	ASA.XSL
Chicago Footnotes (beta - not in zip)	CMSFootnote.XSL
Council of Science Editors (CSE)	CSECitSeq.XSL
	CSENameSeq.XSL
Harvard - AGPS	HarvardAGPS.XSL
Harvard - Anglia	HarvardAnglia.XSL
Harvard - Exeter	HarvardExeter.XSL
Harvard - Leeds	HarvardLeeds.XSL
Humana Press	Humana.XSL
IEEE	IEEE_Alphabetical.XSL
	IEEE_Reference.XSL
Lecture Notes in Computer Science (LNCS)	LNCS.XSL
Modern Humanities Research Association (MHRA)	MHRAFootnote.XSL
Nature	Nature.XSL
Vancouver	Vancouver.XSL

Once these styles have been copied to the Style folder, they will appear in the Style list of the Citations & Bibliography group of the References ribbon (compare Figure 219 to what is shown in Instruction set 45), and can be used as described before.

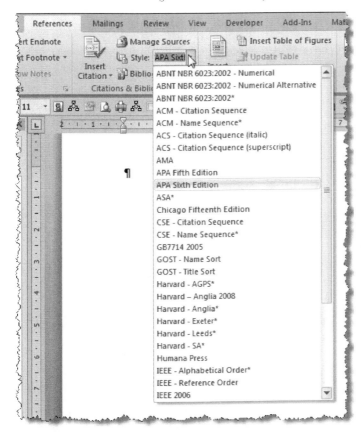

Figure 219   Citation Style list showing extra BibWord styles

Note, though, that if the document is opened on another computer which does not have the styles loaded, the Style will display as Unknown, and any attempt to work with the citations or bibliography will result in Word changing the style to the default style for that computer (Figure 220).

Figure 220   BibWord style not found on computer

A last lifeline from Yves is the BibWord Extender (Figure 221), which overcomes two problems with Word's own referencing system. Firstly, if multiple references are used from the same author(s) in the same year, the convention is to add a date suffix (e.g., 2012a, 2012b, etc.). Word cannot do this. Secondly, while Word can number references in the order they occur in the text (when using numerical referencing styles, of course), Word cannot order the bibliography alphabetically and then assign the numbers in the text accordingly. The BibWord Extender allows both of these possibilities, and it should be noted that the BibWord styles which are suffixed with an asterisk are styles which will benefit from the use of the Extender. Unfortunately, because of the way Word creates citations, making any changes to the references (e.g., adding new sources), may invalidate what has been done by the Extender, requiring it to be rerun. Thus, it is best to use it only when the document has been finalised, and no more changes to the sources will be made. Simply start the tool[92] (it may as for confirmation or an indication of where the bibliography styles are located on your computer), then use the file browser button to load the file to the Word Document text box, and select Extend. Once it has completed, re-open Word, and re-select the same referencing style to force an update of the citation and bibliography fields.

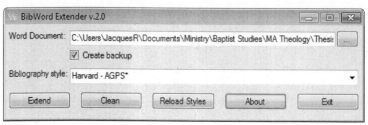

Figure 221   *BibWord Extender*

A nice touch of this tool, which I recommend you use, is that it first creates a backup of the Word document. The backup is indicated with an "_orig" suffix before the file extension.

---

[92] It is an .exe file, so it can be double clicked from Explorer to launch it.

Chapter 14
Going paperless: Using Word's reviewing tools

My promoter has, on several occasions, accused me of slaughtering entire forests on my own. In actual fact, I think he was referring more to the thick statistical printouts I brought him in the course of working for him as a research assistant than to my dissertation, but I do think that, in the process of completing a dissertation, at least a few boxes of paper will have been snuffed out. There are the endless evaluation copies to be given to the promoter and co-promoter(s), meaning that each chapter of the dissertation is printed out at least four or five times, if not more. And then there are the examination copies, *and* the final copies. It is inevitable that a dissertation be printed out (whatever would the library do without it?), but the simple fact is that the technology *does* exist for a dissertation to be completed entirely paperlessly—the only printing that would be needed would be for the final submission copies. In fact, reviewing a dissertation electronically is actually faster, provided that both the student *and* the promoters and examiners mastered the technology. The only drawback would be that the promoters and/or examiners would have to do their work on the computer—no more sitting on the Lazy Boy in front of the fireplace, unless you can take the laptop there!

To date, I have not yet heard of a paperless dissertation, and although I tried it once (as co-promoter[93]) with a student, the student eventually gave up and reverted back to paper (in part also because the chief promoter worked only on paper). Nevertheless, you might become the first student (that I know of) to actually pull it off. Now all you need to do is get your promoter on board!

14.1   Reviewing a document

To understand the process, it helps to review how promoters have (or were supposed to have) reviewed thesis chapters in ages gone by. The student prints out the chapter, presents it to the promoter (sometimes accompanied by a suitable peace offering, but not a bribe!), the promoter then sits with a pen, reads through the chapter, and makes all manner of comments and recommendations in writing on the manuscript. These could indicate changes, a re-ordering of the material, things to be added, or things that should be deleted (I had a lot of those[94]!). This is then returned to the student, who then has to work through the various recommendations, evaluate them, and decide whether to implement them[95].

---

[93] Let me hasten to add that with my current main job description being consultative in nature, I have not acted as promotor or co-promoter for many students at all).

[94] If my erstwhile promoter were reviewing this book, it would be a third shorter, and much the better for it!

[95] Note that I am not advocating that students blindly make all revisions suggested by their promoters. I know this is beyond the subject matter of this book, but in a healthy academic relationship, with a competent student and a competent and well-balanced promoter, the student should be in the position (especially a PhD student) to evaluate the suggestions made by the promoter, and even, on occasion, to disagree. Here much grace is needed in addition to courage—the students should courageously stick to their guns, and the promoters should graciously concede. Unfortunately, this is often where things go wrong (tales of domineering promoters or aggressive, know-it-all students). But examples of dysfunction should not be cause to discard what should be functional, and mutually respectful relationship. Perhaps the best word of advice in this chapter is that both students and promoters should choose carefully whom they will be willing to work with.

In essence, when this takes place electronically, the *process* remains exactly the same. It is only the method that changes. Instead of a pen and paper, the tools now become those tools built into Word for this purpose.

Because of this, the process will be reflected in this chapter. The remainder of the chapter will thus contain four more main sections, including two sections on reviewing, and reworking a document (i.e., working through a reviewed document), respectively. They will be preceded by a section on some necessary preparation, and will be interspersed by a section on the reviewing pane, which is germane to both reviewing and reworking.

14.2 Preparation for reviewing

For the whole process to work smoothly, some things need to be put in place. If this is done, everything will work well. If not, things can start to go awry. Basically, both the reviewer (promoter) and reviewee (student) need to make certain that some things are in place and are done in the proper order or manner. I will also discuss, below, the general options which can be set by either the reviewer or reviewee.

14.2.1 Preparation by the reviewer

Generally, all the reviewer has to do is identify themselves through the Office user name, and turn change tracking on.

14.2.1.1 Setting the Office user name

The most important thing that the reviewer needs to do is to make sure that the Office username is properly set on all the computers on which they will be reviewing the document. Thus, if they intend reviewing the document on a PC at home, and at work, at the very least, the user name should be the same on all of these computers, preferably a properly descriptive name (e.g., their first and last names). This is important, as documents can be reviewed by multiple reviewers, and Word keeps track of each reviewer. It "sees" each computer with a different Office user name as being different reviewers, which is not right.

The username is set in the General tab of the Word Options dialog (Figure 222), and it should be noted that this username applies for all the Office applications. There is a shortcut to this on the Reviewing ribbon (Instruction set 48).

Instruction set 48   Change User Name

302

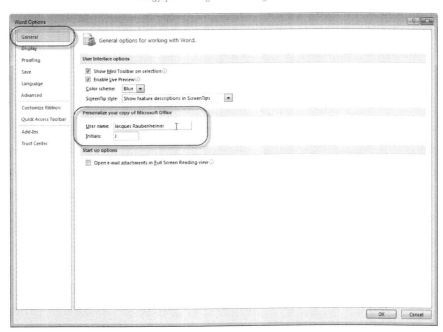

Figure 222   **Change User Name**

Application 14.1   ***Anonymous reviewing***

A request I have had surprisingly often is from journal editors who have sent through an article to a reviewer, and who wish to anonymise the reviewer's work. You will note that if you try to change the reviewer name on a comment, Word will not allow this. Also, if the mouse is held over a change, the reviewer's name appears in a tooltip. As will be explained below, this can be slightly problematic. I have created a tool— included in the Word uTIlities (see section 1.9, p. 7)—which can change the comment author and initials, either for a selection, or for a whole document. However, the reviewer name for tracked changes cannot, ironically, be changed in the same way. There is a method to do it, but it involves some reasonably intricate manipulation of the document's XML structure, and as such, I am not going to describe this here. If you really need it done, see the consultation blurb at the end of this book.

14.2.1.2   Turning Track changes on

The Track changes setting (Instruction set 49) is a toggle—it can be turned on or off at will.

Instruction set 49   Turning Track changes on or off

Shortcut	Ctrl + Shift + E
Keyboard	Alt | R | G | G
Left click	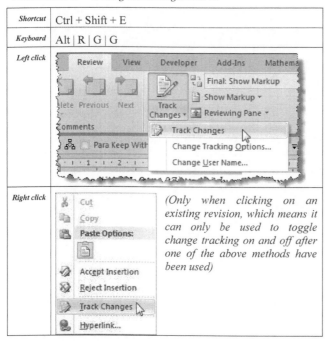
Right click	

(Only when clicking on an existing revision, which means it can only be used to toggle change tracking on and off after one of the above methods have been used)

When the reviewer wants to start reviewing the document, simply turn track changes on—the **Ctrl + Shift + E** keyboard shortcut is very useful here. The reviewer should remember to turn change tracking off when they are finished, and at the very least, the student should check that it is off before starting to rework the document. Note that in certain circumstances, the reviewer may legitimately want to make a change that should not be tracked. In these circumstances, I love using the keyboard shortcut to turn it off, make my change, and then turn it back on. An example[96], to make this concrete, would be the following: Sometimes students don't set the language for their document properly. This may result in a large number of words being indicated as misspelled, when they are, in fact, not (e.g., colour being indicated as misspelled because the language has been set to US English, instead of South African English). Since I do not want to have to keep dealing with these annoyances, the simple thing to do is to set the language for the entire document. However, if I were to select the whole document, and then change the language settings from US English to South African English, that would result in a plethora of unnecessary changes being tracked in the document (try it!). So I would turn track changes off, set the language, and then turn track changes back on. Also, I would add a simple comment at the start of the document to the student indicating that they need to set the language for the document.

---

[96] It stands to reason that there would be no point in a promoter making changes to the document that the student would be unaware of, so an explanation is in order.

14.2.2   Preparation by the reviewee

The reviewee just needs to keep their wits about them managing the various documents (the one they are working on, the one sent to promoter A, the one sent to promoter B, etc.). Remember also that it is not uncommon for a student to work on a document even after they have submitted it to their promoters.

Here are some tips. Firstly, make a backup of the thesis before sending any chapters away. See Application 12.2 on p. 267, together with the uTIlity that I have prepared for that.

Second, copy just the relevant chapter out into a new document, and save the document with an appropriate name (which I would say should include a time stamp)—e.g., "Chapter 2 sent to Prof Soap 2012-03-05.docx." The techniques described in section 12.1 (p. 266) make this a cinch, and especially so when combined with the uTIlity (see section 1.9, p. 7) that allows you to save a selection to a new document. Using this combination, a chapter from a thesis can be saved to a properly named, separate file in less than 30 seconds (really!).

Third, if the document is to be reviewed by multiple reviewers[97], then the student should decide, together with the promoter and co-promoters, whether each will receive a copy of the document and then review it independently (this is the fastest approach), or whether only one document will be sent to the first reviewer, who then reviews it to send it to the second reviewer, and so on until the last reviewer returns the document to the student. This second method allows each successive reviewer to see, and comment on, the previous reviewer's suggestions, but it does obviously not work retroactively, and so this "advantage" is limited.

I will discuss how all the different documents are brought back together again later in this chapter.

14.2.3   Change tracking options

When Word tracks changes, the Track Changes Options dialog (accessed from the Tracking group of the Review ribbon—Instruction set 50), allows you to set both what changes are and are not tracked (within limits), and how the tracked changes are displayed.

---

[97] Just be warned that too many cooks spoil the broth, and that no man can serve two masters!

Instruction set 50   Change Tracking Options

Keyboard	Alt | R | G | O
Left click	

The Track Changes Options dialog is shown in Figure 223, and will be described briefly below. Generally, my recommendation is to learn to work with the default settings, and not to change too much, although the one setting I do personally prefer to make is to turn balloons off. The defaults are: To show insertions as underlined text in a different colour, where each reviewer is given a colour (hence the necessity of setting the Office user name), to show deletions as text struck through and displayed in the reviewer's colour, and to show comments with an "anchor" around the relevant text, and a line to the comment in a balloon in the right margin of the page.

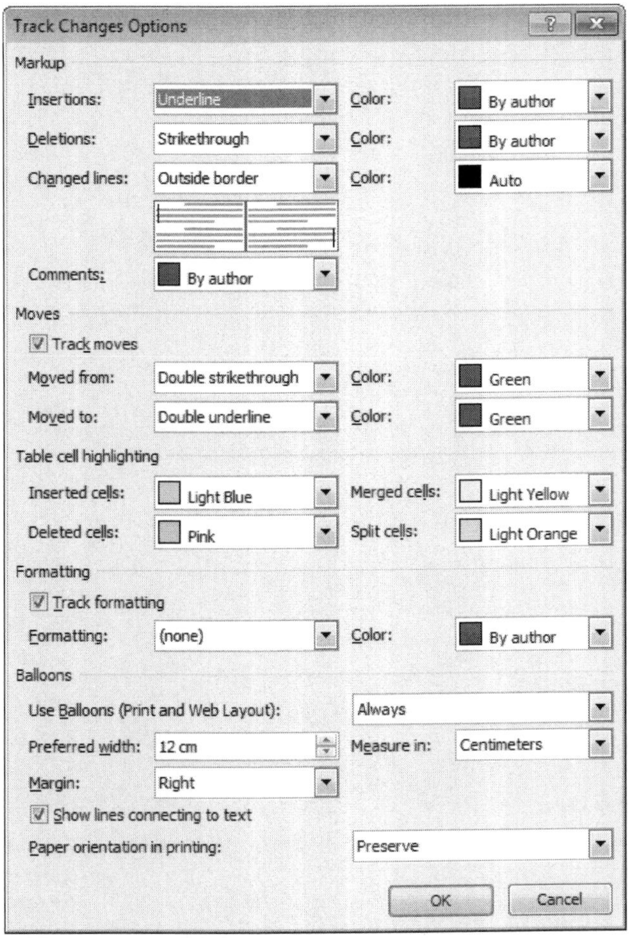

Figure 223   Track Changes Options dialog

The first group of settings relate to the markup—how Word should indicate changes and comments. For Insertions, you can choose from the options None, Colour only, Bold, Italic, (Double) Underline, Strikethrough (the first and last of which make no sense, really)—Figure 224. The options for Deletions are the same as for insertions, with the addition of Double strikethrough, Hidden, Caret (^) or Hash (#), and again not all the options make sense visually. Furthermore, for both of these, a Color can be chosen (Figure 226), but I recommend that you let Word assign a colour to each different reviewer if there are going to be more than one reviewer. Kelly (2010) notes that there are sixteen colours available for users to assign, but that if the setting is left to "by author," Word will select from only eight colours (red, blue, green, violet, dark red, teal, dark yellow and grey). In theory, it is unlikely that you would have so many reviewers for a single document, but if there were to be more than eight reviewers, then Word will start working through the list of eight colours again, so that the ninth reviewer will share the same colour as the first, and so on. Note also that the assigning of colours is somewhat arbitrary, so that there is no guarantee that a certain reviewer assigned a certain colour on one pc will be assigned the same colour on a different pc. In short, I think there are more important things to concern yourself with than which reviewer gets which colour, especially since the whole idea behind tracked revisions is that they eventually be removed (either by accepting or rejecting them), meaning that they are not permanent in any case.

Furthermore, as is the convention when reviewing on paper, a mark is made in the column to indicate the lines in which a change is made. In Word, this takes the form of a simple vertical line in the margin. In the Changed lines section of the dialog (Figure 225) you can choose not to display these, or choose which border to use. The Color of these lines can be set as well (similar to in Figure 226). Generally, I recommend not changing any of these options, least of all the Changed lines options.

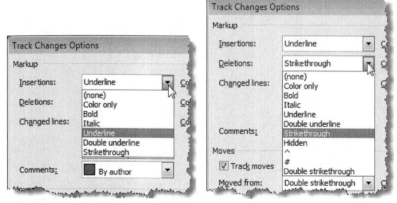

Figure 224   *Track Changes Options dialog: Options for Insertions and Deletions*

Figure 225   *Track Changes Options dialog: Options for Changed lines*

308

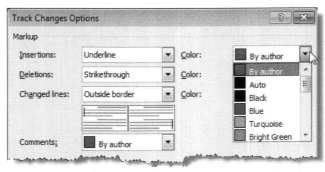

Figure 226   Track Changes Options dialog: Example of setting colour options

When you move text, the Moves section of the dialog allows you to set what the indicators of that move are—remember that in one sense, a move can be seen as a deletion in the original location, and an insertion in the new location, but it is useful to be able to distinguish that text has actually just been moved, not removed and/or added. Remember also that Word also does not always displaying all moves in this manner, but more on that later. As Figure 227 and Figure 228 show, the colour for this can also be set, although it is not a bad idea to keep this distinct from the colours used for insertions and deletions (I normally leave this on the default: Green).

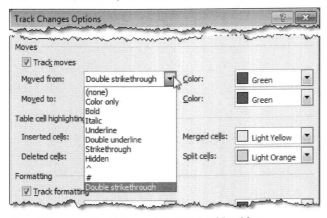

Figure 227   Track Changes Options dialog: Moved from

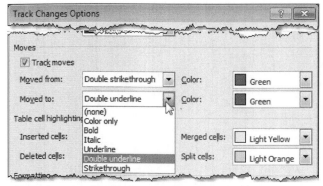

Figure 228   *Track Changes Options dialog: Moved to*

Figure 229 shows that the colours used to indicate when table cells (typically, rows or columns or entire tables) are inserted or deleted, or even merged or split, can also be set.

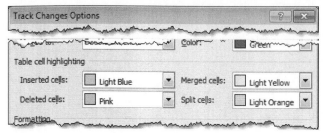

Figure 229   *Track Changes Options dialog: Table cell highlighting*

Furthermore, the Formatting section of the dialog (Figure 230) allows you to control whether Word should keep track of, and indicate, changes made to formatting (i.e., font changes, adding/removing bold, italics, etc.). Normally, these changes should also be indicated, but as I have discussed above, there may be times when they should not. In general, I turn this setting on, and when I do want to make a formatting change that I do not want to be tracked, I turn change tracking off, make the change, and then turn change tracking on again.

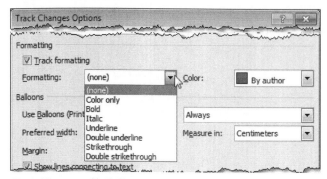

Figure 230   *Track Changes Options dialog: Formatting*

The lower portion of the Track Changes Options dialog (Figure 231) shows settings for the display of balloons. Generally, insertions and deletions can be displayed in the text, or in a demarcated area in the page margin, in a balloon. Comments are normally showed in this area in balloons too, but can be displayed in the reviewing pane. Here you can set which margin, the size of the margin are, and what to use balloons for— Always means for insertions, deletions, and comments, Only for comments/formatting is self-explanatory, as is Never. I find balloons annoying, so I normally turn them off. Note also that balloons are only used in Print Layout view or Full Screen Reading view, and not in Normal view or Outline view.

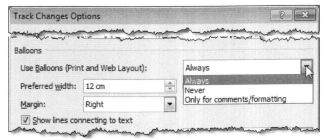

Figure 231   Track Changes Options dialog: Balloons

The last setting in the Track Changes Options dialog (Figure 232) governs how Word prints out documents that contain changes. Because the annoying balloons tend to scrunch up the actual body text, this creates an effect which does not read as easily as it perhaps should. You could choose to force the display into Landscape (no good if you are already using landscape). I find this of limited value, as it does not change the pages printed, but rather flips the actual text page—i.e., the whole portrait page is flipped and shrunk to fit in the smaller height of the landscape page, and the remaining half of the page is divided into two columns, one with the balloons displayed in the left column, and nothing in the right column. Essentially, this would give you space for writing on the right column, but the whole point is to work electronically. To further explain, if the document would print out over ten pages in portrait, with the markup in balloons, forcing landscape will still result in 10 pages being printed, albeit pages on which both the actual text and the markup balloons are smaller—as I said, pretty pointless.

Obviously, if you have turned balloons off, this becomes moot, and the setting is, in fact, not enabled.

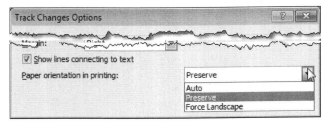

Figure 232   Track Changes Options dialog: Paper orientation

There are one last set of options related to change tracking that are worth being aware of. If you open the Word Options dialog, then go to the Trust Center Tab and select Trust Center Settings..., and then select the Privacy Options tab of the Trust Center dialog, you will with the group of Document-specific settings (Figure 233). Here are two settings, Warn before printing, saving or sending a file that contains tracked changes or comments, and Make hidden markup visible when opening or saving. The former ensures that you don't accidentally (and embarrassingly, or worse) send a document to someone that should not contain revisions, but actually still does. The latter ensures that if a document contains revisions, they will be made visible when the document is opened or saved.

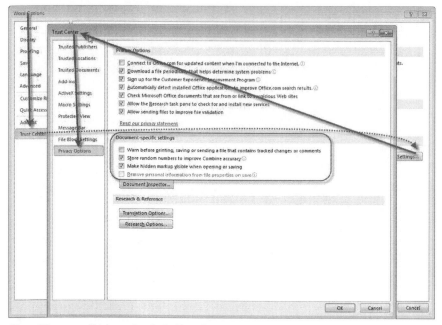

Figure 233   *Privacy options in the Trust Center*

14.3   Reviewing Pane

When not working with balloons, a different method is needed for viewing and working with the revisions and comments (the method of holding the mouse over the item to view the information in the tooltip is not incredibly efficient). I prefer working with the Reviewing Pane, which I still find better than balloons (for example, there is a limit to the length of comments that balloons can display, which the Reviewing pane does not have). The pane is displayed via a toggle button in the Tracking group of the Review ribbon (Instruction set 51).

Instruction set 51   Showing or hiding the Reviewing pane

Keyboard	Alt | R | TP | V (Vertical)
	Alt | R | TP | H (Horizontal)
Left click	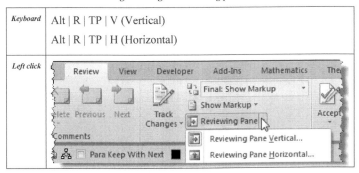

Note that the pane can be displayed at the bottom (Horizontal) or left (Vertical) of the screen, as demonstrated in Figure 234. Also note that the Revision Pane shows a summary of the number of different revisions present in the document (Figure 235). It contains buttons which can be used to hide this summary, update the summary (e.g., for a student working through the revisions), and to close the revision pane.

Figure 234   Reviewing pane showed vertically and horizontally

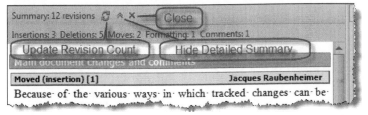

Figure 235   Revision pane buttons

A further useful feature of the Reviewing pane is that you can use it to accept or reject revisions, or to delete comments. All the right click options shown in Instruction set 54, Instruction set 56, and Instruction set 57 are also applicable when right clicking on an entry in the Reviewing pane. Unfortunately, the Follow Move option (see Figure 243, p. 325), while available when clicking on moved text in the Reviewing pane, does not seem to work from there.

14.4   Electronically reviewing a document

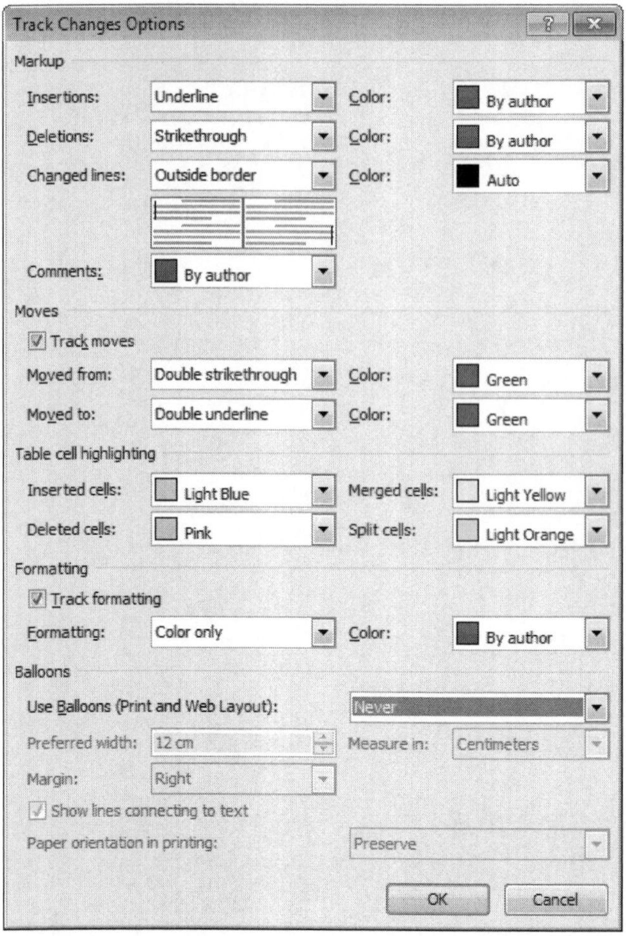

Figure 236   *Track changes options used for the demonstration of tracked changes in this book*

Reviewing a document entails simply reading it, and then either making comments as you go on, or making actual changes to the document, which will then be reviewed and either implemented as is, implemented in a modified format, or rejected by the student. These changes can, of course, be in the form of things deleted, things added, things changed (basically, in terms of Word's change tracking, a concurrent deletion and addition), or things moved.

Because of the various ways in which tracked changes can be displayed (as governed by the settings of the Track Changes Options dialog discussed above), the examples in this section will use the settings as shown in Figure 236.

It should perhaps be added that although changes and comments are dealt with together by Word, there is a basic difference in their intended use in our context. Changes are physical (albeit electronic) changes made to the document. They can be additions, deletions, or changes in formatting. These changes can either be accepted or rejected by the student. Comments, on the other hand, are simply annotations added to the document. They can be printed out, but do not represent actual changes to the physical text of the document. As such, changes can be used by the promoter to indicate what they believe should be done at specific points (without typing the dissertation for the student!), and comments would represent points for the student to consider, and act upon. Unlike changes, comments cannot be "accepted" or "rejected" in the Word context, as they do not represent physical changes to the document.

The various ways that changes and comments can be made will be discussed, and throughout reference will be made to Figure 237.

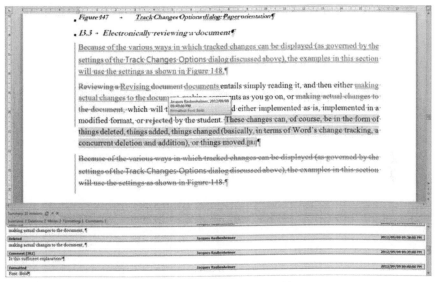

Figure 237   Example of a document changed with change tracking on

The revisions I made to the first two paragraphs of this section (p. 314) for the example will be noted and then an explanation of the methods that can be used for these, will be discussed with each.

*I **replaced** "Reviewing a" with "Revising."* There are several ways to do this. Basically, the job relies on standard Word editing. You could delete the old words, and type the new word. I selected the two old words, and overtyped them with the new word. The end result is the same—a deletion and an insertion are listed (this counts as two changes). It would have been nice if Word could track a single "replacement" instead of the dual deletion and insertion, but that is, at the moment, wishful thinking.

*I **added** an "s" to the end of "document."* This is an interesting special case of what I did in the prior step (which will reveal why I like using this method). If you were just to position the I-beam to the right of the t of document, and type the s, Word would list only one change—the insertion of the s. While this is probably more efficient, it often looks very odd. I prefer to replace whole words (e.g., when a student has misspelled a word). This does mean that the student has to contend with two changes—the deletion and the insertion—but it gives a clearer message to the student of what is required. The question, of course, is what to do with words that should be changed at the end (e.g., the s added here, or words requiring a missing e at the end, etc.). To indicate this, would one not have to type out the whole new word? No. Word actually views, internally, each word as consisting of all the characters that make up that word, and the punctuation mark or space after the word (e.g., if you select a word by double clicking on it, the word and the space are selected). This means that changing the space actually changes the word. Thus, I selected the space after the t of document, and typed "s " (s and space). Word then deletes the whole word "document" and inserts the new word "documents." The same, of course, applies to the converse situation. Although this is not shown in Figure 237, what if I had wanted to change the plural word "documents" to the singular "document?" I could just delete the s, but I could also select the s and the following space, and then just type a space. This will indicate that the whole word "documents" has been deleted, and that the word "document" has been inserted.

*I **moved** the phrase "making actual changes to the document" to just after the word "either" a bit earlier in the sentence.*[98] I did this to show that Word does not list all moves as actual moves. The move could be made in either of two ways—cut and paste (which could, of course, be done with the mouse or the keyboard, and both in multiple manners), or by using the mouse to click and drag the phrase. Regardless of the method used, Word will not indicate it as a move, but as a deletion and an insertion. I don't know why, though?

*I added the **comment** "Is this sufficient explanation?" to the last sentence of the first paragraph.* Comments can be added easily with the keyboard shortcut Ctrl + Alt + M, or from the Comments group of the Review ribbon (Instruction set 52). In contrast to older versions of Word, you cannot insert a comment at a single insertion point (as you can with a bookmark, for example). You must select at least a single character and a comment to that, failing which Word will select the current word, and anchor the comment to it.[99] Note that the comment is indicated by the coloured parentheses, which enclose a shaded are in a corresponding colour. Depending on your Change Tracking options, Word will either open a balloon in the margin or the Reviewing pane, where you can type the comment.

---

[98] Note that I actually need to clean up the sentence a bit more, but left it like this for the sake of the exercise.

[99] A quick tip is that you can select whole sentences by holding down Ctrl while clicking with the mouse, but since this is a book for advanced Word users, you already knew that!

Instruction set 52   Adding a comment[100]

Shortcut	Ctrl + Alt + M
Keyboard	Alt | R | C
Left click	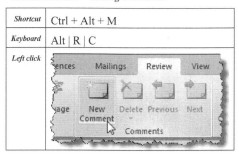

As can be seen in Instruction set 54 (p. 322), right clicking on a comment or comment indicator also has the option of editing a comment. When the Revision pane or balloons are shown, this is senseless, as you could just as easily click in the comment and start typing. However, if balloons are off and the Revision pane is not displayed, selecting this option will open the Revision pane, allowing you to edit the comment.

*I **moved** the second paragraph to before the first paragraph.* Again, this can be done either by cutting and pasting, or by clicking and dragging. Note that now, because I selected a whole paragraph, Word registered it, not as a deletion and insertion, but as a move.

*I **changed** the font of the word "rejected" to bold type.* Nothing strange here. Note that Word listed it as a formatting change.

Note that for each and every revision made, should you hold the mouse over the revision, Word will display a tooltip showing more information about that particular revision. The example in Figure 237 shows the tooltip for the formatting change to bold type.

Also take note of the changed lines, which appear as almost unbroken solid vertical lines just to the left of the text, from the 1st to the 7th, and then the 10th to the 12th lines. Generally, when changes are made to successive lines of text, the bottom and top of the changed lines from the two lines of text will merge.

Finally, remember that not all changes can, at present, be tracked. For example, if you delete a row from a table, Word will happily track that. But if you try to delete a column, you will get the message shown in Figure 238. If Word can't track it, the best advice is to leave it be, and rather add a comment indicating the change you had wanted to make.

---

[100] One interesting tidbit is that older versions of Word allowed one to actually record a sound comment, but as far as I can tell, this functionality has been removed.

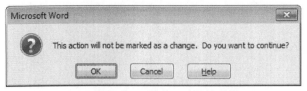

Figure 238   *Word cannot track the deleting of a column*

14.5   Reworking a document

The general idea would be for promoters to receive the document electronically, read through it and make changes and comments, and the send it back to the student, preferably saved under a new name (e.g., "Dissertation—Comments on Ch 2.docx" or "Dissertation—Comments 2005-06-15.docx" or "Dissertation—comments by Prof Dunce.docx," etc.). The simple reason for this is that it is highly unlikely for the student not to make any changes to the dissertation in the time while it is with the promoter (very few promoters are able to give such a short turn-around time on their document evaluation). The disadvantage of this is that the student then has to work with two documents—the reviewed document, and the original. The changes and comments thus have to be viewed in one document, and the changes made in the other. Probably the best solution to this problem is for the student to break the dissertation up into subdocuments and work on only those subdocuments which are not being reviewed. Then the student can receive back the document with the same name, and can accept or reject changes and evaluate comments in one document only. In section 14.5.3 below I discuss strategies for comparing documents.

14.5.1   Viewing markup

Once the student has received the reviewed document, all proposed changes and comments should be evaluated individually.

The first setting is to decide in what way the relationship between the markup and the document should be viewed. This is done using the Display for Review setting in the Tracking group of the Review ribbon (Figure 239).

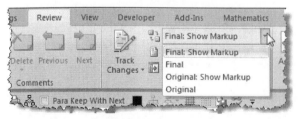

Figure 239   *Display for review*

There are four options, but what you will see depends both on the view you are in, and how you have set balloons (see section 14.2.3 above). Table 18 explains the different options.

Table 18   Display for Review Options

Display for Review Option	If Balloons are used for all markup (i.e., including insertions and deletions)	If balloons are used only for formatting and comments, not for insertions and deletions	If balloons are not used, or for Normal view
Final Showing Markup	Insertions are shown in the text (formatting changes are applied), deletions, formatting changes, and comments are shown in balloons.	All changes are shown in the text (formatting changes are applied), formatting changes and comments are shown in balloons.	All changes are shown in the text (formatting changes are applied and indicated), and comments are indicated with comment indicators only.
Final	Shows the document as it would be if all changes were accepted. No comment indicators or changes are shown (even if balloons are on), but comments and revisions can be seen in the Reviewing Pane.		
Original Showing Markup	Deletions are shown in the text (formatting changes are *not* applied), insertions, formatting changes, and comments are shown in balloons.	All changes are shown in the text (formatting changes are *not* applied), formatting changes and comments are shown in balloons.	All changes are shown in the text (formatting changes are *not* applied but are indicated), and comments are indicated with comment indicators only.
Original	Shows the original, unchanged document (i.e., shows the document as it would be if all changes were rejected). No comment indicators or changes are shown (even if balloons are on), but comments and revisions can be seen in the Reviewing Pane.		

Next, the student can decide whether to view all the markup or only certain kinds of markup (e.g., comments only) from all the reviewers, or only certain reviewers (of course, only if the document has been reviewed by multiple reviewers).

To decide which kinds of markup to view, select or deselect them from the Show Markup tool in the Tracking group of the Review ribbon (Figure 240). Some pointers are in order. Firstly, note that, as is shown in Figure 240, the balloon options discussed under Change tracking options (section 14.2.3, p. 305). Can also be set here. Furthermore, all of Comments, Ink (if any has been used by a reviewer using a stylus[101]), Insertions and Deletions, or Formatting can be displayed or hidden. The last option, Markup Area Highlight refers to the shading of the column in which the balloons appear, which can be turned on or off.

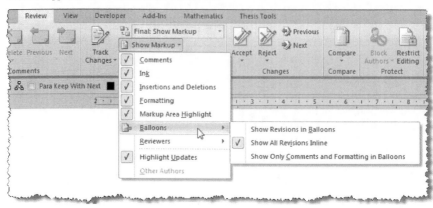

Figure 240   *Show Markup settings*

If the document was reviewed by multiple reviewers, then the student can view markup from any combination of reviewers. Figure 240 shows that markup from each reviewer can be selected or deselected to show or hide that reviewers markup, respectively. There is a handy shortcut to turn on markup from All Reviewers, and, interestingly, the student could even turn off markup from all reviewers in the list. Remember also that each reviewer's markup is displayed in a different colour. Of course, this would require the document to be sent from one promoter to the next, each adding their own comments and changes, and perhaps even commenting on things done by their "predecessors." Alternatively, the student could send a copy to each reviewer, and then merge them all into the working document before working through the revisions, as is discussed in section 14.6.3 below.

---

[101] See, for example, http://office.microsoft.com/en-us/word-help/use-ink-on-a-tablet-pc-HA101841468.aspx?CTT=1.

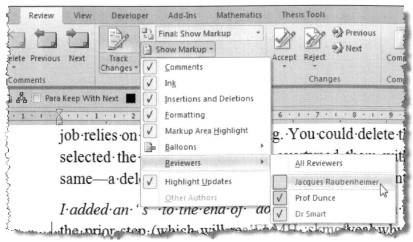

Figure 241   Selecting markup from different reviewers

14.5.2   Working through markup

To work through the revisions made to a document, the student uses the tools on the Review ribbon. When working with comments, the Previous and Next buttons in the Comments group allow the student to navigate backwards and forwards between the various comments (Instruction set 53).

Instruction set 53   Navigating between comments

Keyboard	Alt | R | V (Previous)
	Alt | R | N (Next)
Left click	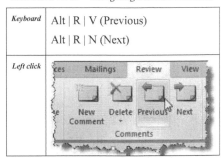

When the student has read (and dealt with) each successive comment, they can delete it using the Delete split button in the Comments group of the Review ribbon (Instruction set 54). The split part of this tool also allows the student to delete all the comments from the document, or all the comments of the selected reviewers displayed.

Instruction set 54   Deleting comments

Keyboard	Alt | R | D | D (Delete) Alt | R | D | A (Delete All Comments Shown) Alt | R | D | O (Delete All Comments in Document)
Left click	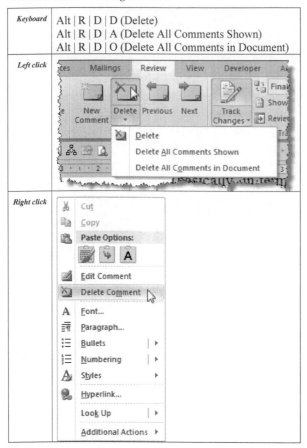
Right click	

Markup will, however, not only consist of comments, but will also include insertions, deletions, and moves[102], and thus some more tools are needed—they are found in the Changes group in the Review ribbon.

The Changes group in the Review ribbon also contains Previous and Next buttons (Instruction set 55) which allow the student to navigate backwards and forwards between all markup instances—i.e., insertions, deletions, moves, formatting changes, *and* comments.

---

[102] And one day, I vainly hope, replacements.

Instruction set 55   *Navigating between revisions*

Keyboard	Alt | R | F (Previous) Alt | R | H (Next)
Left click	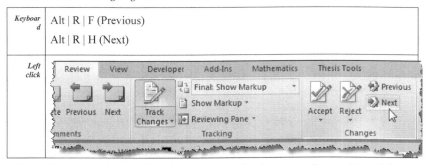

When the student has evaluated each particular instance of something deleted, something inserted, something formatted, or something moved—and decided whether they agree or disagree with the suggested change—they can either implement the revision with the Accept button (Instruction set 56), or reverse the suggested revision with the Reject button (Instruction set 57).

Similar to the case with comments, the split part of this tool also allows the student to accept or reject all the revisions in the document, or all the revisions of the selected reviewers displayed. The top two options will either implement or reverse the revision and move ahead to the next revision (this is the default, and a useful timesaver), or implement or reverse the revision and stay at that point in the document (useful if the student should decide on a third course of action).

Of course, the danger in the Accept/Reject all Changes... buttons should be apparent—a student can accept or reject all suggested revisions without ever having evaluated them. Generally, a conscientious student should never use this option[103], as each recommended change should be evaluated individually by the student—promoters are fallible too (although some would never admit it!).

---

[103] Perhaps suspicious promoters can prevent this by randomly deleting entire portions of the document with track changes turned on. If the student were to uncritically accept all the changes, the dissertation will be ruined with the click of a button! However, I don't think this is sound advice, as the promoter may be held liable (unless they warned the student beforehand). Perhaps better advice is that promoters should select their students carefully, making sure that they only accept conscientious, non-argumentative students!

Instruction set 56   Accepting a revision

Keyboard	Alt | R | A | M (Accept and Move to Next) Alt | R | A | C (Accept Change) Alt | R | A | A (Accept All Changes Shown) Alt | R | A | D (Accept All Changes Document)
Left click	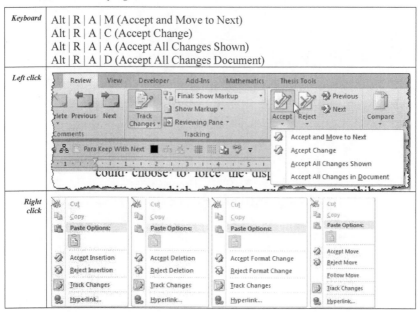
Right click	

Instruction set 57   Rejecting a revision

Keyboard	Alt | R | J | M (Reject and Move to Next) Alt | R | J | R (Reject Change) Alt | R | J | A (Reject All Changes Shown) Alt | R | J | D (Reject All Changes Document)
Left click	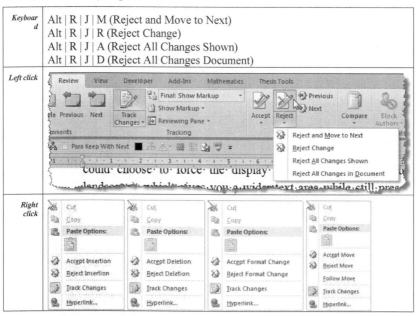
Right click	

In some very exceptional circumstances, revisions themselves may have been changed after being made, but before being accepted. An example follows. The moved paragraph in Figure 237 (p. 315) contains a cross-reference to Figure 148. If something should cause that field to be updated (e.g., printing the document), then the cross-reference will be updated, and when the student wants to accept the move, a dialog like the Tracked Moves Conflict dialog will be shown, where the student will be asked which version of the text they would want to be moved. As Figure 242 shows, sometimes the changes are inconsequential, and the choice is normally easily made.

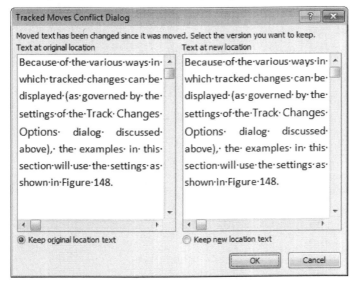

Figure 242   Tracked Moves Conflict dialog

One last tip for working with revisions is that when text has been moved, you might want to see where it has been moved from, or moved to, as the case may be. Right clicking on the moved text (in either the original location or the destination) and selecting Follow Move will take you to the opposite location. Unfortunately, while this option is available in the Reviewing pane, it does not seem to work there.

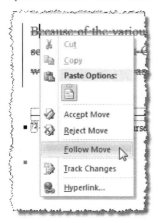

Figure 243   Follow move

The last thing to note is how to confirm that all the revisions and comments have been dealt with. There are several ways, of which I will show two. Firstly, the summary of the Reviewing pane lists the number of markup entries by type. When all of these are zero, there is no more markup (see Figure 235). Also, if you were to click on the Next button in the Changes group (not the Comments group) in the Reviewing ribbon, and you get the message The document contains no comments or tracked changes, well, then guess what? The document contains no comments or tracked changes! You could also use the Document Inspector to note and remove markup.

14.5.3   Printing markup

This is not quite the idea, since the aim is to go paperless, but if, for record-keeping purposes (I'm trying to think of a legitimate reason…) you need to print out the comments on your dissertation, there are two possible ways to go about it. The first is to print the dissertation with the markup. This is done simply by selecting Print markup in Print Preview and Print or Document showing markup in the Print dialog[104] to print the document with all the revisions (Figure 244). If you deselect Print markup in Print Preview and Print or select Document from the Print what list of the Print dialog, only the text will be printed without the revisions.

Note, though, that if you have turned balloons off (see section 14.2.3 above), then insertions and deletions will be displayed in the text, but comments and formatting will not be (their markers in the text will be displayed, but the actual description of the formatting change, or the actual comment, as the case may be, will not be shown). Obviously, if balloons are on, then the settings for what will be displayed in the balloons will govern how the markup will be printed (and comments and formatting, if tracked, will always be printed in the balloons).

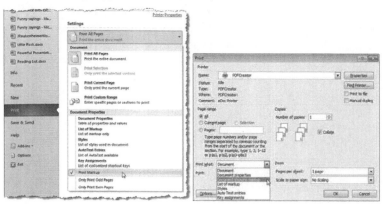

Figure 244   *Printing document with markup*

A more economical method is to select List of Markup from the Print What list box (Figure 245). This prints only a list of the markup, with an indication, for each markup

---

[104] For an explanation of why I give both options, see the discussion in section 19.4.8, p. 369.

entry, of the page on which it is found. Obviously, this can get confusing, since as you work through the document and implement changes, the actual page number could change. Thus, if you want to do this, it would be best to keep a time-stamped backup[105] of the document for reference.

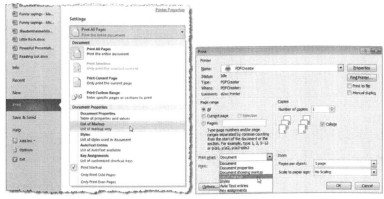

Figure 245   *Printing a list of markup*

14.6   Comparing documents

Sometimes, you may have two versions of a document, and you would need to compare them to each other. For example, if you did not follow a good naming strategy (as described in Application 12.2 on p. 267), or if Word crashed and you have an autosaved document, which might be corrupt, and are not certain whether it differs substantially from the original, etc. Word has a number of tools that can help you find out what the differences are.

14.6.1   Side by side viewing

If you just want to throw the two documents up on the screen next to each other, the View Side by Side tool on the View ribbon (Instruction set 58) is ideal.

Instruction set 58   View Side by Side

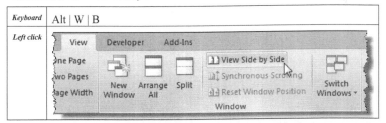

The first thing to do is to open the two documents and the select the tool (if you have more than two documents open, Word will assume that you want to compare the currently active document with one of the other documents, and will present you with a

---

[105] See Application 12.2, p. 193.

dialog to select the one to compare with). Word will then split the screen into two equal windows, and will display each document in one of the windows. One of the problems with viewing two documents in this way is continuously having to scroll the two documents to match the same position in both, and Microsoft has addressed this problem with the Synchronous Scrolling (Alt | W | VS) tool. When it is on, moving one document will move the other in sync. When you do find discrepancies, you can turn this off, and then scroll one to bring them in sync again, and then turn Synchronous Scrolling on to again move them together. Figure 246 shows two documents displayed side by side. Note the similarity in the top page, and the difference in the bottom page just after the heading.

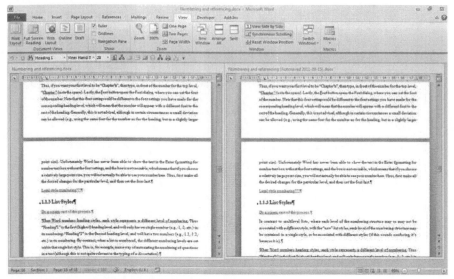

Figure 246   *Two documents displayed side by side*

14.6.2   Legal blackline

Instruction set 59   Compare two versions of a document (Legal blackline)

Keyboard	Alt | R | M | C
Left click	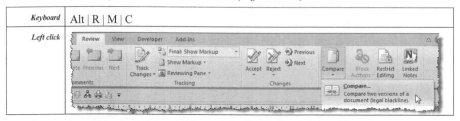

Another option for comparing two documents is to use the legal blackline tool (Instruction set 59). This will open the Compare Documents dialog (Figure 247), where you would generally want to click on the More button to expand the dialog (Word remembers the settings you make in this part of the dialog so that when next you use the tool, the same settings will be applied).

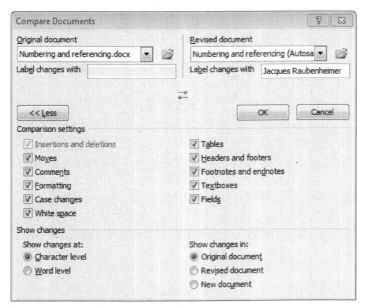

Figure 247   Compare Documents dialog

The procedure is relatively simple: First, select the original document in the list box on the left (if it is not in the list of recent documents Word lists, click on the folder button to the right of the list to open the file browser and select it from your disk, or select Browse... from the very top of the list). Next, choose the newer document from the list on the right, again using the folder button to find it from your disk if it is not in the list. Then you can decide how to label changes which are found between the two documents. In the Comparison settings section, you can decide which document elements you want to compare. I think most of these are quite self-explanatory. The Show changes section requires only two choices: Firstly, how precisely you want to search for differences (at the character or word level). Secondly, you can choose where to show the changes between the two documents—in the original (the one you selected from the left list), in the revised (the one you selected from the right list) or in a new document (which I generally recommend should be the option you choose).

Once you click on OK, Word will compare the two, and show any differences between them using the revisions tool, which is discussed in detail in Chapter 14.

14.6.3   Combining documents

Another application of what is essentially the same tool is to use the Combine Documents option (Instruction set 60).

Instruction set 60   Compare revisions from multiple documents

Keyboard	Alt | R | M | M
Left click	

This will open the Combine Documents dialog (Figure 248) which you will see is the same tool as the Compare Documents dialog. As before, load the original document on the left, the document containing the revisions on the right, check the various settings as required (I recommend not comparing Headers and Footers, and also making certain that the comparison of Fields is on—see the settings I have chosen in Figure 248). This will then load the revisions into the original document, and they can then be worked through in that context. Note that the underlying assumption is that the two documents were roughly the same to start with, but that one has been revised.

Putting this into a practical context. Imagine that our poor student, Hapless Jones, has sent two copies of his second chapter to his two promoters, Prof Dunce and dr Smart. He receives both back, and would like to work through the revisions from both promoters together. All he need do is firstly back up his thesis (see section Application 12.2, p. 267), open the tool and then load first the revisions from one promoter into his thesis, and then repeat the exercise, loading the revisions from the second promoter. Interestingly, if his thesis is in only one document (see the discussion in Chapter 12, p. 265) and he has copied out the second chapter and sent only that to his two promoters (how to do this is discussed in section 12.1, p. 266), he can still do this. Word will show that all that precedes the second chapter, and all that succeeds the second chapter, has been deleted by the two promoters. The student should just reject that[106], and then focus on the revisions for the actual chapter. Admittedly, this is not for the faint of heart, but if you feel that you have mastered the tools, it can be a great time saver.

---

[106] It should now be apparent why I insist on the backup being made first.

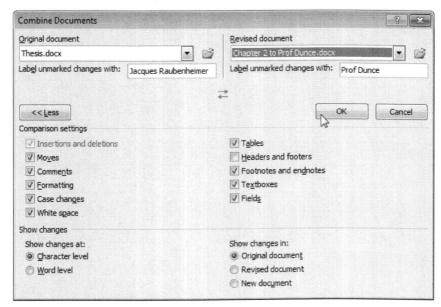

Figure 248   Combine Documents dialog

A last pointer is that if you are using either the Compare Documents or the Combine Documents feature, you can also adjust the display to show various versions of the documents being combined. Figure 249 shows the Word window when both the original and the revised documents are displayed.

Instruction set 61   Showing Source documents when comparing or combining documents

Keyboard	Alt | R | M | S | H (Hide Source Documents) Alt | R | M | S | O (Show Original) Alt | R | M | S | R (Show Revised) Alt | R | M | S | B (Show Both)
Left click	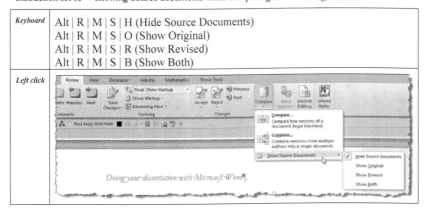

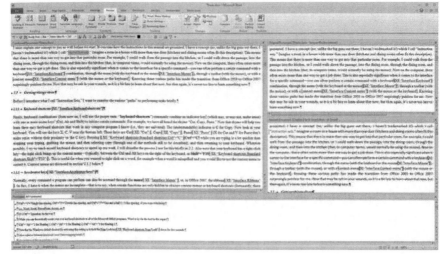

Figure 249 Source documents displayed

Chapter 15
Putting your cards on the table: Getting Tables right

Tables should be something every Word users knows how to create, and in this chapter, I rather want to focus on some more advanced table topics than rehashing the basics.

Just one note before we begin. Because of the nature of working with tables, my instruction sets will work slightly differently in this chapter, and I will be using more figures than instruction sets. As a result, I will not always show the right click options, but take note that many of the functions discussed in this chapter are available from the right click context menu (Figure 250).

Figure 250   *Context menu (Right clicking) for a table*

15.1 Adding tables

Instruction set 62   Adding tables

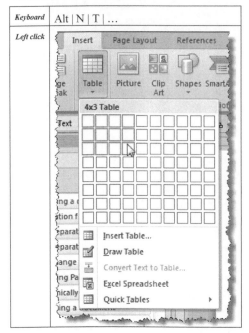

Keyboard	Alt	N	T	...
Left click	

Tables are added with the Table tool on the Insert ribbon (Instruction set 62). The first part of the tool contains a drag list that allows you to add tables with up to eight rows and ten columns (Word will Live preview the table for you as you drag). Additionally, the Insert Table... option will open the Insert Table dialog (Figure 251) which allows you to specify any Number of Rows or Columns, as well as to define the AutoFit behaviour of the table, and finally to use the Remember dimensions for new tables check box to ensure that tables added in future will use the same settings.

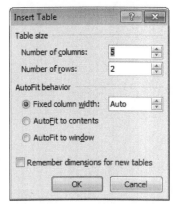

Figure 251   Insert Table dialog

Once the table has been added, Word provides two contextual ribbons which are used to further edit and format the table—Table Tools:Design and Table Tools: Layout. Not all of the tools on these ribbons will be discussed, but the tools that are discussed will be dealt with in their relevant context. Note that because these are contextual ribbons, Word displays them when the insertion point is within a table, and hides them when not.

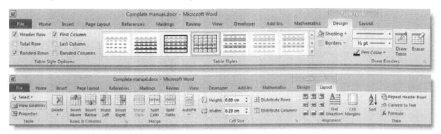

Figure 252   *Table Tools ribbons (Design and Layout)*

Of course, once the table is there, the big work of adding the information to the table comes. We will discuss other ways of getting table data into Word shortly (section 15.3), but note that for the moment, you can simply go to each cell of the table, and type or paste the information there. However, note that it is advisable to have your non-printing characters displayed, so that you can see the end-of-cell and end-of-row markers (shown in Figure 253).

Also remember that while typing, you can easily move to the next cell with the **Tab** key, and to the previous cell with **Shift + Tab**.

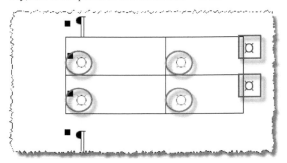

Figure 253   *End-of-cell and End-of-row markers*

15.2   Formatting tables

Once the data has been added, you will in all likelihood have to do some formatting to get the table perfectly right. The best way to do this is to use table styles, which I will discuss in section 15.3, but even if you intend using table styles, you will first have to understand table formatting.

15.2.1   Selecting table parts

Although not always the case, you generally first have to select the part of the table that you want to work with if you intend formatting it (or you at least have to position the insertion point in the relevant cell). There is a Select tool on the Table Tools: Layout ribbon (Figure 254), or you can use the mouse to select parts of the table, as demonstrated in

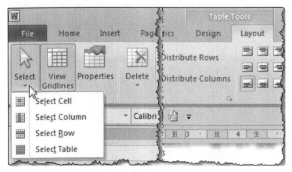

Figure 254   *Selecting table parts from the ribbon*

Instruction set 63   *Selecting table parts with the mouse*

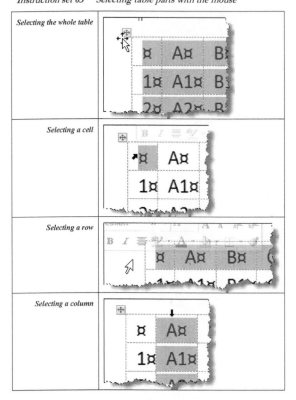

15.2.2   Adding and deleting rows and columns

Rows and columns (and individual cells) can be added and deleted from the Rows & Columns group of the Table Tools: Layout ribbon (Figure 255). Note that columns can be added to the left or right of the column in which the insertion point is found, and rows added above or below the row in which the insertion point is found.

Obviously, when rows or columns are deleted, the row or column in which the insertion point is found is the one deleted.

The Delete tool also contains an item for deleting the whole table, and then there are two tools that allow you to open the Insert Cells dialog (the dialog launcher at the bottom of the Rows & Columns group) and the Delete Cells dialog (the Delete Cells... option in the Delete tool menu). These two dialogs allow you to insert and delete entire rows or columns, but they also allow you to do what you should not: Insert or delete individual cells, thus distorting your table and making, I guarantee, life very difficult for you in the future. You should simply never create tables of the sort shown in Figure 257. Note especially how adding or removing cells column-wise (choosing the Shift cells left option when deleting or the Shift cells right option when inserting) causes other columns to become misaligned. While this table can be rehabilitated, it is often more effort than redoing the table from scratch.

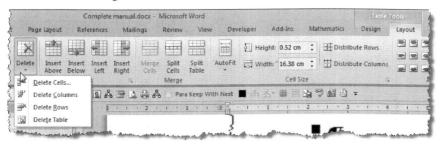

Figure 255   *Inserting and deleting rows and columns*

Figure 256   *Insert Cells & Delete Cells dialogs*

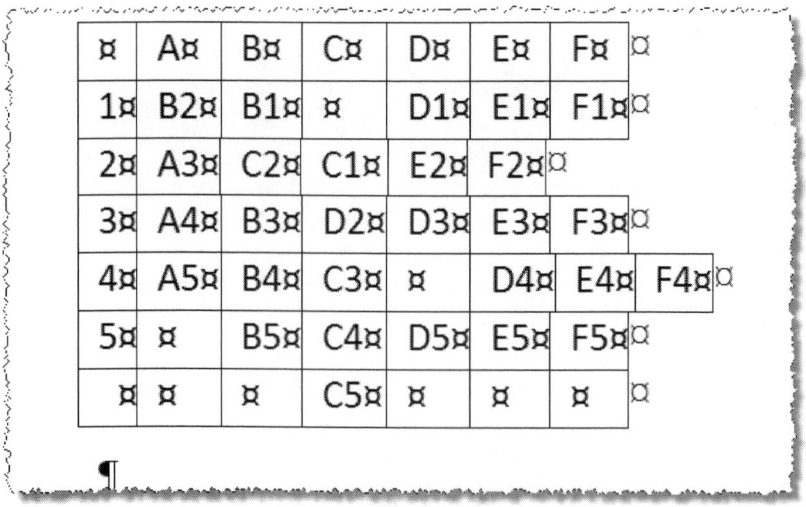

¤	A¤	B¤	C¤	D¤	E¤	F¤	¤
1¤	B2¤	B1¤	¤	D1¤	E1¤	F1¤	¤
2¤	A3¤	C2¤	C1¤	E2¤	F2¤	¤	
3¤	A4¤	B3¤	D2¤	D3¤	E3¤	F3¤	¤
4¤	A5¤	B4¤	C3¤	¤	D4¤	E4¤	F4¤	¤
5¤	¤	B5¤	C4¤	D5¤	E5¤	F5¤	¤	
¤	¤	¤	C5¤	¤	¤	¤	¤

¶

Figure 257   Tabled mangled by inserting and deleting individual cells

Also remember that if you select rows or columns when inserting or deleting, the effect is multiplied. As an example, it is obvious that if three rows or columns are selected, and the delete tool is used, all three will be deleted. But by the same token, if three rows or columns are selected, and the insert tool is used, then three more will be inserted.

If you want to insert rows at the bottom of the table, use the Insert Below option while in the bottom row of the table, and then press **F4** to repeat the action for however many rows you would want, or just select the *x* number of rows from the bottom before inserting. Furthermore, pressing the **Tab** key when you are in the last cell of a table inserts a single new row with the same formatting as the old last row.

15.2.3   Merging and splitting cells

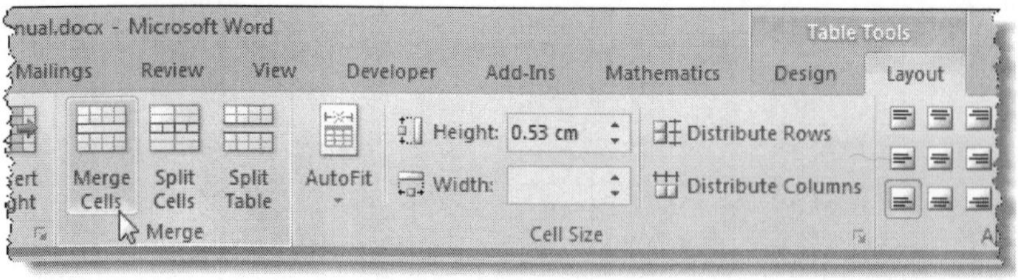

Figure 258   Merging and splitting cells

Word allows you to merge any number of cells in a table—across rows, across columns, or across rows and columns. This is often very useful in aligning table elements properly, such as centre-adding an overarching heading across a number of subheadings. You can also take individual cells and split them into any number of rows and/or columns. There is also a Split Table tool which breaks a table into two above the row in which the insertion point is currently found.

These tools are located in the Merge group of the Table Tools: Layout ribbon (Figure 258).

15.2.3.1   Merging cells

Remember to plan your table layout very carefully. Decide what is going to go where, and also which cells you are going to merge. For merged cells, place the information that will eventually be in the merged cell in the top left cell of the range that you are going to merge. When you merge cells, Word retains all the information in all the cells, but separates it with hard carriage returns. To save yourself the deleting, putting your text there (and only there) will help (note that if a range of cells are merged, and only one of those cells contains text, even if it is not the top left cell, then the effect will still be the same, but it helps to work in an organised fashion nonetheless).

15.2.3.2   Splitting cells

Clicking on the Split Cells tool in the Layout ribbon will open the Split Cells dialog (Figure 259). Word will guess how many rows or columns the cell is intended to be split into, based on the surrounding context and the cell contents, but you can adjust the values if so desired.

Figure 259   *Split Cells dialog*

Bear in mind, though, that as a general design principle, it is normally better to start with the right number of columns or rows, and then only merge those that require merging, than to start with too few rows or columns, and to have to split them—as I stated before, plan your table layout very carefully.

15.2.3.3   Fixing alignment after merging or splitting

If you have merged cells and then find yourself having to insert columns, or unmerge the cells, you may find things going wrong. Word sometimes gets the alignment of cells in the various rows wrong (although I have noticed that this seems to be mostly resolved in Word 2010). Here are some strategies for fixing these.

As an example, consider Figure 260, in which a few cells have been merged and split. The misaligned cell border is clearly visible.

¤	A¤	B¤	¤	¤	C¤	D¤	¤	E¤	F¤	¤
1¤	A1¤	B1¤	¤	¤	C1¤	D1¤	¤	E1¤	F1¤	¤
2¤	A2¤	¤	¤	B2¤	C2¤	D2¤	¤	E2¤	F2¤	¤
3¤	A3¤	B3¤	¤	¤	C3¤	D3¤	¤	E3¶ E4¶ E5¤	F3¤	¤
¤	¤	¤	¤	¤	¤	¤	¤	¤	¤	¤
4¤	A4¤	B4¤	¤	¤	C4¤	D4¤	¤	¤	F4¤	¤
¤	¤	¤	¤	¤	¤	¤	¤	¤	¤	¤
5¤	A5¤	B5¤	¤	¤	C5¤	D5¤	¤	¤	F5¤	¤

Figure 260   *Table with misaligned cell border*

Possibly the worst thing to do with this table is to attempt to correct it by instructing Word to AutoFit the contents. The result is seen in Figure 261.

¤	A¤	B¤	¤	¤	C¤	D¤	¤	E¤	F¤	¤
1¤	A1¤	B1¤	¤	¤	C1¤	D1¤	¤	E1¤	F1¤	¤
2¤	A2¤	¤	¤	B 2¤	C2¤	D2¤	¤	E2¤	F2¤	¤
3¤	A3¤	B3¤	¤	¤	C3¤	D3¤	¤	E3¶ E4¶ E5¤	F3¤	¤
¤	¤	¤	¤	¤	¤	¤	¤	¤	¤	¤
4¤	A4¤	B4¤	¤	¤	C4¤	D4¤	¤	¤	F4¤	¤
¤	¤	¤	¤	¤	¤	¤	¤	¤	¤	¤
5¤	A5¤	B5¤	¤	¤	C5¤	D5¤	¤	¤	F5¤	¤

Figure 261   *Table with misaligned cell border after AutoFitting Contents*

A better option is to use the Distribute Columns option, which results in Figure 262. Although the rows heights have been inflated, the columns are now aligned, and further adjust should maintain this alignment.

¤	A¤	B¤	¤	¤	C¤	D¤	¤	E¤	F¤	¤
1¤	A 1¤	B 1¤	¤	¤	C 1¤	D 1¤	¤	E 1¤	F1¤	¤
2¤	A 2¤	¤	¤	B 2¤	C 2¤	D 2¤	¤	E 2¤	F2¤	¤
3¤	A 3¤	B 3¤	¤	¤	C 3¤	D 3¤	¤	E 3¶ E 4¶ E 5¤	F3¤	¤
¤	¤	¤	¤	¤	¤	¤	¤	¤	¤	¤
4¤	A 4¤	B 4¤	¤	¤	C 4¤	D 4¤	¤	¤	F4¤	¤
¤	¤	¤	¤	¤	¤	¤	¤	¤	¤	¤
5¤	A 5¤	B 5¤	¤	¤	C 5¤	D 5¤	¤	¤	F5¤	¤

Figure 262   Table with misaligned cell border after Distributing Columns

If you just cannot get the spacing of the columns right, then break off the "offending" part of the table using the Split Table tool. Then insert the columns and rows that you need, and remerge the cells. You can then copy the text from the split table back and delete it when you are done.

If you have a problem with cells merged across rows, you can unfortunately not break away the merged columns. You will have to copy the columns, paste them somewhere else, delete them from the table, restructure the table, and then copy and paste back the information into the new cells.

A last resort is to use the Convert to Text tool on the Table Tools: Layout ribbon, and then to immediately use the Convert Text to Table option from the Table tool on the Insert ribbon to convert it back to a table, which should then have proper alignment (although this does not work that well if there were still merged cells resulting in a non-symmetrical table).

15.2.4   Adjusting column width and row height

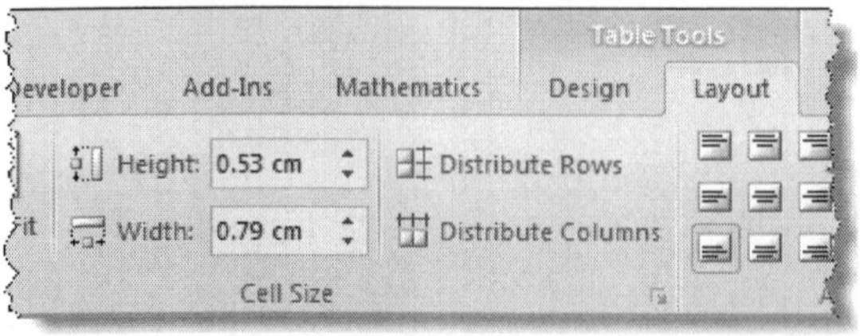

Figure 263   *Cell Size tools*

The height of rows and the width of columns can be set using the tools in the Cell Size group of the Table Tools: Layout ribbon (Figure 263). However, be wary of what is selected. If nothing is selected, the entire row height or the entire column width is adjusted. However, if cells are selected, adjusting the row height will adjust the height of the entire row, but, as Figure 264 shows, adjusting the width will result in only the width of the selected cells being changed, with a misaligned table the result.

Figure 264   *Table mangled by adjusting cell width while cells are selected*

A further technique is to use the Distribute Rows or Distribute Columns tools to divide the row height or column width evenly across the table.

The Cell Size group of the Table Tools: Layout ribbon also contains an AutoFit button, which allows you to instruct Word to adjust the width of the table columns based on the text you add to them (AutoFit <u>C</u>ontents), fit the table to the full margin width, distributing the columns within that based on their content (AutoFit <u>W</u>indow), or to fix the column widths so that Word does not adjust them as you add text (Fixed Colum<u>n</u> Width).

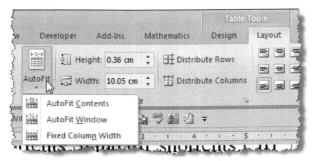

Figure 265   *Table "fit" settings*

All the above notwithstanding, it is also useful to adjust table columns and rows with the mouse. Again, though, make sure that nothing is selected in the table, since this can cause columns to become misaligned.

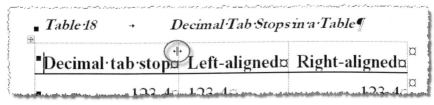

Figure 266   *Adjusting column width with the mouse*

When you hold the mouse pointer over a cell border, it changes to what I call the adjust border pointer (two parallel lines with perpendicular arrows pointing in either directions), which looks like this: ╫. Figure 266 demonstrates this for a column, although it looks much the same for rows. You can then click and drag to adjust the width of a column, or the height of a row[107]. However, it is not quite as simple as clicking and dragging. How you combine the various access keys on the keyboard influences the end result of what will happen to your table.

---

[107] Note that you can only adjust row heights in this way in Print Layout view, not in Draft view. Column adjustment works in both views.

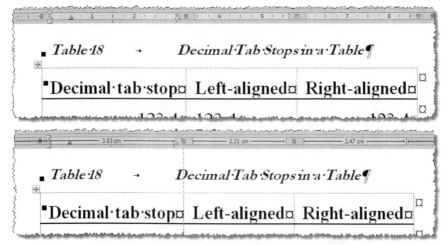

Figure 267   Holding down the Alt key while adjusting column width or row height

The first trick involves the **Alt** key. Holding it down while clicking and dragging to adjust column width or row height will display the exact width of columns, or height of rows, in the ruler, as is demonstrated for columns in Figure 267.

Next, if you hold down nothing (Alt excepted) on the keyboard and click and drag a column width, Word will then adjust the width of the two columns on either side of the border you have adjusted, making one wider, and one narrower (depending on how you drag), but maintaining the total table width. For rows, Word will make the row above the border higher or shorter (depending on how you drag), but will not adjust the height of any of the rows below the dragged border, thus increasing or decreasing the total table height of the table accordingly.

If you hold down the **Ctrl** key before clicking the border, Word maintains the total table width, changes the width of the column to the left of the border as you have set it, and adjusts the widths of all the columns to the right of the border proportionally. Holding down the **Ctrl + Shift** keys before clicking the border, will make Word maintain the total table width, change the width of the column to the left of the border as you have set it, and adjust the widths of all the columns to the right of the border so that they are all equally wide. Finally (my personal favourite), holding down only the **Shift** key causes Word to adjust the column width to the left of the border, and the table width as well (i.e., all column widths to the right of the border are maintained intact). These functions are summarised in Table 19.

Table 19   *Access keys' function when used to adjust table borders*

Key	Function	Works for
Alt	Show measurements	Rows and Columns
Shift	Adjust column widths to the right of the dragged border	Only Columns
Ctrl	Maintain table width	Only Columns

Lastly, **double clicking** on a column or row border will cause Word to autofit the column to the left, or the row above, based on the contents of all the cells in that column or row, and adjusting the total width or height of the table accordingly.

15.2.5   Setting Table properties

Figure 268   *Opening the Table Properties dialog*

The Table Properties dialog can be opened from two different positions on the Table Tools ribbon (Figure 268).

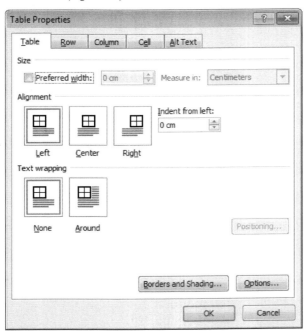

Figure 269   *Table Properties dialog: Table tab*

The Table tab of the Table Properties dialog allows you to set the Preferred width of the table (leaving this out allows Word to autofit the table width). Note that the width can be set in either your local measurement unit, or in a percentage (e.g., if you want the table to be half the width of the page margins, set the width to 50%).

The dialog also allows you to set the position of the table relative to the page margins. By default, tables are left-aligned, although you can easily centre- or right-align tables here, and additionally set an indent from the left (but not the centre or the right).

You can also change the Text wrapping of the table from None to Around, to let the table become a floating object around which you can let the text flow. How this works in principle is discussed for pictures in sections 18.4.1 and 18.4.2 (p. 445–453). When this is set, clicking on the Positioning... button will open the Table Positioning dialog (Figure 270) where you can fine tune the exact positioning of the table. Having said that, while centring or right-aligning tables is not that bad, Word does not actually like floating tables, and too many of them can make your document unstable. Also, if you do go this route, then whatever you do, do not attempt to position multiple tables floating next to each other!

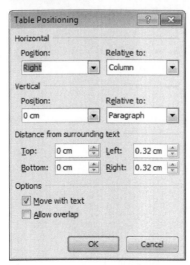

Figure 270   *Table Positioning dialog*

Application 15.1   *Side-by-side tables*

I have just advised against positioning floating tables right next to each other. What to do, then, if you would like to position two tables next to each other? Apart from the question of why you would want to do this, which I shall leave aside, the solution is actually quite simple: Add a single table, with one more column than the two individual tables are to have. Then format the intermediate column to have no top, bottom or middle borders (its left border will be the right border of the last column of the first "table" and its right border will be the left border of the first column of the second "table." You can use the Merge Cells *feature so that the two "tables" need not even have the same number of rows. Even though it is, in reality, one table, it will appear, when printed, as two.*

Although not an exact example, Table 2 uses this technique—instead of one very long, but very narrow, table, I added five columns instead of two, and the third column has no borders. This it seems as if the columns "snake back" for a second set.

Furthermore, the Options... button on the Table tab of the Table Properties dialog will open the Table Options dialog (Figure 271) where you can set default Top, Bottom, Left and Right cell margins (i.e., the spacing between the border of the cell and the edge of the text), as well as (optionally) setting space between cells and setting the autofit behaviour of the table.

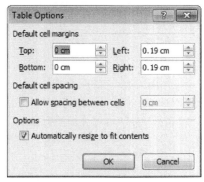

Figure 271   *Table Options dialog*

Although the borders of a table can be set via the tools on the Draw Borders group of the Table Tools: Design ribbon, the Borders and Shading dialog (Figure 272) can also be opened from the same place on the ribbon, or from the Borders and Shading... button in the Table Properties dialog. It is not my goal to discuss this dialog here, although I will mention just three tips in using it for tables:

Firstly, take careful note the Apply to list box. This will allow you to toggle between setting borders for the Text, the Paragraph, the Cell (or selected cells), or the whole Table. Secondly, if the borders for the selection are uniform (i.e., borders all around are the same, and you would want to change the style of one of the borders, you may be frustrated in the process, since changing the style (e.g., from a solid to a dotted line) will result in all the borders being changed. The secret is to break the uniformity—remove the border you want to change, then change the border style, and then add the border again in the new style. Third, remember that while Word does a good job of rendering the borders on paper, if your document is going to be printed by using pdf as an intermediate format, you may want to keep the borders simple and to a minimum, as the borders do not render very well, and also not with much consistency, in pdf.

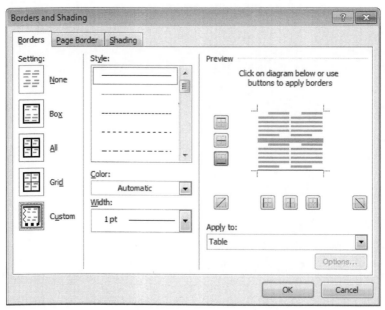

Figure 272   *Borders and Shading dialog: Setting borders for a table*

The Row tab of the Table Properties dialog (Figure 273) allows you to specify either that Word be allowed to autofit your row height (by leaving the Specify height check box deselected), to autofit your rows within bounds (by setting a specified height to an At least value), or to specify an exact height for your rows. You can also, for any number of selected top rows, turn the Repeat as header row at the top of each page setting on and also to specify whether rows may be broken over pages with the Allow row to break across pages setting (these two settings will be discussed in the next section).

Note that if you select multiple rows, the dialog will show the row numbers for all the selected rows at the top of this tab (in Figure 273, it specifies only Row 3). You can then use the Previous Row and Next Row buttons to "break" the grouping and set row heights for each row individually.

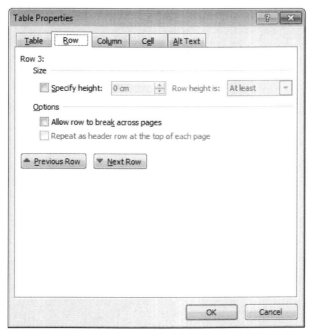

Figure 273   *Table Properties dialog: Row tab*

The Column tab of the Table Properties dialog (Figure 274) allows you to specify either that columns be autofit by Word, or to a Preferred width you supply. However, note that, unlike with rows, you cannot set an exact width here. This may lead to a little frustration in setting your column widths, but if you persevere, you may get the desired result. Note that, as with the Table tab, the width can be set in either your local measurement unit, or in a percentage (e.g., if you have a four-column table, and want all four columns to be equally wide, set the width to 25%).

As with the Rows tab, if you have selected multiple columns, the column numbers for all the selected columns will be shown at the top of this tab (Figure 274 shows Column 2), and you can again use the Previous Column and Next Column buttons to "break" the grouping and set column widths for each column individually.

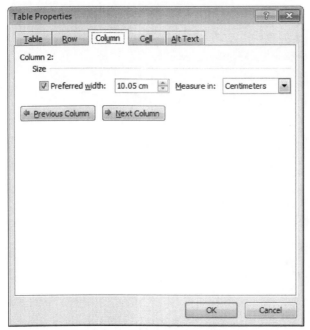

Figure 274   *Table Properties dialog: Column tab*

The Cell tab of the Table Properties dialog (Figure 275) allows you to specify a cell width, much like the column width, and then also in your local measurement unit or a percentage. You can also specify that text be positioned at the Top, Center, or Bottom of the cell.

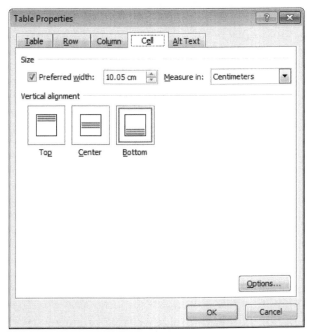

Figure 275   Table Properties dialog: Cell tab

Furthermore, clicking on the Options… button of the Cell tab of the Table Properties dialog will open the Cell Options dialog (Figure 276). Here you specify that the cell use the same text margins as were set in the Table Options dialog (Figure 271), or you can choose difference settings for the selected cells. You can also specify whether text in the cell should be wrapped (if there are words longer than the cell width, then when Wrap text is on, Word will break the word across to a new line, but when it is off, Word will rather adjust the width of the column). You can also instruct Word to Fit text, meaning that Word will adjust the font scaling of text that is longer than the column width, effectively shrinking the text horizontally to force it to fit in (this is only effective if a very small amount of scaling is done, and I think it would probably best be done manually, rather than letting Word indiscriminately apply it through this setting).

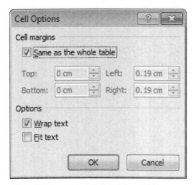

Figure 276   *Cell Options dialog*

Note also that the cell margins, the text direction, and the vertical and horizontal text alignment can all be set from the Alignment group of the Table Tools: Layout ribbon (Figure 277).

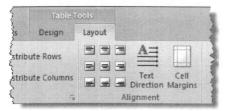

Figure 277   *Table Tools: Layout ribbon—Alignment group*

15.2.6   Dealing with large tables

Sometimes, we have such large tables that they run over several pages. First, a word of warning, and a word of advice. The warning is this: Generally, don't put too large tables into a Word document. A few pages at most should be a limited. I have seen people use Word tables for a columnar layout in policy-style documents, where, instead of using the heading styles to create a proper document hierarchy, the hierarchy was reflected in the table (i.e., the first column was the highest hierarchy level, the second column represented the second hierarchy level, and so on). Not only are these kinds of documents difficult to create and maintain, they are actually difficult to read as well. And, of course, they create unstable documents which eventually crash (which is normally when I get to see them). Now the word of advice. Even style guides (e.g., American Psychological Association, 2010) recommend that when tables get too large, it is best to break them up into a number of individually captioned tables, so that each smaller table will fit onto a single page. Having said that, there are times when we can consider still maintaining, and working with, these large tables. An example is the table of keyboard shortcuts in Appendix A (p. 497).

The first secret is getting the header row(s) to appear on every page. This is very simple—select the rows you want to have repeated (or if it is only the top row of the table, just position yourself in the top row) and then use the Repeat Header Rows tools in the Data group of the Table Tools: Layout ribbon (Figure 278). This feature is then also used in the list of keyboard shortcuts in Appendix A (starting on p. 497).

Figure 278   **Repeat Header Rows**

The next challenge is keeping the rows of the table together. This entails two things—preventing breaks in the middle of a row, and then deciding between which rows you want to allow breaks (there must, after all, be breaks somewhere).

The first is easily dealt with—in the Row tab of the Table Properties dialog, deselect the Allow row to break across pages check box for all rows of the table. This will prevent the table from breaking mid-row (i.e., if a row containing several lines falls over the end of the page, the whole row will be transposed to the next page).

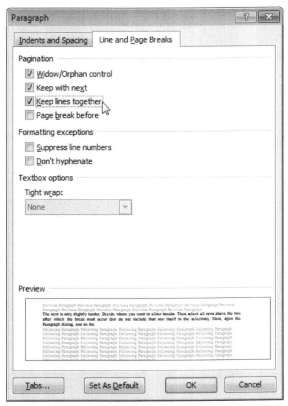

Figure 279   *Paragraph settings to keep table rows together*

The next is only slightly harder. Decide where you want to allow breaks. Then select all rows *above* the row after which the break must occur (but do not include that row itself in the selection). Next, open the Paragraph dialog, and on the Line and Page Breaks tab, select the Keep lines together and Keep with next check boxes (Figure 279).

15.3   Table Styles

When a thesis or dissertation contains many tables, a lot of unnecessary time can be spent formatting tables. Just as you use Paragraph and Character styles to format your text, so also you can use Table styles to format your tables in the blink of an eye.

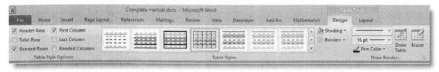

Figure 280   Table Tools: Design

The Table Tools: Design ribbon (Figure 280) consists of only three groups, of which two are dedicated to table styles. The Table Styles gallery contains a large number of galleries that ship with Word, and you can create any number of your own.

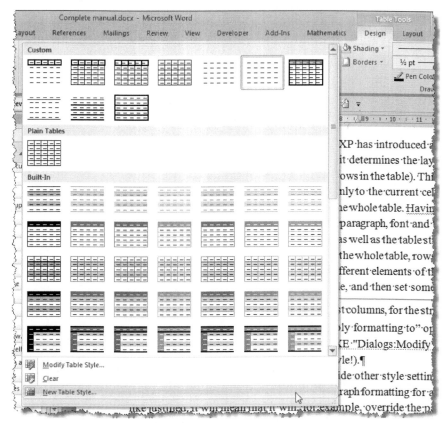

Figure 281   *Table Styles Gallery*

As was mentioned before, table styles can be applied either via the Table Styles gallery on the Table Tools: Design ribbon, or from the Apply Styles dialog (section 6.3.3, p. 97) or from the Classic Styles Gallery (section 6.3.2, p. 95). You can format an entire table simply by clicking on the style you want to format it with. Note also that the bottom of the gallery (Figure 281) contains options for clearing formatting from a table, creating new table styles, and modifying existing table styles.

You can also right click on a style in the gallery (Figure 282) to create new table styles, or modify or delete existing table styles, or to apply table styles while keeping or replacing existing table formatting, or to set a table style as the default for all new tables (which will save you even more time).

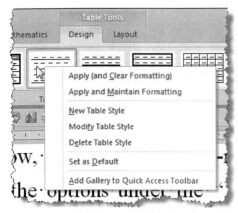

Figure 282   *Context menu (right click) for a style in the Table Style gallery*

Creating a table style is very similar to the process of creating a paragraph style (section 6.4.1, p. 105), barring that the Create New Style from Formatting dialog looks a little different for table styles (compare Figure 81 from p. 105 to Figure 283 below).

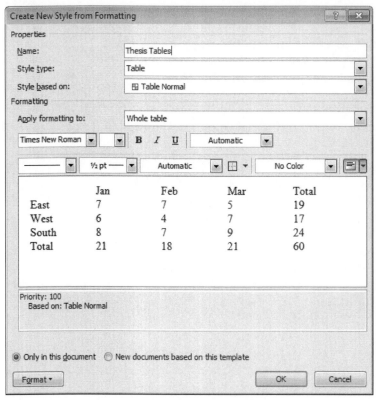

Figure 283   *Create New Style from Formatting dialog: Table style*

The steps, then, are more or less the same as before, with one twist (which should also not be that surprising if you have worked through the process of setting Multilevel lists discussed in 8.1.2.2, p. 151). First give the style an appropriate name that either describes what the style looks like (in an general sort of way) and/or describes what the style is to be used for (e.g., *Thesis tables*). Then also remember to turn on the New documents based on this template setting, so that the style is stored in your template.

Now comes the twist. The Apply formatting to list box lists various parts of a table:

- Whole table
- Header row
- Total row
- First column
- Last column

- Odd banded rows
- Even banded rows
- Odd banded columns
- Even banded columns

- Top left cell
- Top right cell
- Bottom left cell
- Bottom right cell

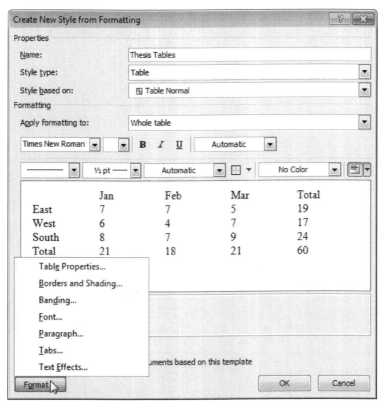

Figure 284   *Create New Style from Formatting dialog: Formatting available for a table style*

Beginning with the Whole table, set the formatting you would want most of the table to assume—Figure 284 shows the formatting available for a table style:

- Table properties
- Borders and shading
- Banding

- Font
- Paragraph

- Tabs
- Text effects

All of these formatting settings have been discussed where relevant, with the single exception of banding, which is set via the Banding dialog (Figure 285), where you set the number of rows and/or columns per band (banding allows different colours to be applied to different bands to facilitate better reading across rows or down columns—see some of the table styles in the gallery).

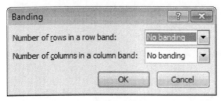

Figure 285   Banding dialog

Once the formatting for the whole table has been set, choose each element that you anticipate using (e.g., header row, first column, etc.) and set only the *differences* between this element and those of the whole table (e.g., making the header row bold).

Once this process is complete, click Ok and the style will be created. The last thing to note is the group of Table Style Options on the far left of the Table Tools: Design ribbon. These setting, as it were, turn the differentiations you specified in the process of defining the various elements of your table style, on and off. Thus, if you specified a bold header row, then the text in the header row will only be bold if the Header Row check box in this group is selected. If not, then the text in the header row will appear as defined for the whole table.

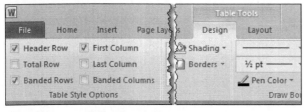

Figure 286   Table style options

Obviously, table styles are also employed in this book. Most of my tables that are captioned as tables use one style (which should be quite apparent see if you compare them), and all the Instruction sets utilise another table style.

15.4   Pasting tables from other sources

The really good news about tables in Word is that you do not necessarily need to type everything that is in every table. Word accepts a lot of input from other sources as tables. In other words, you can copy tables and paste them into your Word document, and they will be tables. Just a word of advice, though. Many statistical programs (e.g., SAS, SPSS, etc.) now provide statistical output in html files by default. Word will happily accept these html tables as tables, but they do not really look that good (the statistical package vendors have other objectives than what you do with your dissertation). Use a table style to perform a one-click reformat of those tables, and your dissertation will look a whole lot better.

15.4.1   Copying and pasting Word table parts

Before discussing copying and pasting from other programs, it would be worthwhile to quickly discuss some principles of copying and pasting from one Word table to another (or from one place in a table to another).

If you will recall, I pointed out displaying your non-printing characters on p. 335 when working with tables. This becomes very apparent when copying and pasting. If you select and copy the contents of a cell, but not the cell end marker, then you are copying and pasting only that text, together with its text and paragraph formatting. If, however, you include the cell end marker in the selection, then you are copying the whole cell, including the cell formatting (e.g., cell margins, cell alignment, etc.). If you select all the cells in a row, but do not select the row end marker, then you are copying merely a group of cells. When you paste it, those cells will be pasted. If you include the row end marker, you are copying a whole row, and then the whole row will be pasted.

1

Key¤	Function¤	Works·for¤
Alt¤	Show·measurements○	Rows·and·Columns○
Shift¤	Adjust·column·widths·to·the·right·of·the·dragged·border○	Only·Columns○
Ctrl¤	Maintain table·width○	Only·Columns○

2

Key¤	Function¤	Works·for¤
Alt¤	Show·measurements○	Rows·and·Columns○
Shift¤	Adjust·column·widths·to·the·right·of·the·dragged·border○	Only·Columns○
Ctrl¤	Maintain table·width○	Only·Columns○

3

Key¤	Function¤	Works·for¤
Alt¤	Show·measurements○	Rows·and·Columns○
Alt¤	Show·measurements○	Rows·and·Columns○
Ctrl¤	Maintain table·width○	Only·Columns○

4

Key¤	Function¤	Works·for¤
Alt¤	Show·measurements○	Rows·and·Columns○
Shift¤	Adjust·column·widths·to·the·right·of·the·dragged·border○	Only·Columns○
Ctrl¤	Maintain table·width○	Only·Columns○

5

Key¤	Function¤	Works·for¤
Alt¤	Show·measurements○	Rows·and·Columns○
Shift¤	Adjust·column·widths·to·the·right·of·the·dragged·border○	Only·Columns○
Ctrl¤	Maintain table·width○	Only·Columns○

6

Key¤	Function¤	Works·for¤
Alt¤	Show·measurements○	Rows·and·Columns○
Alt¤	Show·measurements○	Rows·and·Columns○
Shift¤	Adjust·column·widths·to·the·right·of·the·dragged·border○	Only·Columns○
Ctrl¤	Maintain table·width○	Only·Columns○

Figure 287   *Illustrating the importance of row end markers*

An example is in order. Consider Table 19 above. Figure 287 shows the two different methods of copying, and the two different results. In Frame 1, I select the first three cells, but not the row end marker. I copy them, and position myself at the start of the third row (just before the word *Shift*—Frame 2). When I paste, the result, as Frame 3 shows, is that the three cells of the third row are overwritten by the three copied cells. Frame 4 shows the second method, where I include the row end marker in the selection. In Frame 5 I again position myself in exactly the same position as in Frame 2. When I paste, the result is that a new row (a copy of the second row) is added above the third row (Frame 6).

15.4.2   Converting text into tables

Sometimes (although it is increasingly rare), you could have pure text input that you need to copy and paste into Word, but have it displayed as a table. Word has always been very adept at converting this text into tables, using the Convert Text to Table... option (of course, the text to be converted must be selected before this tool is invoked).

Instruction set 64   Converting text into tables

Shortcut	Use Insert Table... to bypass the dialog
Keyboard	Alt | N | T | V
Left click	

If you select this option Word will open the Convert Text to Table dialog (Figure 288). You can bypass it if you are confident that you won't be changing any settings, by simply selecting Insert Table... instead, which, in this instance, will not open the Insert Table dialog, but will just convert the text to a table automatically. Here you can specify the number of rows and/or columns in the text data, choose in advance the autofit behaviour Word is to apply to the table, and also instruct Word how to separate the text out—Word examines the text and selects the option it believes is best for this, but you can change it if, for some reason, a different option is what is required. Note that you should actually start with this setting at the bottom of the dialog, as changing this will cause Word to repopulate the number of rows and columns options based on its analysis of the text.

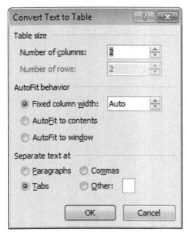

Figure 288   *Convert Text to Table dialog*

15.4.3   Using Excel to create table data

I won't be saying much about this, barring to note that, when creating tables in Word, I often use Excel as an intermediary. The beauty of Excel is that it allows me to use its vast array of formatting tools to format my data first (e.g., adding currency symbols, setting decimal places, and many, many more—even setting borders in Excel is quicker and easier than in Word), also do any calculations I might need to do, and then paste the well-formed table into Word. And Excel cells copied and pasted into Word arrive, by default, not as an Excel object, but as a very good copy of the Excel data, set as a Word table[108]. In fact, you can even take a Word table, copy it to Excel, format it there, and then copy it and paste it back into Word. And if the Excel fonts are not exactly what you were using in Word, then apply a table style is the simple completion to the process. Of course, all of this assumes that you are pasting into a blank paragraph in the Word document, where a new table is then created. See Application 15.2 below for what happens when you want to paste into an existing Word table.

15.4.4   Pasting into existing tables

If you want to paste information from one table into another, the results can sometimes be less that desired. If you select an entire row or column, Word copies the contents of each cell, together with its paragraph formatting, as well as the formatting of the table's cells. This means, for example, that if your two tables do not have exactly the same row

---

[108] Perhaps, for once, after all my griping throughout this book, I should say: "Well done, Microsoft!"

widths, the inserted row will not match the surrounding rows. To prevent this, select only the cells, but not the end-of-row marker. Now when you copy the table content and paste it into the new table, Word maintains the paragraph formatting, but uses the table formatting of the destination table.

Also, be careful of overwriting information in a table when you paste into it. If you have copied five complete rows from a source table, those five rows will be inserted above the current row of the destination table when the cursor is anywhere in the first cell in the row (or if the entire row in the destination table is selected). If the cursor is in any other cell, the rows will be inserted within the destination rows, lengthening the destination rows by the appropriate number of cells. On the other hand, if you have copied only information from five rows (i.e., the end-of-row marker is not selected), then no rows are added, and the information is pasted over the existing information in the relevant five rows of the destination table when the cursor is anywhere in the first cell in the row (or if the entire row in the destination table is selected). If the cursor is in any other cell, the information in the destination table will be overwritten, and the relevant rows of the destination table will be lengthened by the required number of cells (i.e., if information from five cells are copied, and pasted into the 3rd column of a five-column row, then two additional columns will be added for that row).

Application 15.2   Pasting Excel data into an existing Word table

> *Unfortunately, when you paste from Microsoft Excel into an already existing Word table, all the cells selected in Excel are pasted into a single cell in the Word table. The solution to this is, fortunately, quite simple. Firstly, make sure you know the exact size (row and column count) of the range of cells you are copying. Then "prepare the ground" for them: Add that many cells into your Word table. Then select them, and then paste—the Excel cells will be distributed across the Word table cells as hoped. However, be careful to ensure that you have selected exactly the right number of columns and rows in the Word table. For example, if my Excel data consists of four rows, and I select only three in the Word table, then only the first three rows of data will be pasted—the last row will simply be discarded, without even so much as a warning. Conversely, if I were to select five rows instead of four, then the first row will simply be repeated in the fifth row position, again without any indication being given that this is what happened.*

15.5   Other uses for tables

Tables, of course, are a very versatile piece in the armoury of a Word master. Tables serve very well for some other uses as well. For example, not all tables have to be visible to work as tables. All the Instruction Sets in this book are actually tables (note that a specific table style is used, and note how well the tables work as containers for the images used in the Instruction Sets).

Tables are also useful for aligning objects on the page. Quite a few figures in this book are actually borderless (i.e., invisible) tables. Figure 154, (p. 208) is a good example of this, as is Figure 59 (p. 82).

I also mentioned that adding too many continuous section breaks to your document is not a good idea (p. 121). Borderless tables are excellent for creating simply columnar layouts that do not have to "snake." The two bulleted lists on p. 357 (from this very chapter) are a good example of that.

15.6   General tips

Getting the information you want into your table is not always that easy. Here are some tips that can help:

15.6.1   Adding tabs inside a cell

Since the Tab key is used for navigation in a table, people sometimes get frustrated trying to add actual tabs within table cells. Use **Ctrl + Tab** to insert a tab in a table cell!

15.6.2   Table notes

See Application 8.6 (p. 181) for a brief discussion of adding table notes.

15.6.3   Decimal tab stops

Aligning the information in your table is normally quite simple, as it can be done with the paragraph alignment as usual. I prefer to create separate table styles (even if based on my body text style) so that I can fine-tune alignment in my tables through the style(s), without upsetting the rest of my document. However, one rather tricky situation will serve as an illustration for how these settings can be made: Arranging numbers.

A common problem with arranging numbers is that they might not all have the same number of digits before and/or after the decimal (take, for example, accounting data where negative values may be indicated with parentheses). Padding zeros generally help, but might not be the ideal solution in all contexts (they won't work for the accounting example). The solution lies in creating the right kind of tab stops (these tab stops can best be added to the table style or a paragraph style to be used in the table). When doing that, make sure to click on the Clear All button first to remove all the unwanted residual tap stops, and then type in the position of the decimal in centimetres from the left, select the Decimal alignment button, and click on Set (as is shown in Figure 289).

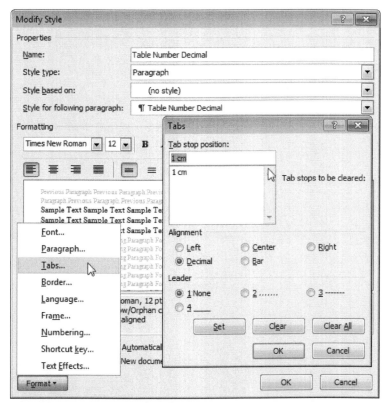

Figure 289   Modifying a style's tab stops

A short demonstration of using decimal tab stops is given in Table 20. Although the numbers look a little unbalanced, they are all aligned along the decimal points, and there can be no confusion in that regard. Bear in mind that numbers in a table are seldom so varied as those chosen here for effect. Note that the decimal tab stops are extremely sensitive. If, for example, the tab stop is wider than the column width (or there is not enough space left in the column for the number of digits after the decimal), then the decimal alignment will be thrown out. It is also best to align the paragraph setting for the style to the left. Then the distance set for the decimal will be measured from the left.

Table 20   *Decimal Tab Stops in a Table*

Decimal tab stop	Right-aligned
123.4	123.4
12.34	12.34
1.234	1.234
1.23	1.23
1.2	1.2
-123.4	-123.4
-12.34	-12.34
-1.234	-1.234
-1.23	-1.23
-1.2	-1.2

Application 15.3   *Adding text above a document-starting table*

I am sometimes asked this: I have a table that is right at the top of a document, but I want to add text above it. How can I get there to add the text?

The answer is amazingly simple: A) Position yourself anywhere in the top row of the table and click on Split Table *(*Table Tools: Layout *ribbon). B) Position yourself at the very start of the very first cell of the table. Press **Enter** (or, for a simple, but complete, keyboard shortcut solution: **Ctrl + Home, Enter**.*

15.7   Table functions

Word's tables can do more than just present data. They can also, to a limited extent, manipulate data.

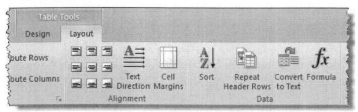

Figure 290   *Table data tools: Sort and Formula*

15.7.1   Sort

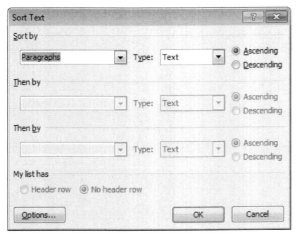

Figure 291   Sort Text dialog

In the Data group of the Table Tools: Layout ribbon is a Sort button (Figure 290), which opens the Sort Text dialog (Figure 291), which allows you to sort the contents of a table by up to three columns. This is also a useful tool for sorting text paragraphs that are not in a table (the tool is also found in the Paragraph group of the Home ribbon).

Note that you should pay attention to whether your table has a header row or not. If there are column headings, and Word thinks your table does not have a header row (Word generally does a good job of guessing this based on your table formatting), then the column headings will end up in amongst the other rows.

Your data can be sorted as text, as numbers, or as dates, and in ascending or descending order.

Using the Options... you can also determine whether the sort must be case sensitive or not (i.e., it treats small letters and capitals differently), what language to use, and how to separate fields (Figure 292).

Figure 292   Sort Options

15.7.2   Formula

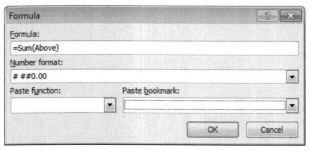

Figure 293   Formula dialog

In the Data group of the Table Tools: Layout ribbon is a Formula button (Figure 290), which add a calculated field to your table (Figure 293). There is a list of functions you can use in the Paste function list box, you can place bookmarks around certain values in your document and then use them in the formulas with the Paste bookmark list box, and you can set certain Number formats (reminiscent of Excel's custom number formats).

Chapter 16
Data Presentation Skills: Creating Charts

Charts are good ways of presenting data in a visual medium. In fact, the appeal of a good chart is that it can fit more data into the same page space than any other medium. Remember though, that both charts and tables serve the same basic purpose—to summarise data in ways which contribute to their interpretation. As such, you should generally choose between a chart or a table as the most appropriate tool for whatever meaning you wish to convey from your data.

Charting is a topic about which whole books can, and have been written. Since Excel has become the default charting application for Word since Word 2007 it would pay, if you are really serious about charts, to read a book such as Walkenbach. Also, for books which generally describe the processes and pitfalls of visually presenting data, you could do much worse than to read the books of Tufte (1983; 1990) or Wainer (1997).

16.1   Graphical excellence

Before we begin, though, let's examine an important concept, again gleaned from Tufte (1983). Tufte uses the term graphical excellence[109], and states (p. 13) that any graphical display of data should:

- Reveal the data
- Show away from the method to the meaning of the data
  (i.e., the graphical method should be self-effacing)
- Never distort the meaning of the data
- Optimise space usage
- Give coherence to large amounts of data
- Encourage comparison of data
- Reveal several levels of detail in the data
  (i.e., encourage micro- and macro readings of the data)
- Server a clearly defined purpose
- "Be closely integrated with the statistical and verbal descriptions of the data."

Furthermore, we would do well to listen to his later (1990, pp. 33–34) comments on the presentation of information:

> We envision information in order to reason about, communicate, document, and preserve that knowledge—activities nearly always carried out on two-dimensional paper and computer screen. Escaping this flatland and enriching the density of data displays are the essential tasks of information design. Such escapes grow more difficult as ties of data to our familiar three-space world weaken (with more abstract measures) and as the number of dimensions increases (with more complex data).
>
> Still, all the history of information displays and statistical graphics—indeed of any communication device—is entirely a progress of methods for

---

[109] His chapter on graphical integrity is also very important.

enhancing density, complexity, dimensionality, and even sometimes beauty....

By giving the focus over to data rather than data-containers, these design strategies are transparent and self-effacing in character. Designs so good that they are invisible. Too many data presentations, alas, seek to attract and divert attention by means of display apparatus and ornament. Chartjunk has come to corrupt all sorts of information exhibits and computer interfaces....

Lurking behind chartjunk is contempt both for information and for the audience. Chartjunk promoters imagine that numbers and details are boring, dull, and tedious, requiring ornament to enliven. Cosmetic decoration, which frequently distorts the data, will never salvage an underlying lack of content. If the numbers are boring, then you've got the wrong numbers.

Tufte (p. 76) goes on to deftly point out that "*Comparisons must be enforced within the scope of the eyespan*, a fundamental point occasionally forgotten in practice." Thus we need to make a distinction between using charts to *present* data in an intelligible and useful format, and simplifying data so as to make it easy to digest, but practically meaningless. Tufte (1990, p. 51) writes:

What about confusing clutter? Information overload? Doesn't data have to be "boiled down" and "simplified"? these common questions miss the point, for the quality of detail is an issue completely separate from the difficulty of reading. *Clutter and confusion are failures of design, not attributes of information....*

So much for the conventional, facile, and false equation: simpleness of data and design = clarity of reading. Simpleness is another aesthetic preference....

What we seek instead is a rich texture of data, a comparative context, an understanding of complexity revealed with an economy of means.

I will leave it to you, the reader, to read his book and discover the full meaning of all those requirements.

16.2   Inserting charts

To insert a chart, simply select the Chart tool from the Insert ribbon (Instruction set 65) and then choose the appropriate chart type. Your screen will split, with Word on the left, and Excel on the right, ready to receive your data. Three ribbons will appear for you to work with, being Chart Tools: Design, Chart Tools: Layout, and Chart Tools: Format.

Instruction set 65   Inserting a chart

Keyboard	Alt	N	C
Left click	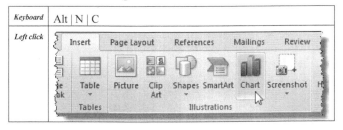

16.2.1   Customising charts

The charting approach since Office 2007 is a top-down, not a bottom-up approach. This means that the instant you insert a chart, you very much have a finished product inserted into your presentation right away. All you need to do is fine tune what you see until you are satisfied. This also means that sometimes, very little customisation will be required to have a display-ready chart in your presentation. Sometimes, of course, you may have to spend a little more time, but even then, this new approach speeds up the process of creating charts dramatically.

16.2.1.1   Chart data

Word uses Microsoft Excel as its charting tool. When you insert a chart, the screen is split into two, with Word on the left half, and Excel, displaying your data, on the right, with irritating sample data which you always have to delete. Note that the data range is surrounded by a blue border. You then either enter your data into the sheet manually, or copy and paste it from an Excel spreadsheet, Word table, html statistical output, or other similar format.

You can close the datasheet when you are done, and can access it at any time if you later need to change the data.

Instruction set 66   Viewing the Microsoft Excel datasheet

Keyboard	Alt	JC	D
Left click	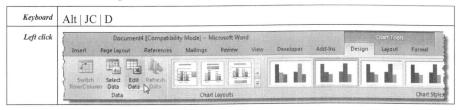

One useful tool that sometimes makes the difference between a chart that is difficult to comprehend or not is the orientation of the data. You can change this by selecting the Switch Row/Column option (Alt|JC|W). You can also use the Select Data tool (Alt|JC|E) to open the Excel data sheet and display the Select Data Source dialog (Figure 294). This tool also allows you to switch (transpose) the data, as well as to arrange the order of your series (which may improve the readability of the chart), and change the settings related to each series and category of data.

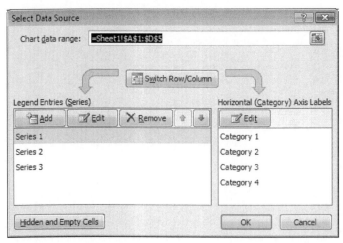

Figure 294   *Select Data Source dialog*

16.2.1.2   Chart type

You can use the Chart Type tool on the Chart Tools: Design ribbon to change the chart type. Different chart types are best suited to different types of data, although certain types of data might be equally well displayed by several chart types. Generally, choose a chart type that does justice to your data, and allows the audience to see what you want them to see from the data. Chart types are discussed in more detail in 16.2.2.

16.2.1.3   Chart options

The Chart Tools: Layout ribbon options cover the Titles, Axes, Gridlines, Legend, Data Labels and Data Table settings of the chart, as well as the option of adding certain statistical analysis indicators (not all of them may be available to you, depending on your choice of chart type), as discussed in Table 21.

Table 21	*Chart Options dialog*
Tab	**Function**
Titles	Set titles for the chart as a whole, and for the horizontal, vertical and depth (if working with a 3-D format) axes.
Axes	Show or hide the values (summarised from your data by Microsoft Excel) for the horizontal, vertical and depth (if working with a 3-D format) axes.
Gridlines	Show lines (which can help with the visual comparison of different data sets, but can obscure of overused) for the horizontal, vertical and depth (if working with a 3-D format) axes.
Legend	Show or hide the legend (A colour-coded box showing the titles of the different data sets) and determine its position. Note that the legend can also be dragged with the mouse to any position in the chart that suits you, regardless of the presets defined here.
Data Labels	Show or hide labels (the actual values of the labels as entered into the datasheet) for the data sets. Data labels can be useful, especially when certain data sets might be difficult to distinguish from a distance, but can also obscure your chart. Which data labels you will be able to use will depend on your chart type, and you may be able to use more than one label (be careful of obfuscation), in which case you can specify with the "Separator" how they are set apart from each other. You can also add or remove the colour-code from the legend using the "Legend key."
Data Table	Show or hide a table underneath the chart which reveals the exact data values as entered into the datasheet, optionally with the colour-code from the legend. Generally, adding a data table makes you chart too small, so as a rule, go either with the chart, or with a table, but not both.

16.2.1.4   3-D Chart Rotation

You can also set the 3-D rotation of 3-D charts with the 3-D Rotation tool in the Format dialog which is also launched from the Chart Tools: Layout ribbon. This will allow you to display data points that may be obscured behind other data points, by changing the chart perspective.

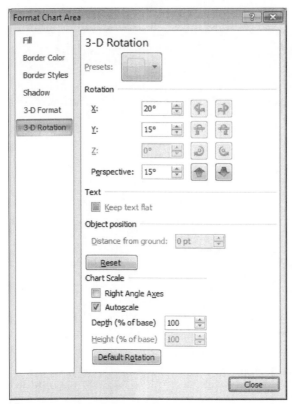

Figure 295   *3-D Rotation of a chart in the Format dialog*

16.2.1.5   Data labels

If you want to display data labels as percentages in column charts, and Word won't let you (users of Harvard Graphics will miss this), you can always do it manually. Simply add the data labels, then click on them once to select them, click on them again to get a square selection box around them, and then click a third time to edit the data label (this is not the same as a double-click and a single click, or a triple click). Then enter the percentage value (which you will have to calculate—this can be done easily in Excel). The picture below shows how one data label has been selected (note the square box). Clicking on it again will allow the user to edit the text. Note that the data labels to the right of this have already been changed.

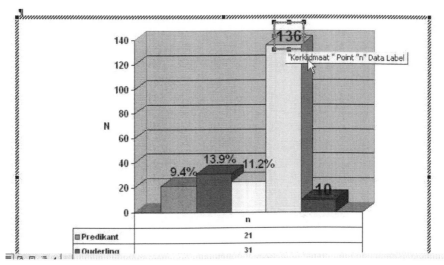

Figure 296   *Editing data labels in a chart*

Another common problem in a chart is when the data labels are obscured behind existing bars. The solution is as is shown in Figure 297: Click on any component of the chart that you can see (the right-most of the front data labels is quickest). Then just press the right arrow until the obscured data label is selected, and click and drag it with the mouse to where it can be seen (sometimes you click miss and then "lose" the label, but just persevere—you will get it in the end).

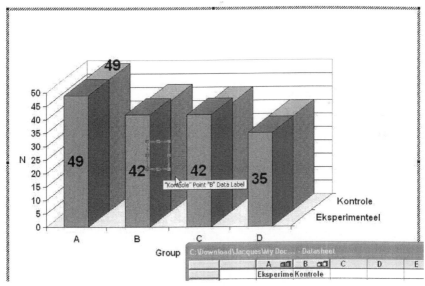

Figure 297   *Data label hidden behind a bar*

16.2.2 Charts—what to use when

One of the most common problems people report when working with charts is that they don't know what charts to use when. Generally, knowing what type of chart works best where is the domain of statisticians[110], but since few of us have that training, that means most of us are in trouble (or should I say you—I am a statistician). But rather than leaving you to wallow in your misery, I am going to try to help you with some general, and then some specific guidelines. Also, as a ray of hope, remember that getting charts right is not a mystical secret harboured by some (statistician) monks living in a cave, only divulged to initiates who have gone through years of suffering to attain their enlightenment. Far rather, getting charts right is a matter of experience. Try, and fail, and learn. And persevere. And eventually, your charts will get better and better, and you, even though not a statistician, can do great charts with the best of them.

16.2.2.1   General guidelines

Let me start by repeating what I said in the manual: Different chart types are best suited to different types of data, although certain types of data might be equally well displayed by several chart types. Generally, choose a chart type that does justice to your data, and allows the audience to see what you want them to see from the data.

16.2.2.1.1 Summarise information

Now for some general guidelines: Firstly, use charts and tables to summarise information. This was something that was drilled into me by my promoter when I was studying. This simple fact is, however, often ignored. Just as useful as charts and tables are for helping us understand complex data, so easily they can be used to obscure important information. Charts are also often misused to present information that can be quite easily understood without them. The general idea is that you only use charts or tables when explaining the data in text will take more space than what the chart or table takes. A common example of this abuse (and we have all done it—even myself), is to present the gender breakdown of a sample by a chart, when something like: "The sample consisted of 124 (52.3%) males and 113 females." This is all I need. I don't need to state that the females constituted 47.7% of the sample, because that is quite obvious (the respondents in the sample can only be male or female, can't they?). I also know that the total sample is 237 (124+113). So that short sentence of text (less than a line on this page), tells me all I need to know, and I don't need a chart to make sense of it. In Word, which is primarily a textual medium, you should stick to this rule almost all the time.

Elaborating just a bit on that, remember that you have a choice: Whether to summarise your information in a chart or a table. The choice can get tricky, because both tables and charts can get cluttered very quickly—and therefore difficult to understand—when you are working with huge amounts of data. Sometimes a chart will be the best way to summarise large amounts of data, but that will also depend on your chart type (see the specific guidelines below). However, two things need stressing: Almost never will you

---

[110] Even that is a bit of a lie. I never had training in how to use charts, although, in the course of representing statistics, you get forced to use charts, and that is how you learn.

use a chart *and* a table to summarise the same data. Thus the Data table function in the chart tool is one that I almost never use (probably 0.01% of my charts get data tables, and then only because I want to point something very specific out). Not only is the Data table unnecessary duplication, it also reduces the available size for your chart. In a way it's a means for you to get the worst of both worlds! The second is that charts can use only two or three dimensions, and can therefore display only information that occupies two or three dimensions.

16.2.2.1.2 Clarify data with the correct choice of chart

The second general guideline, choose a chart type that elucidates (sorry for the big words) the data. In the specific guidelines, I will delve a little deeper into this, but for now, note that some charts work for some types of data, but not for others (I know, I'm repeating myself here).

16.2.2.1.3 Reach your objective with the correct choice of chart

Thirdly, choose a chart type that achieves your objective. The chart must make it easy for people to see what you want them to see, without "cooking" the data. For example, compare the charts in Figure 298 and Figure 299. Both of these charts present exactly the same data: The sales of three regions of a fictional company over four quarters of a year are compared. In Figure 298, the focus is on the quarters, and it becomes very easy for us to see how the four quarters stack up (excuse the pun) against each other, and also how the three regions compared to each other over the various quarters. It is possible, but a lot harder, to see how each region did over the four quarters. That very thing which is hard to see in Figure 298, is a lot easier to see in Figure 299, where the focus is on the regions. There we see the performance of the various regions, with the four quarters repeated for each region. It is harder in Figure 299 (but not impossible) to assess the overall performance per quarter. This clearly illustrates how the choice of the chart type can either clarify or conceal what you want the people to see. Which of these two charts is the right one to use? It depends on your objective. If, for example, you wanted to examine the overall performance of the company over the year, Figure 298 with is focus on the quarters would be best. But if you wanted to compare the performance of the regions with each other, Figure 299 with is focus on the regions would be better.

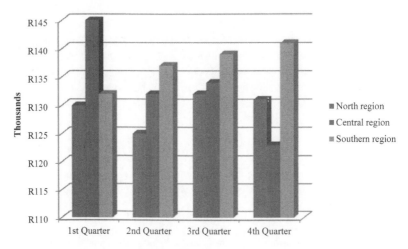

Figure 298   *Chart example: Focus on quarters*

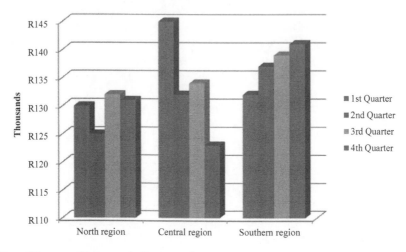

Figure 299   *Chart example: Focus on regions*

As a further example, consider Figure 300–Figure 303, which again present the same data: A fictitious breakdown of the age distribution of a sample. Firstly, note that all of the charts accurately present the information. However, while pie charts are normally the preferred chart format for this kind of information, the strange distribution (a large number of small categories) and the large number of categories in and of itself, makes the chart in Figure 300 a bit harder to interpret. I could add labels to it, as in Figure 301, but the sheer volume of information still makes even this chart a bit "noisy." In order to assist my audience, I turn it into a 3-D column chart, as in Figure 302. This chart is a lot easier to understand, and it is also easy to compare the various categories with each other. Note, also, that I have swung the data around, so that I do not have one series with many points (the default, as is shown in Figure 303), but many series with one point each. If you are a purist, then you will point out that is strictly speaking not correct, but it is a little trick, to make each bar a different colour, which again assists with the interpretation of the chart.

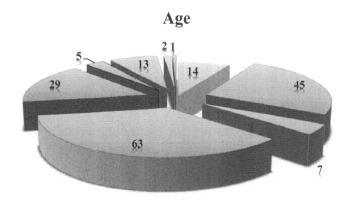

Figure 300　　　　　*Uneven distribution in a pie chart: Legend only*

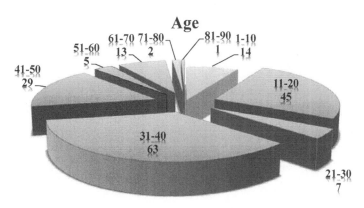

Figure 301　　　　　*Uneven distribution in a pie chart: Full labels*

Age

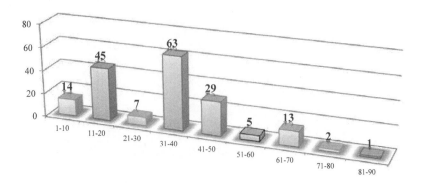

Figure 302   *Uneven distribution in a bar chart: non-uniform*

Age

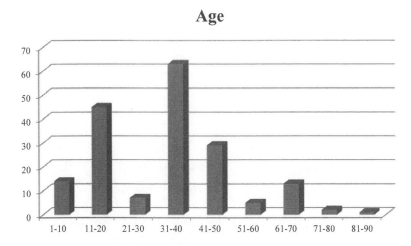

Figure 303   *Uneven distribution in a bar chart: uniform*

As a final example, consider Figure 305 and Figure 304, another two fictitious examples showing the average number of hours of television watched per day by students in their first to fourth study years. The data for these charts is shown in Table 22.

Table 22   *Data for charts in Figure 304 and Figure 305*

	<1 hours	1-2 hours	2-3 hours	3-4 hours	4-5 hours	>5 hours	N
1st years	1	20	14	14	14	4	**67**
2nd years	1	9	18	17	8	4	**57**
3rd years	0	6	11	7	6	1	**31**
4th years	4	25	10	0	1	2	**42**

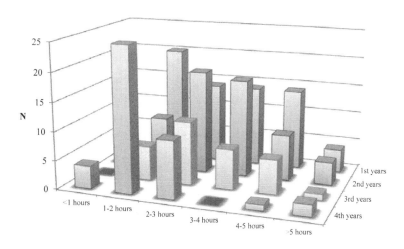

Figure 304   *Bar chart with uneven sample sizes: Actual values*

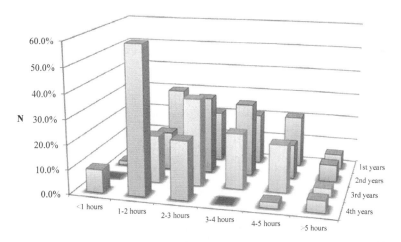

Figure 305   *Bar chart with uneven sample sizes: Percentages*

Figure 304 remains useful, because it provides us with the actual values recorded in the study, but note that because this study contained different sample sizes (as shown in the final column of Table 22), it becomes difficult to compare one group with another in Figure 304. That is a lot easier to do in Figure 305, as all the values have been converted to their within-group percentages. Now group comparisons can be made. Just to highlight one point, compare the various groups in the 4–5 hours category. While in Figure 304 it can be seen that, looking at *actual quantities*, more 1st years fell in this group than 2nd and 3rd years, and the group also contained slightly more 2nd years than 3rd years, who were again more than the 4th year students. But looking at Figure 305, we see that the order in terms of *proportions* is 1st years still most (20.9%, to be exact), 3rd years only slightly less (19.4%), 2nd years much less (14.0%), and 4th years least. Both of these charts are correct, but again, it comes down to the question of objective. Is the main aim to compare the groups (rather use percentages), or to see the distribution of the sample quantities as a whole (rather use the actual values)?

16.2.2.2   Specific guidelines

The most common question about charts is "Which chart should I use where?" Actually, that is a very difficult question to answer, simply because of the general guidelines I have given above. What is your purpose? What does the data look like? All of these questions influence that answer, and so the simple answer to the question "Which chart should I use where?" is always an insufficient answer. But having said that, let's give the simple answer anyway (expanded, by the way, from the Microsoft help files).

16.2.2.2.1 Chart terminology

Let's first get some terminology sorted out. Charts are built on top of data (i.e., they reflect data—numbers) graphically. Charts, then, turn numbers into pictures. To do that, they numbers need to be ordered in some way. That layout is always a tabular layout. In a chart data table (as in any table), we have rows and columns. The rows in a data table normally represent the **categories** in our data (e.g., gender categories, time frames, etc.). The columns in a data table normally represent the **series** in our data. While categories are *normally* independent (but not necessarily unrelated), series are *normally* dependent. To make it clearer, categories are normally mutually exclusive (I cannot belong to the male and female categories simultaneously; My data cannot simultaneously fall into two successive date ranges). Series values, however, occur in all categories (e.g., all males and all females can have height and weight measurements, and the height and weight measurements then each form a series). But these distinctions are not always clear-cut (see the emphasis I put on the word "normally"). This is why you can switch rows and columns in 3-D column charts. As an example, if my categories are sales regions, and my series are quarters of the year, there is no reason why I cannot switch them. While it is so that each sales regions will have sales in each quarter, and the regions are mutually exclusive, the quarters are also mutually exclusive, and each quarter will also have (should!) sales figures for each region. Thus, we have rows (categories) and columns (series). In a table, we know that cells are the intersections of rows and columns. In a data table, these cells are known as **data points**. Each data point will form one element of my chart.

16.2.2.2.2 Column charts

As the name suggests, this chart works well for data that present well in a table (i.e., are neatly organised into rows and columns). They are great for comparison of similar across a range of categories—those categories could be time frames (such as months or quarters or years, etc.), or groups (e.g., male/female). 3-D column charts allow comparison across two groups (e.g., male/female as one category, and age groups as another). These will then form the horizontal and depth axes, and the scale of the values will best form the vertical axis. *3-D column charts* should not be confused with *column charts in 3-D*. In the former, the layout itself is three dimensional (all three axes of the chart are used), and the columns are then, of necessity, three dimensional as well. In the latter, the layout itself is two dimensional (only two axes are used), although the columns are shown as three dimensional objects. Note also that cylinder, pyramid and cone charts are simply stylistic variations on column charts (and are, of necessity, in 3-D), but personally I prefer the simple column charts.

Column charts have some varieties:

16.2.2.2.2.1   Clustered column charts

Clustered column charts help us compare values across independent (but not necessarily unrelated) categories. Thus each category forms one bar in the cluster, and the cluster allow us to compare bars, and we can also compare clusters if there are more than one. The categories used in clustered column charts can be ranges of values, scales, or named groups. If a clustered column chart only has one series, then each cluster also consists of only one bar. Of course, if a chart consists of more than one series, then the choice becomes whether to show it as a multi-cluster 2-D column chart, or a 3-D column chart. Figure 306 shows four variations of clustered column charts. All of the examples use the default sample data provided by Microsoft when you insert a chart. As such, they all display the same data, just in different ways (with the exception that in the single-series clustered column chart, the second and third series of data have been deleted—but the remaining first series is the same as in the other charts).

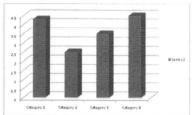

Single-series clustered column chart in 3-D

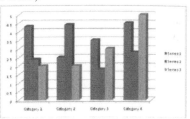

Multi-series clustered column chart in 3-D

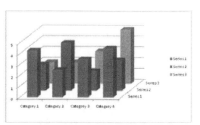

3-D column chart

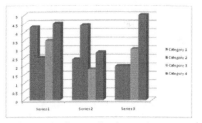

Multi-series clustered column chart in 3-D with categories and series switched

Figure 306   **Clustered column chart examples**

16.2.2.2.2.2   Stacked column charts

Stacked column charts show how individual parts make up a whole. Thus the contribution of each data point to the composition of the whole is compared with the contribution of each other data point. Stacked column charts cannot be 3-D (i.e., they can only use two axes), although the columns can be displayed as three dimensional columns (i.e., they can be displayed in 3-D). A modification to stacked column charts, which works well when you have many series that have largely different values, is a 100% stacked column charts, where the whole is always viewed as 100% (regardless of the actual data count), and the contribution of each data point is expressed as its relative proportion of the whole. These allow better comparison between disparately sized groups (see, for example, the comparison between Figure 304 and Figure 305).

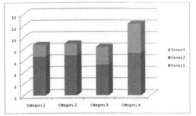 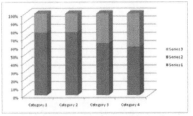

Stacked column chart in 3-D   *100% Stacked column chart in 3-D*

Figure 307   *Stacked column chart examples*

16.2.2.2.3 Bar charts

Bar charts are very similar to clustered column charts, even to having the conical, pyramidal and cylindrical variations. However, there are two main differences: Bar charts can be displayed in 3-D (i.e., the bars are displayed as three dimensional objects), but cannot be 3-D charts (i.e., they cannot use all three axes). Furthermore, bar charts have the scale of the values as the horizontal axis, and the categories as the vertical axis. This works best when the category labels are very long, or when the data values represent time scales. As with column charts, bar charts can be clustered (cf. 16.2.2.2.2.1) or stacked (cf. 16.2.2.2.2.2), and they can be stacked as either normal stacked bars showing the values, or as 100% stacked bars, showing percentages.

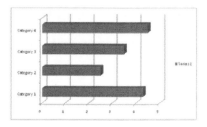

Single-series clustered bar chart in 3-D

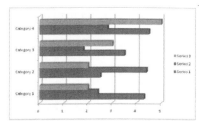

Multi-series clustered bar chart in 3-D

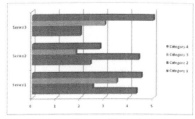

Multi-series clustered bar chart in 3-D
with categories and series switched

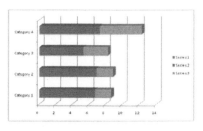

Stacked bar chart in 3-D

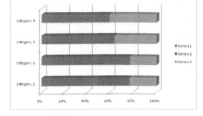

100% Stacked bar chart in 3-D

Figure 308   **Bar chart examples**

16.2.2.2.4 Pie charts

Pie charts work well when you have only one series (i.e., one column and many rows in your data table). This means that the single series charts shown in Figure 306 and Figure 308 can be shown very well as pie charts (but see my comments relating to Figure 300–Figure 303 on p. 378 about having many values in your data series close to, or on, zero). Note also that pie charts cannot display negative values (single series column charts or bar charts can). Pie charts can also get crowded very quickly if your data series has many values (i.e., many rows in your data table)—Microsoft recommends a maximum of seven categories. Finally, note that pie charts only make sense when the various categories are related (even though they may be independent). Thus *Male* and *Female* are related (but independent) categories of gender. Or quarters are related (but independent) categories of a year.

Another advantage in the use of pie charts is their customisability. For example, you have the ability to show both values and/or percentages (since each pie slice makes up part of a whole pie). You can also explode a pie chart to make the individual slices more distinguishable[111], and you can pull any particular slice out of a pie chart[112] to make it stand out from the rest. In a *pie-of-pie* or *bar-of-pie* chart you can take certain values and build a second pie or bar from them. Their combined value is then represented as one slice of the original pie. This can help overcome the problem of values close to or equal to zero.

One final touch to your pie charts: Rotate them so that the smaller slices are in front, and easier to make out (and, if necessary and if possible, order your data so that all the smaller slices either all sit together or are interspersed evenly between the larger slices). An example of this is demonstrated in the last row of Figure 309[113].

Pie chart in 3-D

Exploded pie chart in 3-D

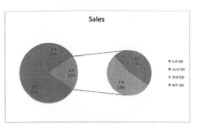

Pie-of-pie chart

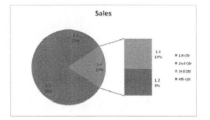

Bar-of-pie chart

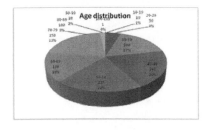

Small slices hard to make out in pie chart

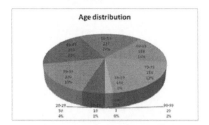

Pie chart rotated to make small slices easier to make out

Figure 309   *Pie chart examples*

---

[111] You can start with a normal pie and click and drag to explode it, or you can choose the exploded format to begin with.

[112] Microsoft's help files say you cannot do this with an exploded pie chart, but you actually can.

[113] Granted, the variable I used—age distribution—would make more sense in a column chart than a pie chart, but the principle of rotation for better visibility is demonstrated.

16.2.2.2.5 Doughnut charts

Doughnut charts are an attempt to do what pie charts cannot do: Show data from more than one series (note that this is already what column and bar charts do, and these charts may be better choices). Doughnut charts show each series as a ring in a set of concentric rings. If a doughnut chart is based on only one series, then it essentially shows the same information as a pie chart, just (in my opinion) in a less appealing format. Doughnut charts are difficult to read (which may also explain why you see so few of them). Doughnut charts cannot be displayed in 3-D, although they can be exploded (which, if you have many categories, just makes things even more confusing).

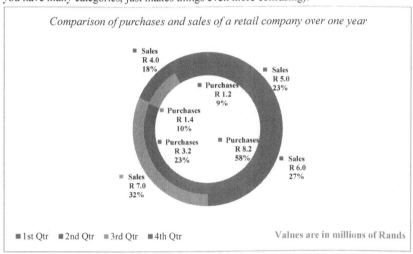

Figure 310   *Doughnut chart example[114]*

16.2.2.2.6 Scatter (XY) charts

The idea behind scatter charts (or scatter plots) is to plot the relationship between two variables. In essence, this means that there are no categories per se in your data—there may be many rows in the data table, and each row does not really represent a category, but simply a *case* or *record*. This also means that, unlike categories, values may be repeated in the first column. The first series of your data table (the first column) contains the values which are plotted on the horizontal axis (these are the X-values). There must be one or more additional columns whose values (the Y-values) are then plotted on the vertical axis against the X-values. As an example (assuming a simple scatter plot with only two columns), this means that for each value in Column A (the X-value), the value in Column B is plotted vertically in line with the X-value on the horizontal axis, and horizontally in line with the Y-value on the vertical axis. Since there may be many repetitions of any given X-value, with the same or different Y-values, this means that for each X-value, a number of Y-values will be plotted on the

---

[114] In all the examples I have done so far, I have just used the default values provided by Microsoft when you insert the chart. In Figure 310 I had to edit the chart substantially to allow for a sensible comparison.

vertical line above it. In this way, the relationship between the variables represented in the X- and Y-columns is examined (note that when there are more than one series, the relationships between the various Y-values is *not* examined, only the relationships between the X-values and each of the Y-values. This means that the X-values serve as reference variables.

Scatter plots are commonly used in physics, statistics, engineering, and a number of other fields. Note that the use of a scatter plot implies a relationship (or at least the possibility of a relationship) between the variables represented in the X- and Y-columns. The nice thing about scatter plots is that they can potentially represent huge data sets, and the actual limit is not how many data points there are, but the scales of the X- and Y-variables (and even then, if a little detail can be sacrificed, quite large scales can be accommodated). In fact, the more data there is, the better scatter plots work (unlike all the chart types discussed prior to this).

The basic idea behind the scatter plot is, as described above, to connect the X- and Y-values with a marker (e.g., a dot) on the chart. While the clusters formed by these markers often are sufficient, scatter plots also allow lines to be drawn from one marker to the next to aid with interpretation, and these lines can be smooth (they curve with the distribution of the markers) or straight (running always in the shortest distance between two successive markers), and the lines can even be shown without the markers.

Another useful tool applicable to scatter plots is the ability to add trend lines. A variety of trend lines exist, and I won't be delving into the mathematical equations underlying the various trend lines, but these are basically further analysis tools which provide us with a means of formulating generalisations based on the results of our scatter plot.

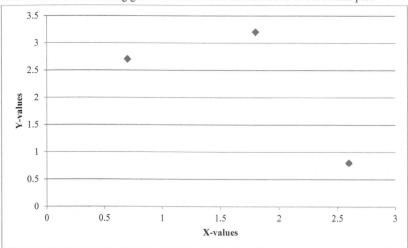

Figure 311   *Scatter plot example*

16.2.2.2.7 Line charts

While the result of a line chart looks very similar to a scatter plot, there are some very important differences. Firstly, in a scatter plot the horizontal axis data are actual values. In a line chart, they are categories. Secondly, in a scatter plot, the X-values need not be evenly spaced—Office will figure out evenly spaced scale points based on the full range of values. With a line chart, the categories must represent evenly spaced values (e.g., months, quarters, etc.) or unique groupings, and it is generally assumed (but not vital) that there is some form of progression (e.g., in time) across those categories—If there is no progression, a bar or column chart might be a better choice. Finally, because scatter plots allow multiple repetitions of the horizontal axis values, while line charts do not, line charts are not suited to as large data tables as scatter plots (Microsoft recommends rather using a scatter plot if you have more than ten categories). Having said that, line charts are great at analysing trends, and even more so at analysing multiple trends (more than one column with data plotted on the vertical axis). Imagine a line chart plotting the oil price, the petrol price, the diesel price, and the paraffin price, over the months of this year. Now that would be interesting!

As with scatter plots, line charts can be shown with or without markers (but obviously not markers only without lines). Also, remember that the markers can get in the way when there are many data values. Furthermore, line charts can present the data in a number of ways not open to scatter plots (see the examples in Figure 312, where all the charts use the same underlying data table). Firstly, line charts can be presented as either two dimensional or three dimensional charts, where the series are plotted along the depth axis in the latter, and in both the scale of the actual data values is plotted on the vertical axis, and the categories on the horizontal axis. Although the categories and series can be switched in 3-D line charts, this makes no sense because of the progression implicit in the categories.

Note that 3-D line charts work best when the different series are measured at the very least by the same measurement unit (e.g., Rands, degrees Celsius, etc.), even if not on the same scale—although using different scales can make things confusing (one series could measure Rands, and another thousands of Rands). The chart works by comparing the different values of the series with each other.

A second feature of line charts not open to scatter plots is that line charts can also be presented as stacked line charts and 100% stacked line charts, although I would almost always prefer stacked bar or column charts instead, as stacked line charts are simply confusing (in other words, I don't consider this a major advantage over scatter plots). If you look at the charts in Figure 312, you will see that while a normal line charts shows the actual values, a stacked line chart works additively. In other words, the value for Series 1 in Category 1 was 4.3. The value for Series 2 in Category 1 was 2.4, which, added to 4.3, gives you 6.7 (the plotted value for Series 2 in Category 1). The value for Series 3 in Category 1 was 2, which, added to the 4.3 for Series 1 and the 2.4 for Series 2, gives you 8.7 (the plotted value for Series 3 in Category 1). And so for each category. This means that in a normal line chart, the series with the highest values will be the highest in the chart, but in a stacked line chart, the last series will be the highest, even if it has the smallest values! I told you stacked line charts were confusing. Using stacked column or bar charts eliminates that confusion. In 100% stacked line charts, the confusion just becomes greater, because now the values for each series with a specific category are converted to percentage values of that category's total (8.7 for Category 1 in this example), and then plotted. The last series will then always lie dead on 100%, as it adds the last bits needed to reach the cumulative total. The last point about stacked line charts is that 3-D line charts cannot be stacked.

And one final tip in helping you choose between line charts and scatter plots: Line charts work great for categorical data (e.g., gender, post levels in an organisation—values that can, for example, not be multiplied or divided[115]), which scatter plots work better for continuous data (e.g., physical measurements, etc.).

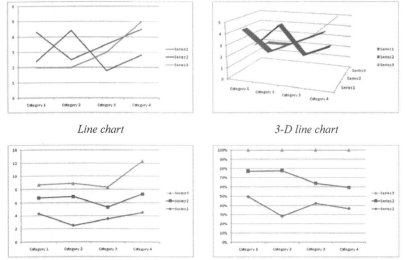

| *Line chart* | *3-D line chart* |

| *Stacked line chart with markers* | *100% Stacked line chart with markers* |

Figure 312　　　*Line chart examples*

16.2.2.2.8 Area charts

Area charts are similar in concept to line charts, although they are better suited to placing the focus on changes over time (i.e., when the progression assumed for line chart data is a time progression), and also allow that progression to be seen as a function of the total value. Area charts are also useful for showing how the whole is a sum of its parts, or for focusing on the relationship each part has to the whole.

As with line charts, area charts are not limited to a single series of data, and as many series can be included as necessary. Two-dimensional area charts can be displayed in 2-D or in 3-D (but then still always only use two axes). When an area chart has three-dimensional data (i.e., more than one series), it can be displayed using two axes (and then in 2-D or 3-D form), where all the series are displayed on the same axis. This often obscures huge amounts of data in a chart, and a line chart may be preferred. However, are charts with more than one series can also be displayed as 3-D area charts (which, can, of course, not be displayed in 2-D), and then the depth axis is used to display the various series.

---

[115] We all know the joke about the average family having 2.3 children!

Two-dimensional area charts can also be displayed in one of three formats: Firstly, they can show the actual values (useful for seeing the actual progression over time for various series)[116]. One problem with this format is that values in one series are often blocked out by the values of other series. And changing the order of the series does not always resolve the problem –it may just result in different values from a different series being hidden. Displaying the chart as a 3-D area chart and rotating it can give the reader a view where all values in every series are visible, but often from a perspective that makes interpretation difficult.

Area charts can also be displayed as stacked charts (in 2-D or 3-D), showing the contributions of the various series to the whole. These have the advantage of not hiding away any values, but can make interpretation of the exact scale of a specific series' values problematic.

Finally, area charts can also be shown as 100% stacked charts (again, in 2-D or 3-D), which is best suited to showing the exact contribution of each series to the whole, but does not allow at all for the exact interpretation of the scale of series values.

These aspects of area charts are all displayed in Figure 313, all of which use the same default data provided by Microsoft, and also the default layout when the chart is entered, with the exception that the 3-D area chart has been rotated to show all the values for both series (which cannot be seen in the area in 2-D to its left), but even in the 3-D area chart, while it is easy to see the progression in each series over time, and also to compare that progression for the two series, it is also evident how hard it is to make sense of the actual value of the series being displayed.

---

[116] This is then also the only format available when a 3-D area chart is used.

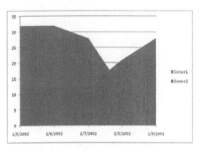

Area chart in 2-D

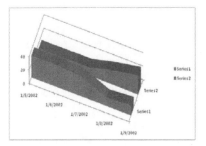

3-D Area chart with rotation

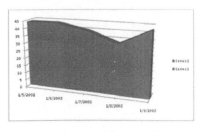

Stacked area chart in 3-D

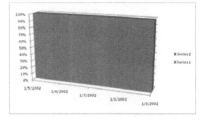

100% Stacked area chart in 3-D

Figure 313   *Area chart examples*

16.2.2.2.9 Surface charts

Surface charts are used to display two or more series of data. The aim with a surface chart is not just to compare the series of data with each other, but to determine what the optimal relationships between the various series are. As such, the layout of the data is very similar to that of a 3-D column chart, but the analysis of the chart data is somewhat different. Figure 314 shows exactly the same data as the 3-D column chart in Figure 306. As you can see, it is more difficult to identify the individual combinations of categories and series in a surface chart (each combination being an individual bar in the 3-D column chart Figure 306), but it is easier to compare to what extent there is agreement amongst those combinations at different levels, as the ranges of the scores are indicated by the colours, as reported in the legend. Note that surface charts may require some rotation to see the full surface, and the chart will not make much sense from an interpretive point of view if the full surface cannot be seen (the default surface chart in Figure 314, for example, does not show the full surface). If no amount of rotation will get the job done, consider using (in order of preference) a wire-frame surface chart (Figure 315), a contour chart or a wire-frame contour chart (the former is shown in Figure 316), or a different chart type completely. Note that, as with column charts, a distinction should be made between the number of dimensions contained in the data, and the number of dimensions used to display the data. Surface charts all use three data dimensions (Categories, Series, and Values), but can be displayed in either 3-D (3-D Surface and 3-D wire-frame surface) or 2-D (contour or wire-frame contour). So, for example, the 3-D surface chart in Figure 314 and the contour chart in Figure 316 use the same data set, but display the data slightly differently.

392

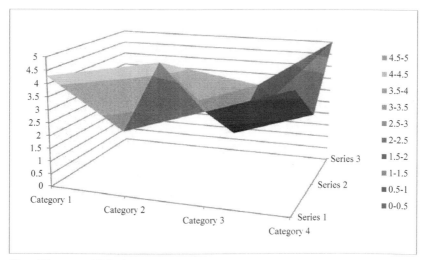

Figure 314   *3-D Surface chart example*

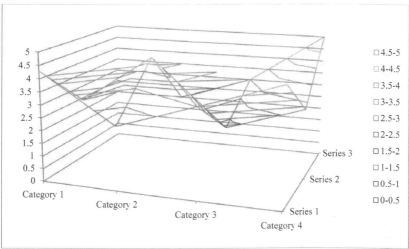

Figure 315   *Wire-frame 3-D surface chart example*

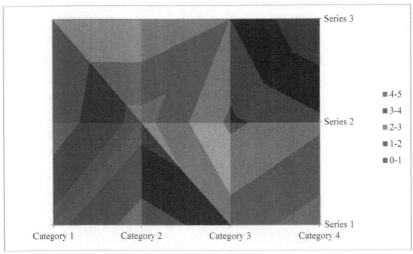

Figure 316   *Contour chart example*

16.2.2.2.10 Radar charts

Think of a radar chart as a 3-D pie chart (note, not a pie chart in 3-D). Whereas a pie chart can only display one series of data (whether in 2-D or 3-D), radar charts can present any number of series. However, the price to pay is that the beautiful symmetry of a pie chart is lost, although there are instances when this is actually desirable. Pie charts of necessity work in percentages—every value in the data series is expressed as a part (i.e., percentage) of a whole. Radar charts, by contrast, use real values, and couldn't actually be bothered with percentages (of course, if you want percentages in your radar chart, work them out beforehand). What's even nicer about radar charts is that the various categories need not even represent classes of the same thing, although they do need to have more or less the same scale (for example, you could list people's scores on measures of depression, self-actualisation, and a number of other personality measures). As such, radar charts have two main applications: As a useful means of comparing a (relatively large) number of aspects of a certain thing which can be represented on at least similar scales, and to compare the relative proportions (on the same set of scales) of a number of different groups (e.g., which business unit has the lowest expenses, highest sales, lowest losses, and highest profits). Note that radar charts can only stand if for pie charts (allowing you to see the relative contribution of each component to the whole) when every axis of the radar chart has exactly the same scale. And even then, you need your thinking cap on. The relative proportion represented by each axis is not indicated by the area, but only by the actual measurement on the axis (i.e., where the "web" crosses the axis).

Radar charts (as is shown in Figure 317) can be displayed as standard radar charts, radar charts with markers (the same as standard, expect each intersection with an axis is also indicated by a marker, which highlights the point made above), or as filled radar charts (which are prettier, but perhaps more misleading in terms of the contribution to the whole, as discussed above). Filled radar charts can, of course, obscure data, unless the fill colours of the upper series are set to be partially transparent.

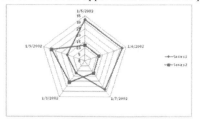 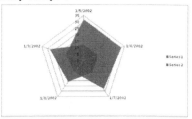

Radar chart with markers

Filled radar chart with semi-transparent series

Figure 317 **Radar chart examples**

16.2.2.2.11 Stock charts

As the name suggests, stock charts were developed to illustrate how stock prices fluctuated over time. Having said that, they can be used in other areas as well, such as giving expression to certain types of scientific data (e.g., fluctuations in temperature, weight, etc.), and also statistical information (e.g., to represent box-and-whisker plots). As with Bubble charts below, the organisation of the data in the data sheet for stock charts is very precise. For a standard stock chart (known as a High-Low-Close chart—see Figure 318), the first column contains the categories. These will be plotted on the x-axis. The second column contains the maximum values for each category. The third column contains the minimum values for each category. And the fourth column contains the middle marker—but note that the value it indicates, while being between the maximum and minimum, need not be in the middle (it could even be as high as the maximum, or as low as the minimum). Rather, it indicates some or other point on the line that has substantive meaning (for example, in a real stock market example, this column is used to indicate the closing values).

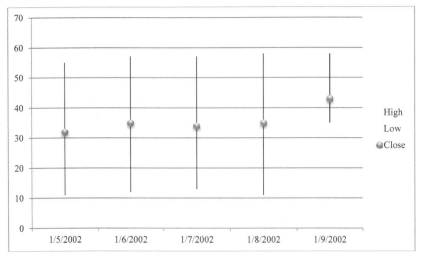

Figure 318   *High-Low-Close Stock chart example*

Some variations on the standard stock chart exist. In an Open-High-Low-Close chart (Figure 319), another data column is added *before* the maximum column, and this column represents a second marker of substantive significance, which may again lie anywhere between the minimum and maximum values. The distance between this first marker and the second marker is now indicated by a box.

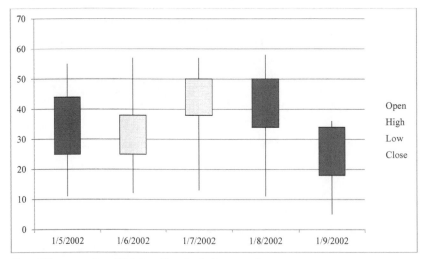

Figure 319   *Open-High-Low-Close Stock chart example*

In a Volume-High-Low-Close stock chart (Figure 320), the first data column from the previous example (before the maximum column) is replaced by another measurement which does not lie on the line between minimum and maximum, but indicates a different aspect of each category. For example, in the case of real stock trading, it is used, as suggested by the name, to indicate the volume of sales. In the scientific example, it might indicate rainfall together with the minimum, maximum, and average or midday temperature). Note that since the substantive measure (volume) is not measured on the same scale as the minimum, maximum, and marker values, two value axes (y-axes or vertical axes) are used: One on the left, and one on the right. Typically, the left axis will indicate the substantive scale (volume) and the right axis the measurement scale for the minimum, maximum, and marker.

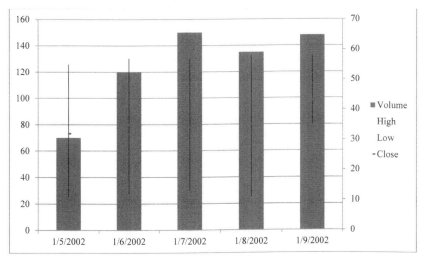

Figure 320   Volume-High-Low-Close Stock chart example

By now you should guess that the Volume-Open-High-Low-Close Stock chart (Figure 321) differs from the standard High-Low-Close Stock chart in that it has two data columns *before* the maximum column, the first indicating the alternative measurement (volume), and the second indicating the starting value of substantive interest (open).

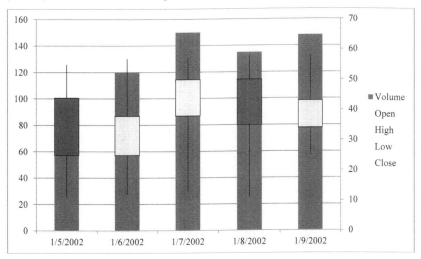

Figure 321   Volume-Open-High-Low-Close Stock chart example

16.2.2.2.12 Bubble charts

Bubble charts are a take on the problem of displaying different types of data related to the same thing that are measured on entirely different scales. Remember that for radar charts, the data for each axis has to be measured on at least relatively comparable scales. But what if you wanted to show the relationship between the weight of something, its temperature, and its volume (to take an example from physics)? For Bubble charts, the data layout is important. The first column represents the x-values (the horizontal axis). The second column represents the y-values (the vertical axis). And the third column represents the bubble size. While only these data points are allowed (note that they are not, per se, series), any number of categories are allowed, and each category will be a bubble. Of course, since there is no category axis (the first axis is used for x-values), the bubbles have to be labelled or colour coded afterwards. Bubble charts can be displayed as plain bubble charts, or bubble charts with a 3-D effect (Figure 322).

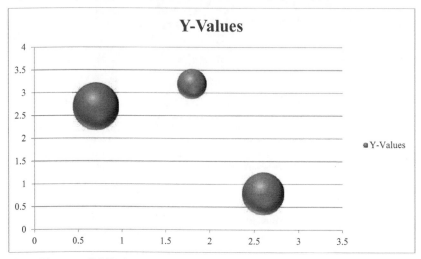

Figure 322   *Bubble chart example*

Chapter 17
Thesis ≈
$\sqrt[3]{\textbf{Knowledge}} \times \log_{10}\{\textbf{Ability}\} \times \lim_{n\to\infty}(\textbf{Perseverance})^2$:
Equations and Mathematics

In many disciplines, you will need to adorn your dissertation with various equations and other mathematical formulae. Here's how.

17.1 Equations

The equation editor of Word should be sufficient for the purposes of all but the most advanced mathematicians, statisticians and physicists. There are proprietary equation software programmes available, but these will not be dealt with here.

17.1.1 Inserting equations

In brief, equations are inserted from the Equation tool on the far end of the Insert ribbon (Instruction set 67) or with the new keyboard shortcut Alt + =. This opens a gallery of built-in (and later custom) equations, and at the bottom, the Insert New Equation option.

Instruction set 67   Adding an equation

Keyboard shortcut	Alt + =
Keyboard	Alt | N | E
Left click	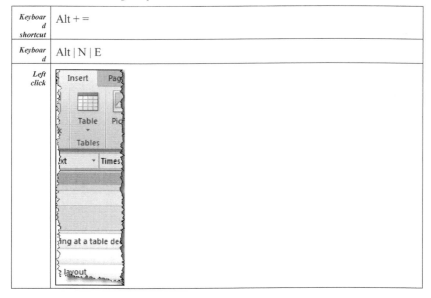

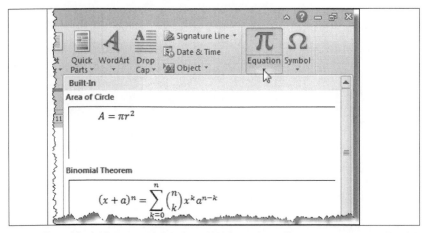

Regardless of whether an existing equation from the gallery, or a new equation is inserted, Word will add an equation object, and will display the Equation Tools ribbon (Figure 323).

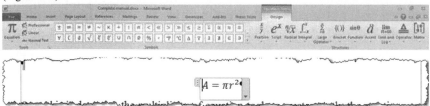

Figure 323   *Equation object with Equation Tools ribbon*

The equation tools on this ribbon are, if you know the equation you want to add, quite self-explanatory. Thus only a brief summary is warranted here.

The Structures group is the most important, as this is what is used to build the various elements of the equation. Each of these elements contains tiny placeholders. Once the element has been inserted, you would click in the placeholder, and then type whatever needs to be entered there. Figure 324 shows how this is done for Einstein's famous formula.

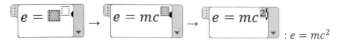

$: e = mc^2$

Figure 324   *Building an equation using the Script Structure*

17.1.1.1   Equation parts

As with normal mathematical calculations, you can, of course, insert structures into the placeholders of other structures (e.g., in the numerator placeholder of a fraction, you could add a bracket structure with a superscript).

The various Equation Tools structures (see also Figure 325) are:

     ≈   Fractions

     ≈   Scripts (sub- and superscripts)

     ≈   Radicals

≈ Integrals
≈ Large Operators (Summation, Products and Co-products, Unions and Intersections, and Other
≈ Brackets (Brackets with separators, Single brackets, and Cases and Stacks)
≈ Trigonometric functions (Trigonometric functions, Inverse functions, Hyperbolic and Inverse Hyperbolic functions)
≈ Accents (Accents, Boxed formulas, and Overbars and Underbars)
≈ Limits and Logs
≈ Operators (Basic operators and Operator structures)
≈ Matrices (Empty matrices, Dots, Identity matrixes, Matrices with brackets, and Sparse matrixes)

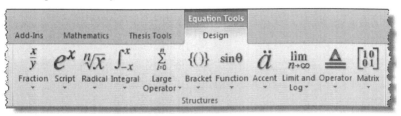

Figure 325   *Equation tools: Structures*

Note also that each of these groups has a further subset of built-in elements, under the title "Common <group name>"—the exception being matrices, where the populated elements are the identity matrices.

17.1.1.2   *Adding symbols to equations*

Further to the structure are a large number of symbols, which are accessed from the Symbols group of the ribbon (Figure 326).

Figure 326   *Equation tools: Symbols*

Microsoft has done a reasonably good job in hiding the fact that this is actually a very extensive gallery of symbols. As can be seen in Figure 327, the title bar of the gallery (which is only visible once the gallery has been expanded) contains a small drop-down, which allows one to choose symbols from these subgroups, the full set of which is displayed in Figure 328:

≈ Basic Math
≈ Greek Letters (Lower- and Uppercase)
≈ Letter-Like Symbols
≈ Operators (Common Binary operators, Common Relational operators, Basic N-ary operators, Advanced Binary operators, Advanced Relational operators)
≈ Arrows

- ≈   Negated Relations
- ≈   Scripts (Scripts, Frakturs, Double-Struck)
- ≈   Geometry

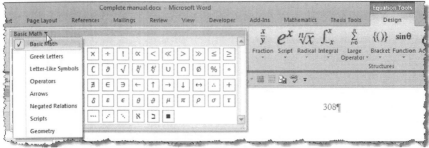

Figure 327   *Equation tools: Symbols subgroups*

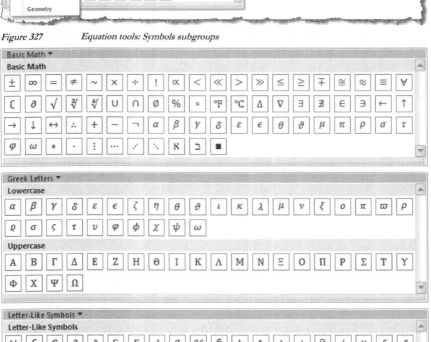

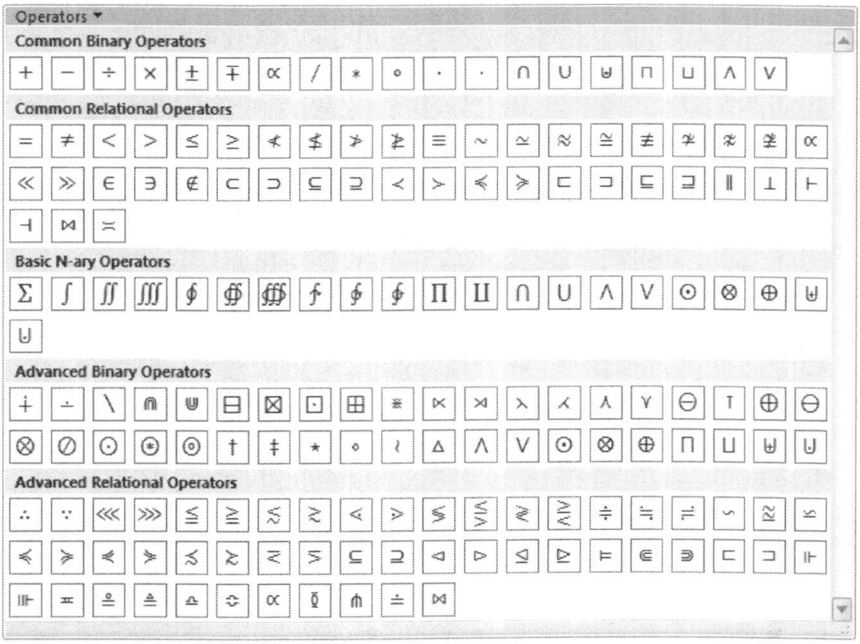

Operators ▼

Common Binary Operators

Common Relational Operators

Basic N-ary Operators

Advanced Binary Operators

Advanced Relational Operators

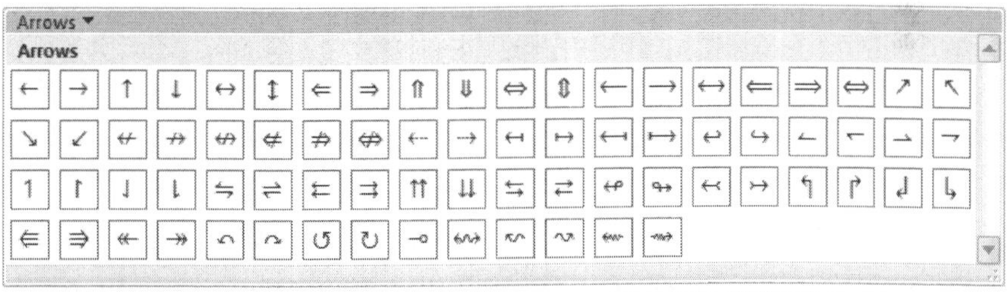

Arrows ▼

Arrows

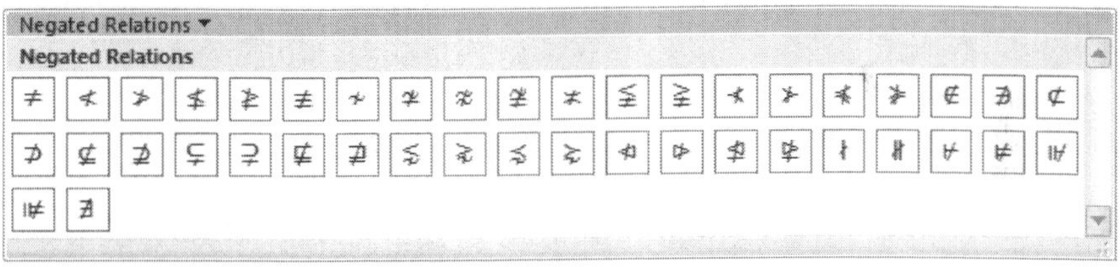

Negated Relations ▼

Negated Relations

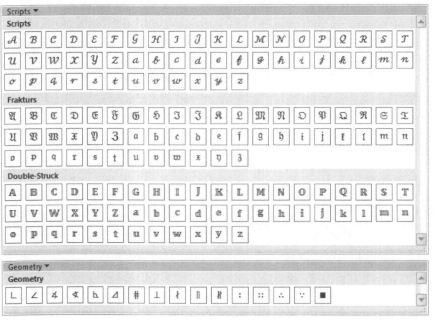

Figure 328   *Full set of Symbols available to Equation Editor*

Note that there may be *even* more symbols that you might want to access, and this will be discussed in the section on Math AutoCorrect below. Once the equation you want has been created, simply move to anywhere outside of the equation border, and Word will remove the ribbon.

17.1.2   Reusing equations

Apart from the fact that equation objects can be copied and pasted, you can also store equations in the document building blocks (Instruction set 68), which will allow you to reuse those equations in different documents with ease. This will open the Create New Building Block dialog (Figure 329), where you can choose the template to which the equation should be saved (accepting the defaults is fine). This will add it to the equations gallery, from where it can be inserted in the future.

Instruction set 68   Saving an equation to the gallery

Keyboard	Alt | JE | E | S

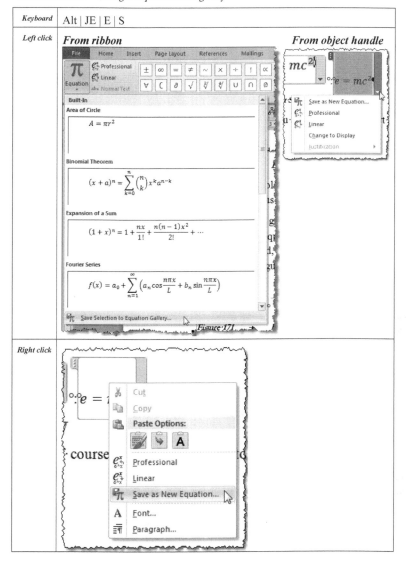

Figure 171

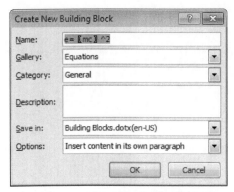

Figure 329   *Create New Building Block dialog*

17.1.3   Equation position

When equations are added, they are added in Display mode, which is a special mode akin to a floating inline object (I know, that doesn't make much sense). What essentially happens, is that the paragraph mark is included in the equation object (you can just see it peeking out in Figure 323 and Figure 324). When an equation is in the display mode, no other text can be included in the same paragraph—if you do add any text, Word automatically changes the equation object to inline mode.

If you want to incorporate the equation into a text paragraph like this: $e = mc^2$, then all you need do is make it an inline equation (see section 18.4.1, p. 445 for a full discussion of inline objects). Figure 330 shows the options available when clicking on the field handle (the first three are also available from a right click). The first thing to notice is that, depending on the existing mode of the equation, the option will be there to switch it to the alternate mode. Secondly, when the equation is in display mode, its position within the paragraph can be determined under the Justification submenu.

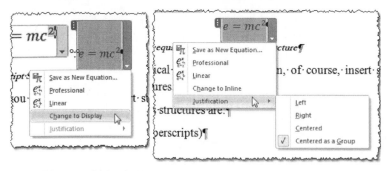

Figure 330   *Setting the display mode of an equation*

17.1.4   Equation alignment

There are several aspects of equation alignment, and I will touch on the two most common.

If you have an equation that extends over multiple lines, you can use display mode and align each line of the equation on a fixed point (e.g., the equals sign).

For a simple example, imagine the following problem: We might know that $\frac{1}{3} \times 3 = 3$, but $0.\dot{3} \times 3 = 0.99\dot{9}$ and is it not so that $1 \neq 0.99\dot{9}$? Or can we construct a proof that shows that $1 = 0.99\dot{9}$?

$$x = 0.\dot{9}$$
$$10x = 10(0.\dot{9})$$
$$10x = 9.\dot{9}$$
$$10x - x = 9.\dot{9} - 0.\dot{9}$$
$$9x = 9$$
$$\frac{9x}{9} = \frac{9}{9}$$
$$x = 1$$

Figure 331   Equation showing alignment

Figure 331 shows such a proof (needlessly elaborated). Note how the various lines of the proof, which are not all equally long, are aligned on the equals signs. This is how it was done: The first task is to create a group from all the lines of the equation. This is done by insert soft carriage returns (Shift + Enter) at the end of each line, so that the whole equation is contained in one paragraph. The next step is to select the equals sign in each line of the formula, and then to right click on it and select Align at this Character from the context menu. Word will then insert an alignment point to the left of the equals sign. This, and the completed equation showing the alignment points, can be seen in Figure 332.

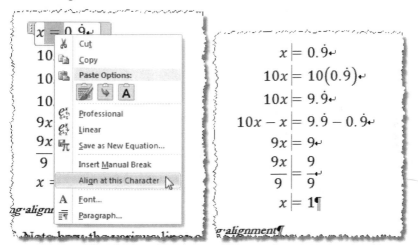

Figure 332   Aligning different lines of an equation

If you are creating a matrix equation, then right clicking on the equation will reveal the Matrix spacing... option, which will open the Matrix Alignment and Spacing dialog (Figure 333). Here you can set the alignment of the elements in the matrix, as well as the row height (distance between baselines) and column width (distance between column edges), as well as the space in between columns). Note that two of the alignment options are available directly from the right click menu.

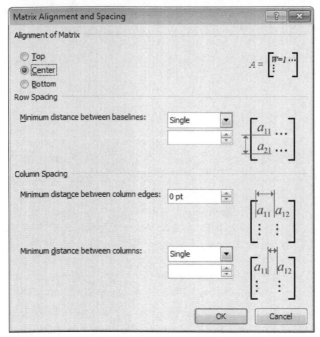

Figure 333   *Matrix Alignment and Spacing dialog*

17.1.5   Customising equations

As you work with the different kinds of equations, there are a host of changes that you might want to make. Many of these can be made by changing font (e.g., raising or lowering text) or paragraph (e.g., line spacing) settings (the Font... and Paragraph... options are always available when you right click on any part of an equation). However, the more specific type of equation modifications are not available on the ribbon, but apparently only by right-clicking on the relevant equation or equation part. Since there are so many, a summary of these options is presented in Figure 334 and Figure 335. Furthermore, a summary of the main options available for various equations and equation parts is presented in Table 23.

Fractions

Scripts & Trigonometric functions

Radicals

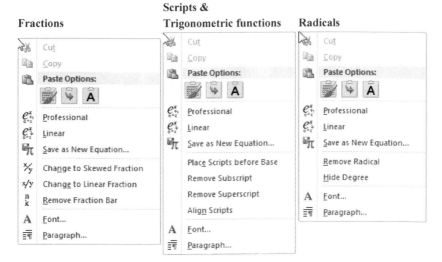

Integrals & Large operators

Brackets

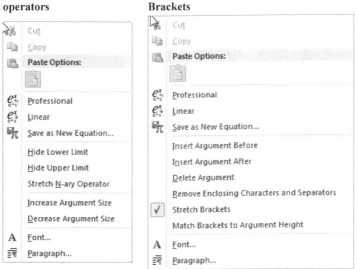

Figure 334   *Context menus for various types of equations (A)*

Overbars & Underbars

Boxed formulas

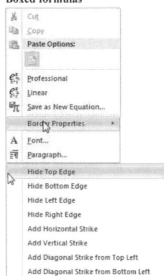

Matrices

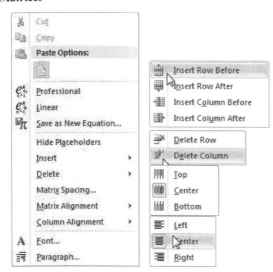

Figure 335   *Context menus for various types of equations (B)*

Table 23   Modifications to Equations

Equation type/part	Modification
Fractions	Change format between Skewed/Linear/Stacked
	Remove bar (for stacked only)
Scripts	Remove script
	Place before/after base
	Align
	Increase/decrease argument size
Trigonometric functions &	Remove script
Limits & Logs	Increase/decrease argument size
Radicals	Remove radical
	Hide degree
	Increase/decrease argument size
Integrals &	Hide Upper/lower limit
Large Operators	Stretch N-ary operator
	Increase/decrease argument size
Brackets	Remove enclosing characters and separators
	Delete argument
	Insert argument before/after
	Stretch brackets (toggle)
	Match brackets to argument height (toggle, only if Stretch is on)
Accents	Remove accent
Bars	Remove bar
	Place bar above/below base
Matrices	Delete Rows/Columns
	Insert Rows (Above/Below)
	Insert Columns /(Before/After)
	Matrix/Column alignment
	Matrix spacing
	Hide/Show placeholders

17.1.6   Equation options

There remains one more group of settings that can be set for equations. However, these settings are set globally—i.e., for the document as a whole, not for each individual equation. To access the equation options, use the dialog launcher from the Tools group of the Equation Tools ribbon (Instruction set 69). The dialog is shown in Figure 336. Most of the settings in this dialog are self-explanatory, and will thus not be discussed. Note, though, the three non-standard buttons. Defaults... allows you to make the settings apply, not only to the current document, but to all new documents based on the underlying template (templates were discussed in Chapter 5). Math AutoCorrect... opens the AutoCorrect dialog on the Math AutoCorrect tab and the Recognized Functions... button opens the Recognized Math Functions dialog, which is also normally opened from the Math AutoCorrect tab of the AutoCorrect dialog. These two groups of settings will be discussed in section 17.3 below.

Instruction set 69   Equation Options

Keyboard	Alt | JE | T
Left click	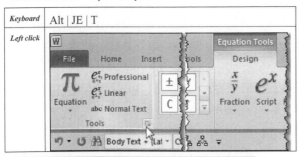

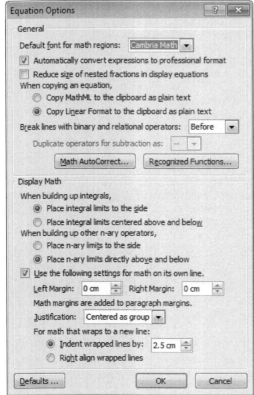

Figure 336   Equation Options dialog

17.1.7   Numbering and Captioning equations

Theses and dissertations in certain disciplines (mathematics, statistics, physics, chemistry, etc.) will of necessity contain a large number of equations, and as such the equations will have to be numbered, and then listed. Furthermore, the most commonly used convention is for these equation numbers to include the chapter number, and to appear on the right of the equation, typically aligned to the page margin.

It seems, from my research, that there are no easy ways to do this, so much so that even the Word team at Microsoft seem stumped in coming up with a really good solution.

One solution that has been touted (e.g., Michelstein, 2011; Wyatt, 2010) is to combine either a numbered list, or the SEQ field , with an invisible table—you basically add a borderless 1x3 table. However, if you were to read comments posted on the Word blog entry for Michelstein's explanation of this method (http://blogs.office.com/b/microsoft-word/archive/2006/10/20/equation-numbering.aspx), then you will see that users remain dissatisfied[117]. Another Microsoft employee—Dong Yu (2010)—has provided a macro approach that pretty much automates a variation of the above suggestion (see http://research.microsoft.com/en-us/people/dongyu/Office2007EqnNumber.txt). But this also seems unsatisfactory. The main drawback to these approaches is that they do not easily allow the generation of a list of equations—the ideal way to do this is not to use the raw SEQ field, but the Caption tool (discussed in section 8.4, from p. 161)[118].

Here's my suggested method. I admit that it still requires more manual labour than I feel should be necessary, but I do believe it presents a more robust solution than that presented by Microsoft's employees. The first step is to add two blank paragraphs, position yourself in the first of these, and then add the equation. Then position yourself to the right of the equation (i.e., just before the first of the two paragraph marks), and press **Ctrl + Alt + Enter** to add a Style Separator . Now add a tab, and then insert an Equation caption (remembering to set the numbering so as to include the chapter number, and the caption itself so as to E̲xclude the label from the caption)—Figure 337. The convention, again, is for the equations to be enclosed in parentheses, which can now be added.

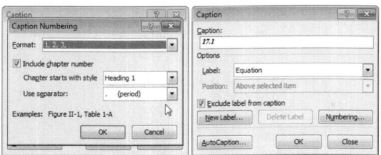

Figure 337   *Adding an equation caption*

However, these parentheses bring up the problem associated with bookmarks, as the left parenthesis will be swallowed into any cross-reference to the equation, so you will need

---

[117] See also (Lewis, 2009)—http://ist.uwaterloo.ca/ec/equations/equation2007.html—who states bluntly that "Word 2007 does not have built-in support for equation numbering, and at this time, we do not have a preferred solution."

[118] I am fully aware that the Caption tool is merely an automated tool for inserting SEQ fields, and that it is thus slightly unfair of me to group Wyatt's method with the others, but the Caption tool does more than just create a SEQ field (amongst others, it changes the paragraph style to the built-in Caption style), which is why I suggest it's use.

to consult Application 11.2 on p. 245 to correct this.[119] This will leave you equations, properly centred on the page, with auto-numbering equation captions properly aligned, that can easily be used to generate a list of equations[120] using the method described in section 9.2 (from p. 190).

By this stage, you should have something similar to the left image of Figure 338. The last thing that needs to be done is to align the equation number. By some quirk, it seems that, while the Style separator does allow you to combine two paragraphs into one, only the first paragraph's tab stops seem to apply—since Microsoft has totally neglected documenting the Style separator, we are left at a loss as to whether this is by design or by oversight. And yet, if you close and save the file, and re-open it, you may find Word wanting the tap stop for the second "paragraph." Thus, the safest thing to do seems to be to add the same tab stop on both sides of the Style separator—you need to position the I-beam both to the right and the left of the Style separator, and then add a right tab stop[121] equal to the text width of your page (e.g., if the ruler width is 16 cm, then add a 16cm right tab stop), as is demonstrated in Figure 339. The end result should be something like the right image of Figure 338.

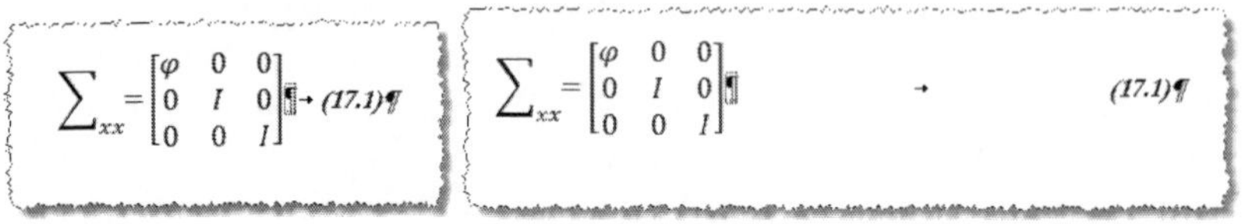

$$\sum\nolimits_{xx} = \begin{bmatrix} \varphi & 0 & 0 \\ 0 & 1 & 0 \\ 0 & 0 & 1 \end{bmatrix} \P \rightarrow (17.1)\P \qquad \sum\nolimits_{xx} = \begin{bmatrix} \varphi & 0 & 0 \\ 0 & 1 & 0 \\ 0 & 0 & 1 \end{bmatrix} \P \qquad \rightarrow \qquad (17.1)\P$$

Figure 338   *Adding and aligning an equation caption*

---

[119] I think I can blame this extra work squarely on Microsoft.

[120] Admittedly, this may not be an ideal list, as the fact that the actual caption "Equation" is excluded from the caption, means that the list will not contain entries like "Equation 2.1   p.13," but rather "(2.1) p.13."
However, using the bookmark-modification techniques I discuss in the section on bookmarks (see specifically section 11.2.4, p. 169), the parentheses can easily be removed from the reference, and with some creativity, the remaining list can be formatted quite effectively. Also, very often the idea behind numbering is not to generate a list of the actual equations, but rather to have an auto-numbering list that can be cross-referenced. Because the Caption tool uses the SEQ field, it remains ideal for this purpose.

[121] Remember that the Tabs dialog can easily be opened with Alt, O, T.

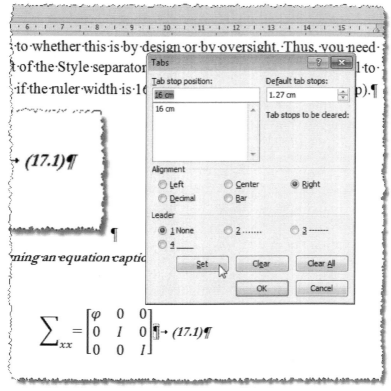

Figure 339   *Adding a tab stop to align an equation caption*

If you will forgive the double caption, Figure 340 shows such an equation with its caption numbering (there only being one such caption-numbered equation in this book, I have decided to forego the list of equations!).

$$\sum_{xx} = \begin{bmatrix} \varphi & 0 & 0 \\ 0 & I & 0 \\ 0 & 0 & I \end{bmatrix} \qquad\qquad (17.1)$$

Figure 340   *Equation 3.13 from Tucker and MacCallum (1997, p. 25)*

And, in closing, if you have to add many equations, all that work can get quite tedious, which is why I have created a simple macro to automate the work for you. Section 19.4.8 (from p. 484) explains how to add a macro like this to your Normal template. However, I have already added it to the Word uTIlities (see section 1.9, p. 7)—the tool is named Numbered equation.

Macro Listing 2   AddCaptionedEquation

```
Sub AddCaptionedEquation()
' Created by J. Raubenheimer, 2012
'Adds an empty equation box and a right-aligned equation caption
    With Selection
        .TypeParagraph
        .TypeParagraph
        .MoveUp Unit:=wdLine, Count:=2
```

```
        .OMaths.Add .Range
        .MoveRight Unit:=wdCharacter, Count:=1
        .InsertStyleSeparator
        .TypeText Text:=vbTab
        .TypeText Text:="("
        .InsertCaption Label:="Equation", ExcludeLabel:=1
        .TypeText Text:=")"
        .HomeKey Unit:=wdLine
        Dim intPos As Integer
        With .PageSetup
            intPos = .PageWidth - .LeftMargin _
            - .RightMargin - .Gutter
        End With
        .ParagraphFormat.TabStops.Add Position:=intPos, _
        Alignment:=wdAlignTabRight, Leader:=wdTabLeaderSpaces
        .HomeKey unit:=wdLine
        .ParagraphFormat.TabStops.Add Position:=intPos, _
        Alignment:=wdAlignTabRight, Leader:=wdTabLeaderSpaces
    End With
End Sub
```

17.1.8   Professional vs. Linear equations

Generally, you would want to use the professional format for your equations, but in certain instances (e.g., as is commonly used in mathematical or statistical e-mail discussion forums, or in preparation for a journal article), you may want to submit the equation in a linear format, where the various elements of the equation have been reduced to a notation which does not require any special layout. Figure 341 shows the distinction between those in a simple formula.

$$e = mc^2 \qquad e = \llbracket mc \rrbracket \, {}^\wedge 2$$
Professional equation   Linear equation

Figure 341   Professional vs. Linear equations

You can switch back and forth between these two formats with relative ease—Instruction set 70. Of course, this suggest an alternative method for writing complex formulas which may be quicker than the point-and-click interface of the equation editor—simply type out the equation in linear format, and switch to Professional. If you did it right, Word will convert the equation for you. Easy, but it requires pedantic accuracy and a high degree of proficiency in writing out the equation notation (i.e., for maths pro's only!). You could, of course, do the equation piecemeal, and switch often to see that Word is rendering it properly in the professional format.

Instruction set 70 Switching between Professional and Linear equation formats

Keyboard	Alt | JE | P
	Alt | JE | L
Left click	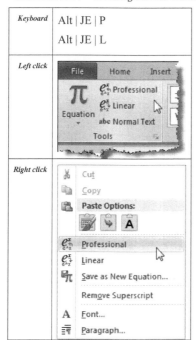
Right click	

17.1.9   Cambria Math

It is important to remember that Word uses what is called a Math region for its equations. These regions are specially defined, and, for example, the Math Authocorrect options to be discussed in section 17.3 only apply, by default, inside math regions. Furthermore, Math regions use the Cambria Math font (installed with Office). While this does allow you access to a large number of mathematical operators and symbols in the font, the drawback to this is that the font of your equations will be different to the font used for the rest of your text. This shouldn't be too much of a problem, unless your equations contain a lot of normal text, or if you position them within your text paragraphs. While you can change the default font used for maths in the Equation Options dialog discussed in section 17.1.6 above.

Furthermore, note that the Tools group of the Equation Tools ribbon also contains a Normal Text button which allows you to insert normal text into the equation (e.g., to add comments to elements of the equation). The style of that text will be the same as that of the surrounding paragraph.

17.2   Legacy equations

There have, through the years, been several ways in which equations could be created in Word. Because some of these still exist in some documents, and even still have their uses in certain contexts, they are discussed briefly in this section.

17.2.1   Microsoft Equation 3

For compatibility, the Equation editor from Word 2003 and earlier (Equation 3.0 or Equation 3.1) is also included. You can still access it, although I prefer using the never tool. Ito insert an old Equation 3 object, select Insert, Object, and from the Create New tab, select Microsoft Equation 3 from the Object type list box (Figure 342).

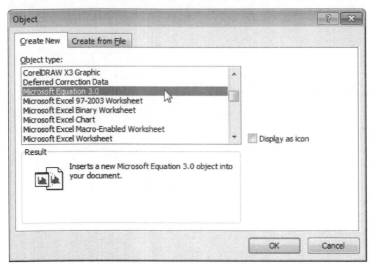

Figure 342   *Insert Object dialog: Insert Microsoft Equation 3.0 Object*

You can also still edit Equation 3 objects by double clicking on them, which will open the Equation 3 object, with the Equation toolbar (which for some strange reason I cannot get a screen capture of). For more advanced editing, right click on the equation, and then select Open from the Equation Object submenu (Figure 343). This will give you the Equation Editor (Figure 344), although I will not go into a discussion of this tool here.

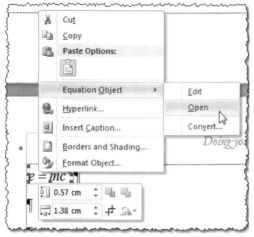

Figure 343   *Opening the Equation 3 Editor*

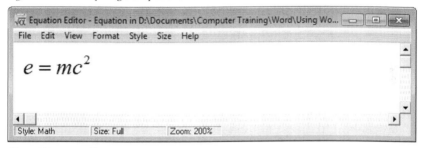

Figure 344   *Equation 3 Editor*

If you have equations created in earlier versions of Word, these are unfortunately not updated to Word 2007/2010 equations, but remain as Equation 3.0 objects. If you want to upgrade them, you will have to redo them manually.

17.2.2   EQ field

Equations have come a long way in Word, and as we progress through this chapter, we seem to be travelling back in time—the Equation 3 object was shelved with the introduction of Word 2007, and it was in itself an upgrade to the EQ field. However, both are still included for compatibility reasons, and there are some very interesting applications for the EQ field. The EQ field is built from switches, which define the placement of the various elements that make up the equation. The basic way in which the EQ field works is that you can string together any number of switches, even nesting some switches within others (see my example in Figure 345 and its explanation). Many of the switches are themselves modified by "sub-switches"—the only rule here is that these sub-switches generally need to be included within the parentheses for the switch that they modify). Table 24 shows the EQ field switches, copied (Microsoft, 2012).

Table 24 *EQ field switches[122]*

Group	Switch	Function	Modifying switches	Modifying switch function
Array	\a()	Arrays elements in multiple columns; elements appear in order by rows.	\al	Aligns left within columns.
			\ac	Aligns centre within columns.
			\ar	Aligns right within columns.
			\co$N$	Arrays elements in n columns (the default is 1).
			\vs$N$	Adds n points of vertical spacing between lines.
			\hs$N$	Adds n points of horizontal spacing between columns.
Bracket	\b()	Brackets a single element in a size appropriate to the element. The default brackets are parentheses.	\lc\C	Draws the left bracket using the character c.
			\rc\C	Draws the right bracket using the character c.
			\bc\C	Draws both bracket characters using the character specified for c. If the character you specify is {, [, (, or <, Word uses the corresponding closing character as the right bracket. If you specify any other character, Word uses that character for both brackets.
Displace	\d()	Controls where the next character following the EQ field is drawn. Note that empty parentheses follow only the last option in the instructions.	\fo$N$ ()	Draws to the right n points.
			\ba$N$ ()	Draws to the left n points.
			\li ()	Underlines the space up to the next character.

---

[122] Copied from http://office.microsoft.com/en-za/word-help/field-codes-eq-equation-field-HP005186148.aspx.

Group	Switch	Function	Modifying switches	Modifying switch function
Fraction	\f(,)	Creates a fraction with the numerator and denominator centered above and below the division line, respectively. If your system uses a comma as the decimal symbol, separate the two elements with a semicolon (;).		
Integral	\i(,,)	Creates an integral, using the specified symbol or default symbol and three elements. The first element is the lower limit, the second is the upper limit, and the third is the integrand.	\su	Changes the symbol to a capital sigma and creates a summation.
			\pr	Changes the symbol to a capital pi and creates a product.
			\in	Creates the inline format with the limits displayed to the right of the symbol instead of above and below it.
			\fc\C	Substitutes a fixed-height character specified by c for the symbol.
			\vc\C	Substitutes a variable-height character specified by c for the symbol. The symbol matches the height of the third element.
List	\l()	Uses any number of elements to create a list of values separated by commas or semicolons, so that you can specify multiple elements as a single element.		
Overstrike	\o()	Places each successive element on top of the previous one. Any number of elements is permitted. Separate multiple elements with commas. Each character is printed within an invisible character box. Options align the boxes on top of one another.	\al	Align at the left edge.
			\ac	Align in the center (the default).

421

Group	Switch	Function	Modifying switches	Modifying switch function
Radical	\r(,)	Draws a radical using one or two elements. The first element is the radical itself, and the second is placed in the box.	\ar	Align at the right edge.
Script	\s()	Places elements as superscript or subscript characters. Each \s code can have one or more elements; separate the elements with commas. If more than one element is specified, the elements are stacked and left-aligned.	\ai*N* ()	Adds space above a line in a paragraph by the number of points specified by n.
			\up*N* ()	Moves a single element above the adjacent text by the number of points specified by n. The default is 2 points.
			\di*N* ()	Adds space below a line in a paragraph by the number of points specified by n.
			\do*N* ()	Moves a single element below the adjacent text by the number of points specified by n. The default is 2 points.
Box	\x()	Creates a border for an element. When used without options, this code draws a box around the element.	\to	Draws a border above the element.
			\bo	Draws a border below the element
			\le	Draws a border to the left of the element.
			\ri	Draws a border to the right of the element.

A last note when using the EQ field is to make sure that you have deleted the space between the end of the equation and the closing brace, so that you don't get an unintended space after your equation—compare the space at the end of: $0.\dot{3} \times 3 = 0.99\dot{9}$ with $0.\dot{3} \times 3 = 0.99\dot{9}$, the two EQ entries being: { EQ 0.\O(3,') x 3 = 0.99\O(9,') } and {EQ 0.\O(3,') x 3 = 0.99\O(9,')} respectively.

The question, of course, is whether you should use the EQ field or the new equation objects as a matter of course? The answer is complex, because the determinant[123] is what you want to achieve. For run-of-the mill equations, the equation object is quicker to learn, and runs less risk that your document might contain elements which will not be supported in the future. For complex equations, the equation object is probably also more pliable and offers more functionality. It might be that the EQ field is useful in certain contexts though (see, for example, Application 17.1 below). Another context where the EQ field is the clear winner is when you want numbered equations (see the discussion in section 17.1.7 above). After all that, note, though, that when the two are used inline within paragraphs, certain differences also become apparent. Take the following paragraph from p. 407, which, by the way, was done using the EQ field:

> For a simple example, imagine the following problem: We might know that $\frac{1}{3} \times 3 = 3$, but $0.\dot{3} \times 3 = 0.99\dot{9}$ and is it not so that $1 \neq 0.99\dot{9}$? Or can we construct a proof that shows that $1 = 0.99\dot{9}$?
>
> For a simple example, imagine the following problem: We might know that $\frac{1}{3} \times 3 = 3$, but $0.\dot{3} \times 3 = 0.99\dot{9}$ and is it not so that $1 \neq 0.99\dot{9}$? Or can we construct a proof that shows that $1 = 0.99\dot{9}$?

The first instance of this paragraph uses the equation object, and the second, the EQ field. Note that the line spacing on the former is more compact (and is thus to be preferred), but that the EQ field uses the paragraph font, instead of the Cambria Math font (and is thus to be preferred from that angle). I could tighten up the line spacing in the latter paragraph (I did on p. 407), but it will never be as tight as in the former. Conversely, I do not know of a simple way to change the font of the equation object. This means that, in at least one context, even in Word 2010, the EQ field is probably still the clear winner: Creating fractions that are not available from the symbol set. If, thus, I wanted something like $\frac{3}{11}$, it is a simple matter to add {EQ \f (3,11)}, whereas the equation object will be lost more complex to use. Note, though, that this results in a large line gap for the line in which the fraction occurs, so you would want either to set the line spacing for the paragraph, or, as I did in this paragraph, set the font size of the fraction smaller (I changed it to $\frac{2}{3}$ of the paragraph font size).

---

[123] Please excuse the pun!

I will thus leave it to you to decide which you would prefer to use, but perhaps the best would be to learn to use both, each in the context which bests suits your desired outcome.

Application 17.1   X-Bar

One of the things I gest asked most frequently is this: How do you get X-bar? Yes, you could use the Equation Editor (it has overbars in the Accents group), but that is clumsy, especially in the middle of a paragraph or in a table.

There are actually several alternate ways in which this can be done. In each of the three methods shown below, the X-bar character you see was produced using the method being discussed—you can compare them visually to see the differences in each method's result (for each, I suggest some possible "tweaks," but to be fair, they are all presented here "un-tweaked"). My personal favourite is the second method, using the EQ field, as it provides the X-bar in the same font as the text you are using with the minimum of fuss. Note also the past paragraph of this section if you are going to be using the X-bar often.

*Firstly, the $\overline{X}$ character can be found in the **MS Reference Sans Serif font** (also a lowercase and another variant). I have discussed elsewhere how to go about getting and adding fonts (see section 3.1, p. 35), but beware the problems associated with fonts when it comes to printing (see especially section 19.2.1, p. 470). You may also want to adjust the font size for this symbol.*

*Another option is to use the **EQ field** with the overstrike switch (\o) to place the macron (overbar) character (Unicode: 00AF or ASCI: 0175) above the X. Thus {EQ \o (X, ⁻)} will produce $\overline{X}$. You may have to tweak the height of the macron in the Character Spacing tab of the Font dialog to get it just right. The hardest part may actually be getting the overbar—you will find it in the Latin-1 Supplement subsection of the Normal Text character set in the Insert Symbol dialog. Fortunately, there is now a slightly easier method too—the overbar is now also included in the maths autocorrect discussed below (section 17.3).*

*A third option is to switch to the **Symbol font** (Ctrl +Shift +Q) , then type the ` character (grave accent). Next, switch back to your text font, and type the X. This will produce $\overline{X}$. Again, you may want to tweak the font size with this one. You may also need to delete the space after the word preceding the X-bar, which might lead to spelling errors....*

A last idea is to create an autotext entry (see section 4.4, p. 75) or a maths autotext entry (see section 17.3 below) for the X-bar (I would suggest \xbar for the maths autocorrect) so that you need not go through the whole process each time. Simply create the X-bar using the method of your choice from the above, then select it, and create the AutoText or AutoCorrect entry.

Application 17.2   Recursion

Another interesting problem is the indication of recursion. Again, the EQ field with the overstrike switch comes in handy: Insert the Bullet Operator (Unicode: 2219) from the Mathematical Symbols *subsection of the* Normal Text *character set in the* Insert

> *Symbol dialog, and then use the Character Spacing tab of the Font dialog to raise the character by about 6pt (depending on the font size you are using).*
>
> *Thus {EQ \F(2,3) = 0.\O(6, ̇)} allows me to write $\frac{2}{3} = 0.\dot{6}$.*

As a final, concrete example of how to use the EQ field, my trite little formula[124] for the chapter title, which was done using a Word Equation, is repeated in the top part of Figure 345. Then, the bottom part of the same figure repeats the equation using the EQ field:

{EQ Thesis ≈ \r (3,Knowledge) x log\s\do8(10)\b\bc\{(Ability) x \o(\s\do10(n→∞),lim) (Perseverance)\s\up8(2)}. Both versions are presented "untweaked," meaning that both could benefit aesthetically from some minor adjustments (e.g., setting font size or adjusting the vertical position of some of the individual elements), but the way in which they are presented allows better comparison of the raw functionality of each method.

Word 2007/2010 Equation $\text{Thesis} \approx \sqrt[3]{\text{Knowledge}} \times \log_{10}\{\text{Ability}\} \times \lim_{n\to\infty} (\text{Perseverance})^2$

EQ field $\text{Thesis} \approx \sqrt[3]{\text{Knowledge}} \ \text{x} \ \log_{10}\{\text{Ability}\} \ \text{x} \ \lim_{n\to\infty} (\text{Perseverance})^2$

Figure 345   Comparison of Equation vs EQ field

17.3   Math regions and Math autocorrect

Remember that while math is all about equations, not all of math is about equations. When an equation is inserted, what is actually added is a special document part called a math zone or math region. There is a lot that you can do with these math regions, much of which has already been discussed. However, it should be noted that within a math region, a special set of autocorrect settings apply. The chief thing to note is that—if you learn the necessary nomenclature—you can learn to type math in these areas, using Word's special math autocorrect. How to access the autocorrect settings was discussed in section 4.3 (p. 64). Figure 346 shows the Math AutoCorrect tab of the AutoCorrect dialog. Note that here, you can even change the settings so that you can type formulas in your text (they will be expressed as text, not as math region equations) using the various math autocorrect entries, by activating the Use Math AutoCorrect rules outside of math regions setting. Note that the Recognized functions... button opens a dialog (Figure 347) which allows you to specify text terms which will not be italicised (the way normal text is) within a math region.

---

[124] Or is it, many a true word is spoken in jest?

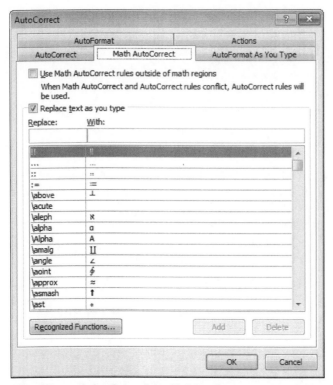

Figure 346   *AutoCorrect dialog: Math AutoCorrect*

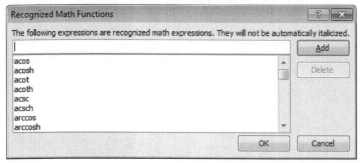

Figure 347   *Math AutoCorrect: Recognized Math Functions*

Table 25 provides a listing of all the built-in Math AutoCorrect symbols (Microsoft, 2012; Microsoft, 2012), but you can, of course, add your own, as was discussed in section 4.3 (p. 64).

Table 25   *Math AutoCorrect Symbols*[125]

Symbol	AutoCorrect entry	Symbol	AutoCorrect entry
...	...	⊥	\above
ℵ	\aleph	α	\alpha
Α	\Alpha	Π	\amalg
∠	\angle	≈	\approx
↑	\asmash	∗	\ast
≍	\asymp	⁞	\atop
‾	\bar	˙	\Bar
⟦	\begin	⊤	\below
⊐	\bet	β	\beta
Β	\Beta	⊥	\bot
⋈	\bowtie	□	\box
⟨	\bra	ˊ	\breve
•	\bullet	∩	\cap
∛	\cbrt	·	\cdot
⋯	\cdots	ˇ	\check
χ	\chi	Χ	\Chi
∘	\circ	⊣	\close
♣	\clubsuit	∯	\coint
≅	\cong	∪	\cup
ℸ	\dalet	⊣	\dashv
ⅆ	\dd	ⅅ	\Dd
⃛	\ddddot	⋮	\dddot
˙	\ddot	⋱	\ddots
°	\degree	δ	\delta
Δ	\Delta	⋄	\diamond
◇	\diamondsuit	÷	\div
˙	\dot	≐	\doteq
...	\dots	↓	\downarrow
⇓	\Downarrow	↓	\dsmash
ℯ	\ee	ℓ	\ell
∅	\emptyset	⟧	\end
ε	\epsilon	Ε	\Epsilon
■	\eqarray	≡	\equiv
η	\eta	Η	\Eta
∃	\exists	∀	\forall
⊞	\funcapply	γ	\gamma
Γ	\Gamma	≥	\ge
≥	\geq	←	\gets
≫	\gg	ℷ	\gimel
ˆ	\hat	ℏ	\hbar
♡	\heartsuit	↩	\hookleftarrow
↪	\hookrightarrow	≍	\hphantom
˜	\hvec	ı	\ii
∭	\iiint	∬	\iint
ℑ	\Im	∈	\in
Δ	\inc	∞	\infty
∫	\int	ι	\iota
Ι	\Iota	ȷ	\jj
κ	\kappa	Κ	\Kappa
⟩	\ket	λ	\lambda
Λ	\Lambda	⟨	\langle
⌈	\lceil	⟦	\lbrack
...	\ldots	/	\ldivide
		≤	\le
←	\leftarrow	⇐	\Leftarrow

---

[125] Copied from http://office.microsoft.com/en-za/word-help/linear-format-equations-and-math-autocorrect-in-word-HA101861025.aspx.

Symbol	AutoCorrect entry	Symbol	AutoCorrect entry
↼	\leftharpoondown	↽	\leftharpoonup
↔	\leftrightarrow	⇔	\Leftrightarrow
≤	\leq	⌊	\lfloor
≪	\ll	↦	\mapsto
■	\matrix	∣	\mid
⊨	\models	∓	\mp
μ	\mu	M	\Mu
∇	\nabla	⨇	\naryand
≠	\ne	↗	\nearrow
≠	\neq	∋	\ni
‖	\norm	ν	\nu
N	\Nu	↖	\nwarrow
o	\o	O	\O
⊙	\odot	⨌	\oiiint
∯	\oiint	∮	\oint
ω	\omega	Ω	\Omega
⊖	\ominus	⊢	\open
⊕	\oplus	⊗	\otimes
∫	\over	‾	\overbar
⏞	\overbrace	⏜	\overparen
‖	\parallel	∂	\partial
◇	\phantom	φ	\phi
Φ	\Phi	π	\pi
Π	\Pi	±	\pm
⁗	\ppprime	‴	\pprime
″	\pprime	≺	\prec
≼	\preceq	′	\prime
Π	\prod	∝	\propto
ψ	\psi	Ψ	\Psi
℆	\qdrt	x=(-b±√(b^2-4ac))/2a	\quadratic
⟩	\rangle	∶	\ratio
}	\rbrace	]	\rbrack
⌉	\rceil	⋰	\rddots
ℜ	\Re	▭	\rect
⌋	\rfloor	ρ	\rho
P	\Rho	→	\rightarrow
⇒	\Rightarrow	⇁	\rightharpoondown
⇀	\rightharpoonup	⁄	\sdivide
↘	\searrow	∖	\setminus
σ	\sigma	Σ	\Sigma
~	\sim	≃	\simeq
∕	\slashedfrac	⌐	\smash
♠	\spadesuit	⊓	\sqcap
⊔	\sqcup	√	\sqrt
⊑	\sqsubseteq	⊒	\sqsuperseteq
⋆	\star	⊂	\subset
⊆	\subseteq	≻	\succ
≽	\succeq	Σ	\sum
⊃	\superset	⊇	\superseteq
↙	\swarrow	τ	\tau
T	\Tau	θ	\theta
Θ	\Theta	×	\times
→	\to	⊤	\top
↤	\tvec	▁	\ubar
∎	\Ubar	▁	\underbar
⋯	\underbrace	⏝	\underparen
↑	\uparrow	⇑	\Uparrow
↕	\updownarrow	⇕	\Updownarrow
⊎	\uplus	υ	\upsilon
Υ	\Upsilon	ε	\varepsilon
φ	\varphi	ϖ	\varpi
ϱ	\varrho	ς	\varsigma

Symbol	AutoCorrect entry	Symbol	AutoCorrect entry
ϑ	\vartheta	∣	\vbar
⊢	\vdash	⋮	\vdots
→	\vec	∨	\vee
∣	\vert	‖	\Vert
░	\vphantom	∧	\wedge
℘	\wp	≀	\wr
ξ	\xi	Ξ	\Xi
ζ	\zeta	Ζ	\Zeta
		(space with zero width)	\zwsp
∓	-+	±	+-
←	<-	≤	<=
→	->	≥	>=

Although the scope and intent of this book prevents this single chapter from becoming a whole book on using math in Word, if you would like to read more, you could do a lot worse than to start with Murray Sargent's blog: http://blogs.msdn.com/b/murrays/archive/2012/01/09/math-in-office-links.aspx.

17.4   More with math

But wait, there's more! Microsoft has put in a lot of effort into developing the math capabilities of the various applications in the suite. And this extends the capabilities of what you can do in Word, mathematically speaking, quite a bit.

17.4.1   Microsoft Mathematics

One great tool, which is not a Word tool per se, is Microsoft Mathematics. It can be downloaded from: http://www.microsoft.com/en-us/download/details.aspx?id=15702. This tool allows you to work with, resolve, and graph equations. Working with Microsoft Mathematics is a topic on its own, and will not be dealt with here, although it should be noted that whatever you have created in Microsoft Mathematics can be exported to Word easily from the File tab of the Microsoft Mathematics application.

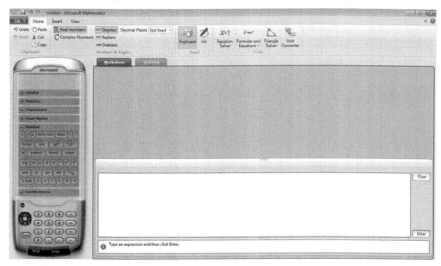

Figure 348   Microsoft Mathematics

Microsoft Mathematics also has an accompanying Word Add-In, which can be downloaded from: http://www.microsoft.com/en-us/download/details.aspx? displaylang=en&id=17786. This Add-In loads a Mathematics ribbon in Word, which can then be used to access much of the same functionality from within Word.

Figure 349   *Microsoft Mathematics Add-In for Word: Mathematics ribbon*

17.4.2   Windows Math input

Perhaps not that essential to this chapter, and not about Word per se, but if you are doing math, and you work on a tablet device, you could use Windows 7's Math Input Panel (just type Math Input" in the search bar) to interpret hand-written math equations, and add them to Word.

For example, Figure 350 shows a horrendous formula written on my PC with the mouse, and how the Math Input Panel has interpreted it. Simply clicking the Insert button on the bottom right (with Word open, and the correct location in the document selected, of course) will insert the interpreted equation into your document.

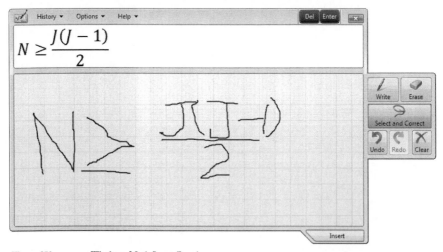

Figure 350   *Windows Math Input Panel*

If your handwriting is like mine, then you may need to coach it a bit—Figure 351 shows how I used the Select and Correct tool to change the incorrect Σ to $\geq$.

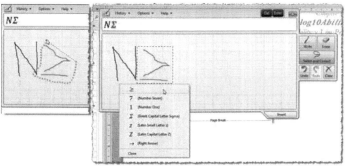

Figure 351   *Correcting Math Input in the Windows Math Input Panel*

Chapter 18
Releasing your inner artiste:
Doing Drawings in Word

Various graphic objects can be created with Word: WordArt objects, pictures, organization charts, and regular drawing objects. Most of these are accessed from the Insert ribbon, with Instruction set 71 showing how to insert a drawing shape.

Instruction set 71   Inserting a drawing shape

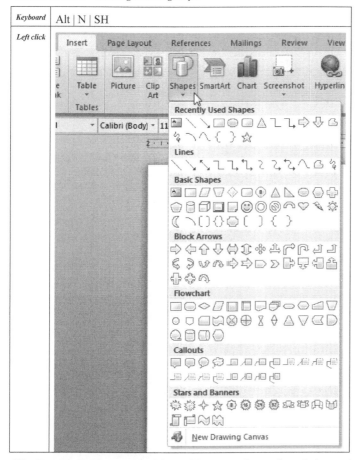

The Drawing Tools: Format ribbon will appear when a shape is inserted, and contains specific buttons for inserting a wide variety of these object types, as well as a dizzying array of tools to use.

18.1   Selecting drawing objects

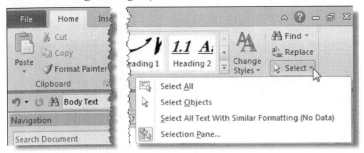

Figure 352   *Selection tools on Home ribbon*

When you have one or more drawing objects in your document, you may at times want to select them. Individual shapes can easily be selected with the mouse. Multiple shapes can be selected by holding down the Shift key as you click on each successive shape. Alternatively, you can use the Selection tools on the Home ribbon (Figure 352). For example, the easiest way to select objects and ensure that you miss nothing, is to click on the Select Objects tool on the Home Ribbon, and then to click at one corner (e.g., above and to the left of the top, left-most object), and then drag across to the opposite corner (e.g., down and to the right, covering the bottom, right-most object). As you drag, a dashed rectangle will form, and any objects included in entirety within the selection area will be selected. Thus, the right-most square from Figure 353 will be selected, but not the middle square. When the selection is completed (i.e., when you release the mouse button) the selection handles (little circles on the corners and in the middle of the sides) will appear on all the successfully selected objects.

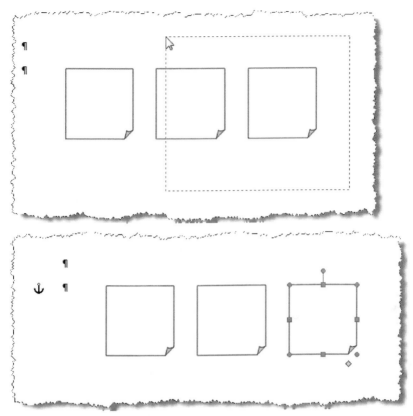

Figure 353   Selecting multiple shapes

Another way to select objects is to use the Selection pane (also found on the Home ribbon—see Figure 352). Figure 354 shows the Selection pane for the objects included in the drawing shown in Figure 357. Here, you can click on any item to select that shape in the drawing (e.g., note that the cloud is selected, and that in the Selection pane, AutoShape 25 is selected). Interestingly, to select multiple objects in the Selection pane, you do not hold down the Shift key, but the Ctrl key. You can also temporarily hide objects (or reveal them again after being hidden) by clicking on the eye icon to the right of that object, or with the Show All/Hide All buttons at the bottom of the pane which will apply to all the listed objects. The remaining tool of the Selection pane will be discussed in the sections below on Grouping and Drawing layers.

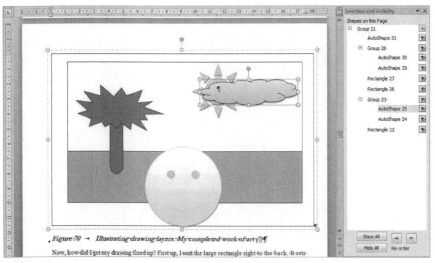

Figure 354   *Selection pane*

18.2   Grouping

If you create a complex picture consisting of multiple drawing objects, their relation to the text becomes critical to the integrity of the greater picture. If you modify the text, you could find the elements of your carefully constructed artwork floating apart! The best way to prevent this is to select all the elements, and then to right-click on any one of them (be careful not to deselect the others—this can happen easily if you left-click on any one of them again), and then to select Group from the Grouping option. This fuses the elements together, and Word will treat them as a single whole. You can, at later stages, ungroup or regroup the objects at will.

If you have grouped, or even just selected a number of objects together, you can also move and/or resize them simultaneously. Note the groups displayed in the Selection pane in Figure 354.

Instruction set 72   Grouping and ungrouping drawing objects

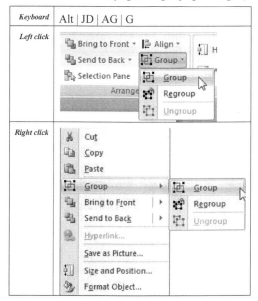

Further tricks for working with multiple objects are discussed in section 18.4.1 below.

18.3   Drawing layers

For various technical reasons, Word has to manipulate the contents of a document in what are called layers. Primarily, there is the text layer and the drawing layer, although the drawing layer itself will consist of as many "sub-layers" as there are images. Simply put, imagine that every object on a page (text box, chart, equation, drawing, etc.) was drawn onto an old overhead projector's transparency sheet (each sheet is thus a "layer"). To get the final composite, all of these transparency sheets are put on top of each other. It stands to reason that if there is any overlap by any of the objects, then the order in which the sheets are stacked will determine the end result.

The way in which these layers relate to each other can, however, be manipulated quite extensively. For example, multiple drawing objects can be stacked in a precise order, allowing you to create various overlapping effects. Simply right-click on the object and then select the desired setting from the Order option (Figure 355), or use the tools in the Arrange group on the Format ribbons[126].

---

[126] i.e., Drawing Tools: Format, or Picture Tools: Format or SmartArt Tools: Format, or Chart Tools: Format, etc.

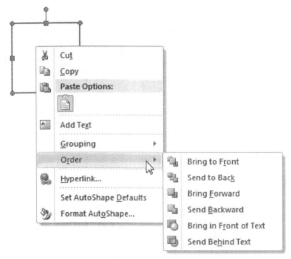

Figure 355   *Ordering drawing objects*

In Word we have six ordering options, four to determine the position of each object within the various drawing sub-layers, and two more to determine the order of the drawing layer in relation to the text layer, as explained in Table 26:

Table 26   *Ordering Objects*

Ordering option	Function
Bring Forward	Take this object and move it to one layer higher within the drawing sub-layers (or switch this object and the object above it in their layer positions).
Bring to Front	Take this object and move it to the highest of the drawing sub-layers (right in front of all other objects).
Bring in Front of Text	The object floats over the text (how exactly it floats is further determined by its wrapping)
Send Backward	Take this object and move it to one layer down within the drawing sub-layers (or switch this object and the object below it in their layer positions).
Send to Back	Take this object and move it to the lowest of the drawing sub-layers (right behind all other objects).
Send Behind Text	The object floats beneath the text (how exactly it floats is further determined by its wrapping)

Sometimes you will find that you have called an object forward (note, not to the front) but it is still stuck behind another object. This is not because the program has failed to execute your command. It just means that the object obscuring the one you want to move is more than one layer above it, and you may have to move it several times to get it in the position you want it in. This will be discussed in more detail in section 18.3.4 below. Note that the Selection pane (Figure 354) lists the drawing objects in their layer-order—the item at the very top of the pane is in the uppermost layer (The Front) and the item at the bottom of the list in the pane is in the lowest layer (Back). The Selection pane also has two spin buttons (with the caption Re-order) with which you can also manipulate the layers of the various objects.

18.3.1   Why layers?

My aim here is to elaborate a bit on the topic of drawing layers, so that you have a better idea of the concept, and how it works. This should help you create diagrams and other graphics more quickly, and also more professionally, by avoiding some of the most common mistakes based on a failure to grasp this principle.

I am going to over-simplify things a bit in this explanation, but I want to put in lay terms the reason why the concept of layers in necessary in the first place. My hope is that understanding the underlying necessity will help you understand the concept. Now, when you type text into the computer, that text is transmitted and stored in a certain encoding format (you may be familiar with the most common of those formats— ASCII[127] text). When you add pictures, those pictures cannot be stored in that same format, as it is a text only format (although the format does include a few options for text formatting and control characters). Rather, pictures are stored as raster graphics[128] (have you heard the term bitmap?), where the picture is basically made up of a rectangular grid of dots. Each dot is known as a pixel, and each dot has a certain colour. If you take a newspaper picture and hold it up close, you will see this effect in action. The picture's resolution indicates how many pixels are included in a certain surface area, and the more pixels, the better quality the picture. In other words, to the computer, pictures and text are two radically different things. Text is from Mars, and pictures are from Venus.

Now for the computer programmers, that creates a huge problem. The computer users, after all, demand to be able to use text and pictures together, and they couldn't care two hoots about lame excuses of different encoding. So the computer programmers simply had to come up with a resolution (excuse the pun) to the problem. Of course, you may not even be aware of this problem, so well have the computer programmers resolved it (if you worked with versions of Word like Word 5 for DOS, then you would know that Word has not always been able to accommodate pictures, although don't be fooled into thinking that this is a problem which only the creators of Word had to solve—every computer program that allows you to create graphics has the same issue).

Furthermore, the problem is not only about how to accommodate text and graphics together. Even when you use two or more pictures together, you have the same problem. Remember that a raster graphic is a rectangular grid of coloured dots. But what if you draw two things (each having their own grid), and then put them on top of each other? What's the poor computer to do? If pixel 1,1 is red in the one graphic, and green in

---

[127] American Standard Code for Information Interchange. Although I hate using Wikipedia as a reference, you might read this article for some background if you are that way inclined: http://en.wikipedia.org/wiki/Ascii.

[128] Again, look here for a less-than-satisfactory explanation: http://en.wikipedia.org/wiki/Raster_graphics.

another, the computer could burn itself out or at least go schizophrenic trying to resolve the dilemma. The same dot cannot be two colours at the same time.

The solution, of course, to all these problems lies in the use of layers[129] (and almost all programs I know of that allow graphics and text use the layers concept, although I do not know who came up with it first).

18.3.2   What is a layer?

Basically, layers are there to keep things apart. Every picture occupies its own layer, and the text has its own layer. Think of layers as transparent surfaces on which text or drawing objects are placed, and layers can be stacked on top of each other in any order desired. A low tech example (if you're old enough to relate) is transparency sheets used on an overhead projector. The way we would do a drawing is to take one sheet, a bunch of pens, and draw everything on that one sheet. Lines of different objects can intersect quite happily in the process. What the computer does is to place each single object on one sheet, and then stack the sheets very precisely on top of each other to create the final effect. Here no drawing objects can intersect. The end result, of course, is exactly the same. But the different processes reflect the different realities of the real world and the computer world.

18.3.3   The text layer and the drawing layer

When you work in a program like Word, you have two layers—the text layer and the drawing layer. Actually, the drawing layer can contain as many sub-layers as you want, but think of it in general terms for now. As an analogy, I like to think of the ground and the sky. The text is on the ground, and the clouds are up in the sky (and different clouds can form at different heights), and never the two shall meet, but the clouds can cast their shadow onto the ground. It's important to know about these two layers, because Word does allow you to move even the drawing layer behind the text layer (and so there my analogy of ground and sky begins to fall apart!). Note, however, that the text layer in Word is more flexible than I have made it out to be up till now. The text layer can contain Frames, which can float above the text. The text layer can even contain pictures, although these pictures are then known as inline pictures, and they do not float above the text, rather, they move with the text and even obey certain text formatting rules (like paragraph alignment, etc.). However, all drawing objects and text boxes in Word automatically reside in the drawing layer.

Note that Excel, of course, doesn't have a "text layer" in the same sense as word. There are the cells, on a layer of their own, and then there is the drawing layer. PowerPoint, because it works towards graphical images displayed on a screen, not text printed on a page, also has no text layer. You cannot just type text anywhere on a slide, but rather need to place all your text in text boxes. Note, however, that in PowerPoint, it's not that the text layer has been replaced with something else (like the cell layer, for want of a better word, in Excel). Far rather, there simply is no text layer in PowerPoint, only a drawing layer. Of course, considering the different medium you are working in, that

---

[129]   And   again,   another   less-than-satisfactory   summary   can   be   found   here: http://en.wikipedia.org/wiki/2D_computer_graphics

makes perfect sense. The one implication of this, of course, is that the concept of frames, which float but can be placed in the text layer, is unique to Word. Word has frames and text boxes. Excel and PowerPoint have only text boxes.

18.3.4   Using layers

That's all fine, but if this isn't going somewhere, I'm going to be putting you to sleep. Let's do a little drawing to illustrate the concepts (allow me to apologise in advance: I'm no artist—I only do drawings that could, with a little luck, be entered into kindergarten drawing competitions). Let's say that we want to draw a face standing in front of a window, with a cloud and a tree and the sun all visible in the window. Seeing as I am typing this in Word, I will be illustrating it as it is done in Word, but the process is identical for PowerPoint and Excel. First up, my drawing shapes, as seen in Figure 356. I will be using some of these shapes to construct my drawing. The important thing to remember is that each shape gets a layer of its own. In the process, I will also be recapping some of the other drawing skills we looked at in the course.

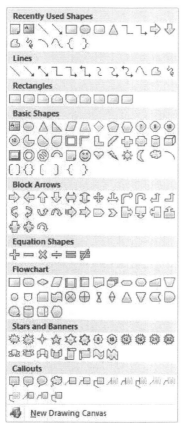

Figure 356   *Drawing shapes*

What I want to do is analyse my picture (Figure 357) step by step, so that you can see how I did it. The first thing I did was to draw the frame of the window. I used the rectangle tool for that. Then I right-clicked on the frame and selected Format so that I could tell Word, in the Colors and Lines tab that this frame should have no colour. Next I used the face tool to draw the face. I held down the Shift key as I drew it, so that the face would come out as a perfect circle (which is perhaps less than realistic). I used the Shape Styles to add the shaded colour to the face. Next up was the tree. First I drew a cylinder as the tree trunk. Then I used the explosion callout to draw the canopy (I'm using my imagination here). I used the standard colours to make the canopy dark green, and then the colour picker to make the trunk brown. Then I drew another rectangle inside the first one, and used the standard colours to make it light green. This would be the grass. Then I realised that my tree was too big, so I selected first the canopy by clicking on it, and then the trunk together with the canopy by holding down the Shift key and clicking on it. I then used the Group tool to group them together. Now I can move and resize them as a unit. I maintained the perspective that I had by holding down the Shift key while clicking on one of the corner sizing handles and dragging the tree smaller. Then I used the cloud shape to draw the cloud, and then the sun picture for the sun (again holding down Shift as I drew to get a perfectly round sun). Finally, I realised that I did not have the proper "context" for my diagram, so I drew an even larger rectangle than the very first one, so that it now looks as if my window is actually in a wall.

Of course, if you did all of that, you would realise that the result up to there looks nowhere near my work of art (I flatter myself, don't I?). That's because I haven't used layers. In fact, what I have at this point in time is a big white rectangle, only! That's because the "contextual" rectangle that I drew last is right on top of everything. Whenever you do drawings like this, the computer will automatically assume that each new part of the drawing belongs on top of the previous one. Of course, the big problem is that that is not how our minds work. When you work with the Order tools (the tools you use to manipulate your layers), you have two directions (forward and backward), and two scales of movement (one at a time, or all the way in one go). These are plotted in Table 27, and also illustrated in Figure 358, which is best examined after you have read the explanation of how I did drawing. Note that in Word (the only of the main Office applications with a true text layer), you also have the added options of taking your drawing objects in front of, or behind the text (layer). One final thing here: When you have grouped objects together, they still maintain their individual layers, although those layers now move together. If, for example, you have grouped two objects together (like my tree trunk and canopy), and their order is wrong, you will first have to ungroup them, re-order them, and then re-group them.

Table 27   *Drawing Order Tools*

		Scale	
		One at a time	**All the way**
Direction	**Up**	Bring forward	Bring to front
	Down	Send backward	Send to back

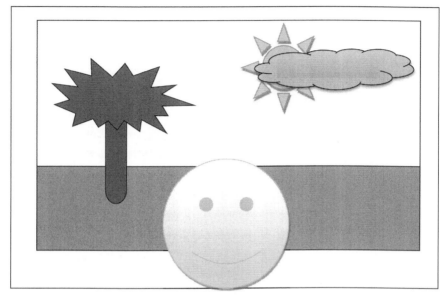

Figure 357   *Illustrating drawing layers: My completed work of art (!)*

Now, how did I get my drawing fixed up? First up, I sent the large rectangle right to the back. It sets my context, so that is exactly where I want it to be. Now my grass rectangle was in front of the tree, which could not be. So I moved the tree forward. I had to do this a few times, because the first time it moved past the sun (which had been drawn after it, and was thus above it). Then I had to move it past the cloud (same reason). Then I had to move it past the grass. And there it was, in the right place. Then I had to move my sun backward (not right to the back, because that would put it behind the large rectangle), so that it would peep out from behind the cloud (clouds can't be behind the sun, can they?). And, of course, last but not least, I had to bring my face right to the front (it was still partially behind the grass at this point). Now if you were able to, and you flipped my drawing on its side, it would look like eight transparencies or sheets of glass stacked on top of each other. And each of those contains only one of the eight drawing objects used to make my picture. You can see a representation of this in Figure 358.

Figure 358   *Illustrating drawing layers: My "work of art" imaginatively flipped on its side*

The last thing I did (and I generally recommend it, unless you want to fiddle with the text wrapping of the individual drawing objects), is to select the whole lot by encompassing it with the select tool, and then grouping it all together into one unit. This should help you realise, of course, that grouping is flexible and cumulative—you can even group different groups together (as I have done). And that, of course, is how I did it. Easy, if you understand layers.

18.3.5   Conclusion (layers)

After you have read this section on layers, the job is not done yet! It will help if you persevere through to the next section, to gain an understanding of inline and floating objects in Word.

I hope that this little introduction has helped you grasp the basic principles involved in using the drawing tools. My advice now is to go out and practise some of your own drawings. And, if you struggle, to persevere, as well as to try and read up a bit more. A good place to start is this: For a bit of an introduction to drawing objects in Word, which also deals with the topic of text and drawing layers, see http://word.mvps.org/faQs/DrawingGraphics.htm. Two other very nice demonstrations of certain drawing tool principles in PowerPoint (but which apply equally to all the other Office applications) are: http://www.echosvoice.com/beziercurves.htm and http://www.pptworkbench.com/html/3d_catchment.htm. Now go out and draw!

18.4   Pictures

Any picture that you have on disk can be added to your documents. Use the Picture tool on the Insert ribbon (Instruction set 73).

Instruction set 73   Inserting Pictures

Keyboard	Alt | N | P
Left click	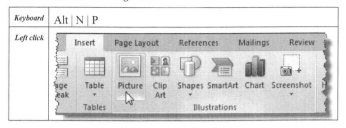

18.4.1   Inline vs. Floating pictures (and objects)

When a picture is inserted, it is inserted inline by default. I recommend that you keep most of your images inline. An inline image is inserted into the text layer[130]—i.e., it becomes part of a paragraph. Although you cannot format it the way you would format text, it does follow the paragraph formatting applied to its host paragraph (e.g., if the paragraph is centre aligned, the picture will be centred horizontally on the page). Working with inline pictures is both more stable, and also results in less file size bloat.

Application 18.1   Captioning floating objects

> *If you have a floating object, you can still caption it. I do, however, recommend that you add the caption to a normal paragraph, and then just anchor the object to that paragraph. The alternative is to select the object, and then insert the caption. Word will, in the Insert Caption dialog, ask you whether to place the caption above or below the object, and will then insert the caption within a floating text box. Older versions of Word would not include those captions in a list of captions, but this problem has been resolved, and these captions will also appear. In short, you can do this, and for certain effects this may be the only way to get the desired result, but I still recommend mostly using inline objects, and using inline captions without exception.*

18.4.1.1   Object anchors

When an object is not placed inline, it is still anchored either to a paragraph or to the page. This means that as that paragraph moves (e.g., if other paragraphs are added or deleted from before it), so the object will move with it. The object anchor can only be seen when non-printing characters are displayed *and* when the object itself is selected. The bottom section of Figure 353 shows a selected drawing shape, and the object anchor in the margin next to the paragraph. Note that when the anchoring paragraph is deleted, the anchor is deleted with it, together with the anchored picture (or object)— even though it may be a floating picture. You can also click and drag on the anchor to anchor the object to a different paragraph.

---

[130] You can see that the term "text" layer is rather flexible....

An interesting situation occurs when you want to add a picture and label it in Word (see Figure 4 on p. 13 as an example). You will notice that you cannot group an inline picture with the floating text boxes or other shapes that you have used for your labels (it would not make sense if you could, as a matter of fact). You might not want to make the picture floating, as that creates a whole new set of problems. The solution is to insert a drawing canvas (Instruction set 74). A canvas is basically an object frame which can contain any number of other objects. So you can add all your pictures, align them, group them, etc., within the canvas. But the canvas itself can be left inline in a paragraph (canvases can, though, also be set to float, which is also useful).

Instruction set 74   Inserting a Drawing Canvas

Keyboard	Alt	N	SH	N
Left click	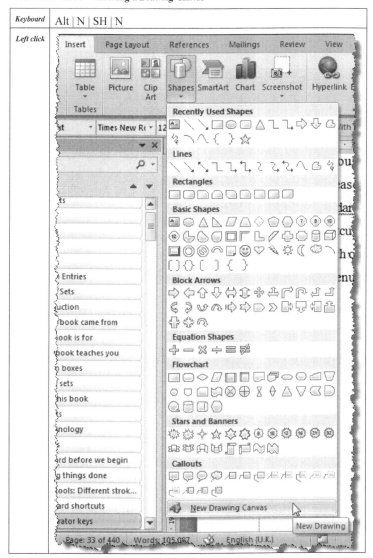

18.4.1.3   Using tables to organise pictures

One last trick for getting pictures to play along nicely is to insert them into the different cells of a table which has no border formatting. Some examples of the use of this technique are Figure 59 (p. 82), Figure 108 (p. 148), Figure 109 (p. 149), most of the chart examples in Chapter 16 (from p. 369), and almost all of the instruction sets (such as Instruction set 74 above).

18.4.2 Picture layout and Text wrapping

When working with pictures, there is actually quite a lot that you can do to determine their exact position on the page and their relationship to the surrounding text. All of this is dealt with, generally, in the picture's layout. While you can access the Position and Wrap Text tools from the Picture Tools ribbon, and while both of these have a More Layout Options button at the bottom of their list of options, you can also right click on the picture, and select Size and Position....

Instruction set 75   Accessing picture layout

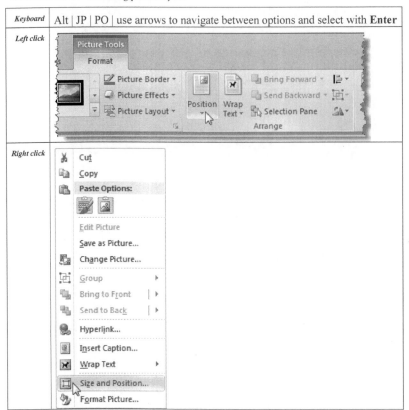

Keyboard	Alt | JP | PO | use arrows to navigate between options and select with **Enter**
Left click	
Right click	

I will thus discuss the various settings from the context of the Layout dialog, although once you are familiar with the tools, you will be able to access them from the ribbon or context menu as well. The first setting to look at is the sizing of the picture (Figure 359). You can resize a picture by clicking and dragging on any of the sizing handles, or in the dialog or the ribbon, where you can set the size in very precise units, or as a proportion (larger or smaller) of its original size. When you lock aspect ratio (on by default for pictures, off by default for drawing shapes), then the height and with change in equal proportions simultaneously. When resizing with the mouse, you can enforce aspect ratio by holding down the Shift key while clicking and dragging on a corner sizing handle (it stands to reason that middle sizing handles ignore aspect ratio).

You can rotate a picture by clicking and dragging on the rotation handle (Figure 360), or on the ribbon or this tab of the dialog.

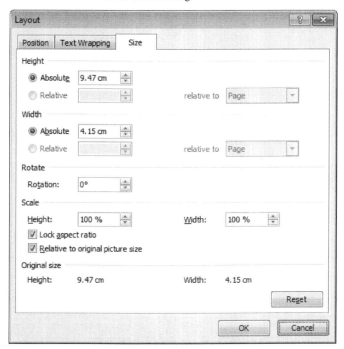

Figure 359   *Layout dialog: Size tab*

Figure 360   *Rotation handle*

In the Text Wrapping tab of the Layout dialog, you can determine the object relates to text. Any option other than In line with text will cause the object to be moved from its inline position in the text layer, to a floating position in the drawing layer. When in this position (floating) text can "move" around the picture, and this setting governs exactly how that happens. The four positions Square, Tight, Through, and Top and bottom will all allow you to determine whether text should be wrapped on both sides or only one of the sides of the image, and if so, exactly how far the text should be from the image.

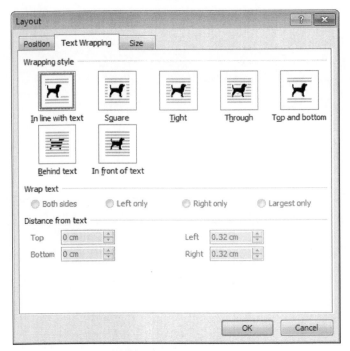

Figure 361   *Layout dialog: Text Wrapping tab*

Perhaps the best way to illustrate the various text wrapping options is by example: Figure 364 shows the same paragraph of text with the same shape in exactly the same position in each paragraph, but each time with a different text wrapping option set. Note that, depending on the exact image you have chosen, you would often not be able to tell the difference between tight and through wrapping.

It should be added that you can manually manipulate how the text wrapping is done as well. From the Wrap Text submenu of the context menu for an object, select Edit Wrap Points (Figure 362). This will display a wrap boundary around the object as a red line, with black points which you can click and drag into, or away from, the object, to change how the wrapping takes place. Figure 363 Shows how some of these points were (sequentially) manipulated to obtain a tighter wrapping, and with further manipulation, the wrapping could be made even tighter (note the mouse captured in the process of dragging points in the middle two images).

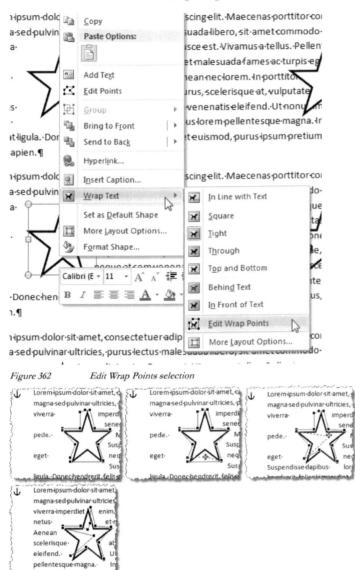

ιipsum·dolα ... scing·elit.·Maecenas·porttitor·co
a·sed·pulvin ... suada·libero,·sit·amet·commodo·
a· ... isce·est.·Vivamus·a·tellus.·Pellen
. ... et·malesuada·fames·ac·turpis·eg
. ... hean·nec·lorem.·In·porttitα
ιs· ... ırus,·scelerisque·at,·vulputate
. ... venenatis·eleifend.·Ut·nonu
ιt·ligula.·Dor ... us·lorem·pellentesque·magna.·Ir
apien.¶ ... t·euismod,·purus·ipsum·pretium

ιipsum·dolα ... scing·elit.·Maecenas·porttitor·co
a·sed·pulvin ... do·

Copy
Paste Options:

Add Text
Edit Points
Group
Bring to Front
Send to Back
Hyperlink...
Insert Caption...
Wrap Text
Set as Default Shape
More Layout Options...
Format Shape...

Calibri (E ⌄ 11 ⌄ A˘ A˘
B I

In Line with Text
Square
Tight
Through
Top and Bottom
Behind Text
In Front of Text
Edit Wrap Points
More Layout Options...

·Donec·hen ... us,
ι.¶

ιipsum·dolor·sit·amet,·consectetuer·adip ... co
a·sed·pulvinar·ultricies,·purus·lectus·male ... odo·

Figure 362   *Edit Wrap Points selection*

Figure 363   *Editing text wrapping points*

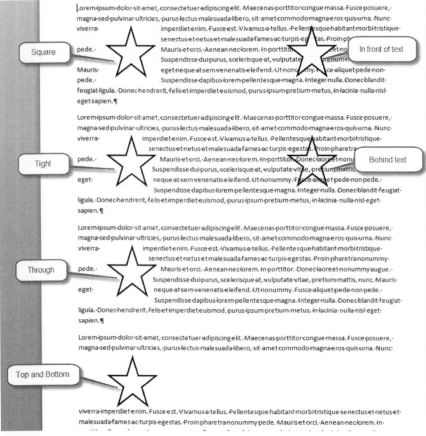

Figure 364　　　*Text wrapping options demonstrated*

The Position tab of the Layout dialog (Figure 365) allows you to determine the exact position of the object, relative to the page, margins, paragraph, etc. Which options you have available here will depend on which type of wrapping you have selected, and where (in what surrounding context) the image has been placed. The options are quite self-explanatory, though.

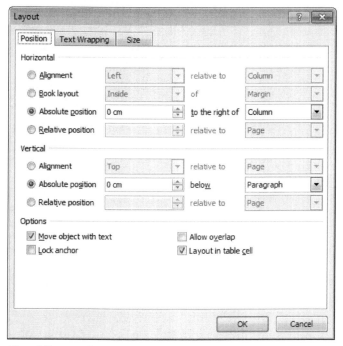

Figure 365   *Layout dialog: Position tab*

18.4.3   Editing pictures

Just remember that Word is a word processing program, not a photo editor. If you want to do serious photo editing, then get something like Photoshop. But all that aside, Word can do some basic retouching of images that you add to your documents, that eliminates the hassle of having to get a second program involved. Figure 366 shows a photo I took while hiking the Otter Trail (http://celtis.sanparks.org/parks/garden_route/camps/ storms_river/tourism/otter.php). The size of this photo (taken with a 5Mb point-and-shoot digital camera—the Panasonic DMC-FZ5, if you must know) is 2 104 429 bytes. The following sections will all edit this photo in some or other way.

Figure 366   Photo to be edited

18.4.3.1   Removing image background

The ability to remove the background of a picture (Instruction set 76) is a welcome addition to the tools included in Office 2010.

Instruction set 76   Remove Background tool

Keyboard	Alt | JP | E
Left click	

The tool has its own ribbon (Figure 367).

Figure 367   *Background Removal ribbon*

The process of removing an image's background is quite simple, if at times painstaking. The tool will recognise objects within the image, and then draw a rectangle around that

454

object, showing in purple tint what will be removed, and in the original colour, what will be retained (Figure 368).

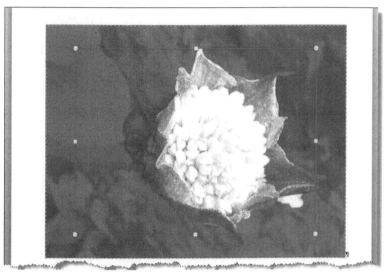

Figure 368   *Initial background detected for removal*

If the wrong object has been identified, or portions of the object mistakenly excluded, you can adjust the rectangle to indicate what you want to keep (compare how Figure 368 selects the flower, while Figure 369 selects the beetle).

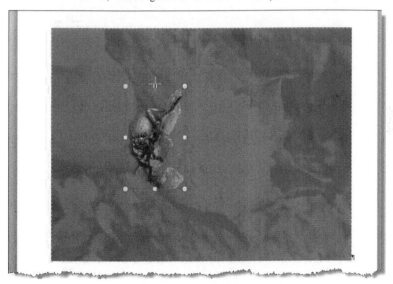

Figure 369   *Identifying a new object for background removal*

However, some images may need some further "tweaking." If parts of an image are still retained when they should be removed, you can use the Mark Areas to Remove tool, and if some parts of an image are excluded when they should be retained, you can use the Mark Areas to Keep tool. Since they work in much the same way, only one will be demonstrated below. Figure 370 shows how some areas have been marked, and you will notice the mouse pointer drawing a line over a part of the background which should be removed—you can either single click on certain portions, and the tool should identify the parts to keep and remove, but if it needs a little more guidance, you can click and drag to identify portions. You can also delete these editing marks, or simply undo one if the tool removes too much, for example. Once you have successfully identified what must be kept and what must be removed, you can click on Keep Changes to remove the background.

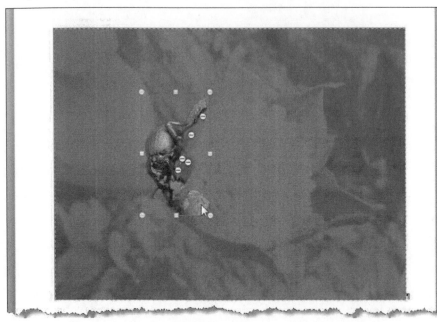

Figure 370   *Indicating background areas to be removed*

Once the background has been removed (Figure 371), the image will still be the same size as before, but all removed portions will be invisible (i.e., if the image floated over text, the text would be visible through the removed areas). You can, of course, crop away large portions of such images should you want to.

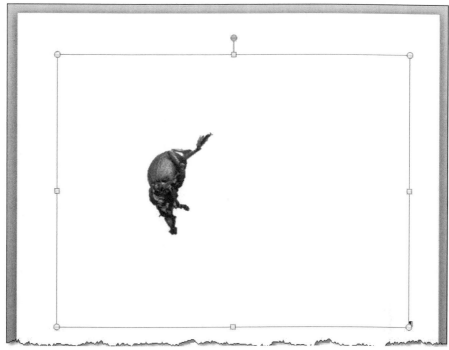

Figure 371   *Image with background removed*

18.4.3.2   Cropping images

Similar to resizing is cropping (Instruction set 77). However, with resizing, the whole picture changes size. With cropping, the end result is also not the same size as the original, but here part of the picture that you do not want displayed is cut away.

457

Keyboard	Alt | JP | V | C
Left click	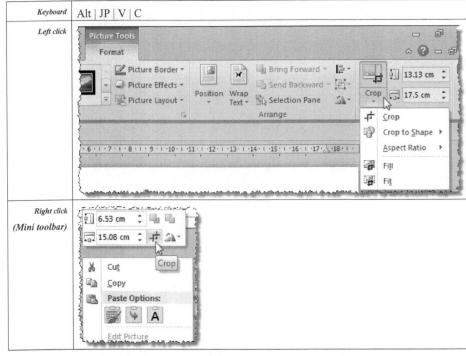
Right click (Mini toolbar)	

The crop tool places a crop border around the picture, with crop handles in the same locations as the sizing handles were. When you now click and drag on one of the handles, that part of the picture is cut away (Figure 372). Basically, you can drag each handle, to the position you want, and then when you click on Crop again, those parts of the picture are made invisible. However, take note that they are not actually cut away— they are just made invisible. The problem with that is, of course, that you might imagine that if you have cropped away half of a 2Mb file, the resulting file size will be approximately 1Mb less, while in reality it stays the same, since the cropped portion is still there in the document (occupying file space), it is just invisible. The advantage to this is that you can later un-crop a picture. If you want to delete the cropped portions of an image, then you need to do that during compression, as discussed in the next section.

Figure 372   *Cropping a picture*

However, take note that Word 2010's cropping tool includes a host of new cropping features (see the submenus that are visible in Instruction set 77) that allow you to crop to certain shapes, aspect ratios, or other.

18.4.3.3   Compressing images

When you add a picture to a document, that file is literally included into the xml file structure of a Word document. Which means that if your picture is 2Mb, you automatically increase the file size by that amount when the image is added. However, Word already compensates for this by compressing all the pictures you add when the document is saved. This behaviour is governed from the Image Size and Quality group of the Advanced tab in the Word Options dialog (Figure 373). Here you can disable image compression for the document, or you can set the level of compression to use for all images in the document. Note that compressing pictures is a compromise to the file size problem: It reduces the size of the inserted pictures, and can sometimes have a dramatic effect on file size. But at the same time, something of the quality (which may not always be noticeable) might be lost.

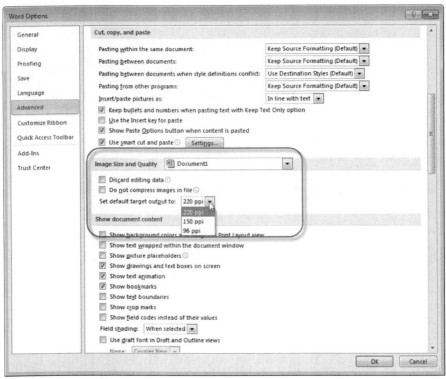

Figure 373   *Word Options: Image compression settings for the entire document*

If you have decided to turn compression off for a document, then you can compress images in your document manually. The tool is on the Picture Tools: Format ribbon in the Adjust group (Instruction set 78) and opens the Compress Pictures dialog (Figure 374).

Instruction set 78   Compress Pictures

Keyboard	Alt | JP | M
Left click	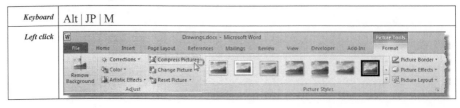

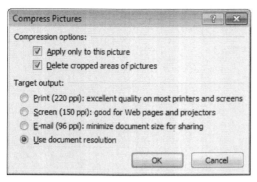

Figure 374   *Compress pictures dialog*

The process of compressing is fairly simple: You can compress only the currently selected picture or all the pictures in the document. You can also choose to permanently remove parts of pictures which have been cropped off, which will also help reduce file size, and which makes sense, as the reason you have cropped them is that you no longer want them to be displayed in the document. The Target output section allows you to choose for what purpose you intend using the document, which will impact on how much compression is done (the lower the resolution, the lower the quality, but the smaller the resulting file). I generally recommend that you go for the Print setting, which is the least amount of compressions, and thus also the smallest reduction in file size, but which, in reality, already represents quite a substantial amount of compression.

18.4.3.4   Setting a transparent colour

One or more of the colours in the picture can be made transparent by using the Set Transparent Color tool (Figure 375). When you click on the tool the mouse pointer will change to a stylus. Whichever colour you click on in the picture will be made transparent (Figure 375). However, there are two caveats which you should be aware of. Firstly, it would be nice if you could use the tool multiple times to make several portions of an image transparent, but each time you click on a new colour, the old colour which was transparent, becomes visible again—only one colour can be transparent at a time. Secondly, it works best with images that have very uniform colours—Figure 376 shows how the effect has been applied to the sample image, but often the result might not be what you had expected. While the tool has, in some ways, been superseded by the remove background tool, it can still be used to create some surreal picture effects (e.g., Figure 377).

Figure 375   *Set Transparent Color*

Figure 376   *Transparent colour in an image*

Figure 377   *Transparent colour in an image (take II)*

18.4.3.5   Format Picture Dialog

Finally, the Format Picture dialog can be used to set many of the settings discussed above (e.g., sizing, rotation, cropping), often with much finer precision, albeit somewhat remotely. This dialog is accessed either from the context menu or the dialog launcher on the Picture Styles group of the Picture Tools: Format ribbon. The important thing to note about this dialog is that it is a modeless dialog—i.e., the adjustments you make in the dialog are made in real time to the image. Thus, you can keep the dialog open, and change the settings, and see exactly how they impact on the image as you make the changes.

Instruction set 79   Format Picture

Keyboard	Alt	JP	O
Left click	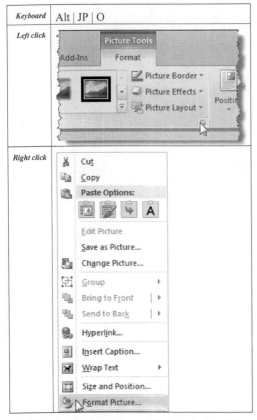
Right click	

I will here only discuss two of the tabs in this dialog.

The Picture Corrections tab (Figure 378) allows you set the brightness and contrast of the picture, as well as to sharpen or soften the image. Both of these have presets, which may help you find the effect you are looking for quicker, and the Reset button will allow you to revert back to the unadjusted image.

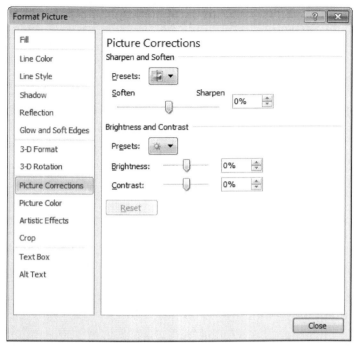

Figure 378   *Format Picture dialog: Picture Corrections tab*

The Picture Color tab allows you change the colour saturation or tone of the image, and also to recolour the image in a number of different ways. Again, there are presets for all of these which help find the right setting quickly (the greyscale, sepia and washout presets of the Recolor tool deserve special mention), and again the image can be reset to its unadjusted format very easily with the Reset button.

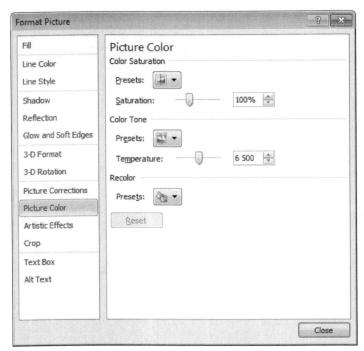

Figure 379   *Format Picture dialog: Picture Color tab*

18.5   Clip art

Inserting clip art is essentially the same as inserting a picture, except that it comes from a different source. A certain amount of clip art is installed on your computer together with Microsoft Office, courtesy of Microsoft. Each piece of clip art is tagged with one or more descriptive word, and the Insert Clip Art pane contains a search function which allows you to search for pictures according to your desired objective. You can also search for, and download clip art from the Internet if you are connected. Once a clip art is inserted, it can be manipulated in precisely the same way as any other picture.

Instruction set 80   Inserting Clip Art

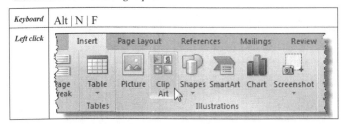

You can find good clipart pictures on sites like www.office.microsoft.com or www.clipart.com.

Chapter 19
Putting your thoughts on paper: Printing your dissertation

It's a sad fact of life that, after all the blood, sweat and tears required for writing a dissertation, there lies one last steep mountain ahead: Printing the whole thing out. There are many reasons for this.

Firstly, you will have printed sections of your dissertation out piecemeal to present to your promoter, and will probably have printed the whole thing out a couple of times in this manner by the time you are finished (thus, as my own promoter only half-joked, sentencing an entire forest to destruction). However, the chances are good that you will never have printed it as a single whole on one occasion. Despite the wonderful technology at our disposal, it is rarely so easy an achievement to print the whole thing out as a single unit and not experience any problems. And there are a myriad things that could go wrong—from page spacing to page numbering, to missing fonts and missing graphs and pictures, etc. These are the issues we will address in this chapter. If you know what the issues are, and can plan around them, then your printing process will go a lot smoother.

A second reason why printing your thesis is such a daunting task is that it is much more work to type a dissertation than to print it (take heart!), but a dissertation is normally typed over a period of many months, even years. A dissertation, on the other hand, is (normally!) printed out in the period of a single, heart-stopping day, and that day is normally already a few days after (or, for the students more capable of planning, only a few days short of) the final submission date!

A further problem is caused by the length of a dissertation. If your document is only three pages long (e.g., a letter) it is quite a simple task to get everything properly spaced and ordered. When your document is three hundred pages long, this becomes a totally different challenge. Even just the size of the document has a huge influence on the time taken to print one copy. Think of it. A typical desktop printer will print about 6 pages per minute (ppm), and that is for a "typical" page—(i.e., in printer marketing terms) one not heavy on graphics. But even at 6ppm, that would come to 10 seconds per page, which means a 300 page dissertation would take 50 minutes to print! And that is without the time needed to clear the print output tray, or load more paper into the paper tray, as a typical desktop printer will not have space for that many pages. But even at 50 minutes per copy, that means five copies would take well over four hours to print! Granted, most students these days are not brave enough to print their dissertations out on their home printers, so these get taken to a copy shop where they will be printed on high-speed printers. However, even these printers can, from start to end, take a fair amount of time to print. Firstly, there will be a queue of other students' dissertations also waiting to be printed. Next, these large print machines are normally connected via network cables, which means the dissertation needs to be sent to the printer over the network (a process called "ripping") which can, if there are many graphical elements (images or even just tables), take a very long time (the total time for five copies of a 300 page dissertation should, though, be much less than four hours).

This last scenario leads to one final cause of much heartbreak on printing day—because few of us have the luxury of having printers at home (where we most likely typed our dissertation) that are capable of printing out such a large document in one go, most of us need to take the dissertation to be printed out somewhere else. This means that we need to take the file(s)[131] to a different computer, with a different printer, and this is where the fun begins.

19.1 Choosing a printer

Word is a WYSIWYG program—it will, in Print Layout view and Print Preview , always attempt to display (non-printing characters aside) the document exactly as it would be printed on paper with the currently selected printer. Thus it may be a good idea, if you can do this at such an early stage, to identify the printer on which you will print your dissertation even before you start typing it. This is in itself fraught with the potential for disappointment, as the three year or more period in which you type your dissertation will give the printer's owner ample time to decide to replace it. But at the very least you should obtain some information about the destination printer before you go to print your dissertation. The best time to do this, then, is probably a few months before you start putting the whole thing together for the final version.

19.1.1 Printer drivers

Allow me to explain: In the early DOS days of computers (If you can't remember those days, you were probably still at school when I was doing my dissertation, or even younger!), each software program had to manage the printer on its own. It could not call on DOS to carry out that task. This means that early DOS versions of, for example, Word and Word Perfect™ had their own, built-in printer drivers. If your printer was not recognised by the program, tough luck[132]. Then, when the first version of Microsoft Windows appeared, a revolution took place. Windows itself took care of the printing task, and all the installed programs could call on Windows to print out whatever document they had. This meant also that printer manufacturers could now supply printer drivers with the printers (instead of sending it to Microsoft et al), and you could install the driver, and viola—your printer would work!

The bad news of this revolution is that different printers have different print settings (some printers, for example, can print closer to the edge of the page than others). Word is extremely printer-dependent—e.g., it won't allow you to print preview a document if you do not have a printer installed on your computer. Without going into too much detail[133], this means that the same document might print out differently on two different printers (even two printers linked to the same computer). Although the differences are normally very slight, they can make a difference on large documents such as

---

[131] Plural, of course, if you are working with a master document and sub-documents (cf. section 12.2.1).

[132] The common workaround for this problem was to see if another printer driver could work on your printer—a workaround still used today in Windows!

[133] For those more interested in the technical side of this, Word continuously compares the document you are working on with the "device context." The device, of course, is the printer, and the context is what the printer can and cannot do, and if it can, *how* it will do it. Word tries to display the document (especially if you are working in Print Layout view) as it will be printed on the *currently selected* printer.

dissertations. To illustrate, a typical problem that you might have encountered is the following message from Windows:

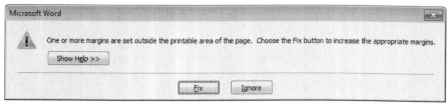

Figure 380   Margins outside of printable area

This is related to the printer driver you are using, and when your margins are on the limits of the printer's capability, you may get this message with one printer, but not with another.

Now, to return to the original topic, if you can identify the printer you will be using, get its installation CD or download its drivers from the manufacturer's website, and install that printer's drivers onto your computer (even if the printer itself is not attached). This will "fool" your computer, and you can then see what the document would print out like from that printer when you look at it in print preview. This technique may even be of help if you have already finished typing the dissertation, but don't have a lot of time to spend at the printer—you can check the layout of the document with that printer set as the printer for the document (see section 19.4.2 below), the evening before.

One final word of warning in this regard concerns printing your dissertation on multiple printers (e.g., you have colour graphs that need to be printed at a professional print shop, but you want to print the black-and-white pages somewhere else because of cost). Because of the different printer driver settings, you may find the pages printed on one printer will have one or two fewer or more lines on than the same pages printed on the other printer. Allow me to quote the Microsoft Word MVP John McGhie (2000):

> It is worth mentioning that in Word, pages do not exist in the document file. Like a professional typesetter, Word makes up its pages on the fly when it displays or prints a document. Word uses measurements from the installed fonts and the installed printer driver to do this. It is almost impossible to get two machines so exactly similar that a document will paginate with exactly the same page breaks on each.

The best thing to do is to first print out the smaller set of pages on the one printer (e.g., the colour pages), and then, when you print the many remaining pages on the other printer, check that they match up. You may need to use a variety of strategies to enforce this, such as to insert page breaks to force a few lines down to the next page, or break a paragraph up and set the Keep lines together setting of the paragraph formatting or set up the document with manual page breaks before and after the required page). Another option is to create a pdf version of the dissertation and take that to the print shop, but this also has some potential liabilities to it. This will be discussed in section 19.7 on p. 492.

19.1.2 Printer memory

One last thing needs to be said about the printer you are printing on. Make sure that it has sufficient memory for the job at hand. Although a complete discussion of how your computer and your printer share the burden of printing things out (including the memory burden) is not warranted here, it should be noted that sometimes, if the printer does not have enough memory available, it may split the contents of one page into two pages (breaking it down to make it more manageable). Of course, this will never happen with your text, but if you have large charts or other graphic objects, then you may find the printer printing out the top portion of the image on one page, and the bottom portion at the bottom of a second page whose top half is blank. If you can't resolve the problem there, then you may have to start the whole thing over on a new printer, with all its attendant problems!

19.2 Fonts

Another problem associated with printing your dissertation out on a different printer attached to a different computer is that you may be using some fancy fonts that are available to you on your computer, but have not been installed on the other computer (as technology advances, a problem that is thankfully becoming less common is that some printer drivers cannot print some fonts). There are various potential solutions to this problem. Firstly, you could try to embed the fonts. If that doesn't work, then you could copy the fonts, take the font files with you, and then install them on that computer [134]. The problem, of course, is knowing where to find them.

19.2.1 Font substitution

First en explanation of exactly what happens when you use a font in a document that is not found on the computer on which the document is opened. What Word will do is to choose another font that is available on the host computer, and use that in the place of the missing font. How Word will do that is, of course, determined by Microsoft, but the basic principle is that fonts can be classed into generic font categories (e.g., serif fonts, sans serif fonts, etc.). Word will then choose another font from the same basic category. Of course, some substitution rules for specific font names might also be defined at the operating system level, or could even be defined internally. The end result, though, is the same. Because a different font has been used, the finished product is not what you had in mind. Lastly, on the topic of font substitution, Word now allows you to easily check whether any of the fonts in your document have been substituted. In the Show document content group of the Advanced tab of the Word Options dialog, select Font Substitution... (Figure 381). Word will scan the document and alert you if any of the fonts have been substituted.

---

[134] Bear in mind also that fonts, like most computer programs, are not free, and it may actually be a contravention of copyright to install a font on a different computer.

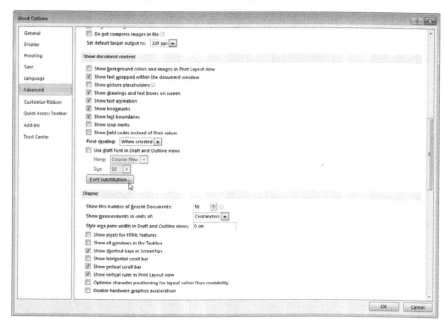

Figure 381   Word Options: Advanced tab, Font Substitution

19.2.2   Embedding fonts

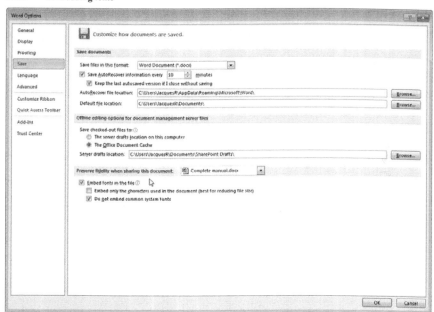

Figure 382   Word Options: Embed fonts

You can instruct Word to embed fonts into a document in the Save tab of the Word Options dialog (Figure 382). What this means is that the font file is saved as part of the document—it obviously increases the file size, but it also means that when the document is taken to another computer, the font is available, even if the font has not been installed onto that computer. There are two sub-settings that you can use to potentially reduce the file size. Firstly, if you choose to only embed the characters used in your document, then only a portion of the font is included, and this limits the file inflation. However, should you later edit the document on a different computer without that font installed, and should you then use a new character for the first time, that character will not be available.

Secondly, you could choose not to embed common system fonts—i.e., those fonts commonly installed on most Windows PCs. If you want to check this for yourself, then Microsoft provides lists of which fonts are installed with which programs here: http://www.microsoft.com/typography/fonts/default.aspx.

There are some caveats, however. Not all types of fonts can be embedded (e.g., PostScript fonts cannot be embedded, TrueType and OpenType Fonts can be embedded), and font creators can protect their fonts against being embedded in a document, so it will not necessarily work for all potentially embeddable fonts either. To find out whether a font can be embedded, you would have to go to the Windows Fonts folder, right click on the font file, and select Properties. Note, though, that the Fonts folder groups font families together, so if you right click on a font and do not see the Properties option, then first double click on the font to open the family, after which each individual font in the family will be displayed. This is shown in Figure 383.

Microsoft (Microsoft, 2009) lists "four levels of embedding permissions:"

- 📖 'Print and preview' fonts can be embedded in a document, provided the user reading the document cannot edit the content of the document.
- 📖 'Editable' fonts can be embedded within content that can be edited by the user.
- 📖 'Installable' fonts within a document may be permanently installed by the user reading the document or a client application. In practice, installable fonts are treated like editable fonts by most client applications.
- 📖 'No embedding permissions' prevent fonts from being embedded in a document.

Also, Microsoft has made available a tool (Font properties extension) that gives you additional information concerning fonts, which is quite useful. It is described, and a download link provided, here: http://www.microsoft.com/typography/TrueTypeProperty21.mspx.

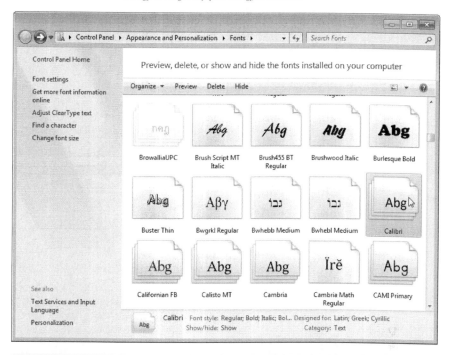

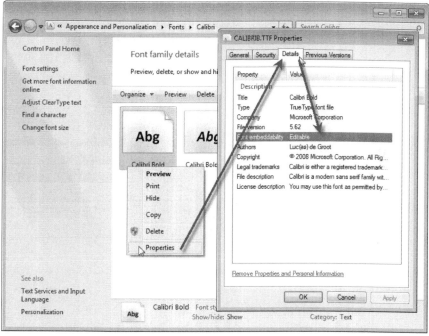

Figure 383   *Font properties: Font embeddability*

19.2.3   Finding your fonts

Should you want to install a font on another computer, you first have to check that you have legal permission to do this. If you do, you should be able to download the font off the internet. You could also, with the appropriate permission, copy the font off your computer and install it on the host computer.

The first thing you want to do is make a list of all the fonts you have used in your dissertation. Next, go and compare that list to the printing computer, and identify any missing fonts. Then, on your computer, go to the Windows Fonts folder from the Control Panel. Here you will see all the fonts installed on your computer. Find the font you need to copy, right click on it, and then select Properties from the shortcut menu. This will give you the Properties dialog, showing you, amongst others, the name of the font file[135] and its location (typically, C:\WINDOWS\Fonts). So now all you need to do is go there, copy the file to a disk, and take it to the new computer. Just remember that if a font is actually a family of fonts, you would need to copy all of those font files making up the family.

If you can't seem to find the fonts folder where the Properties dialog says it should be, you may need to select the Show hidden files and folders option on the View tab of the Tools, Folder Options dialog in Windows Explorer. A brief tutorial showing how to install a font can be found here: http://www.microsoft.com/typography/ TrueTypeInstall.mspx.

19.3   Printing options

Apart from sorting out the hardware, you also need to be aware of the software settings involved in printing out a document. There are numerous places where these settings are accessed, as will be discussed below.

Oddly, Word's print options are set in two distinct places in the Word Options dialog. The first is on the Display tab (Figure 384). Some of these settings that will be discussed in the context of the new print settings in Word below. Those that should be noted here are: You can instruct Word to Update fields before printing. This will ensure that all your cross-references, page numbers, tables of contents, etc. will be right each time you print, although this does take a short while to complete. When you are doing your final layout, you might want to set this off (after having manually updated all your fields, of course), so that Word will stop updating things which could lead to a reorganisation of content on your pages.

It is worth noting that if you have used hidden text, you can instruct Word to print out your document showing that hidden text.

---

[135] An alternative (and easier) approach is to change the View setting of the Fonts folder to "Details" (on the menu bar). This will Show you the name of the font, the name of the font file, the size of the file, and its modification date.

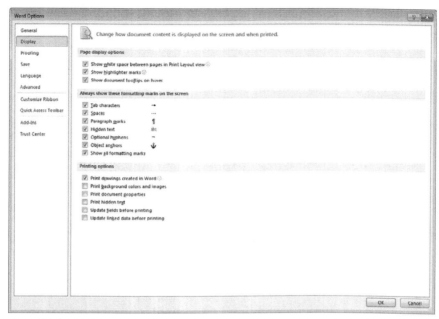

Figure 384   *Word Options: Display tab*

The second group of print settings are found in the Print group of the Advanced tab of the Word Options dialog (Figure 385). It is not necessary to discuss all the options given here. What is relevant to the printing of your dissertation is that you may want to check the setting of the Scale content check box, as this may lead to problems in certain instances (see Application 7.1, p. 128), and also this is the area where the very brave can attempt manual duplex printing.

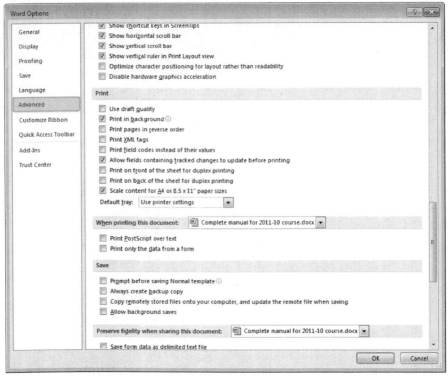

Figure 385   *Word Options: Print group of the Advanced tab*

19.4   Print settings

Word 2010 no longer defaults to the Print dialog (which I missed dearly), instead offering a much more cumbersome Print preview and Print (Figure 386), which is jack of all trades, master of none—it doesn't preview as well as the old print preview did, and it doesn't print as well as the old Print dialog did. Its only advantage is that it has combined these two processes into one. What I will thus do is first discuss the various print settings in the context of the new tool provided by Microsoft (consider it my way of at least giving recognition to the pointless effort they have put into this), and then I will show you how to reclaim the old tools.

Instruction set 81 **Print Preview and Print**

Shortcut	Ctrl + P or Ctrl + F2
Keyboard	Alt | F | P
Left click	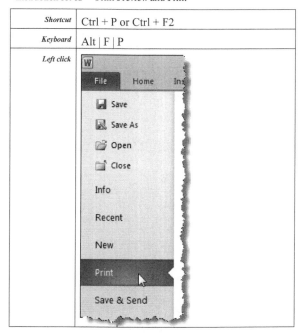

When you access either Print (**Ctrl + P**) or Print Preview (**Ctrl + F2**)—Instruction set 81—Word will take you to Print Preview and Print (Figure 386) of the Office 2010 Backstage view.

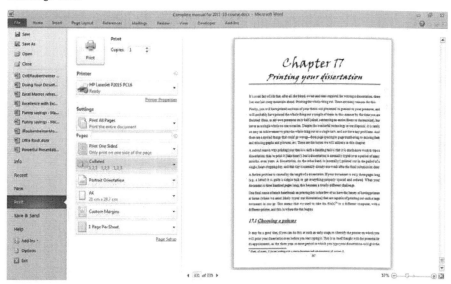

Figure 386   *Print preview and Print*

19.4.1   General functions

The Print Preview and Print has a large button on which you can click to actually send the document to the printer. Alongside this is the spin button combo box where you set the number of copies you would like to print (see Collation below). Furthermore, at the bottom centre of the screen is a page counter, with buttons to move forward or backwards through the document, or where you can type in a page number that you would like to go to—the page number to use here is the physical sheet count, not the printed page number. At the bottom right of the screen is the zoom slider which you can use to zoom in and out of the page or document.

19.4.2   Printer properties

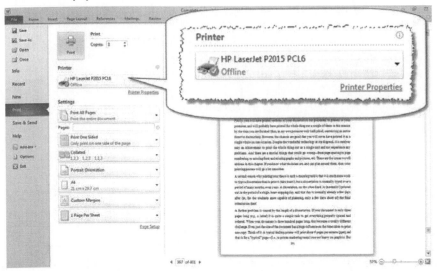

Figure 387   *Printer list*

Next to the Printer name list box (where you can choose which printer you are going to use to print the document), you will find the printer properties button. The settings here vary from printer to printer, but some of the settings you may want to look out for are the resolution (typically 300DPI or 600DPI) and toner saver settings, which will together influence the sharpness and clarity of the printing, with an inverse effect on the printer's toner. There are many others here, but you may want to browse through all the settings available before you start printing, so that you are confident that nothing untoward will befall your printed document (e.g., printing colour in monochrome, etc.).

19.4.3   Print Range and Print What

Two portions of the old Print dialog have been combined in the new Print Preview and Print interface.

19.4.3.1   Print range

The print range setting is very useful. For example, your printer's memory may not be able to handle the full number of pages all in one go (especially if it is a network-linked printer), and you will want to print your dissertation a few pages at a time (especially when they contain many graphics), or you could want to print some pages on a black printer, and some on a colour printer.

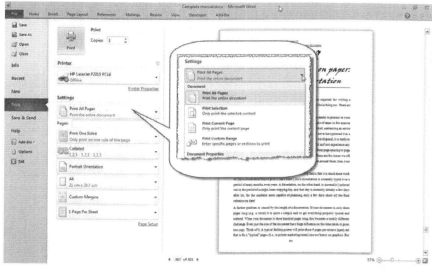

Figure 388   Print Range

The page range settings allow you to print your document in various ways. The most commonly used setting is, of course, to Print All Pages. You can also select a certain amount of text, and then select Print Selection to print only that. The page ordering will be altered—i.e., the selected text starts printing from the top of the page, regardless of its position on the actual pages of the document.

You could also choose to print only the Current Page, another useful setting.

Lastly, you can also print only certain pages by selecting Print Custom Range and then typing the range in the Pages text box. Some examples are given below:

Table 28   Examples of Print Ranges

Range	What will print
2, 5	Pages 2 and 5 of the document
2-5	Pages 2 to 5 of the document
2, 5-8	Page 2 and pages 5 to 8 of the document
p1s1, p3s1	Pages 1 and three of Section 1 (in this instance, also the 1st and 3rd pages of the document)
p1s2, p3s2	Pages 1 and three of Section 2 (in this instance, not the 1st and 3rd pages of the document)
p1s1-p5s2	From Page1 of Section 1 to Page 5 of Section 2
s1	All the pages in Section 1
s2, s4	All the pages in Sections 2 and 4
s2-s4	All the pages in Sections 2, 3 and 4

You should concentrate when using these ranges, however, as it is difficult to relate them to your page numbering. Thus, if your document contains ten "preliminary" pages, and the numbering only starts in a new section, on the physical eleventh page of the document, then that is Page 11, although it is numbered Page 1 (or, it could be Page 1 Section 2, assuming that it is in Section 2). The best way to check exactly where you are is to look at the status bar (the bar at the very bottom of your Word screen). For example, the picture below shows that the user is working on the page that is numbered 229 (and is in Section 26), but is the 253rd page of a 347 page document.

Page: 229 Section: 22 Page: 253 of 347 Words: 95 098 English (South Africa)

Figure 389   *Formatted vs actual page number*

19.4.3.2 Print what

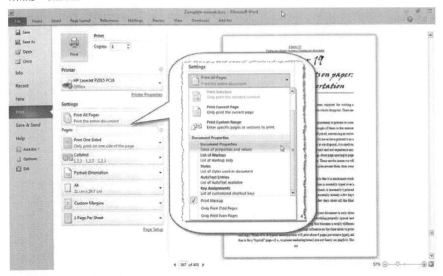

Figure 390   *Print what*

Focusing first on the bottom portion of the list, you can choose to print the document properties (normally a one-page table with the basic properties of the document), or a list of the markup (tracked changes and comments), or a list of the styles contained in the document. Two more lists can be printed. The first is a list of AutoText entries, although this is not specific to the document (i.e., it reflects the customised AutoText entries available in Word, and this will be the same from pretty much any document (global templates aside). The second is a list of customised keyboard shortcuts, showing both those that are globally available in Word, as well as those (if any) that are unique to the document in question.

The very bottom portion of the list allows you to specify whether your document should be printed showing the markup or not (only applicable if you have chosen a page range to print from the top portion of the drop-down list, not if you have chosen to print one of the meta-data lists just discussed). You can also, in this section of the list, attempt to do manual duplex printing (i.e., print on both sides of the page) by choosing to print the odd and even pages separately. This is not advisable for large documents such as a dissertation—rather get a printer (e.g., in a print shop) that can automatically print on both sides of the page). If your printer cannot print on both sides of the page, you can still achieve this through this setting. Basically, you will print all the even pages, then flip the pages around, re-insert them into the printer, and print all the odd pages. Note that this can be quite labour intensive, and when the printer starts jamming or crumpling your re-inserted pages, you really start having fun…. Note also that this is a document setting—i.e., after having set this to print, for example, odd pages only, each time you print the setting will remain in force, and you will print only the odd pages, until you switch to printing the even pages, or turn the setting off.

19.4.4   Print output

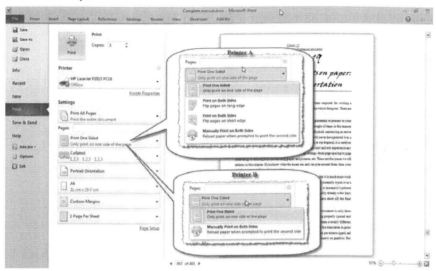

Figure 391   Print Output

Underneath the Print range tool, you can specify how the pages should be sent to the printer. This will be informed by the printer driver. For example, the accompanying screen capture shows the same setting for two different printers. The first can print on both sides of the page, which adds two options to the list. Both lists, though, have the option of choosing manual duplex printing, which was discussed above. Note, however, that here it is a once-off instruction, not a document setting.

19.4.5   Collation

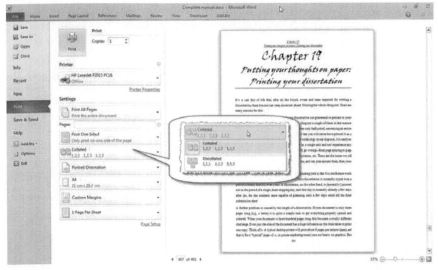

Figure 392   *Collation*

This setting will normally be on, and all it does is tell Word to print multiple copies (if you are printing multiple copies) of the document, one copy at a time. In other words, the first copy of the whole document will be printed, then the next copy, and so on. If you take this setting off, the first page of all the copies will be printed, then the second page of all the copies, etc. However, I would recommend that, even if you are printing multiple copies of your dissertation, you print one copy out first, then check it thoroughly before printing any further copies. Where you might want to turn the collate setting off is, for example, when you are printing only the pages of your document that contain colour. You can then easily divide all copies of the same page into however many sets you need.

Note also that there is a significant difference in speed, with non-collated printing being much faster. The reason for this is that each page is sent to the printer's memory, printed, and then cleared, before the next page is sent, and so on. When the printer has to collate, for example, 10 copies, then that means the time (even if it is only a fraction of a second) spent loading and clearing each page from memory is multiplied by 10. If the document is not collated, then each page is loaded once, 10 copies are printed, and that page is then cleared, only once. On a large document of hundreds of pages, this makes a huge difference. Remember that when next you go to the print shop and have to have multiple copies printed in a hurry. Of course, if collation is off, then you will have to build however many sets you have printed manually (i.e., from our previous example, take all 10 copies of page 1 and divide them into 10 separate piles, then take all 10 copies of page 2 and repeat, etc.). Even so, it may still be faster than collated printing, as you can assemble your sets as the printer spits out the pages.

19.4.6   Page Setup settings

Figure 393   Page Setup settings

A fair number of the page setup settings are repeated in this portion of the Print Preview and Print area. Specifically, you can change the page orientation, the page size, and the margins for the section to which the page that is currently being viewed, belongs. If the page should contain a section break, Word will apply the changes made here to the topmost section on the page, even if you have placed the cursor in the bottom section. There is, of course, a link from which you can launch the Page Setup dialog proper.

19.4.7   Scaling

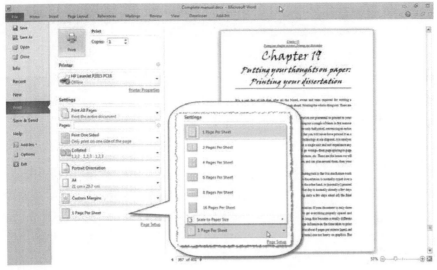

Figure 394   Scaling

Word allows you to natively (i.e., through the Word Print interface, not through the printer settings), choose to scale your output so that anything from 1, 2, 4, 6, 8, or 16 pages are printed on a single sheet. This can be useful when you want to do a quick printout of a certain portion of work and want to save toner and/or paper. You could also use the Scale to Paper Size setting to change the printed output from what is set in the document to any of the many other paper size you find listed there (the paper size set in the document's page setup will remain unchanged).

19.4.8   Reclaiming the Print dialog and Print preview

One of my biggest peeves with the new Print Preview and Print has to do with speed. Firstly, not all the submenus discussed above are keyboard enabled, meaning that if you want an option from that submenu (e.g., to print only the current page), you have to use the down arrow and move down the list one item at a time until you reach that option.

Or use the mouse, which is still slow. In the old Print dialog, printing the current page, for example, is as simple as pressing **Alt + E**. Secondly, each time the Print Preview and Print loads, it has to render the pages (i.e., Word determines afresh what content will go on what page). With a large document numbering hundreds of pages, this can take quite a few seconds, even on a decent pc, while the Print dialog doesn't need to do this, and loads immediately. Even cancelling is slower, as Word has to re-render the input for Print Layout view, which means you may sometimes see, when exiting Print Preview and Print, the message displayed in Figure 395. By contrast, cancelling the Print dialog is quick.

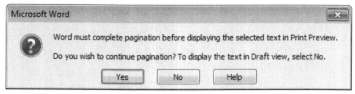

Figure 395 *Word needs time to render pages according to printer driver*

To get the old print preview back is relatively easy. You can modify the Quick Access Toolbar as was discussed in section 2.1.4 (p. 18). From the list of All commands, choose Print Preview Edit Mode (Figure 397).

Reclaiming the old Print dialog has proved to be a bit harder. Search as I might, I could not find this in the list of commands. But, where there's a will, there's a way. To do this, we have to create a macro—but don't worry, the process is quite easy. First, from the Developer ribbon (cf. Figure 63, p. 86), open the Macros dialog (**Alt + F8**)— Instruction set 82.

Instruction set 82   Accessing the Macros dialog

Shortcut	Alt + F8
Keyboard	Alt | L | PM
Left click	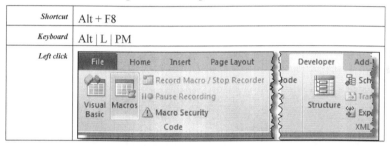

Next, in the Macro name text box of the Macros dialog, type "PrintDialog" (Figure 396) and click on Create.

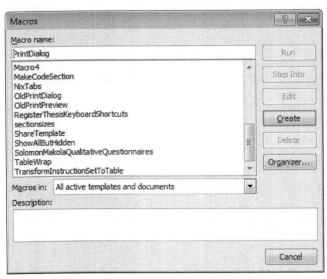

Figure 396   *Macros dialog: Creating the PrintDialog macro*

This will open the VBA Editor, with the Sub and End Sub statements for the macro already created. All you need to add is one line of code: Application.Dialogs(wdDialogFilePrint).Show. It should look as shown in Macro Listing 3.

Macro Listing 3   *PrintDialog*

```
Sub PrintDialog()
'Created by J. Raubenheimer
'Accesses the Word 2007 and earlier Print Dialog for Word 2010
    Application.Dialogs(wdDialogFilePrint).Show
End Sub
```

Now go and add that macro to the Quick Access Toolbar as is shown in Figure 397. You can also click on the Modify... button to give the macro the printer icon.

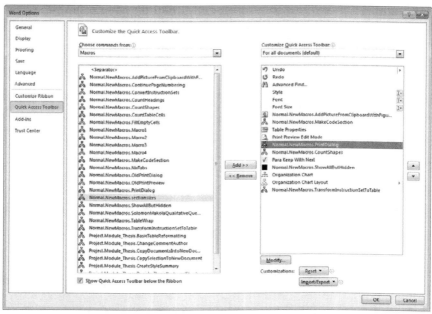

Figure 397   *Adding the PrintDialog macro to the Quick Access Toolbar*

The end result will be as is shown in Figure 398—two buttons that you can use to access the old print preview and the old print dialog, as is respectively shown in Figure 399 and Figure 400. If you really want to, you can reassign the **Ctrl + P** keyboard shortcut back to this dialog—this was demonstrated in section 11.6.3 (p. 253) where the **Ctrl + F** keyboard shortcut was reclaimed. It really will do no harm to do this, as the **Ctrl + F2** keyboard shortcut which referred to the old print preview in Word 2007, still points to the new Print Preview and Print in Word 2010. In fact, I also reassigned **Ctrl + Shift + F2** to PrintPreviewEditMode (the old print preview).

Figure 398   *Print Preview Edit Mode and PrintDialog on the QAT*

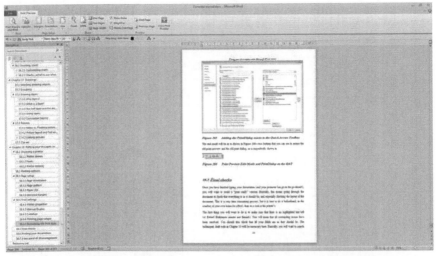

Figure 399   Old Print Preview

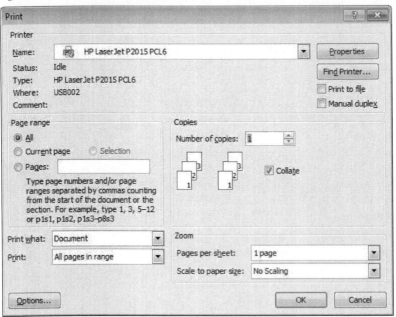

Figure 400   Old Print dialog

Since the various print settings have already been discussed in the context of the new interface, these will not be repeated here: They function the same in the Print Dialog, it is just more keyboard friendly, and can thus result in a faster print than the new method. However, the use of the old Print Preview will be briefly discussed.

19.5   Print Preview Edit Mode

Print Preview Edit Mode (just Print preview in Word 2007) is useful in that it provides an easy to navigate interface where the document is displayed exactly as the printer would render it. Because of this, it is very useful to check through your document in this mode to make 100% certain that all is as it should be.

There are some pointers here that do bear mentioning. Firstly, it has several things in common with the new Print Preview and Print from the Backstage view of Word 2010. Both have certain tools available that are useful: The Zoom slider, the ability to set margins, page size and orientation, etc. However, Print Preview Edit Mode has these additional options: The Ruler, the ability to display non-printing characters if so desired, the Magnifier as a tool to quickly zoom in and out of specific sections of a page, and, of course, the ability to turn off the magnifier and make a quick edit to the text while in Print preview.

When in Print Preview Edit Mode, the Print Preview ribbon (Figure 401) is made available (most other ribbons are hidden).

Figure 401   *Print Preview ribbon*

Many of the settings on this ribbon are self-explanatory—there are navigation buttons that take you to Print Preview and Print, and to the Print settings in the Word Options dialog (cf. Figure 385 on p. 476). There are page setup tools that allow you to set the Margins, page orientation, and –size, as well as to open the Page Setup dialog proper.

There are zoom tools with various zoom options, as well as a button to open the Zoom dialog itself (and the zoom slider is at the bottom right of the screen as well). The Preview group of tools allows you to turn the ruler on or off, to switch the mouse pointer between its true self and the magnifier. The magnifier is useful, as you can hold the magnifying glass which has replaced the mouse pointer over any part of the page, and simply click to zoom in on that portion of the page, or click again to zoom back out. You can turn non-printing characters on or off with the **Ctrl + Shift + *** keyboard shortcut. Also, when the magnifier is turned off in the ribbon, you can click in the text and edit it—not the ideal mode in which to do these kinds of changes, but useful for making quick corrections without having to quit Print preview. Lastly, there is a Close button (or just press Esc) to return to Print Layout view.

The question does need to be answered, though—why do we need Print preview, when Word already shows us what the document will be printed out like in Print Layout view? Well, firstly, it should be remembered that in Word, the concept of a page does not really exist. The structure of a document is any number of sections, which contain any number of paragraphs. How those paragraphs are distributed across the pages is determined by Word on the basis of the currently selected printer driver. This means that Word makes up the pages "on the fly," and that content which would appear on one page, given a certain printer, might end up on another page, given a different printer. Of course, as the capabilities of printers converge with better technology, these differences can be expected to diminish (and indeed, it is my experience that they have), but the fact remains that they are there. Now, when Word displays a document in Print Layout view, it is definitely displaying the document as it would print on the given printer, but Word still gives preference to editing requirements. This means that *most of the time*, Print Layout view will give an accurate rendering of the document as it would print. But there are exceptions. Print preview always gives preference to the printer driver requirements, meaning that Print preview will *always* give an accurate rendering of the document as it would print. This is most often evident when you have "abnormal" document components, such as graphics, and also end- and footnotes. Also, by default Print preview shows the document without the non-printing characters, which is, of course, desirable in that context—it is generally a good method of operation to have the non-printing characters visible in Print Layout view, and not visible in Print preview.

19.6 Final checks

Once you have finished typing your dissertation (and your promoter has given the go-ahead!), you will want to create a "print ready" version. Basically, this means going through the document to check that everything is as it should be, and especially checking the layout of the document. This is a very time consuming process, but it is best to do it beforehand, in the comfort of your own home (or office), than in a rush at the printer's.

The first thing you will want to do is to make sure that there is no highlighted text left (cf. Application 11.1, p. 239). This will mean that all outstanding issues have been resolved. You should also check that all your fields are as they should be. The navigation techniques dealt with in Chapter 11 will be necessary here. Basically, you will want to search for, and deal with, all highlighted items, and then you will want to go to each and every field in your document (after updating all the fields with **Ctrl + A, F9**) and check that there are no messages such as the following "Error! Reference source not found."[136] This message indicates that the item the cross-reference field was referring to, has either been deleted or changed in such a way that Word no longer recognises it, and can thus no longer associate it with the field. If you are unfortunate enough to find these, you will have to figure out what the reference once referred to, and then either re-create that thing, if it should not have been deleted, or if it should, delete the reference as well. Note that these broken references can be anywhere—in tables of content, in references to figures or tables, in cross-references, etc.

If you are using Reference Management Software (cf. Chapter 13), then the next thing you will want to do is update your list of references, and make sure that your reference list and in-text references are correct.

---

[136] You can search for this message (make sure you type it correctly). If the search comes up empty, then no news is good news.

You should also check the numbering of the pages—not to check your table of contents, as Word will ensure that it will be right—but to make sure that all the pages that should be numbered are, and are numbered in the right manner (e.g., with Arabic numerals instead of Roman, or vice versa, etc.).

The final task is to check the layout of your document—it just doesn't make sense to do this at an earlier stage, and you shouldn't let your promoter bully you into wasting time with this at any earlier stage of the process. If there are big blanks on pages between tables and text (e.g., if a table has been forced to print on one page only, and has left half of the preceding page blank as a result), then leave them be—until now, that is. Remember, as was just pointed out in the previous section, that Word makes up the individual pages on the fly. A dissertation is always in flux (it will probably undergo one more revision after the examination copy is printed, before it is finally laid to rest, and that will hopefully be a small one), and as such, any changes to the layout may be nullified by changes made to prior sections of the document. Now when it is finished, and no more changes are anticipated, the right time has come to fine-tune the layout. It is also for this reason that all changes to fields (including reference list fields, if Reference Management Software is used) be done prior to checking the layout, as even small changes made to a large number of fields can considerably alter the layout of the text.

Thus, first make a backup of the unmodified document (see Application 12.2 on p. 267). Then make sure that you first select the actual printer driver with which you will be printing (cf. 19.1 above), and then work through the document, from the start, checking that your text flows properly, and checking that figure and table captions are with their respective elements, etc. Now, if there are big blanks on pages between tables or figures and the rest of the text, then now is the time to correct them. What you want to do at this stage is basically order the text so that it will present neatly as a printed document. You should make a backup, and save regularly, so that you can find a useful return point should you mess things up too much. At this point, you will find yourself cutting paragraphs from after tables, graphs and pictures, and pasting them in front of the aforementioned, so as to fill up any annoying blanks. You should do all of this in Print Layout view, and should start from the beginning, and work your way to the end, as changes made at the beginning will affect the layout of all the rest of the text, at least to the end of the current chapter. You may even have to resize some graphic objects, and generally "tweak" your document until you are happy with the aesthetics of the final product.

The last thing you want to do is then save this "print ready" version, and then copy it to a disk (preferably a flash disk, or then a CD or DVD if possible). This is what you will take with you to the printer. Save it with a new name, such as "Dissertation – Print Version.docx" so that you now have two versions with identical content, but different layout—your normal one on your hard drive, and the one on the disk. You may still change the disk version at the printer, and if changes have to be made to the dissertation before the final copy is submitted, then it is generally best to make them to the first copy on your hard disk, not the printer-modified one (although this is not necessarily always the case). Remember to copy your template to the disk as well, together with any fonts you will need (cf. 19.2, although it may be less stressful for yourself if you install the fonts on the printing computer ahead of time).

19.7   Creating a pdf version of your dissertation

The disadvantage to the way Word structures a document is that it has no inherent pages—pages are just made up as Word interprets the constraints of the printer driver. This does mean that, from printer to printer (or even from earlier to later versions of drivers for the same printer), your content can "float" from page to page. One very popular solution is to create a pdf version of the document. In fact, most universities these days require a pdf copy of the dissertation to be submitted alongside the hard copies.

19.7.1   Creating a pdf copy of your dissertation

Instruction set 83 shows how a pdf file can be created from within Word.

Instruction set 83   Saving as a pdf

The Save As dialog will be opened (now titled Publish as PDF or XPS—as seen in Figure 402), with the Save as type list box set to PDF[137] (you could also choose XPS). Of course, you could just press **F12** and select the type yourself, which may actually be quicker. The process is very similar to just saving a file—you choose the location on your drives to save it to, you give the file a name (the Word file name is chosen as a default, and it is a good idea to keep the pdf name the same), and you click on Publish (or Save).

---

[137] Word does not always seem to get this right, leaving the setting at .docx. I believe this error was corrected in the Office 2010 Service Pack 1.

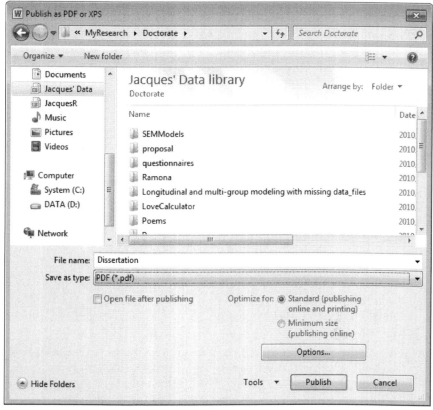

Figure 402   *Publish as PDF or XPS dialog (Save As dialog)*

Note, however, that there is a choice to optimise the document for Standard use (better quality, larger resultant file size) or Minimum size (lower quality, smaller resultant file size). I recommend, at this stage, going for the former. You can also choose to Open the file after publishing, which will open the file in your pdf reader, so that you can see the resultant output—a nice time saver. Lastly, there is an Options... button, which allows you to set some detail on what will be output, as is shown in Figure 403. These will be reminiscent of the print settings already discussed, and should thus not be too hard to understand. A useful feature is the ability to add bookmarks to help readers navigate through the pdf document (this will result in a structure very reminiscent of the Word Document Map—see section 11.6.4, p. 256). A last useful feature is the ability to password protect the document, although your university will probably not want you to do this.

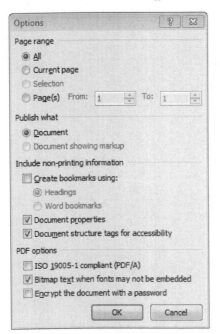

Figure 403   *Options dialog for saving as PDF*

19.7.2   Alternative methods of creating pdf files

A large number of products can be used to convert Word documents to pdf documents. Top of the list, of course, is the original: Adobe Acrobat (www.adobe.com). Another popular alternative is the open-source PDF Creator (www.sourceforge.net/pdfcreator). This program allows you to create different passwords so that, for example, you can allow anyone to open your pdf document, but disallow them from copying text or printing it. However, I have found that the quality of the output sometimes lags behind that of Microsoft's tool.

19.7.3   Caveats to using pdf

Before you start thinking that pdf is the end-all solution to all your printing woes, it pays to be aware of some problems that linger. Firstly, because the Word XML file format is already a compressed format, I have found that the pdf versions of my Word documents are generally not smaller than the original Word documents, and, in some instances, are significantly larger.

Secondly, I have found that the process of conversion to pdf does result in a slight loss of quality—in other words, if a Word document is printed out directly, and a pdf of the same document is created and then printed, the pdf version may provide a slightly worse quality end result. This is especially noticeable with tables, where the thickness of the lines tends not to be uniform in pdf files, but it is also discernible in other graphic objects and diagrams. For more information on this, I can recommend reading through these two white papers:

http://www.dclab.com/white_papers/converting_from_pdf.asp

http://www.dclab.com/white_papers/pdf_conversion.asp

Thirdly, Acrobat reader also employs font substitution (discussed in section 19.2.1 above).

19.8   *Printing your dissertation*

Printing your dissertation is normally a two-day process. The first day is spent checking everything in advance, as has been described, and on the second day you will do the actual printing. Make sure you have a good supply of coffee, enough time to do the job right, enough paper to print out the whole document, and extra for mistakes (I would say about double the amount of pages in the document as a minimum is safe), enough toner (you may have to check this with the owner of the printer), and perhaps even either a stimulant or a sedative, as the case may be....

When you get to the printing computer, it is generally best to copy the documents to that computer's hard drive, and then work with them from there. Any changes can be saved, and the files transferred back to the disk (if possible). You will then want to run through the document again, checking especially the fonts and the layout (this is the thing most likely to change as a result of the foreign printer driver). Once you are happy that everything is as it should be, you may proceed with printing. Having said that, you may have to deal with a number of unforeseeable problems, such as printers not printing the odd page section start on the odd page (requiring you to add another page break), printers jamming on your graphics (requiring you to send perhaps one page at a time, at best, or find another printer, at worst), paper jams, and other such heart-stoppers. Good Luck!

Of course, if you have created a pdf or xps version of your document, you should (*should!*) be able to print this out without too much concern about the layout of the end product (but see the caveats from the previous section).

19.9   *A last word of discouragement!*

And if you think all this has been a lot of hard work, remember that you will have to print the thing out twice—once for evaluation, and then the final copy submitted after the recommended changes have been made. Pray that you will have no changes, because if you do, you will have to go through the whole process again!

Appendix A
Complete Listing of Word Keyboard Shortcuts

Access key	Key	Function	group	Scope	Toggle	Alternative
Alt	F3	Create Autotext entry	Autotext	Word	No	
	F3	Complete Autotext entry	Autotext	Word	No	
Ctrl	F3	Append (by cutting) selection to the Spike (undo to restore text)	Autotext	Word	No	Alt + Ctrl + v
Ctrl + Shift	F3	Insert Spike's contents into the document and clear Spike	Autotext	Word	No	
"Spike" (i.e., type the word "spike")	F3	Insert Spike's contents into the document without clearing Spike	Autotext	Word	No	
Shift	F7	Check spelling	Spelling	Word	No	
	F7	Thesaurus	Spelling	Word	No	
Ctrl + Shift	*	Show non-printing characters	Display	Word	Yes	
Alt + Ctrl	S	Split the screen	Display	Word	Yes	
	F6	Switch to other pane in split screen mode	Display	Word	Yes	
Alt + Ctrl	N	Switch to Normal View	Display	Word	No	
Alt + Ctrl	O	Switch to Outline View	Display	Word	No	
Alt + Ctrl	P	Switch to Print Layout View	Display	Word	No	
Alt + Ctrl	E	Insert Endnote	Footnotes and Endnotes	Word	No	
Alt + Ctrl	F	Insert Footnote	Footnotes and Endnotes	Word	No	
Alt + Shift	C	Close the Footnote/Endnote box in Normal View	Footnotes and Endnotes	Word	No	
Alt+Shift	D	Insert a DATE field	Fields	Word	No	
Ctrl +Alt	L	Insert a LISTNUM field	Fields	Word	No	
Alt+Shift	P	Insert a PAGE field	Fields	Word	No	
Alt+Shift	T	Insert a TIME field	Fields	Word	No	
Ctrl	K	Insert Hyperlink	Fields	Office System	No	
Alt + Shift	X	Insert Index entry	Fields	Word	No	

Access key	Key	Function	group	Scope	Toggle	Alternative
Ctrl	F9	Insert Field	Fields	Word	No	
Alt	F9	Toggle field codes in whole document	Fields	Word	Yes	
Shift	F9	Toggle field codes for selected field	Fields	Word	Yes	
	F9	Update field	Fields	Word	No	
Ctrl + Shift	F9	Unlink field (permanently replaces field with its current value)	Fields	Word	No	
Shift	F11	Go to next field	Fields	Word	No	
	F11	Go to previous field	Fields	Word	No	
Ctrl	F11	Lock field	Fields	Word	No	
Ctrl + Shift	F11	Unlock field	Fields	Word	No	
Ctrl	F4	Close current document	File operations	System	No	
Alt	F4	Close Word	File operations	System	No	
	F12	File, Save As…	File operations	Office	No	
Ctrl	O	Open file	File operations	System	No	
Ctrl	N	Open new file	File operations	System	No	
Ctrl	S	Save	File operations	System	No	
Ctrl	P	Print	File operations	System	No	
Ctrl	F6	Switch to next open Word document	File operations	Office	No	
Ctrl + Shift	F6	Switch to previous open Word document	File operations	Office	No	
Ctrl + Shift	G	Word Count	Word Count	Word	No	
Alt	C	Recount Word Count toolbar	Word Count	Word	No	Ctrl + Shift + R
Ctrl + Shift	End	Go to end of document, selecting all text between current position and end	Selection	System	No	
Ctrl + Shift	Home	Go to start of document, selecting all text between current position and start	Selection	System	No	
	F8	Turn on Extend mode (not a toggle - use Esc to turn Extend mode off)	Selection	Word	No	

Access key	Key	Function	group	Scope	Toggle	Alternative
Ctrl + Shift	F8	Turn on Extend mode for a vertical selection (similar to holding the Alt key while selecting with the mouse)	Selection	Word	No	
	Any character	In extend mode, extend to that character	Selection	Word	No	
Shift	F8	Increase selection	Selection	Word	No	
Ctrl + Shift	F8	Decrease selection	Selection	Word	No	
	↑	Select all characters to the left of the current character, right to the beginning of the paragraph	Selection	System	No	
Ctrl + Shift	→	Select all characters to the right of the current character, right to the end of the paragraph	Selection	System	No	
Ctrl + Shift	←	select one word to the left	Selection	System	No	
Ctrl + Shift	→	select one word to the right	Selection	System	No	
Shift	Page down	Select all text from the current position to one screen down	Selection	System	No	
Shift	Page up	Select all text from the current position to one screen up	Selection	System	No	
Shift	Home	Select all text from the current position to the beginning of the line	Selection	System	No	
Shift	End	Select all text from the current position to the end of the line	Selection	System	No	
Ctrl	A	Select entire document	Selection	System	No	
Ctrl	X	Cut	Manipulation	System	No	
Ctrl	C	Copy	Manipulation	System	No	
Ctrl	CC	Open Office Clipboard	Manipulation	Office / System	No	
Ctrl	V	Paste	Manipulation	System	No	
Ctrl	Backspace	Delete whole word to the left of the cursor	Manipulation	System	No	
Ctrl	Delete	Delete whole word to the right of the cursor	Manipulation	System	No	
	F2	Move	Manipulation	Word	No	
Shift	F5	Cycles through the last five working places	Navigation	Word	Yes	
Ctrl	F	Find	Navigation	System	No	

Access key	Key	Function	group	Scope	Toggle	Alternative
Ctrl	G	Goto	Navigation	System	No	F5
Ctrl	H	Replace	Navigation	Office	No	
Ctrl	End	Go to end of document	Navigation	System	No	
Ctrl	Home	Go to start of document	Navigation	System	No	
Ctrl	←	Move one word to the left	Navigation	System	No	
Ctrl	→	Move one word to the right	Navigation	System	No	
Ctrl	↓	Move to the top of the next paragraph	Navigation	System	No	
Ctrl	↑	Move to the top of the paragraph	Navigation	System	No	
Ctrl	Page up	Repeats the last search upwards	Navigation	System	No	
Ctrl	Page down	Repeats the last search downwards	Navigation	Word	No	
Alt	↑	Top of the current page, except when in a table	Navigation	Word	No	
Alt		Start of previous cell in a table, but without selecting cell contents	Navigation—Tables	Word	No	
Alt	→	Start of next cell in a table, but without selecting cell contents	Navigation—Tables	Word	No	
Alt	Home	Left-most cell in a table row	Navigation—Tables	Word	No	
Alt	End	Right-most cell in a table row	Navigation—Tables	Word	No	
Alt	Page up	Top cell in a table column	Navigation—Tables	Word	No	
Alt	Page down	Bottom cell in a table column	Navigation—Tables	Word	No	
Shift	Tab	Previous table cell, with contents selected	Navigation—Tables	Word	No	
	Tab	Next table cell, with contents selected	Navigation—Tables	Word	No	
Shift	Tab	Insert new table row at bottom of table, only when used in last cell of table	Tables	Word	No	
Ctrl	Tab	Inserts a tab in a table cell	Tables	Word	No	
Ctrl + Shift	E	Toggle Track Changes	Reviewing	Word	Yes	
Ctrl	\	Expand/Contract subdocuments in Master document	Master Documents	Word	Yes	
Alt + Shift	K	Check for errors in Mail Merge document	Mail Merge	Word	No	
Alt + Shift	M	Merge to Printer	Mail Merge	Word	No	
Alt + Shift	N	Merge to New Document	Mail Merge	Word	No	
Ctrl + Shift	S	Activates the Styles list box	Styles	Word	No	

Access key	Key	Function	group	Scope	Toggle	Alternative
Alt + Ctrl	1	Make the paragraph Heading 1 style	Styles	Word	No	
Alt + Ctrl	2	Make the paragraph Heading 2 style	Styles	Word	No	
Alt + Ctrl	3	Make the paragraph Heading 3 style	Styles	Word	No	
Ctrl + Shift	L	Make the paragraph List style	Styles	Word	No	
Ctrl + Shift	N	Make the paragraph Normal style	Styles	Word	No	
Alt + Ctrl	!	¡	Symbols	Word	No	
Alt + Ctrl	?	¿	Symbols	Word	No	
Alt + Ctrl	C	©	Symbols	Word	No	
Alt + Ctrl	R	®	Symbols	Word	No	
Alt + Ctrl	E	€	Symbols	Word	No	
Ctrl	,	Adds a cedilla to selected following characters (e.g., ç when followed by a c, Ç when followed by a C)	Symbols	Word	No	
Ctrl + Shift	<	Adds a circumflex to selected following characters	Symbols	Word	No	
Ctrl + Shift	@	Adds a degree symbol above the letters a and A; used primarily in Danish, Norwegian, and Swedish	Symbols	Word	No	
Ctrl + Shift	:	Adds a diaeresis or umlaut to selected following characters	Symbols	Word	No	
Ctrl	`	Adds a grave accent to selected following characters	Symbols	Word	No	
Ctrl	/	Adds a slash through the letters o and O; used primarily in Danish and Norwegian	Symbols	Word	No	
Ctrl	~	Adds a tilde to selected following characters	Symbols	Word	No	
Ctrl	'	Adds an acute accent to selected following characters	Symbols	Word	No	
Ctrl + Shift	&	Creates combination or Germanic characters based on selected following characters (e.g., æ when followed by an a, Æ when followed by an A)	Symbols	Word	No	
Alt	130	é	Symbols	System	No	
Alt	136	ê	Symbols	System	No	
Alt	137	ë	Symbols	System	No	
Alt	147	ô	Symbols	System	No	

Access key	Key	Function	group	Scope	Toggle	Alternative
Alt	148	ö	Symbols	System	No	
Alt + Ctrl	T	™	Symbols	Word	No	
Alt		Accesses the menu. Then use the underlined letter of the menu items to access the function you need. e.g., Alt, f, v gives you print preview; Alt, o,s gives you styles and formatting; Alt, a, c, t selects the entire table; etc.	Task control	System	Yes	F10
Alt	Esc	Minimise	Task control	System	No	
Shift, (Alt)		Holding down the Shift key changes certain menu items (e.g., File, Close changes to File, Close All)	Task control	Office	No	
	F1	Help	Task control	System	No	
Ctrl	F1	Toggle ribbon display	Task control	Office	Yes	
Ctrl	Y	Redo	Task control	System	No	
Ctrl	F4	Repeat the last action (redo)	Task control	System	No	
Ctrl	Z	Undo	Task control	System	No	
Ctrl + Alt	K	AutoFormat	Text formatting	Word	No	
Ctrl + Shift	Q	Changes the font to Symbol	Text formatting	Word	No	
Shift	F3	Cycle through available case settings (All uppercase, all lowercase, capitalised)	Text formatting	Word	Yes	
Ctrl	[	Decrease point size by one point	Text formatting	Word	No	
Ctrl	]	Increase point size by one point	Text formatting	Word	No	
Ctrl + Shift	<	Decrease point size to next available point size (as seen in point size list)	Text formatting	Word	No	
Ctrl + Shift	>	Increase point size to next available point size (as seen in point size list)	Text formatting	Word	No	
Ctrl + Shift	J	Distribute text across the line (applies to whole paragraph)	Text formatting	Word	No	
Ctrl	B	Bold text	Text formatting	System	Yes	
Ctrl	I	Italicise text	Text formatting	System	Yes	

Complete listing of Word keyboard shortcuts

Access key	Key	Function	group	Scope	Toggle	Alternative
Ctrl	U	Underline text	Text formatting	Office System	Yes	
Ctrl + Shift	D	Double Underline text	Text formatting	Word	Yes	
Alt + Ctrl	- (Minus)	Insert em dash	Special characters	Word	No	
Ctrl	- (Minus)	Insert en dash	Special characters	Word	No	
Ctrl + Shift	- (Hyphen)	Insert Non-breaking hyphen	Special characters	Word	No	
Ctrl + Shift	Space	Insert Non-breaking space	Special characters	Word	No	
Ctrl	- (Hyphen)	Insert Optional hyphen	Special characters	Word	No	
Ctrl	Enter	Insert Page Break	Special characters	Word	No	
Ctrl + Shift	Enter	Insert column break	Special characters	Word	No	
Shift	Enter	Insert soft carriage return (line break)	Special characters	Word	No	
Ctrl + Shift	H	Make text hidden	Formatting	Word	Yes	
Ctrl + Shift	C	Copy formatting (not content)	Formatting	Word	No	
Ctrl + Shift	V	Paste formatting (not content)	Formatting	Word	No	
Ctrl	E	Centre paragraph	Paragraph formatting	Word	No	
Ctrl	J	Justify paragraph	Paragraph formatting	Word	No	
Ctrl	L	Left-align paragraph	Paragraph formatting	Word	No	
Ctrl	R	Right-align paragraph	Paragraph formatting	Word	No	
Ctrl	M	Left-indent paragraph with one tab stop more per time	Paragraph formatting	Word	No	
Ctrl + Shift	M	Left-indent paragraph with one tab stop less per time	Paragraph formatting	Word	No	
Ctrl	T	Make paragraph hanging indent with one tab stop more per time	Paragraph formatting	Word	No	
Ctrl + Shift	T	Make paragraph hanging indent with one tab stop less per time	Paragraph formatting	Word	No	
Ctrl	1	Make paragraph single spacing	Paragraph formatting	Word	No	
Ctrl	5	Make paragraph 1.5 spacing	Paragraph formatting	Word	No	
Ctrl	2	Make paragraph double spacing	Paragraph formatting	Word	No	
Ctrl	Q	Removes additional formatting (i.e., formatting not defined by the style) from the paragraph	Paragraph formatting	Word	No	
Ctrl	0	Set Paragraph, Spacing Before to 12pt (one line)	Paragraph formatting	Word	Yes	
Ctrl	=	Make text subscript	Text formatting	Word	Yes	

Access key	Key	Function	group	Scope	Toggle	Alternative
Ctrl + Shift	+	Make text superscript	Text formatting	Word	Yes	
Ctrl + Shift	K	Makes text small capitals	Text formatting	Word	Yes	
Ctrl	D	Open text formatting dialog	Text formatting	Word	No	
Ctrl + Shift	Z	Removes additional formatting (i.e., formatting not defined by the style) from the text	Text formatting	Word	No	
Ctrl + Shift	F	Set Font (Font list box)	Text formatting	Word	No	
Ctrl + Shift	P	Set point size (Font Size list box)	Text formatting	Office System	No	
Ctrl + Shift	A	Toggles All uppercase	Text formatting	Word	Yes	
Ctrl + Shift	W	Toggles underline single words	Text formatting	Word	Yes	

Reference List

American Psychological Association. (2010). *Publication Manual of the American Psychological Association* (6th ed.). Washington: American Psychological Association.

Booth, P. F. (2001). *Indexing: The Manual of Good Practice*. K G Saur.

Carey, G. V. (1951). *Making an Index* (2nd ed.). Cambridge: Cambridge University Press.

Carey, G. V. (1961). No room at the top. *The Indexer, 2*(4), 120–123.

Kelly, S. (2010, September 3). *How does Track Changes in Microsoft Word work?* Retrieved September 12, 2012, from Making the most of Word in your business: http://www.shaunakelly.com/word/sharing/howtrackchangesworks.html

Kelly, S. (2010, August 15). *How to create numbered headings or outline numbering in Word 2007 and Word 2010*. Retrieved January 24, 2011, from Shauna Kelly: Making the most of Word in your business: http://www.shaunakelly.com/word/numbering/numbering20072010.html

Knight, G. N. (1988). *Indexing, the Art of: A Guide to the Indexing of Books and Periodicals*. Routledge.

Lewis, W. (2009, October 2). *Theses & Long Documents: Creating and Numbering Equations with Microsoft Word 2007*. Retrieved July 24, 2012, from University of Waterloo, Information Systems & Technology: http://ist.uwaterloo.ca/ec/equations/equation2007.html

McGhie, J. (2000). *Word's numbering explained*. Retrieved 10 25, 2010, from The Word MVP site: http://word.mvps.org/FAQs/Numbering/WordsNumberingExplained.htm

Michelstein, J. (2011, October 20). *Equation numbering*. Retrieved July 23, 2012, from Word blog: http://blogs.office.com/b/microsoft-word/archive/2006/10/20/equation-numbering.aspx#

Microsoft. (2008, January 15). *How to move AutoCorrect entries in Word 2007 from one computer to another computer*. Retrieved March 8, 2011, from Microsoft Support: http://support.microsoft.com/kb/926927

Microsoft. (2009, June 26). *Microsoft Typography: Font Redistribution FAQ*. Retrieved March 17, 2012, from Microsoft.com: http://www.microsoft.com/typography/RedistributionFAQ.mspx

Microsoft. (2012). *Control the formatting when you paste text*. Retrieved September 21, 2012, from Office.com: http://office.microsoft.com/en-us/word-help/control-the-formatting-when-you-paste-text-HA010215708.aspx

Microsoft. (2012). *Field codes: Eq (Equation) field*. Retrieved 07 23, 2012, from Microsoft Office: http://office.microsoft.com/en-za/word-help/field-codes-eq-equation-field-HP005186148.aspx?CTT=1

Microsoft. (2012). *Field codes: Index field*. Retrieved September 23, 2012, from Office.com: http://office.microsoft.com/en-za/word-help/field-codes-index-field-HA102017394.aspx?

Microsoft. (2012). *Field codes: Ref field*. Retrieved September 21, 2012, from Office.com: http://office.microsoft.com/en-us/word-help/field-codes-ref-field-HA102017423.aspx

Microsoft. (2012). *Linear format equations and Math AutoCorrect in Word*. Retrieved September 8, 2012, from Microsoft Office: http://office.microsoft.com/en-za/word-help/linear-format-equations-and-math-autocorrect-in-word-HA101861025.aspx?CTT=3

Microsoft. (2012). *Math AutoCorrect symbols*. Retrieved July 23, 2012, from Microsoft Office: http://office.microsoft.com/en-za/word-help/math-autocorrect-symbols-HA010064598.aspx?CTT=5&origin=HA010200498

Microsoft. (n.d.). *Field codes Index field - Word - Microsoft Office*. Retrieved 02 02, 2011, from Office.com: http://office.microsoft.com/en-gb/word-help/redir/HP005186209.aspx?queryid=ad95f37925534feea0669d7bfd39cc97&respos=0&CTT=1

Microsoft. (n.d.). *Field codes TA (Table of Authorities Entry) field - Word - Microsoft Office*. Retrieved 02 02, 2011, from Office.com: http://office.microsoft.com/en-gb/word-help/field-codes-ta-table-of-authorities-entry-field-HP005186214.aspx?CTT=1

Microsoft. (n.d.). *Field codes TC (Table of Contents Entry) field - Word - Microsoft Office*. Retrieved 02 02, 2011, from Office.com: http://office.microsoft.com/en-gb/word-help/redir/HP005186197.aspx?queryid=d55a6e311c104ed497fb95430b093f14&respos=0&CTT=1

Microsoft. (n.d.). *Field codes TOA (Table of Authorities) field - Word - Microsoft Office*. Retrieved 02 02, 2011, from Office.com: http://office.microsoft.com/en-gb/word-help/redir/HP005186215.aspx?queryid=13fef5369c1348658064af8083d59094&respos=4&CTT=1

Microsoft. (n.d.). *Field codes TOC (Table of Contents) field - Word - Microsoft Office*. Retrieved 02 02, 2011, from Office.com: http://office.microsoft.com/en-gb/word-help/redir/HP005186201.aspx?queryid=e445208029e3444bb6d213357facefd1&respos=3&CTT=1

Microsoft. (n.d.). *Field codes XE (Index Entry) field - Word - Microsoft Office*. Retrieved 02 02, 2011, from Office.com: http://office.microsoft.com/en-gb/word-help/field-codes-xe-index-entry-field-HP005186216.aspx?CTT=5&origin=HA102110133

Microsoft. (n.d.). *Find and replace text or other items*. Retrieved 08 23, 2011, from Office.com: http://office.microsoft.com/en-us/word-help/find-and-replace-text-or-other-items-HP005189433.aspx

Microsoft Word Team. (2009, June 25). *Multilevel Lists vs List Styles*. Retrieved February 11, 2011, from Word Blog: http://blogs.msdn.com/b/microsoft_office_word/archive/2009/06/25/multilevel-lists-and-list-styles.aspx

Mulvany, N. C. (2005). *Indexing Books* (2nd ed.). Chicago: University of chicago Press.

Neville, C. (2007). *The complete guide to referencing and avoiding plagiarism.* Maidenhead: Open University Press.

Spiker, S. (1964). *Indexing your book: A practical guide for authors.* Madison: University of Wisconsin Press.

Stuple, S. J. (2007, March 08). *The Many Levels of Lists.* Retrieved July 29, 2009, from Word Blog: http://blogs.office.com/b/microsoft-word/archive/2007/03/08/the-many-levels-of-lists.aspx

Tucker, L. R., & MacCallum, R. C. (1997). *Exploratory Factor Analysis.*

Tufte, E. R. (1983). *The visual display of quantitative information.* Cheshire: Graphics Press.

Tufte, E. R. (1990). *Envisioning information.* Cheshire: Graphics Press.

Vandenberg, R. J., & Lance, C. E. (2000). A Review and Synthesis of the Measurement Invariance Literature: Suggestions, Practices, and Recommendations for Organizational Research. *Organizational Research Methods, 3*(1), 4-70. Retrieved January 23, 2008, from http://orm.sagepub.com/cgi/content/abstract/3/1/4

Wainer, H. (1997). *Visual Revelations: Graphic tales of fate and deception from Napoleon Bonaparte to Ross Perot.* New York: Copernicus.

Wellisch, H. H. (1996). *Indexing from A to Z* (2nd ed.). Niso Press.

Wyatt, A. (2010, April 27). *Numbering Equations.* Retrieved September 5, 2012, from WordTips: http://word.tips.net/T000273_Numbering_Equations.html

Yu, D. (2010, September 1). *Equation Number in Office 2007 and 2010.* Retrieved July 26, 2012, from Microsoft Research: http://research.microsoft.com/en-us/people/dongyu/Office2007EqnNumber.txt

Index

Tools!

Don't forget to go to
http://insight.trueinsight.za.com/word
to download the thesis examples and Word uTIlities
discussed in this book.

This page will also contain more information on
using Word for your thesis or dissertation, tips, dates
of presentations on the content of this book, and
more.

Do you want to get it first hand?

Dr Raubenheimer is available to offer hands-on training sessions covering all the material in this book, at your own venue.

Send a mail to trueinsight.consulting@gmail.com with the subject line "MSWord thesis training" to enquire about costs and availability.

Need help?

If you are struggling and want help with the MSWord formatting of your thesis or dissertation (sorry, we can't write your thesis for you), send an e-mail to trueinsight.consulting@gmail.com with the subject line "Thesis formatting help" to find out about the current availability of help and the costs involved.

Printed in Great Britain
by Amazon.co.uk, Ltd.,
Marston Gate.